DANGER DISASTER AND HORRID DEEDS

Prepared by the Staff of Yankee, Inc.
Editor: Clarissa M. Silitch
Art Director: Carl F. Kirkpatrick

DANGER DISASTER AND HORRID DEEDS

Published MCMLXXIV by
Yankee, Inc., Dublin, New Hampshire

FIRST EDITION

ISBN 0-911658-62-9
Library of Congress Catalog Card No. 74-83983
Manufactured in the United States of America

CONTENTS

1710-1973 . . . being
A CHRONOLOGICAL CALENDAR OF THE
DANGERS, DISASTERS, AND HORRID DEEDS
covered in this book

1710-1718
Black Sam Bellamy harries the Northeast Coast, attempts to found a "Pirates-Only" colony at Machias, Maine, and finds his Maker when his ship *Whydah* is dashed to bits on the rocks of Wellfleet, Massachusetts.

1755
April 14
Little Lucy Keyes is lost in the Wachusett woods; no trace of her is found. A strange death-bed confession years later tells of her dreadful and undeserved end.

1756
June
Molly Finney, a fair young thing of 14, is captured by marauding Indians, marched off to Quebec, and sold into slavery to an old French trader.

1757
September
Bold and dashing Captain McClellan of the British merchantman *Rose* spirits Molly Finney away—out of slavery.

1839
December 15
HURRICANE!! The most disastrous gale in history to date hits New England; it runs up and down the coast for almost a week and plays ducks and drakes with the ships in Gloucester harbor.

1842
February 25
Birth of Ida Walley Zoradia Lewis, Newport's heroic lifesaveress, America's Grace Darling, who was to cheat the sea of more than forty lives.

1845
October 27
Scapegrace scion Albert Tirrell of Weymouth, Massachusetts, murders his mistress Maria (to all appearances) and runs off to sea.

1846
March 24
Albert Tirrell's trial begins; resourceful lawyer Rufus Choate successfully defends the accused and makes legal history.

1850
December 22
Dauntless seaman Roger Elliott battles through icy rocks and giant drifts to Owl's Head Light, Maine, to alert the keeper to the plight of a young couple frozen in a block of ice to the taffrail of a wrecked schooner. The couple survive!

1851
April 17
Minot's Light topples from its rocky perch in the Atlantic; its keepers perish.

1862
September 10
The bark *America* embarks on a whaling voyage out of Holmes Hole, Martha's Vineyard, with one George Welden aboard. George is not what he seems.

1863
January 9
George Welden flogged for quailing at his duty. But everyone felt differently about him when he lost his shirt.

1865
September 25
Langdon Moore, apparent inspiration for Denman Thompson's perennial play, "The Old Homestead," robs the Concord, Massachusetts, bank

1866
May 3
The extreme clipper *Hornet* burns to a crisp in mid-Pacific. Captain Josiah Mitchell and twenty-nine men set out for Hawaii, two thousand miles distant, in a long boat and two life boats.

1872
November 9
The Great Boston Fire—flames consume 65 acres in the heart of Boston, Massachusetts.
December 4
(December 5, sea time) Brig *Mary Celeste* is found off the coast of Portugal, mysteriously abandoned though the table is set for dinner.

1873
April 30
Enraged citizens of Mapleton lynch "Bloody Half Acre" murderer Cullen at Maine's first and only necktie party.

1876
January 26
A fortune is efficiently lifted from the Northhampton (Massachusetts) National Bank by a canny gang of masked burglars.

1877
Fall
Bicyclist finds refuge from a storm in an old stagecoach tavern. Grisly experience in the Octagon Room.

1880
June 11
Floating steam palaces *Narragansett* and *Stonington* collide in Long Island Sound. The crews look out for themselves, with terrible consequences for the passengers.

1883
June 13
Everything goes wrong at Mystic's (Connecticut) ceremony to dedicate its newly erected Civil War statue.

1885
A strange series of extremely odd petty thefts begins in Chester, Vermont.

1891
December 4
Four trains crash in five minutes at one spot in East Thompson, Connecticut.

1893

Summer

A gentlemanly thief impoverishes the men and fascinates the ladies of Stockbridge, Massachusetts.

1896

July 14

Bloody murder on the high seas aboard the *Herbert Fuller.*

1897

February

The Reverend Prescott Jernegan astounds his hand-picked audience of wealthy would-be investors by making gold out of sea water.

October

Arson, robbery, and murder in West Peabody (Massachusetts). Is town half-wit Tom Ducey the firebug? Crazy like a fox in fact?

1898

February 3

The milk train meets the fast freight head on and climbs aboard its mighty Mogul engine.

July 23

An *irreverent* Prescott Jernegan skips off to France with his family and an extra hundred thousand.

1899

August 6

Day of the Peck's Mill Pond trolley tragedy.

December 13

Young Mr. XYZ, poor but dishonest, comes to a violent and anonymous end.

1901

July

Jolly and capable, Nurse Jane Toppan comes to Cataumet on the Cape, where she proves herself skillful and killful.

1902

July 29

C.H. Waterman of Chester, Vermont, springs a trap on the rat that's been stealing his grain.

1903

March 20

The famous Fall River Line loses its only passenger in the grinding crash of its *City of Taunton* with handsome steamer *Plymouth* of the same line. *Plymouth's* shattered deck serves as an impromptu parade ground for United States Marines.

March 28

Two lionesses at large terrorize the town of Pittsfield, Massachusetts—except for one lady who tells them to "Scat!"

1911

October 14

Avis Linnell, Hyannisport choir girl, dies suddenly—NOT by her own hand, and with benefit to the clergy.

1914

June 25

"E.V.," supremely competent and studiously unheroic insurance executive, mans the last ramparts against the raging flames of the Great Salem Fire.

1916

September 28

That devious and unpleasant little fellow, Frederick Small of Mountainview, New Hampshire, endeavours to add to his income and get rid of his wife by one fell stroke.

1918

August 13

Dr. William Kendrick Dean of Jaffrey, New Hampshire, is killed and stuffed down a well by a person or persons unknown. German spies?

September 6

Sad suicide of a German submarine.

1919

January 15

Molasses traps people like flies in Boston.

1923

April 6

Veteran pogie steamer *John Dwight* goes down off Cuttyhunk Island. Coast Guardsmen find no bodies, no crew, no wreckage, no life boats.

April 7

Eight bloody corpses are fished out of Vineyard Sound—all murdered, and all members of the *John Dwight* crew??

1926

April 9

"George Washington" is throttled by a Boston strangler.

1927

November 13

The Wheeler Reservoir bursts its bonds and flattens the town of Becket, Massachusetts. A brave telephone operator miraculously escapes.

December 17

Despite official silence, reporter McIntyre learns by semaphore signals of the tragic loss of the U.S. S-4 rammed by another U.S. vessel. No survivors.

1937

May 6

The era of the dirigible ends abruptly when the giant German zeppelin, *Hindenburg*, explodes into flame upon landing at Lakehurst, New Jersey.

1938

September 21

The terrible Hurricane sweeps through New England. Shrieking wind! Driving rain! Roaring water! Havoc is wreaked.

1942

December 8

Unsolved enigma of World War II, the tattered wreck of a P-40 fighter plane flies out of the blue, from the wrong direction—Mindanao.

1944

July 6

One of the country's most heartbreaking fires claims the Ringling Bros., Barnum and Bailey Big Top in Hartford, Connecticut, while the circus is in full swing.

1946

November

Partridge snatches hunter from the jaws of frozen death.

1952

February 18

Tankers *Pendleton* and *Fort Mercer* break apart in the sea—within 40 miles of one another.

1953

June 7

The Worcester Tornado.

1956

July 25

Death of an ocean liner. The "unsinkable" *Andrea Doria* is rammed by the *Stockholm* and goes to the bottom, where she remains.

1972

February

Robert D. Hall, Jr. lives through a real snow job on Willey's Slide.

1973

Summer

The third attempt to salvage the "unsalvageable" *Andrea Doria* comes to naught.

1.
STRANGE ACCIDENTS OF FATE

The S-4 by Semaphore

United States submarine S-4 at the Boston Navy Yard.

by John Mason

The Navy wasn't talking, but McIntyre remembered the code for the saddest scoop of his life.

SATURDAY AFTERNOON IS THE DULLEST TIME OF the week in a newspaper office; the regular staff knocks off early and only those in charge of Sunday editions stick around the City Room.

On Saturday afternoon, December 17, 1927, it was unusually quiet at the *Boston American*. Two photographers were making prints in the dark rooms, and a small group of reporters played penny ante. Colonel Burt Ford, on his way to the comp room with corrected proofs, stopped to clap a friendly hand on the shoulder of Mark McIntyre, who stood smoking a cigarette and kibitzing the card players.

"Well! The new editor couldn't keep away from the old mill, eh? What's the matter, Mark, things too quiet in Harvard Square?"

McIntyre had recently been promoted from the *Boston American* reportorial staff to be editorial manager of the Hearst paper in Cambridge, but on Saturdays he still dropped into his old office in Winthrop Square, Boston, to chew the fat with his pals, who kidded him good-naturedly about his new job.

McIntyre dished it right back and rubbed it in. "Confidentially, fellers, this being boss is O.K.! I never realized what it would be like to have a banker's hours . . . and salary!"

That sally was greeted with a chorus of expertly executed Bronx cheers, but McIntyre ignored the insult and continued in mock seriousness: "Stormy nights, when I'm snuggled down in my little beddie all nice and warm, I think of you poor palookas, impatiently waiting for a bull to break loose in the Brighton abattoir, or a three-bagger over in Chelsea. I say: 'Mark, old man, you'll never have to go sloshing round in the sleet and snow any more. Now you're an editor!'"

He was interrupted by Burt Ford with a piece of pulp in his hand, on which he had hastily scrawled: "4:05 P.M. Provincetown??? Short while ago. Coast Guard??"

The players looked up from their cards as Ford said: "Just got a phone call from Provincetown. Something's happened on the Cape, but nobody knows what. Coast Guard's tearing around like mad, but they're not talking.

"I'm sending Turner to make pictures, and I guess you better go along, Brockbank, in case it's a shipwreck."

McIntyre blinked, gulped and stammered: "Don't you want an old Navy man to go too? You know I did a three-year hitch in Uncle Sam's Navy!"

"Hear! Hear!" said one of the gang. "Make way for Admiral McIntyre!" But Burt Ford shook his head, went back to his desk, pulled out the assignment sheet and scribbled: "12/17/27 4:30 p.m.—Brockbank and Turner to Provincetown."

McIntyre leaned over Ford's desk and whispered eagerly: "Put me down too, Boss! My Buick's outside with a tank full of gas, and I've nothing to do till Monday. No kiddin', Burt, I do know the Navy lingo. . . ."

Ford thought a moment and said: "O.K. Editor McIntyre! You asked for it, and here 'tis. You'll take the boys in *your* car, and I don't want to see 'transportation' on three swindle sheets. If you find anything, phone me around seven, so we can flash the morning AD, then get a good follow-up for the bulldog, and if it's big, we'll want a different story and layout for Monday's *Record*. That rolls Sunday afternoon. There's your triple assignment, Mark. Watch the ice on the road."

But McIntyre was already out in the hall buzzing the elevator and yelling for Frank Turner and Burt Brockbank to get a move on. He had a feeling this was going to be something *big*—and *his*!

It was too cold in McIntyre's open roadster to do much talking, so the three newsmen sat huddled and silent, tapping their feet on the frosty floorboards and holding gloved hands over tingling ears. In spite of Saturday night crowds in Quincy, Kingston and Plymouth, they made good time, speeding up to seventy when the road was bare, slowing down for the stretches of ice. Only at Orleans and Wellfleet did snow-

drifts delay them, and they pulled into Provincetown at 7:30.

"Ford'll be expecting a phone call," Mark said, pulling up to the Post Office where the Coast Guard was located.

"Burt may have asked for a call, but he knew better. Three hours to P-town is damn good going, if you ask me. Coffee?"

In the lunchroom there was buzzing comment on the commotion out in the harbor, but no definite information. As usual, rumors were a dime a dozen. The boys from the *Boston American* had hoped they were first on the scene, but they soon spied Charlie Drury and Jimmy Jones of the *Herald*, George Hill of the *New York Times*, Larry Goldberg of the *Post*, and some *Globe* men. They confirmed the earlier report that the "Navy wasn't talking" and said they'd promised to issue a statement before long.

Some of the press boys were trying to collect $100 to hire a fishing boat and sail out to investigate, but McIntyre had his own idea. "No soap. I guess I'll stay here." Far out in the darkness toward Wood End, he had spotted a cluster of moving lights which, to his practiced eye, looked like one Navy ship towing another. As soon as the crowd moved off he drove to the municipal pier, and backed his Buick into an open shed that faced the harbor. He tossed a blanket over one headlight, and stood in front of the other.

For a chap only twenty-six, McIntyre had had a varied career. At sixteen he had run away from home to join the Navy, and when the first units of the Atlantic Squadron sailed for Europe in 1917, Mark was a member of the overseas Armed Guard. He was soon promoted to signalman, and at the end of his first year he could send and receive so fast he was transferred to the submarine service, and saw plenty of action at the Azores, Bizerte, Casablanca and on the English Channel. When he was later transferred to the destroyer squadron, he was one of the fastest semaphore men in the whole outfit.

Now, as he stood stamping his freezing feet on the snow-covered wharf in Provincetown, he figured the distant lights were on a ship which had anchored. He removed his hat, took a good grip on the brim, and held it in front of the headlight of his car. Then he yanked it rapidly

Above: Submarine interior drawn for the *Boston Sunday Globe,* Jan. 11, 1931.

Below: Reminders of tragedy at the New London submarine base are (right)
the clock from the S-4 and (left) the clock from the S-51, lost Sept. 25, 1926.

back and forth, covering and uncovering the headlight, spelling out (with two dots, two dashes, two dots) the customary code interrogatory flash, followed by: "WHAT SHIP? WHAT SHIP?"

His heart gave a jump when immediately the yardarm blinkers on the distant craft opened up and winked back. "U.S.S. PAULDING. WHO INQUIRES?"

Now, this was a delicate spot for an ex-Navy man to be in. Should he try to kid the operator on the *Paulding* into thinking he was a Navy official or a ship in port, or should he tell the truth? To gain time while he made this decision, Mark repeated his question: "WHAT SHIP? WHAT SHIP?" And back from the answering blinkers came: "U.S.S. PAULDING. WHO WANTS TO KNOW?"

Mark decided to play fair. To indicate the message was private and not official, he prefixed his answer with the letters "P.V.T." and with his old felt hat flying to and fro, he sent his message. "THE PRESS. WE WOULD LIKE DETAILS OF WHAT HAPPENED. MARK MCINTYRE."

No answering flash came back from the destroyer, so Mark switched off the headlights to save the battery, climbed into the car, and lit a cigarette. He knew it would take several minutes for the kid in the shack to take his request to the C.O. As he smoked and waited and watched and smoked, he had a horrible thought —suppose the Navy had already broken the story uptown? Should he return to Coast Guard headquarters, or stay on the wharf?

He played his hunch and waited. When half an hour had slipped by, he turned on the lights and sent his message again, changing it to sound more formal and official. "TO COMMANDING OFFICER U.S.S. PAULDING. PLEASE GIVE BRIEF DETAILS OF WHAT HAPPENED."

Immediately the yardarm blinkers split the darkness with a terse: "WHILE RETURNING FROM MANEUVERS OFF PROVINCETOWN 3:37 PM TODAY WE RAMMED AND SANK SUBMARINE S-4. BELIEVE CREW OF 40 ABOARD." Without taking his eyes from the rapidly flashing signals, Mark scribbled the message on the back of an envelope,

and it wasn't until he reread that tragic dispatch that the full import struck him.

Forty men—boys, many of them—helplessly trapped in a sunken sub on the floor of the ocean. Mark had been on too many subs not to realize what they were going through at that very moment. A cold, intense blackness. Silence broken by sobs and the sound of seeping water. The stifling stink of the batteries. The skipper's tired voice: "Take it easy, men, and don't move around. They'll be after us soon." A groan, a curse, mumbled prayers.

Mark didn't feel any better when he realized that probably by now the reporters on Main Street had the news, and were blubbering into telephones while he sat freezing his fanny on that fish pier. In his mind's eye he could see the big presses, vomiting big black headlines—and the bylines were his rivals'. He said to himself: "Smart guy, eh? Cambridge editor!" and he jumped from the roadster and walked rapidly toward the center of Provincetown.

A blank stare and a straight face may fool the average person, but it seldom works with a dick or a trained reporter, and the boys pounced on Mark as soon as they saw him. "Hey! Where ya been? Whaja dig up? Come on, GIVE!"

Was it possible they didn't know? His spirits rose slightly as he shrugged them off. "Wait till I get some smokes."

In the drugstore, he made sure no one followed him as he slid into a phone booth, dropped his nickel and whispered: "Long distance. Liberty 4000, and make it snappy, sister!" Before the clink of coins had ceased, he was asking breathlessly: "City Desk? This is McIntyre in Provincetown. Listen—have you had any report of what happened here this afternoon? YOU HAVEN'T? Well, here it is! And official! Ready? At 3:37 this afternoon the submarine S-4 was returning from manuevers. She came to the surface off Wood End Light and whango! the destroyer *Paulding*, PAULDING, P as for *Peter* yep, *Peter*, and PAUL-DING. You know, DING-DING-DING, P-A-U-L-D-I-N-G that's it. Well, the *Paulding* slammed into the sub and sent her to the bottom. Got it?" Then his voice choked as he added: "There's forty men on board the S-4. Yeah, looks pretty bad, poor devils. No, I haven't talked to headquarters yet, but I will right now. Sure, I'll keep calling. Goodbye!"

Ex-Navy man Mark McIntyre had completed his first assignment. He turned his mind to the second.

* * * * *

The next few days were trying ones for the reporters and photographers.

The only information from the Navy Department concerned the plans for rescue, and even a personal trip in an open boat, three miles out from Provincetown, in a heavy sea, availed almost nothing.

What was the fate of those forty men, trapped like rats in their steel coffin 200 feet below the surface of that angry sea?

Were they still alive?

Would the Navy reach them in time?

These and a thousand other questions were constantly before the newspaper boys, who suffered terribly from exposure and sea-sickness, as they braved the elements in open boats in order to make their last editions.

On Sunday afternoon, the sister ship of the S-4, the S-8, dropped her signal devices down alongside the S-4 and reported that some of the crew were still alive.

A buoy was attached to mark the final resting place of the submarine and then on Monday, as the storm increased to hurricane force, the ships rolled and pitched so violently that it was not safe for the divers to work. Mud hooks were dragging, and rather than lose additional lives, the Navy Department ordered all ships into port until the storm had passed.

With the first streak of dawn the next day, two Navy boats were seen patrolling the harbor. Back and forth they passed.

From the press boat, the reporters inquired if the S-4 had been lost, but Admiral Brumby had given orders that no more information was to be given out, and the reporters did not dare to say that the sub had been lost unless they were sure of it.

Every newshound on the job tried to think of some way of getting the Navy to talk, but to no avail. So they stood on the deck of the rescue ship *Falcon*, watching the divers as they prepared to go below.

There was Lieutenant Commander Ellsburg,

awarded the distinguished service medal for raising the S-51, Michaels and Eadie, two of the greatest divers that ever lived, and with them, Jimmie Ingram, a Navy diver, and a personal friend of Mark McIntyre.

Jimmie was getting ready to go down and look for the S-4. Just before they put his helmet on, McIntyre caught his eye and slowly moved his hands in front of him.

If any of the press boys noticed Mark, they thought he was buttoning his coat or putting his mittens on, but to the trained eye of a Navy man, the maneuvers of Mark's mittens meant much.

Over and over again, as he apparently fumbled with his coat, he was slowly spelling in Morse code the question, "Is she lost?" One of the Commanders picked up a megaphone and yelled, "Down Stage." The heavy diving helmet was lifted from the deck, and for a moment McIntyre feared that Jimmie Ingram would not have a chance to answer him.

But Ingram decided to stretch his tired muscles before he descended into that cold, green water. He stretched his arms and kicked his legs and lifted his hands high above his head, three or four times, and each time that he did it, the movements of his arms spelled Y-E-S.

When the water had closed over his friend the diver, a stream of bubbles marking his passage down into the darkness where forty men were slowly dying, McIntyre shoved off from the *Falcon* and went ashore. He said he was going "to get some dry mittens and a cup of coffee."

He had a lump in his throat and an ache in his heart when, for the second time in 48 hours, he called his office in Boston and gave them a scoop on the S-4—there would be no survivors.

END

The Great East Thompson Train Wreck

**Strange overtones of
coincidence—four trains wrecked
with only two lives lost . . .**

by Francis D. Donovan

WHEN THE HOARSE SCREAM OF ENGINE 175's whistle echoed out over the quiet little settlement at East Thompson, Connecticut, at 6:48 A.M., it occasioned no particular interest, for train whistles were common enough at this busy junction point. But when the sound of the whistle abruptly terminated in a rending crash, the inhabitants knew the worst had happened— a train wreck! They had no way of knowing at that moment that what they had heard was only the beginning—that within a few minutes, the cold, foggy morning of December 4, 1891, was to be remembered ever after as the day of the four-train wreck at East Thompson.

In 1891, the New York & New England Railroad was fighting for its very existence. Its double-tracked main line from Boston through Walpole, Franklin, Blackstone, Putnam and Willimantic to its New York connections at Fishkill, Wilson's Point, and Norwich was justifiably known as the "air-line route." Although the road's curves and grades taxed the skill of every engine crew, the New England trains made remarkably fast time to New York. This was the line of the New England Limited (six hours, Boston to New York,) the famous White or "Ghost" Train (five hours and 40 minutes,) the plush Long Island & Eastern States Express, the Norwich Boat Train, the Washington Express, and other trains noted for their speed and appointments, all hammering over the line that the New York and New England used as

The yard at East Thompson, Connecticut, on December 5, 1891—the day after the wreck.

its only weapon against its powerful competitor, the New York, New Haven & Hartford Railroad.

The New York & New England had its back to the wall, but it fought back with everything that steam and men could do. It was a time of high-wheeling engineers and high-wheeling locomotives; the "fast runner" was lionized by young and old alike—*if* he was a capable engineer—and the aura of glamour that built up around men like Gene Potter, engineer of the Ghost Train, long outlived their mortal activity. (See *Yankees Under Steam*, Yankee, Inc., 1970, p. 28.)

But to return to our story—the morning of December 4, 1891, dawned cold and damp, and a dense fog enveloped the whole countryside west of Douglas.

At East Thompson, the Southbridge Branch Local stood on the westbound main track, and engineer Joe Page awaited Conductor Sibley's signal to pull off the main line and head up the branch to Webster and Southbridge.

Still farther west, at Putnam, the weather had caused delays. Eastbound train No. 8, the Long Island & Eastern States Express, awaited clearance to leave for Boston, and beside it, headed in the same direction but standing on the westbound main, its headlight gleam almost lost in the fog yellowed by smoke and steam, was the special Fast Freight, drawn by engine 175. Engineer Harry Wildes and Fireman Boyce in the

cab of 175 found nothing strange in being headed east on westbound tracks—they knew that well before they reached East Douglas, the Long Island & Eastern States would have passed them on the adjoining track. This type of operation was simply an expedient to get the trains over the road, and, covered by the proper orders, had been performed successfully innumerable times previously.

Wildes and Boyce talked briefly with engineer Harry Taber and fireman Jerry Fitzgerald in the cab of engine 105 of the Long Island and Eastern Express. Wildes had expressed surprise at seeing Taber handling the 105 from Putnam to Boston, but Taber explained that the regular engine assigned to the express had developed mechanical trouble coming up from Hawleyville and had to be taken out of service. When Taber's engine, the 105, was assigned to complete the run, Taber insisted on being at the throttle of "his" engine. His affection for the locomotive and the indulgence of the motive power superintendent were to cost Taber his life. Taber smiled as he related to the other three men that his regular fireman, Mike Flynn, had refused to fire the 105 to Boston because of a strong premonition of disaster, and because of this, Jerry Fitzgerald signed on for what was to be his last run.

Engineer Wildes received his go-ahead, and before his train had little more than cleared Putnam yard, Harry Taber opened the throttle

Left photo: Taber and Fitzgerald were killed in engine #105, shown here after it had "reeled like a crazed colt" and hurtled off the track.

Center photo: Fire left nothing of #62's wooden cab.

Right photo: Engine #175, righted after it had plowed into #31, the badly damaged front end of which is seen left.

of his 105 and train #8 eased out onto the main line and soon picked up speed.

Not far behind them, and working steam, the fast Boat Freight with Ed Hurley and Will Louden in the cab of engine 62 came pounding up from the Norwich line into Putnam, and finding everything clear for them, swung onto the eastbound main behind Taber and hammered on toward Boston.

Thus was the stage set for one of New England's most noted train wrecks. On the eastbound main track were trains #8 and #10, only minutes apart; on the westbound main, and being slowly overtaken by #8, was the extra freight—all three trains burning up the rails toward Thompson and Douglas. The early morning light had little effect on the murky fog, but all three engineers, conscious of the fact that they were behind time, batted the stacks off their engines to gain precious minutes.

At East Thompson, Joe Page on engine #31 listened hard—then he heard it again—a locomotive whistle ahead of him to the west. The thought crossed his mind that what he had heard was probably the long-overdue Long Island & Eastern States Express, but even as he turned to fireman Cook to mention it, the orange glow of a headlight warned him that a train was approaching at high speed, and coming head-on into him! There was time only to shout a warning, and Page and Cook jumped

—an instant before Henry Wildes' engine #175 plowed into the 31.

The loud hiss of live steam escaping from ruptured boilers, the dust and smoke of the reverberating crash momentarily stunned those present. Smashed cars, engines, and cargo littered the East Thompson yard and spilled across the adjoining eastbound tracks. Within moments, train #8 ploughed into the debris. Taber's 105 reeled like a crazed colt and hurtled sideways, almost burying itself in the gravel alongside the track. Steam escaping from the 105's broken safety valve dug a huge crater in the dirt and hurled gravel and stones with such force as to ruin a dwelling across the highway. Taber and Fitzgerald were killed instantly, the only recorded casualties of the wreck.

By this time, confusion reigned supreme. The passengers in the sleeping cars "Cato" and "Midland" struggled from their careened coaches and wandered aimlessly about. Wildes and Boyce, badly injured, had not yet been dragged from their crushed and burning engine. Smoke and steam from the wrecked locomotives were soon implemented by more smoke from burning freight and cars. The bone-chilling fog all but obliterated the light thrown from the trainmen's lanterns.

Even when they thought of it, there was no time to flag down the Boat Train; it roared into the long curve west of the junction, and within seconds crashed into the rear of the

E. THOMPSON, CONN.
4-TRAIN WRECK
DEC 4, 1891 - 6:50 AM
NY & NE RR

LEGEND!
① SOUTHBRIDGE LOCAL
   ENG 31
   ENGR. JOE PAGE
   FIREMAN: F. COOK

② EXTRA FREIGHT EASTBOUND
   ENG 175
   ENGR WILDES
   FIREMAN BOYCE } INJURED

③ #8 - LONG ISLAND & EASTERN
   STATES EXPRESS - EASTBOUND
   ENG 105
   ENGR: HARRY TABOR
   FIREMAN: J. FITZGERALD } KILLED

④ #10 - BOAT TRAIN
   ENG 62
   ENGR: ED HURLEY
   FIREMAN: WILL LOUDEN

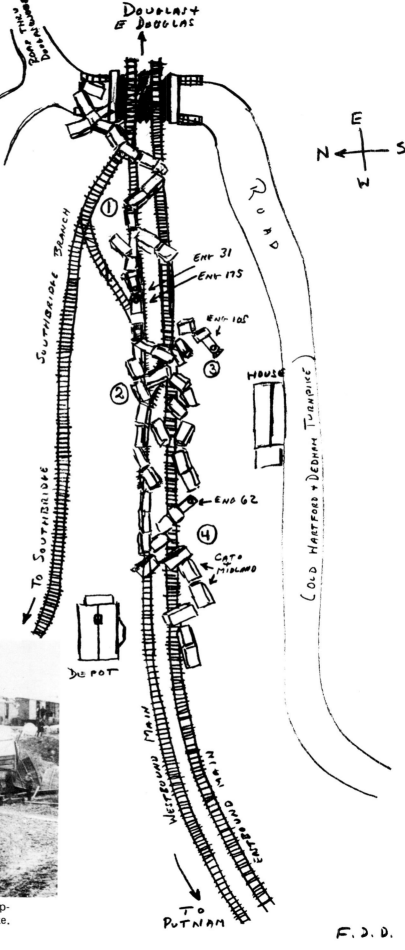

DOUGLAS & DOUGLAS

ROAD THRU DOUGLAS

E
N ← → S
W

Road

① SOUTHBRIDGE BRANCH

ENG 31
ENG 175

ENG 105

③ HOUSE

②

OLD HARTFORD & DEDHAM TURNPIKE

ENG 62

④

CATO & MIDLAND

TO SOUTHBRIDGE

DEPOT

WESTBOUND MAIN

MAIN

EASTBOUND

TO PUTNAM

F.D.D.

The cars of the Southbridge Local dropped off the bridge, blocking the turnpike.

wrecked Long Island & Eastern States Express; Engine 62's wooden cab caught fire almost immediately, but miraculously, Hurley and Louden climbed unhurt out of the twisted remains of their locomotive.

Word of the crash was flashed to Webster and Putnam, and fire-fighting and medical equipment were dispatched to the scene at top speed.

First reports of loss of life and property were greatly exaggerated; it was not until afternoon that it was definitely established that Taber and Fitzgerald were the only ones killed. The damage to rolling stock, however, was extensive. Norwood wreckmaster Hunton Bradley drily observed that the four engines, shorn of cabs and piping, "looked for certain like a row of plucked chickens. . . ."

The curious came from miles around—in special trains from Worcester and Blackstone and Putnam, in horse-drawn rigs, on bicycles, and on foot. Souvenir hunters—and others— helped themselves to Pullman car fixtures, lamps, and blankets.

It seemed to all incredible that the loss of life was so small in view of the scene of utter devastation that they beheld. The cars of the Southbridge-bound local had dropped off the bridge over the old Hartford & Dedham Turnpike road, further complicating travel in the area. Bales of cotton burned for hours, keeping a pall of smoke over the site, hampering clean-up operations. The track was clear by late afternoon, and the Ghost Train was the first train through.

And what about responsibility for the four-train wreck? The official investigations were no less exhaustive than the roundhouse discussions. Some said that the Putnam dispatcher had overlooked the practice of the Southbridge Local crew in using the westbound main to make up their train, but no evidence pointed to any such oversight. Some said that engineer Wildes should have slowed his train coming into East Thompson on a westbound track—but he was running a fast freight, he was behind time, and he held orders that gave him a clear track for the 15 miles between Putnam and East Douglas.

Some said that the Southbridge Local should not have remained on the westbound main so long—but nothing was due behind it, and the few minutes it stood there were well within timecard allowances. One thing that was never really settled was whether or not the operator or agent was on duty at East Thompson; if he was, and the dispatcher at Putnam had called him *after* allowing the three trains to start for Boston, and couldn't reach him, then no warning could have been given to the Southbridge crew. But in all the investigations, no mention was made of any operator's failure at East Thompson, so it is reasonable to assume that the station was not open.

What happened at East Thompson was probably the result of an odd combination of timing and operating procedures. It happened in the time when there were no automatic block signals or protective devices—in a time when railroad-operating practices seem nothing less than primitive—but in a time when such practices were the best available. Trains were operated on telegraphic and written orders, but once out "on the iron," a train could be stopped only by manual means. Trains delayed by bad weather and then hurled on toward Boston on only a few minutes' clearance . . . a local standing on a track on which no train was expected . . . no automatic warning signals . . . these were the factors in this and other train wrecks of the period.

The affair was not without overtones that were more than passing strange; Harry Taber killed because he would not let another man run his engine, and the engineer in question, Jim Brennan, alive for the same reason; Mike Flynn, Taber's regular fireman who lived because of intuition—the *second* time in his life had been saved by a premonition, and Reverend Joseph Jackson, the diminutive Methodist minister who performed superhuman feats of strength in clearing wreckage and leading passenger after passenger to safety from the burning coaches. Probably the strangest thing of all was that only two lives were lost in a wreck involving four trains, three of them moving at high speed.

But eerie or ordinary, it is all in the past, and is but a memory. The branch to Webster no longer exists, and only a little-used single track through East Thompson, where once high-wheeling trains roared through in the palmy days of railroading, attests to the former glories of the New York & New England Railroad.

END

by T. M. Prudden

The Light That Was Perfectly Safe

**"The lighthouse won't stand over tonight—
she shakes two feet each way now."**

MUCH HAS BEEN WRITTEN ABOUT THE OVER-turning of Minot's Light in the great storm of April 16, 1851.

But there is still more to the story than has been told.

Minot's Ledge, off Cohasset, Massachusetts, lies in a particularly dangerous position. It is so situated that vessels entering Boston Harbor, especially those from the northeast, could run afoul of it, and they frequently did when the weather was thick and Boston Light could not be seen. So the Government decided to mark these ledges with a lighthouse, the first one being completed in November, 1848.

It was a spidery-looking structure consisting of eight iron legs plus a central iron core, and two stories of living quarters and the light on top. It was common sense that such an open-work design would offer less resistance to huge waves than would a solid masonry construction. But evidently the power of such waves was underestimated. Those officials who visited the finished light could only do so on fairly calm days, and therefore they did not have the chance to observe the shocking power of a great storm.

Within a year the Light had shown a tendency to whip back and forth in a storm, so much so as to frighten the first keeper, a Mr. Dunham of West Bridgewater, Massachusetts. An interview given by Mr. Dunham to the *Boston Journal* on April 18, 1851 (the day after the Light fell), says: "He set forth his views and opinions as to the security of the structure in a communication to the proper authorities in May of last year after witnessing the effects of the several storms of the preceding 4 or 5 months. He, at the same time gave notice that he should resign his post the following October unless measures were adapted for the better security of the structure. His suggestions for the better protection of the work were not complied with and he was taken at his word, and is now in retirement."

Other whispers of the weakness of the Light

The spidery ironwork lighthouse first constructed on the dangerously shallow Minot's Ledge off Cohasset soon showed a tendency to whip back and forth.

were the occasional reports of failure of the tie-rods diagonally bracing the iron legs. Apparently these tie-rods were all too frequently dismounted and sent ashore for straightening and welding. An editorial in the *Boston Evening Transcript* of April 17, 1851, says: "A visitor who was present during the great gale of last December wrote, 'Of the Lighthouse I was coolly told that it was very doubtful if it stood through this winter, as one of the iron supporters had split the rock'."

At the time of the disaster, and for some time previously, the keepers were a Mr. Bennett (salary $1,000 per year) and two young assistants, Joseph Wilson and Joseph Antonio (salary $550 per year each).

It is of the greatest interest that these same two assistant keepers were alone in the Light just a month before its overturning, and lived through a storm of almost equal intensity. Mr. Bennett was ashore during both storms, and away on official business. One of these two

assistants came into the office of the *Boston Daily Journal* and told of his experiences. Thus he reported first hand the horrors and fears which were repeated a month later when the Light fell. It is most unusual to have a story told by a participant of an experience which was duplicated a month later, and which caused his death.

The interview was printed March 22, 1851, and is quoted here: "The following facts gathered from one of the assistant keepers of the Lighthouse on Minot's Ledge have thrilling interest. It is well known that this Light is constructed with a light iron frame, the posts being set in the rocks, drilled for that purpose at low water, the ledge being 3 miles distant from the shore. The late storm commenced on Sunday morning about 2 o'clock, the wind blowing from the northeast, accompanied with heavy snow and preventing objects from a distance of ½ mile being seen. During the day the storm increased, and on Monday morning the oscilla-

23

Above: Overwhelmed by the fury of the elements, the iron spider falls.

Below: Found in a floating bottle, this note hastily scrawled by Assistant Keepers Wilson and Antonio is now the proud possession of the Hingham (Mass.) Historical Society.

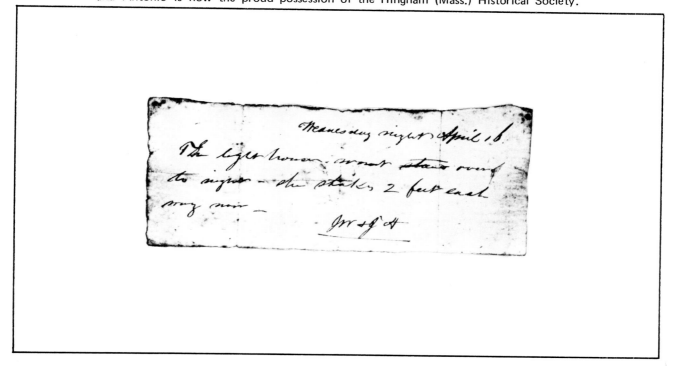

tion of the Lighthouse became so great from the action of the sea, that the inmates could with difficulty keep upon their feet and indeed were frequently knocked down. They were finally obliged to retreat to the store room, the next below, their cooking utensils having been broken, and it being impossible to remain where they were. Here they remained for 4 days without sleep and compelled to live on dry bread and uncooked meat. The (lamp) chimneys in the Light were continually being thrown out and, of course, broken, and the difficulty of ascending to replace them may be inferred from the fact the person who was compelled to perform this hazardous duty was several times thrown from the ladder in consequence of the vibration of the building, caused by the storm. The spray ascended to the receiving deck, a distance of some 50 feet, and thoroughly soaked the provisions and everything contained in that division—making it necessary to secure or remove them to the store room above.

"Thus for four days and nights the persons in charge of this Light were not only in imminent danger of losing their lives but subjected to hardships that would have discouraged most men.

"On Thursday morning the storm abated, and the wind changing to the north broke the sea.

"The only danger to this novel Light is by storms from the east-south-east. No protection is afforded in that quarter, being a free and unobstructed opening from the sea. From other points comparative protection is afforded by the shore and rocks."

On April 17, 1851, the Light overturned. The tragedy was reported in the *Boston Courier* of April 18. It is quoted here.

"Minot's Light was regarded as a structure of great strength but it could not withstand the fury of the elements on Wednesday night; although unharmed, it had sustained the shock of many severe gales. The structure was composed of iron throughout—whole height from the Ledge 75 feet. Diameter of lantern 11½ feet and it contained 15 reflectors of 21″ each.

"The last time the Light was seen standing was about half past three o'clock on Wednesday

afternoon, and the Light was not seen burning that night.

"About 4 o'clock yesterday (Thursday) morning, Mr. Bennett the Keeper, was on the beach and discovered strewn all around, fragments of the building. Parts of the residence room and of the lantern itself were on the beach, and also portions of the bedding, Mr. Bennett's clothes, etc. One of Mr. Bennett's life buoys came up on the shore having the appearance of having been

Gaining access to the "new" Light, completed in 1860, was tricky in rough weather.

25

used by one of the unfortunate men who were in the Lighthouse.

"The Keeper himself was not on the Light at the time of the disaster. One of his boats was swept off in the last storm, and he came up to purchase another, under the direction of the collector, and not returning soon enough to enable a boat safely to convey him from the shore to the Ledge, he providentially escaped.

"The two who were lost were Joseph Wilson and Joseph Antonio (a Portuguese). Wilson we learn was about 20 years of age; Antonio was 25 and formerly kept a boarding house at Cohasset. They were both true and faithful men.

"It is but a few weeks since, when the public was much excited in relation to the safety of this structure, that the engineer under whose superintendence the lighthouse was built, in a long communication published in the *Advertiser*, demonstrated on scientific principles that the building was perfectly safe. The communication contained a most ungenerous sneer at the fears which had been expressed by Mr. Bennett.

"We were confirmed in our opinion as to its insecurity by the testimony of pilots, fishermen and other nautical men who were aware of the dangers to which it was exposed, and of the fearful force of the waves by which it was washed, so that it oscillated at least 12 inches each way in a gale. It now appears by the testimony of Mr. Bennett that where strength was most required the braces were of cast iron (Note: this cannot have been so, the braces must have been wrought iron).

"A few days after the great gale of March last, young Wilson—a modest and unassuming young man—called at our office, and gave us an account of the fearful and appalling scenes through which he passed during the 4 or 5 days which the gale lasted. We remarked to him that probably it would be difficult to keep the Light if Mr. Bennett should leave it. 'Yes, sir' said the brave fellow, 'I shall stay as long as Mr. Bennett does, and when we leave the Light it will be dangerous for any others to take it'."

There are a few chinks to fill in, to round out the story.

One eyewitness report tells of seeing the Light tilted over 30° before a succeeding wave smashed it down. This seems unlikely since the consensus was that the Light fell during the night —a very dark and stormy night—and the Light was three miles offshore. Residents of Glades, however, reported that they heard the furious ringing of the tower's bell during the night and that the ringing suddenly ceased just before one o'clock in the morning of April 17.

The body of one of the keepers was found in a cleft on a tiny rocky islet outside Cohasset Harbor. It is reported that the position of the body indicated that the man was alive when cast ashore, and he died from injury and exposure.

The two keepers wrote out a message on a piece of paper, and signed it with both of their initials. It reads:

Wednesday night April 16
The lighthouse wont stand over tonight— she shakes 2 feet each way now.   JW & JA

This was put in a bottle and tossed overboard. Some fluke of the tide and wind washed it into Hingham Harbor (some say it was picked up in Massachusetts Bay). It is now a prized possession of the Hingham Historical Society. Its existence seems to be largely unknown except for a few history enthusiasts.

Shortly after the overturning of the Light, the underwriters decided to send the steam towboat *R. B. Forbes* to Minot's Ledge to remain until a permanent lightship could be provided.

Four years after this tragedy the construction of a second light of stone was started, the new iron framework being inserted in the holes left by the wrecked tower. After one season of work "a fearful gale obscured the Ledge, and when the seas moderated it was seen that the work had shared the fate of the first tower."

* * * * *

The present-day Light was finally completed and illumination first poured forth on August 22, 1860. It has withstood everything Mother Nature has had to offer—including giant seas which have, on occasion, swept clear over the top of the 97-foot structure.

On May 1, 1894, a new lantern was installed with a one-four-three flash—which romantic souls have decoded as representing "I love you." Since then, Minot's Ledge Light has been known as "Lover's Light" along the Cohassett shore.   END

The 97-foot 1860 Light has thus far withstood the giant seas which on occasion sweep right over its top. *Courtesy Edward Rowe Snow.*

by Carol W. Kimball

Mystic's Disastrous

An embarrassing chapter in local history . . .

ON A BEAUTIFUL JUNE DAY IN 1883, 18 YEARS after the Civil War, Connecticut G. A. R. veterans turned out peaceably to dedicate a memorial to the honored dead, but marched once more into artillery fire to see their ranks mowed down and their comrades fall beside them. For a while, action was so lively that some old-timers thought it would be their last parade.

Civil War monuments are common in New England towns, and the statue in Mystic, Connecticut, is not at all unusual in appearance. At the crossroads of East Main Street and Broadway a uniformed soldier leans on his gun atop a granite pedestal, gazing calmly to the southeast. There is nothing in his bearing to suggest the startling hubbub which accompanied his debut on June 13, 1883, but the chances are that no other memorial had such a dedication. Not only were the artillery shots misplaced, but both seats and platform collapsed during the program—all in all the dedication proved to be an embarrassing chapter in local history.

To begin with, the unveiling was planned for Decoration Day of that year, but had to be postponed when the New England Granite Company of Westerly, Rhode Island, could not deliver the statue in time. Ceremonies were rescheduled for Wednesday, June 13, with the whole county invited. The extra holiday was hailed with enthusiasm. Special trains were arranged, the steamer *Julia* planned a special trip from Westerly, and the Sound steamer *Block Island* announced her first gala excursion of the season from Norwich to Mystic.

Hosts for the occasion, the Williams Post of the Grand Army of the Republic of Mystic, began preparations in April, appointing five prominent members to make arrangements. Their chairman was Captain John Knight Bucklyn, founder and principal of a fashionable preparatory school, Mystic Valley Institute, veteran of 41 battles during the war, and about to be involved in his 42nd. Working with him were Postmaster J.A. Rathbun (wounded at Richmond), hardware merchant Parmenas Avery (21st Regiment), Deacon John Green Packer (Port Hudson), and C.H. Rowe (Heavy Artillery). The committee planned a day-long program beginning with literary exercises at 11 A.M. followed by a parade and luncheon.

Afterwards the men recalled ruefully, "The first advice we received was to spend as little money as possible."

Their plans were completed well in advance. They contacted a host of celebrities and patriots. For chief orator they engaged the popular Connecticut Senator, General Joseph R. Hawley. Governor Thomas Waller, who lived in New London, also agreed to attend. Neighboring G. A. R. posts promised to be on hand, along with the National Guard, an artillery company from Fort Trumbull, and several marching bands.

June 13 was perfect, weatherwise, and early in the day crowds converged on Mystic by foot, train, and carriage. At 11 A.M. an expectant 2000 waited near the draped monument, gift of the prominent Mallory family in honor of the vil-

28

Dedication

it was Bull Run all over again!

Capt. John Knight
Bucklyn, Officer
of the Day.

lage's brave men. A few miles west at Groton Bank, streets were deserted. Everyone was at the dedication.

General Hawley was already on hand. Everyone loved the former governor, commander of the First Connecticut Regiment at Bull Run and more recently president of the 1876 Centennial Commission.

But then came the first rumor of trouble. Other honored guests did not arrive on schedule. Governor Waller's train was late, and so was the *Block Island* with the Norwich delegation.

The audience stirred uneasily. Their uncomfortable seats had been put together somewhat hastily the afternoon before. Ordered to keep expenses down, Captain Bucklyn had to depend on volunteer labor to construct benches and platform. Although 25 fellow veterans had promised to give him a hand, only two of them showed up when the time came. The discouraged captain assembled some of his students to wield hammer and saw. By suppertime Tuesday, rows of makeshift plank seats surrounded the monument, and a shaky platform stood in front of the pedestal.

Bucklyn's complaints at the special G. A. R. meeting that evening got little sympathy. The post was busy mustering in new members for the big parade. Instead of listening to the captain's grievances, they appointed him Officer of the Day.

And so, just after 11 o'clock the next morning, while the audience waited impatiently, things began to go wrong. According to the editor of the New London *Day*, "During this vexatious delay occurred the first in a series of mishaps which marred the occasion."

Seated with other newsmen to the left of the speakers' stand, the editor heard a sharp crack. A portion of the improvised platform collapsed before his eyes, depositing several dignitaries on the ground. Fortunately, they didn't have far to fall. But next excitement spread to the audience when a whole row of Bucklyn's seats gave way, spilling a number of spectators onto the soft grass.

Victims picked themselves up and order was restored as the tardy New London train chuffed slowly into Mystic station, just down the street from the monument, bringing the Governor with the National Guard and a band. And while the Governor was escorted up Broadway from the depot, the steamer *Block Island* made port. She docked gingerly at the old wharf below the bridge, the largest vessel to steam up the tortuous channel, but she carried nearly 1000 excursionists and 150 Norwich Grand Army boys in their best uniforms.

As Governor Waller and his staff reached the tottering platform, certain Mystic veterans were hurrying three blocks west to the steamboat dock to welcome the Norwich delegation. To martial drumbeat, the visiting troops disembarked and, preceded by their Mystic escort, started for the ceremonies. Stepping smartly down Front Street, they made a right turn into East Main. The monument was almost in sight. Passing Willow Street, the first intersection, they could see the waiting crowds.

Right: Capt. Robert Palmer Wilbur, whose gold watch saved his life.

Below: Mystic's Civil War monument, some years after its disastrous dedication.

At the next corner, Jackson Avenue, Officer of the Day Bucklyn had stationed the Fort Trumbull artillery battery, ready to fire a 38-gun salute, one for each state in the Union, when the monument was unveiled. The guns were on the east side of the street, muzzles pointing westward toward the bridge and the advancing troops. Instructions were to fire when the speeches were over, and all hands were forming the parade a safe distance beyond the monument.

But during the awkward pause as belated guests assembled, the artillery officer, Lieutenant Fish, thought it would be appropriate and diverting to fire a salute in honor of Governor Waller. He asked for and obtained Captain Bucklyn's permission for this unscheduled volley.

Thus it happened that Fish gave the order to fire this salute at the exact moment the Mystic veterans were passing Jackson Avenue, happily escorting the Norwich troops to places of honor. The procession was not more than 20 feet from the gun muzzles when the opening shot was fired.

30

The first discharge of powder poured into the Mystic platoon. As the men fell away in confusion, their Norwich comrades bore the brunt of the second shot. Fortunately, the artillery refrained from firing a third time.

It was Bull Run all over again. Twenty-eight men were felled, struck by coarse grains of powder, their clothing torn and scorched. Some were marked and scarred by powder burns, others hit with pieces of wadding. There were no fatalities, but several required medical attention, including three Norwich visitors. Captain J.C. Brewer was badly cut and burned about face, legs, and body. Lieutenant Carruthers, assistant postmaster at Norwich, suffered a concussion and an eye injury from a heavy charge of powder in the face. Charles Young bled profusely from a severed leg artery.

Three Mystic men, Captain Henry Latham, Warren Burnett and Frank Cleveland, were wounded about the face. But of the hosts, Captain Robert Palmer Wilbur was the worst hurt. The well-known shipmaster, just retired from the sea, had commanded ships *Dauntless* and *M. P. Grace*, but never met such rough treatment on the ocean.

The first blast cut Captain Wilbur's face; grains of powder ignited his shirt. Then a piece of gun wad penetrated his pants' leg, set his canton flannel underdrawers afire, and raised a large blister under his knee. In his vest pocket the captain carried a fine gold watch presented to him by Queen Victoria's government for his rescue of 80 officers and men from a sinking British ship. A large fragment of waste struck the captain's chest, hitting the watch with such force that the gold case was badly dented. The hands stopped at 11:26. Captain Wilbur always believed the watch saved his life.

Casualties were carried at once to the nearby house of sparmaker James B. Sutton, and doctors were soon in attendance. Latham and Burnett were back in circulation at lunch, but the other victims remained out of action for the day.

Yet in spite of the accident, the dedication went on. The program proceeded as planned, punctuated at intervals by collapsing of platform and seats, which continued to break until they were a perfect wreck. "Of frailest description," wrote the New London reporter, "seats were supported on starch boxes and other light materials. A lit-tle more common sense might have been expended in their construction."

After the literary exercises, the monument was unveiled at last, and without benefit of the 38-gun salute! Then the parade wended down East Main, crossing the bridge over Mystic River to West Main Street, around the block, and over the bridge again. The crowd wound up at Jackson Avenue, happily this time, for there, in a 140-foot tent, lunch was served to 1300 marchers and guests. Mystic women had prepared lobster, baked beans, piles of ham and tongue sandwiches, and an assortment of cakes for dessert. At each of the 1300 places was a buttonhole bouquet. Using steam from Mr. Morgan's nearby machine shop, the ladies brewed eight barrels of delicious coffee. The lavish luncheon was easily the most pleasant chapter of the dedication.

At 4 P.M. a sudden shower broke and everyone scrambled for home or shelter, bringing the Dedication Day to a fitting close.

The countryside argued about the affair for weeks. Lieutenant Fish blamed Captain Bucklyn, saying that he had wanted to place his guns down by the river, but the captain said there were sick people close by who would be disturbed. Fish said he warned the committee there would be danger if the guns were pointed up the street, but claimed he was told it would keep the crowds back. Bucklyn retorted that he supposed Fish knew his business and would have enough sense to elevate his guns when he saw troops approaching. Most of the public agreed with Bucklyn.

"Either Fish did not know what he was about or didn't care," was the general conclusion.

Mystic's disastrous dedication with misplaced cannon fire and ramshackle seats was not soon forgotten. The only untarnished success of the day was the luncheon. "Perhaps it would have been well to allow the women to handle *all* the details," jibed the New London *Day*.

But in spite of a bad start, Mystic's Civil War soldier still stands in the same spot today, although his quiet corner is now a tiny island in the center of U.S. Route 1, surrounded by streams of traffic. Yet he continues to gaze thoughtfully to the south, his dignity unaffected by events of the past or present. June 13, 1883, is forgotten.

END

A roaring wall of molasses snapped the trestle of the Boston "El" (see sagging track, center) just seconds after the crowded elevated train whizzed by.

The Molasses Flood

by Alton Hall Blackington

Rupture of the giant molasses tank caused a very sticky situation

As LONG AS PEOPLE WORK AND LIVE AND PLAY IN the vicinity of North End Park in Boston, no winter will pass without someone recalling the catastrophe that took place there on January 15, 1919.

The scene of this tragic accident was that low-lying section of Commercial Street between Copps Hill and the playground of North End Park.

Looking down from Copps Hill on that mild, winter afternoon, you saw first the tracks of the Boston elevated—and the old, old houses nearby. Across the street were the freight sheds of the Boston and Worcester and Eastern Massachusetts Railways, the paving division of the Public Works Department, the headquarters of Fire Boat 31, and the wharves with patrol boats and minesweepers moored alongside. In the background to the left, the Charlestown Navy Yard. Towering above the freight sheds was the big tank of the United States Alcohol Company—bulging with more than two million gallons of crude molasses.

In the Public Works Department, a dozen or more horses munched their oats and hay, as flocks of pigeons fluttered around to catch the stray kernels of grain that fell from the feed bags. Stretched out on the running board of a heavily laden express truck, "Peter," a pet tiger cat, slept in the unseasonably warm sunshine.

This was the fourth day that the mercury of the thermometer on the sunny side of the freight shed had been climbing. On the 12th of January it was only two degrees above zero. But, on the 13th, the temperature rose rapidly from 16 degrees to 40; now, at 12:30 P.M. on Wednesday, the 15th, it was 43 above zero, and so warm in the sun that office workers stood around in their shirtsleeves (talking about the weather). Even the freight-handlers had doffed their overcoats, and sailors from the training ship *Nantucket* carried their heavy pea jackets on their arms.

Mrs. Clougherty put her blankets out to air

These two photos give a panoramic view of Boston's Commercial Street as it appeared a few hours after the two-million-gallon, 58-foot-high tank split wide open.

and smiled at little Maria Di Stasio gathering firewood under the freight cars. She waved to her neighbor, Mrs. O'Brien, dusting her geraniums on a dingy window sill.

In the pumping station attached to the big molasses tank, Bill White turned the key in the lock and started uptown to meet his wife for lunch. He bumped into Eric Blair, driver for Wheeler's Express, and said, "Hello, Scotty. What are you doing around here at noontime? Thought you and the old nag always went to Charlestown for grub?"

The young Scotsman grinned, "It's a funny thing, Bill. This is the first time in three years I ever brought my lunch over here," and he climbed up on the bulkhead and leaned back

against the warm side of the big molasses tank —for the first and last time.

Inside the Boston and Worcester freight terminal, Percy Smerage, the foreman, was checking a pile of express to be shipped to Framingham and Worcester. Four freight cars were already loaded. The fifth stood half empty on the spur track that ran past the molasses tank.

Mr. Smerage had just told his assistant to finish loading the last car when a low, deep rumble shook the freight yard. The earth heaved under their feet and they heard a sound of ripping and tearing—steel bolts snapping staccato, like a machine gun—followed by a booming roar as the bottom of the giant molasses tank split wide open, and a geyser of yellow-

34

The fallen roof of the huge tank is seen on the ground at right. Twenty-one people perished in the disaster.

ish-brown fluid spurted into the sky, followed by a tidal wave of molasses.

With a horrible, hissing, sucking sound, it splashed in a curving arc straight across the street, crushing everything and everybody in its path.

In less time than it takes to tell it, molasses had filled the five-foot loading pit, and was creeping over the threshold of the warehouse door. The four loaded freight cars were washed like chips down the track. The half-loaded car was caught on the foaming crest of the eight-foot wave and, with unbelievable force, hurled through the corrugated iron walls of the terminal.

The freight house shook and shivered as the molasses outside, now five feet deep, pushed against the building. Then the doors and windows caved in, and a rushing, roaring river of molasses rolled like molten lava into the freight shed, knocking over the booths where freight clerks were checking their lists.

Like madmen they fought the onrushing tide, trying to swim in the sticky stuff that sucked them down. Tons of freight—shoes, potatoes, barrels and boxes—tumbled and splashed on the frothy-foaming mass, now so heavy the floors gave way, letting tons of the stuff into the cellar. Down there the workers died like rats in a trap. Some tried to dash up the stairs but they slipped—and disappeared.

As the 58-foot-high tank split wide open,

The ruins of the firehouse demolished by the tidal wave of molasses. The shine of sweet death on the wall reaches up two stories.

more molasses poured out under a pressure of two tons per square foot. Men, women, children and animals were caught, hurled into the air, or dashed against freight cars only to fall back and sink from sight in the slowly moving mass.

High above the scene of disaster, an elevated train crowded with passengers whizzed by the crumbling tank just as the molasses broke loose, tearing off the whole front of the Clougherty house and snapping off the steel supports of the "El" structure. The train had barely gone by when the trestle snapped and the tracks sagged almost to street level.

The roaring wall of death moved on. It struck the fire station, knocked it over on its side, and pushed it toward the ocean until it fetched up on some pilings. One of the firemen was hurled through a partition. George Leahy, engineer of Fire Boat 31, was crushed to death under a billiard table.

In the Public Works Department, five men eating their noonday meal were smothered by the bubbling, boiling sludge that poured in upon them.

Up at fire headquarters, the first alarm came in at 12:40 P.M. As soon as Chief Peter McDonough learned the extent of the tragedy, he sounded a third alarm to get workers and rescue squads.

Ladders were placed over the wreckage and the firemen crawled out on them to pull the dead and dying from the molasses-drenched debris.

Amidst a mass of bedding and broken furniture, they found the body of Mrs. Clougherty —killed when her house collapsed. Nearby lay the body of "Peter."

Capt. Krake of Engine 7 was leading his men cautiously along the slippery wreckage under the elevated when he saw a mass of yellow hair floating on a dark brown pool of molasses. He took off his coat and plunged his arms to the elbows in the sweet, sticky stream. It was Maria Di Stasio, the little girl who had been gathering firewood.

Over by the Public Works Building, more than a dozen horses lay floundering in the molasses. Under an overturned express wagon was the body of the driver.

Fifteen dead were found before the sun went down that night, and six other bodies were recovered later. As for the injured, they were taken by cars and wagons and ambulances to the Haymarket Relief and other hospitals.

The next day the firemen tackled the mess with a lot of fire hoses, washing the molasses off the buildings and wreckage and down the gutters. When hit by the salt water, the molasses frothed up in yellow suds. It was weeks before the devastated area was cleaned up.

Of course, there was great controversy as to the cause of the tank's collapse. About 125 lawsuits were filed against the United States Industrial Alcohol Company.

The trial (or rather the hearings) was the longest in the history of Massachusetts courts. Judge Hitchcock appointed Colonel Hugh W. Ogden to act as Auditor and hear the evidence. It was six years before he made his special report.

There were so many lawyers involved that there wasn't room enough in the courtroom to hold them all, so they consolidated and chose two to represent the claimants.

Never in New England did so many engineers, metallurgists and scientists parade onto the witness stand. Albert L. Colby, an authority on the amount of structural strain a steel tank could sustain before breaking, was on the witness stand three weeks—often giving testimony as late as ten o'clock in the evening.

Altogether, more than 3,000 witnesses were examined and nearly 45,000 pages of testimony and arguments were recorded. The defendants spent over $50,000 on expert witness fees, claiming the collapse was not due to a structural weakness but rather to a dynamite bomb.

When Auditor Ogden made his report, he found the defendants responsible for the disaster because the molasses tank, which was 58 feet high and 90 feet across, was not strong enough to withstand the pressure of the 2,500,000 gallons it was designed to hold. In other words, the "factor of safety" was not high enough.

And so the owners of the tank paid in all nearly a million dollars in damages—and the great Molasses Case passed into history.   END by Leo T. Molloy

Tragedy at Peck's Mill Pond

Something was radically wrong— two wheels left the rails of the trestle. Horror mounted as the car lurched from left to right.

ONE OF THE WORST ELECTRIC-STREETCAR DISASters in New England, if not in the nation, occurred on the sultry Sunday afternoon of August 6, 1899, in Stratford, Connecticut, when a car loaded with passengers ran off a 65-foot-long trestle and plunged 50 feet into a swamp called Peck's Mill, causing instant death to many and eventual death to the seriously injured, to the number of 32. Men, women and children were among the victims.

The single-trolley track extended from the Bridgeport terminal, a distance of about 15 miles to the present City of Shelton (then the Town of Huntington). It had been opened only four days earlier. The line provided convenient public transportation to Stratford and Bridgeport from Shelton and the Lower Naugatuck Valley cities of Ansonia and Derby and the towns of Seymour and Oxford on the opposite side of the Housatonic River, which was spanned between Shelton and Derby by a wide, steel vehicular and passenger bridge.

The track ran along the main road from Shelton to Stratford through mostly open country of widely scattered homes and farms on its west side, while on its east side the Housatonic River, augmented at Derby by the confluence of the Naugatuck River, became a tidal stream which flowed placidly southeast to empty into Long Island Sound between Stratford and Milford.

In those days the cars were small and open, with seats extending the width of the car and two running boards on the east side, from one of which the motorman collected the four five-cent fares to Shelton. The lower running board provided a convenient step for passengers boarding or alighting from the car. It was a single-truck car with four wheels and a four-ton motor attached underneath the floor.

A happy, expectant crowd had assembled at the Bridgeport terminal, seeking relief from the intense heat during the trolley ride through the country and along the river with its occasional breeze. The women wore light summer dresses, stylish hats, and some carried shawls on their arms. The men mostly carried their coats on their arms and wore straw hats. Thus they were prepared for the chilly ride home in the evening hours.

At 3 o'clock, 26-year-old Conductor John Carroll, a recent bridegroom, gave the starting signal bell to Motorman George Hamilton, 40. A few passengers were picked up along the five-mile run to the center of Stratford, where more passengers boarded the car, including a number from Milford. As the car left Stratford, nearly every seat had been taken and some of the passengers were standing to be near relatives or friends.

The car proceeded at good speed for a mile before the unguarded trestle spanning Peck's Mill Pond came in sight. There was a slight incline of about 25 feet approaching the trestle, and Motorman Hamilton made no effort to slacken the car's speed. The four wheels of the truck under the car landed safely on the rails of the trestle and had gone about ten feet when the flange on one of the wheels on the east side of the car climbed the rails. Still the car went on with undiminished speed in this precarious position.

Two wheels on the east side of the car then left the rails, slipping outside and dragging the two wheels on the west side with them. The car ran along a stringer intended as a guard on the side of the trestle for a short distance.

The passengers, aware that something was radically wrong, by this time were in panic.

The unguarded trestle over Peck's Mill Pond, where the Bridgeport trolley jumped the rails.

WHERE CAR LEFT BRIDGE

WRECKED CAR AFTER BODIES WERE REMOVED

WHERE CAR LANDED

Many stood up grasping the back of the seats in front of them. There were cries and screams to stop the car but it continued to run along the edge of the trestle. Horror mounted as the car lurched from left to right, then left the trestle, hung in the air for a moment, and plunged down into the swamp, overturning as it did so, spilling out some of the passengers and landing upside down.

William Kelley of Bridgeport, John Cruite and George Canfield of Derby, and Motorman Hamilton leaped free of the car and landed safely in the knee-deep mud below. They were about to go to the relief of the passengers when they saw the upturned floor of the car, with its heavy burden of truck, wheels, and motor crash down upon the helpless victims, entrapping them and crushing out the lives of most of them.

Kelley waded through the mud to the lower road and hailed a man driving a horse and carriage. The man glanced at the wreckage, whipped up his horse, and sped off to Stratford to give the alarm.

In five minutes, three doctors were at the scene administering to the injured as the news of the disaster spread and a crowd began to assemble. Efforts to lift the floor of the car were without result. The would-be rescuers waded through mud to the now crimson pool which surrounded the wreckage. An hour later a block and tackle succeeded in shifting the floor to one side of the wreckage, revealing the grotesque pile of human bodies.

Meanwhile, nearby farmers with haywagons arrived; in these the dead were placed and driven into Stratford, where a temporary morgue had been set up in the Town Hall.

Three ambulances from the Bridgeport Hospital soon arrived. The badly injured were placed in these and rushed the six miles to the hospital. Two died en route, and four others died in the ensuing weeks. A dozen others responded to treatment and were eventually discharged from the hospital. By nightfall most of the dead had been identified and turned over to their family undertakers to be prepared for burial. Town Clerk Howard Wilcoxson of Stratford, also Registrar of Vital Statistics, eventually recorded a total of 32 killed in the wreck.

The Bridgeport-Shelton trolley line was ended in 1928 when bus service was instituted. In a short time the two trestles were dismantled and the tracks taken up. Thus the grim reminder was removed. END

A Terrifying Hour

**In Pittsfield, Massachusetts, two perilous
pussies ran loose and at large!**

by John Mason

NEVER WAS THE OLD SAYING, "WHAT YOU DON'T know won't hurt you," better illustrated than in Pittsfield, Massachusetts, on March 29, 1903. It was a foggy Saturday night and among the late shoppers hurrying home with their Sunday dinners were Mr. and Mrs. Patrick J. McCarty.

Mrs. McCarty held onto a basket of vegetables with one hand and onto Pat with the other. Under her arm (instead of over her head) she carried a big umbrella. Pat had quite a load, too—a dozen bottles of beer in a paper bag and ten pounds of rib roast loosely done up in paper.

As they felt their uncertain way through the fog and drizzle, they came suddenly to what they thought was Henry Piper's big dog, "Prince," right in the middle of the sidewalk. Mr. Mc-Carty thought the dog looked bigger than usual, but, as things frequently do get bigger and fuzzier on a foggy Saturday night, he said affably, "Hello, Princey Old Boy! 'Ows the old doggie woggie tonight?"

The huge, tawny animal, sitting on its haunches, licking its chops, and sniffing at the fresh meat Pat was lugging, gave a loud growl, and, swinging an enormous paw in Pat's direction, missed him by a millionth of an inch.

That was too much for Mrs. McCarty. Believing that even dogs should have good manners, she put down her basket, walked up to the beast, and scolded, "You're a BAD dog, Prince! Now get out of me way! Go on home, d'you hear? G'WAN!"

When the animal bared its long white teeth and gave no sign of departing, Mrs. McCarty lifted her umbrella and smacked the critter right between its big furry ears. With a surprised "yelp," the animal leaped over the hedge and disappeared in the darkness.

The next morning, when Mrs. McCarty opened her Sunday newspaper, she couldn't believe her eyes. Across the front page in big, black headlines were these words: "TWO BIG LIONS

40

ESCAPE FROM CIRCUS! PITTSFIELD CITIZENS HAVE NARROW ESCAPES! Enraged beasts kill one horse—Injure others—Hundreds flee as Lions Roam Streets."

In fact, two big lionesses had escaped from the Bostock Animal Show, in Pittsfield, Massachusetts, and for several hours that section of Berkshire County was in an uproar. The story was carried by the Boston papers the following Monday, but the general public didn't know that one of the lionesses had attacked and nearly killed her keeper on Saturday afternoon. Here's what happened.

The F. C. Bostock Animal Show had arrived in Pittsfield to play a week's engagement at the Academy of Music before moving on to Fitchburg. Big crowds had packed the Auditorium every day, and at the Saturday matinee there was a full house—mostly women and children. The youngsters clung to their mothers as they watched Madame Barlowe step courageously into the big cage where four enormous lionesses paced back and forth. One of them (named "Victoria") kept snarling and whining. Victoria weighed about 600 pounds, and there was a reason for her bad disposition. She was with young, and, as all wild animals are dangerous at such a time, the attendants kept a "sharp eye" on her.

When it came time for the lionesses to climb the ladder and walk the "tight rope" (which was really a plank suspended in mid-air) the other three lionesses went through their routine perfectly, but Victoria refused to budge. She snarled, showed her wicked teeth, and, when Madame Barlowe approached her, she crouched as if ready to spring. Madame Barlowe finally had to fire her pistol to scare the beast into doing her stuff.

But no amount of coaxing or threatening would get Victoria across the tight rope that afternoon. When the show was over, Madame Barlowe called William Crawford, one of the trainers, and said, "Bill, I think it's about time that Victoria was confined to her cage. She was tricky this afternoon and very ugly."

About an hour later, when Crawford stepped into the cage to toss chunks of horse meat to the lionesses, Victoria was still snarling, and the moment he turned his back she sprang for him. Crawford jumped, but one of the lioness' long claws caught him on the chin and ripped it wide open. As he was knocked headlong against the bars, he felt a stinging pain in his shoulder. Luckily, there was a pike pole handy. With it, Crawford forced the enraged beast back into her corner and tripped the gate.

When it clanged down, the trainer, bleeding badly from a dozen cuts, staggered backstage and collapsed.

Three physicians responded to a call for help. The injured man was removed to a doctor's office, where it was found that his shoulder and arm had been badly lacerated. To prevent blood poisoning, his wounds were cauterized. Several stitches were taken in his chin, his arm was put in a sling, and he returned to the Academy for the evening performance.

Calling the stagehands together, Crawford said, "Boys, you have to watch Victoria tonight—every second. She's tasted blood and there's no telling what she may do. If anything happens, don't shoot unless you have to. She's a valuable animal and we don't want to lose her or the cubs."

(Full-grown lions at that time were bringing between $1,500 and $2,000. Her "kittens" were worth $500 apiece.)

The stagehands did watch Victoria every minute. It was not until after the show was over and the animals had been paired off and put into smaller cages to travel, that somebody was very careless indeed!

Usually all theatrical equipment and scenery was hoisted from truck wagons in the courtyard in back of the Academy to the third-floor stage entrance by block and tackle. But when the Bostock show arrived, the manager of the Academy had a hunch, and he forebade the stagehands to hoist the animals in what he called "those old, flimsy packing cases." Actually, they were wooden cages or boxes with iron bars at each end. With two animals to a cage, the cage weighed about 1,300 pounds.

So when the show moved in, the animal cages were lugged up the fire escape and onto the stage—instead of being hauled up by ropes.

Well, when it began to rain that Saturday night, it looked like too much of a job to move the animals down three flights of fire escape, so a crew of carpenters put up a big, heavy beam that projected out from the upper-story stage entrance. A block and tackle was hung so the cages could be lowered onto the express wagons below.

About 11 o'clock that night, after the scenery, baggage and props had been let down, the cages were lowered. After supervising the landing of his panthers, jaguars, and a big, black "Nubian" lion, Signor Arnoldo started down the fire escape just as the cage containing Victoria and another lioness named "Sappho" was being pushed toward the open stage door to be lowered.

Looking down into the dimly lit courtyard, Arnoldo saw two express wagons drawn up to the loading platform. The bigger wagon had two horses; the smaller, only one. A crowd of 30 to 40 bystanders stood with upturned faces watching the cage containing Sappho and Victoria as it swung out from the third story and started slowly toward the ground.

When it was two-thirds of the way down, the rope snapped. The cage crashed to the concrete. The top flew off, the sides caved in, and both lionesses leaped out, into the crowd.

According to eyewitnesses standing safely above the lionesses, no human beings ever moved faster than those folks. The Monday edition of *The Berkshire Eagle* said, "As some of those spectators haven't been seen since Saturday night, it is presumed they are still running."

For a second or two both lionesses stood as if dazed. Then Victoria rose to her full height—just as you've seen lions pictured on circus posters—and sprang for the horse on the smaller express wagon.

With a blood-chilling roar that could be heard for blocks, the enraged lioness sank her teeth in the horse's throat and, slinging a giant paw over the animal's back, pulled it to the ground.

At the same instant, Sappho leaped for the horses harnessed to the other express wagon. Snorting and thrashing, they tried to get free from their harnesses and the wreckage of the splintered cage, but Sappho had a death grip on the nigh horse, and they couldn't get loose.

Hoping to frighten the lionesses away from the horses, Signor Arnoldo and J. Warren Chase dashed down the fire escape discharging revolvers, but the lionesses paid no attention.

Then Arnoldo ran into the courtyard and fired at Victoria point blank. He either missed or the bullets glanced off. It was several minutes before she left the mangled horse and crawled under the express wagon.

Sappho, meanwhile, ambled out of the courtyard and onto Cottage Row where, like a big dog, she trotted down the sidewalk—sniffing of this and that as she padded along.

(If one is to believe all the stories about that exciting Saturday night, Sappho was seen "on every street" and in "every back yard" in Pittsfield!)

The most surprising part of the whole affair is that, instead of staying indoors, folks got up, dressed, and ran out to chase the lionesses. In vain did police, firemen, and circus attendants warn them of what might happen if the beasts were cornered. They paid no attention. Armed with sticks, brooms, and guns, they patrolled the dark, foggy streets—prodding the thickets and poking all likely places where a lioness could hide.

Back in the courtyard, where Victoria was still under the wagon, Signor Arnoldo crept forward with his gun. When a few feet from the lioness, he aimed and fired several times. The lioness came out, leaped over the horses, ran a short distance, and dropped. Arnoldo then started off to search for Sappho.

When a local reporter learned that his boss, Editor William J. Oatman, had gone to a diner for his midnight cup of coffee, he phoned the lunch cart to warn Mr. Oatman not to leave because a lion was sitting outside on the pavement.

Mr. Oatman, however, had already left. He reached his office while the reporter was still phoning. "So", he said, *"that's* what I brushed against a few minutes ago. I thought it was a shaggy dog!" (The McCartys had thought so, too.)

The lioness caused the most excitement when she appeared from the shadows of Cottage Row and headed for North Street Bridge. There she stopped, sniffed a few times, and trotted across the bridge toward the Central Garage where she disappeared behind a vine-covered lattice. It was pitch dark back there, and the crowd circling and closing in did not know just where she was hiding.

Every so often some prankster would pitch a stone into the bushes, and, with screams and yells, men, women, and children went tumbling

The old Academy of Music in Pittsfield, Massachusetts, where the Bostock Animal Show was performing. *Courtesy The Eagle Publishing Company.*

all over each other to get out of the way. Then they would close in again, ready with such suggestions as: "Build a big fire," "Ring the church bells," or "Send for the militia."

Fortunately, Henry Jeffers, the night man at the garage, came along and opened the side door. Apparently Sappho liked the smell of tires and gasoline, for she made her way in. When the door closed behind her, the crowd gave a great shout. Now all they had to do was capture her and take her to the train!

The stagehands fetched a cage and placed it against the sliding door as Arnoldo stepped inside. Sappho, seeing her reflection in the door of a highly polished car, took a swipe at it with her paw and then sank her teeth in a tire. It exploded with a bang, and the terrified beast—like a cat in a fit—leaped up the sides of the garage and over the cars, turning the place into a shambles.

When she finally quieted down, Arnoldo spoke to her as you would speak to a kitten—and darned if she didn't trot right up to him. He patted her throbbing head and led her to the cage. In she went—glad to be in familiar surroundings.

All that night, Sappho wailed and moaned for her missing companion, Victoria—her pitiful cries sending shivers down the spines of all who heard them.

Meantime, the dead lion was skinned and the hide sold to a taxidermist. It would have brought more than $75 had it not been mutilated by souvenir hunters, who also took the teeth and claws as mementoes of that exciting night.

Many tall tales have been told about the Pittsfield lionesses' escape. It is said, for example, that when Drs. Roberts and Millett removed the lion cubs from their dead mother they were found to be alive and were brought up on milk bottles, later becoming favorite attractions at an upstate zoo.

And then there was the chap who is alleged to have broken the all-time record in the Berkshires for high jumps. When the lion was breathing down his neck, did he really clear that nine-foot fence?   END

The Marlboro Cornfield

DUSK ON FEBRUARY 3, 1898, CAME AS A HOWLING snowstorm. Engineer George Fairbank, along with fireman Frank Walford and conductor George Moffet, was urging his Mogul type engine No. 823 along behind a huge snowplow southward from Fitchburg, Massachusetts, to Framingham. As this was a single track on the old New Haven Railroad (and a busy one), a great deal of maneuvering and switching was required by the tower men to make way for the heavy snowplow.

A while earlier, conductor Joe Boudreau in Framingham had signaled his engineer Charles Eaton, and their 4-4-0 type No. 684 engine, with Eaton and his fireman Clarence Wheeler, had rolled the daily three-car milk train northward toward Fitchburg. As the milk train was an important run and the snow accumulation had not become too heavy, dispatcher Perry White wired the agent in West Berlin, midway along the route, to set a red signal against the plow train and have the Mogul take a siding for the more important shipment of milk on the 684.

But the telegraph tapped on deaf ears—heard only by the "Back In 10 Minutes" sign left on the door by the agent when he went to a nearby store for his evening meal. The 823 saw the customary "clear road" signal and rolled past. A mile north of Marlboro Junction the inevitable happened. In railroad circles they called it a "cornfield meet."

No carnival hell-driver has ever accomplished what happened next. At 40 miles per hour the milk engine ran right up the front of the big plow and came to rest on the boiler of the 823. While no one was seriously hurt, fireman Wheeler was nearly drowned when water from the 684's tender came cascading down. As the men started climbing down, engineer Fairbank hollered at the crew above, "You've got a damned nerve to be on this track!"

The next morning the smashed plow, which had protected the 823's smokebox front, was towed away—leaving the unbelievable scene in the photo.   END

44

Meet

by Richard D. Leggee

**The telegraph tapped on deaf ears . . . Then—
"You've got a damned nerve to be on this track!"**

2.
PIRATES, SCOUNDRELS AND ARTFUL DODGERS

Black Sam Bellamy, Buccaneer
The Great Sea-Water-into-Gold Swindle
Castine's Fake Baronet
The Oddities of Mr. Small

Black Sam Bellamy, Buccaneer

To make his dream a reality, Black Sam felt he needed more men, some women, and another ship as a back-up . . .

Illustration by Austin Stevens

by John J. Leane

THE STORY OF THE PIRATE COLONY OF MACHIAS, Maine, is a part of the story of Charles (sometimes called Samuel) Bellamy—adventurer, pirate, orator—who made his appearance in the nefarious and bloody business of piracy off the islands of the Antilles in 1717. He was also known as "Black Sam" because of the color of his beard and the shoulder-long, jet-black hair that hung from beneath his red bandanna.

Very little is known of the origins of Charles Bellamy. Some old records of seafaring and piracy suggest that he was born in England and spent his youth working on fishing boats that plied the shores of Newfoundland, Nova Scotia and Maine. Later he turned up in the Caribbean, where he engaged in salvaging gear from old ships and wrecks along the islands of the Antilles.

Not finding the salvage business very lucrative, Black Sam decided to turn pirate and take by force the treasure he had never been able to find in the coral-encrusted hulks of wrecked Spanish galleons. With a partner named Williams, he outfitted two small sloops and, after collecting a band of fortune-seeking cutthroats, set out to take prizes along the shipping lanes of the Atlantic.

Bellamy did not have far to go to find his first and greatest prize. Outside the Mona Passage that lies between the Dominican Republic and Puerto Rico, he came upon a British merchantman named the *Whydah*. The ship was on her way to England laden with a million-dollar cargo of gold, silver, coffee, spices, mahogany, sugar and other merchandise. Black Sam quickly noted, as did his fellow pirates, that the English ship carried 28 guns. They knew that a direct attack on her would be suicidal; their small boats would be blown into matchsticks by a single cannonade from the merchantman.

The two sloops hoisted the tricolor of England and sailed to the north. The *Whydah*, a few miles to the starboard, sailed to the northeast, ignoring what seemed to be two ordinary-looking trading boats out of New England.

When the topsails of the merchantman were barely visible on the horizon, the sloops turned to the east and trailed after her. After the sun went down and the bright stars of the tropic night began to circle the heavens, the sloops put on more sail and crept closer to the unsuspecting *Whydah*.

About an hour before dawn, when the bright stars of the tropic night began to fade and the sea-level darkness became a little darker, the two sloops came up on the stern of the *Whydah*. Grappling hooks were flung over the rails and Black Sam and his buccaneers swarmed aboard. The watch on the *Whydah* had been lax. There were only a few men on deck, some of them sleeping beneath the tarpaulins covering the deck guns. They surrendered without firing a pistol or lifting a cutlass. The captain was found sleeping in his cabin beneath the poop deck. When he violently protested the seizure of his ship, Black Sam ran him through with a cutlass and had his gored body flung overboard. The rest of the *Whydah's* crew was trapped below decks.

Shortly after sunrise, the crewmen of the *Whydah* were herded together on the aft of the main deck. Black Sam, looking down on them from the railing of the poop deck, gave forth with one of his anti-establishment harangues.

"Ye miserable scum of the earth, ye cowardly poltroons who serve kings, princes, and lords for a miserly pittance scarce big enough to keep body and soul together. Ye are yellow-livered swine, numskulls, and craven cowards to serve those who trample on ye with laws they make to protect their ill-gotten power and wealth. They make their laws to rob ye as they wish and enforce their foul laws upon ye with sword and musket. They banquet in the fine halls of their castles and mansions and leave ye to feed on the few crumbs and the gristle they cannot eat. To ye I say, *I* am no slave and as a free man I have the *right* to make war on them as they do on me. To all of ye I say, make one with me against these vultures who look upon us as swine and cattle. . . ."

With his fists pounding the railing and rivulets of sweat pouring from his forehead into his beard, Black Sam continued the tirade for almost an hour. When it ended, the men of the *Whydah* found themselves with the choice of becoming pirates or prisoners. Most of them, figuring it was better to be a live pirate than an ill-treated or perhaps a dead prisoner, joined the buccaneers.

All hands were put to work. The two sloops were stripped of their gear and supplies, and scuttled. By mid-morning the *Whydah* was under full sail and headed to the northwest.

Along the coast of Florida and the Carolinas, three schooners, a brigantine and two sloops fell into the clutches of the pirates. The vessels were looted and scuttled. Black Sam grinned and rubbed his hands together with satisfaction as their cargoes were lowered into the holds of the *Whydah*: casks of molasses, bags of coffee, sacks of beans, barrels of salted fish, chests of tea, sides of salted pork, hardwood lumber, bales of tobacco, and several iron-bound chests of gold and silver. The crews were then given the usual Bellamy harangue from the poop deck and a choice of becoming pirates or prisoners.

Until then, few who had not been actually attacked by the *Whydah* knew of its existence. But Black Sam made a mistake by which he forfeited this helpful obscurity. While taking on fresh water at the mouth of a small river in South Carolina, he stranded 20 prisoners on a lonely beach. He reckoned it would be to his advantage to have fewer to feed on the *Whydah*, but some of the marooned sailors made their way to Charleston and spread news of the depredations of Bellamy and his pirates.

All went well with Black Sam and his buccaneers until they were cruising off Cape Hatteras. The trade wind that had been fairly steady from the southeast died away and the *Whydah* floated on what seemed to be a calm slate-grey sea. Black Sam, standing on the poop deck of his ship, noted the change in the weather. Beneath his feet he could feel a faint stern-to-bow movement of the *Whydah*, as if far beneath her hull rolling waves were moving to the north. He noted the grey-white mist that shrouded the blue of the sky and the faintly luminous ring that circled the afternoon sun. He had seen weather phenomena like this before and knew that a storm could be expected. He set his crew to work. Drooping sails were furled and clewed to the yardarms. Deck guns were doubly lashed to their platforms. Below deck, the barrels, sacks, and crates of looted cargo were made secure.

The storm broke before sunset, and immediately the *Whydah* was scudding and rolling before gusts of wind of hurricane force. The sails that had been lashed to the yardarms blew away in tattered shreds, and rigging and ropes showered down on the main deck to be swept into the sea by mountainous waves of thrashing water. Incessant thunder crashed and rolled overhead while lightning bolts ran ragged patterns of fire down the black sky.

Three days passed before the fury of the hurricane spun itself out, and on the fourth day the *Whydah* was rolling on a comparatively calm sea about 50 miles east of Montauk Point at the tip of Long Island.

Undismayed by the storm damage to his ship, Black Sam set his men to repairing smashed yardarms and replacing lost rigging. He then spread fresh sail and cruised to the southwest. Off the Capes of Virginia, he captured two schooners and a brig and added their cargoes to his collection of loot. Also, after his usual oration on the iniquities of kings, lords, and governments, he added many more sailors to his collection of pirates.

By this time the *Whydah* needed a complete overhauling. She had been long at sea and had been blasted and battered by a hurricane. Her hull leaked, she needed new masts and spars, and her bottom was encrusted with barnacles. Black Sam needed a snug harbor where timber could be obtained and where his ship could lie unobserved during the several months it would take to accomplish the overhauling. He knew that putting into any cove along the southern Atlantic coast or in the West Indies would invite attack and probably bring about his capture or death, since news of his deeds and a description of his pirate ship had now spread far and wide in southern waters.

Bellamy turned the *Whydah* to the northeast and in a few weeks was sailing along the rugged coast of Maine. Several times he put in at what seemed to be snug coves but hurriedly departed when he found inhabitants in the areas.

The *Whydah* continued to the northeast and eventually came to Machias Bay and the mouth of the Machias River. It was here that Bellamy found the haven he was seeking. In a small shallop he explored upstream and found no settlements or inhabitants. At the same time he found that the river was deep enough to take the *Whydah* several miles inland from the coast. In the surrounding woods he noted tall pine trees that would make stout masts for his ship. From past experience he knew that these northern waters would provide codfish, salmon and trout to help feed his crew. Fresh meat could also be obtained by hunting deer, otter, beavers and wild turkeys.

About three miles inside the mouth of the Machias, the *Whydah* was anchored near a beach that lay between two hills. Defense of the anchorage became the first order of business for Black Sam. From dawn to dusk his prisoners worked at digging trenches and erecting breast-works on a slope overlooking the river. Five cannon were mounted on wooden platforms behind the breast-works to command the river. Other pirates and prisoners built huts of logs and canvas to provide shelter and to house supplies.

When Bellamy was satisfied that his position on the Machias was secure, the *Whydah* was careened on the beach, and her crew pressed forward with the work of transforming her into a seaworthy vessel.

It was about this time that Black Sam conceived the idea of making his fortified position on the Machias a permanent pirate settlement. During the spring, summer and fall, he could make forays into the Atlantic to take prizes, and in the winter, when few ships would be sailing the sea lanes, he and his men could hibernate in their hideaway on the Machias. To make this dream a reality, he felt he needed more men, some women if he could find them, and another ship as a back-up for the *Whydah*.

Four months after Bellamy arrived at Machias, the *Whydah* was ready to put to sea. Leaving 50 men behind as a garrison for his anchorage, he sailed out of Machias Bay and cruised along the coast of Nova Scotia to Newfoundland. On the way he captured a few fishing boats and plundered them of their salted codfish and sailing gear. The captain of one boat defied Bellamy and denounced his oratory as blustering nonsense. Black Sam cut him down with a cutlass and threw his bloodied body into the sea. After that there were no more protests from captured fishermen.

Outside Placentia Bay in Newfoundland, the lookouts on the *Whydah* sighted what seemed to be a French merchantman. To Black Sam the ship looked like a fat prize. He pressed on all sail and bringing the *Whydah* up beside her fired a halting shot across her bow. The answer was devastating. The French ship dropped canvas from along her sides and Black Sam and his pirates found themselves looking into the snouts of a line of heavy guns. In a thunder of smoke and flame, chain shot and grape shot raked the decks of the *Whydah*. Tattered pieces of sail, broken spars, and chewed-up rigging showered down on some dozen dead and wounded pirates who lay on the *Whydah* deck, their blood flowing into the scuppers.

The French ship, a 36-gun frigate taking a company of soldiers to their garrison at Quebec, pressed her advantage and drew close to the *Whydah*. Some French sailors and soldiers flung grappling lines to her rails and scrambled to her main deck. Here they were beaten back by the swinging cutlasses of Bellamy's men, who knew they were fighting for their lives. By this time some of the guns of the *Whydah* were in action, and a lucky shot smashed the mizzen mast of the Frenchman. Sails, yardarms and rigging came crashing down on her deck. In the confusion that followed, the pirates hacked away the French grappling lines, and the *Whydah* drew away from the battle. Black Sam had no intention of continuing a fight in which his ship would be battered and pounded by the heavy cannon on the frigate. He turned the *Whydah* to the southwest and returned to his anchorage on the Machias River.

About a month later he sailed out of Machias Bay again and steered to the south. Off Nantucket Sound he captured a schooner named the *Mary Ann*, laden with casks of whisky and wine. After putting a prize crew of ten pirates on board the captured vessel, Black Sam began to navigate to the north along the outside of Cape Cod. While he was giving his usual harangue to the crew of the *Mary Ann*, his pirates were swilling tankards of the looted wine and whisky. By nightfall most of the pirates were staggering drunk. When a high wind and a fog swept in from the east, they scarcely knew north from south.

The end of the *Whydah* came about midnight when she crashed on a reef near Wellfleet on Cape Cod. One version of the story has it that the captain of the *Mary Ann* wrenched the *Whydah's* wheel away from a drunken pirate and deliberately steered for the craggy reef. Jagged rocks tore ragged holes in her hull, and in a few minutes she disappeared beneath the foaming surf. The *Mary Ann*, following a lantern hung on the stern of the *Whydah*, foundered on a sandbank close by and, rolling on her side, went down in an avalanche of pounding waves.

The captain of the *Mary Ann* was the only survivor of the *Whydah*. Six of the men on the *Mary Ann* reached the temporary safety of a beach. Within a few days, the pirates were taken in a round-up and sent to Boston to be tried. On evidence presented by the captain of the *Mary Ann*, they were convicted of piracy and hanged.

During the following weeks, more than a hundred bodies from the two wrecks were washed ashore and were buried behind the dunes on Cape Cod. One of the bodies may have been that of Charles Bellamy, who had dreamed of establishing a pirate colony on the Machias River only to have his dream vanish in a flood of looted liquor that sent his pirate ship to her doom.

There are no records of what happened to the garrison that Black Sam left behind at Machias. It is believed that as the months went by and the *Whydah* did not return, they trekked away in small bands to seek settlements in Maine and New Brunswick. In such settlements they could pass themselves off as shipwrecked sailors and conveniently forget that they had sailed as pirates with Black Sam Bellamy. The huts and shelters they had built rotted away, and the cleared sites where they had stood were soon covered with brush and scrub; the protective ramparts above the river became rain-washed mounds of earth and boulders.

What happened to the treasure of the *Whydah*? No one knows. Did it go down with the *Whydah* or did Black Sam bury it in the hills around Machias or on some lonely island on the coast of Nova Scotia? It has never been found.

END

The Great Sea-Water-into-Gold Swindle

One small box extracted five dollars in pure gold from the ocean in a single night . . .

LATE IN THE AFTERNOON OF A COLD, RAW DAY in February, 1897, the Reverend Prescott F. Jernegan paced impatiently on the platform of the Providence, Rhode Island, railroad station. He had just come up from Florida, and he minded the stinging cold. He kept tapping his thinly-gloved fingers against his top coat pocket, and tracing the outline of a bottle-like bulge obtruding from it.

He wondered, as he awaited the arrival of his friends' train from Connecticut, if they would bring their bottles and the box which he had designed for their experiment.

When the men stepped from their train, clad in fur coats, earmuffs and mittens, he noted that one carried a strange package. He also observed that they were carrying a heavy basket, a lantern, and two small oil stoves.

Jernegan helped them stow the odd assortment of items into his sleigh. Then he picked up the reins and they drove off at a fast clip out of the city proper and towards the waterfront. Shortly, he drew into a shed and hitched the horse. While he lighted a lantern, his companions picked up their bundles, and then followed their former pastor over a long, rickety wharf that jutted into the harbor. On the end of the pier, high above the ocean, stood a small

Klondike,
No. Lubec, Me.

by Alton Hall Blackington

Left: Hiram Comstock's grist mill which became "Klondike Plant No. 1" in North Lubec, Maine. The tide waters passed under the structure and through Jernegan's magic boxes.

Below: Prescott F. Jernegan.

shack. Jernegan produced a key and unlocked the door. They went in out of the dark and wind and extremely bitter cold.

Except for a couple of broken chairs and a small table, upon which rested some storage batteries and wires, the room was empty. The one tiny window was heavily curtained, and a trap door in the floor was bolted. As soon as they had the oil stoves going properly, Jernegan took off his gloves, reached into his pocket, and, withdrawing a small glass-stoppered bottle, he placed it on the table.

"All you have to do," he said, "is to put your quicksilver in the box, then add the chemicals from this vial, close the cover, attach the wires from this battery, and lower away. I'll come for you as soon as it's daylight. And oh yes, don't forget to throw the switch. Well, good night, gentlemen! And good luck!"

A moment later, the Reverend Prescott Ford Jernegan (whose name was soon to be head-lined in newspapers all over the world) was in his sleigh, driving towards his Providence hotel.

His friends prepared for their great experiment. The box they had brought with them had been carefully constructed according to specifications furnished by Jernegan. It was made of wood and lined with zinc, and the

53

cover had several large holes so that water could flow in and out.

Into this box they dumped the contents of the three bottles of quicksilver which they had purchased, added the chemicals supplied by Jernegan, attached the wires, closed the cover, and opened the trap door in the floor.

A blast of cold, damp air rushed into their faces. The tide was rising and a few small ice cakes bumped against the slimy pilings beneath them. Slowly and cautiously they lowered the box into the ocean, closed the trap door, turned on the switch, and then settled down for a long, cold, anxious night.

One of the waiting men was Andrew N. Pierson, founder of the world's largest greenhouses of the day, in Cromwell, Connecticut. The other, Arthur B. Ryan, was a successful jeweler and a deacon of the First Baptist Church in Middletown, Connecticut. Ryan had helped Jernegan get his first pastorate after graduation from Newton Theological School, and he had been very much upset when the parishioners in Middletown had objected to Jernegan's high-handed method of preaching and forced him to resign.

Jernegan's next church was in Deland, Florida. He hadn't been there very long, however, when he wrote Arthur Ryan a very surprising letter, reading something like this:

> My Dear Deacon Ryan: A few nights ago I had a dream during which it was revealed to me that GOLD can be extracted from the ocean by passing a current of electricity through . chemically treated quicksilver. The dream was so vivid, I tried the experiment in a small way, AND IT WORKS!
>
> Now if we could get someone to finance a factory for doing this work on a big scale, we would soon be millionaires.

All evidence points out that no two men of finer caliber ever lived than Andrew Pierson and Arthur Ryan. They were intelligent, generous, God-fearing gentlemen, and their word was as good as their bond. Ryan, being an expert jeweler, knew a lot about gold, quicksilver and acids, and by consulting his encyclopedia he learned that in every ton of sea water there is an infinitesimal amount of gold, silver, and other metals. He also knew that for centuries scientists had been trying to find some inex-

pensive method of getting that gold out of the ocean. And here was a letter from his protegé Jernegan, claiming the secret had been revealed to him in a dream!

If this exciting information had come from some unknown, Ryan probably wouldn't have given it a second thought, but here was a young man whom he knew personally and respected. Jernegan belonged to one of the oldest and finest families on Martha's Vineyard Island, Massachusetts. He had been graduated with honors from Brown University, and he was an ordained Baptist minister. Therefore, if the Reverend Mr. Jernegan said he could get gold out of the ocean, that was all Deacon Ryan wanted to know.

He suggested to Jernegan that he come north and put on a demonstration. And that is how Arthur B. Ryan and his wealthy friend "Andy" Pierson happened to be huddling over two smoky oil stoves in a shaky, shivery shed on the Providence waterfront in February of 1897.

At dawn the next day, the two half-frozen men opened the trap door to find the rope and wires below encased in ice, for it was several degrees less than zero. They had barely hoisted the box and opened it, when Jernegan arrived to drive them back to the city. Examination of the box showed that some quicksilver had, mysteriously, leaked away, but there was still enough to fill one bottle. When this had been sealed and safely tucked in Pierson's pocket, they left the shack and drove to Jernegan's hotel for a hot breakfast.

All during the meal Jernegan kept impressing upon them that they had built the box in Connecticut and brought their own quicksilver. "And," he added, "you know, gentlemen, that I haven't the faintest idea which chemist you have chosen to analyze your mercury."

All of which was true! So after breakfast Ryan and Pierson went to a laboratory that Pierson had picked. Ryan did the talking.

"How long will it take," he asked the chemist, "to find out if there's any copper or silver or gold in this quicksilver?"

The chemist shook the bottle and said, "Oh, better give me till tomorrow noon. Takes quite a while to make a complete test." They left the quicksilver with him and drove back to the hotel to talk things over and to rest.

Wholly unknown to Ryan and Pierson, another friend of Jernegan's was also resting up in the same hotel. He was Charles E. Fisher, former floorwalker in a Brooklyn, New York, dry-goods store, more recently employed as a deep-sea diver. He too had been busy the night before on the Providence waterfront.

Next day the chemist reported that he had found "quite a bit of zinc, a trace of copper, a few cents' worth of silver, and *gold to the amount of $4.50.*" Ryan and Pierson all but fainted!

Jernegan just smiled. "If one small box and a bit of mercury can accumulate almost $5.00 in pure gold from the ocean in a single night," he said, "just think what we could do with, say, one thousand of those little boxes!"

They did think about it. In fact, they didn't think about anything else! But before they would say anything to their friends about investing money to build a factory, they demanded other demonstrations. Jernegan staged them with the same astounding success. Tests were held in Rhode Island and in Connecticut, and one very promising demonstration was conducted on the desolate shores of Block Island. While the amount of gold varied in these tests, there was always more than enough to warrant going after it in a big way.

Each time Jernegan furnished the "magic" chemicals which he said "did the trick," and, although Fisher was never seen, he was a part of the "magic" formula, walking on the floor of the ocean in his diving suit to "salt" the box.

On the fifth of November, 1897, a group of excited businessmen met in Levi Turner's law office on Exchange Street in Portland, Maine, to form a corporation "to get gold out of the ocean." With the exception of Fisher, who had suddenly appeared on the surface as a dear friend of Jernegan's, every one of the men involved was outstandingly successful in his particular field of business, and many of them were prominent members of the Baptist Church.

Jernegan had a slick-sounding name all picked out for his new enterprise. "We'll call it the Electrolytic Marine Salts Company," he said, "and I think, gentlemen, we should capitalize it for ten million shares at a par value of one dollar a share."

The directors agreed, the papers were signed, and each director purchased one share of stock. The remaining 9,999,995 shares were made available to Jernegan and Fisher, who were to hire agents to sell the stock to the public.

The officers of the newly-formed, ten-million-dollar corporation, with five dollars cash on hand, were as follows:

President, Arthur B. Ryan; Vice President and General Manager, P. F. Jernegan (he had

Nothing now remains of the Klondike plant. The arrow in the photo points to the site of the one-time grist mill.

One of Jernegan's "gold accumulators" was donated to the library in Lubec, Maine.

dropped the "Reverend" by this time); Asst. General Manager, Charles E. Fisher; Treasurer, W. R. Usher; and Clerk, A. P. Sawyer. The last-named two were respected business men of Newburyport, Massachusetts.

Andrew Pierson (who is said to have kicked in $25,000 to start things going) was made manager of construction.

When the directors of the new Electrolytic Marine Salts Company asked Jernegan where the first plant was to be erected, he had that answer ready too.

"Brother Fisher and I," he said "have made extensive exploration, and we have found an ideal location at North Lubec, Maine, on Passamaquoddy Bay. The tides are very high up there, and they will furnish us with millions of tons of gold-bearing sea water. Then too, the natural isolation of that section of Maine is greatly to our advantage. With a secret process like ours, we can't afford to have inquisitive competitors poking around."

You bet their boots they couldn't have anyone poking around! And the first thing they did, after taking over the old Comstock Grist Mill at North Lubec, was to build a board fence ten feet high all around their property, with three strands of barbed wire on top. And they armed the guards at this "Klondike Plant" with rifles and shotguns.

How the scheme was worked. (Drawn for an 1898 edition of the *Boston Sunday Herald*.)

In short order, several large basins were built, and a 700-foot dam put in, with automatic gates to control the "gold-bearing sea water." Under the Grist Mill was a sluiceway, and to this were attached 243 of the "magic" boxes.

When the contents of these "accumulators" were analyzed by the U.S. Assay Office in New York and found to contain gold at the rate of $308.61 worth every 24 hours, the rush to invest was on.

Another, bigger dam was built at the canal, and a rickety old wooden bridge was replaced with an iron structure, all at the expense of the E.M.S. Company. New offices, stables, and cottages were put up fast, while the officials of the company purchased several fine year-round residences to live in.

The very air was electric with the ring of hammers, saws, drills, and chugging pumps. When the noonday whistle blew, more than 600 workmen knocked off to eat.

President Ryan told the out-of-state visitors, "To date, we've spent $50,000 on this 'Klondike Plant.' The new one at the canal will cost ten times as much. At present, we have 243 machines working, and each one collects about $1.27 worth of gold out of the ocean every 24 hours."

But there came a day, in July 1898, when there was no gold in the "accumulators" for Mr. Arrington to make into bricks!

The reason? Well, there was no Mr. Fisher to put gold into the boxes when no one was watching. Fisher, it seems, had gone away without telling anyone he was going. Then Jernegan also disappeared!

They had often been away before on business. Jernegan made frequent trips to New York to confer with various bankers, while Fisher had to traipse all over the country to get old gold (stick pins, wedding rings and discarded watch cases) that could be melted down for him to put in the accumulators under the cover of darkness.

This time it was different! No word was ever heard from Fisher again. It was later learned that he had fled to New South Wales, where he died a few years later—penniless and unmourned by his respectable relatives.

But Jernegan made the headlines in a big way. He had deposited sizable sums of money in the Fourth National Bank of New York, and the King's County Trust Company. Two days after he made the deposits, he wanted the money back "to buy platinum wire"—he said. The New York bank officials got suspicious and telephoned the National Shawmut Bank in Boston to ask about Jernegan's credit. The report came back as "O.K."—and he withdrew $90,000, with which he bought a lot of government bonds and held the rest as ready cash.

Shortly afterwards, the New York banks became more suspicious and put Pinkerton's on Jernegan's trail. He was located in the office of the French Line buying a ticket to Europe under the alias of "Louis Sinclair."

On July 23, 1898, Jernegan sailed for France with his wife, little son, and about $100,000. Ryan presently received a letter from Jernegan, mailed in New York before sailing, in which he said, "Fisher had disappeared with the formulas. I'm afraid he had fooled us all, and I'm going to Europe to try to find him."

It was a dark day for Pierson when the news was relayed to him. For several days neither he nor Ryan could bring himself to believe that he had been so cleverly and completely hoaxed. Both men lost heavily, as did hundreds of other investors.

Oddly enough, Jernegan returned $75,000 of the stolen swag to his American investors, from Brussels, Belgium. This, plus the sale of the company's assets and the scrupulous honesty of its directors, permitted the stockholders eventually to collect 36 cents on every dollar invested. The sea-water-gold scheme was trotted out again in England, but the Britons proved warier game, and Jernegan lost $30,000 of his ill-gotten gains in the attempt to fleece them. The shock seems to have persuaded him to "go straight," for he ended up as an able and respected school teacher in the Philippine Islands!

END

by Francis W. Hatch

Castine's Fake

IN MARCH, 1863, THE BRIG MAUD BRIGGS RAN through Fort Point narrows and hove to off Bucksport, Maine. She found a berth and in a short while her skipper, Captain Jordan, was barking orders for tying up. One of the crew was a 22-year-old Englishman. A month earlier, in a West Indian port, he had appeared on board with a plea to work his passage north. Captain Jordan, a thrifty man, could use a hand with no wages involved, and signed him on. In the log he entered the name, "Charles Cecil Jocelyn." Jocelyn was thinly clad and destitute,

and Captain Jordan fitted him out with odds and ends from the slop chest. The *Maud Briggs* headed north, keeping well off shore from Confederate raiders. For Jocelyn, Bucksport was the jumping-off place. After two days occupied with unloading, he turned in his sea-going gear. Donning his light West Indian cotton clothes, he inquired directions to the town of Penobscot and took off on foot. In his pocket he carried messages and trinkets from a homesick boy he had met in the Bahamas, a Penobscot lad serving before the mast on a ship bound for South

Baronet

View of Castine, Maine, from the sea (from an old print).

America. Learning that Penobscot was a neighboring town to Bucksport, Jocelyn readily agreed to act as messenger. He was ill equipped to tussle with March, Maine's meanest month.

Two hours later, in a sorry state of exhaustion and chill, he arrived where the road forks at North Castine. In desperation, seeing a light in a house on the shoulder of the hill to the right, he forgot about his Penobscot errand and took the right fork. Had he chosen the Penobscot road to the left, it is likely that he could not have survived. The light shone from the house windows of Eliakin Hutchings, a farmer who lived with his wife Lizzie and daughter Annie. Mrs. Hutchings, answering Jocelyn's knock, opened the door. Touched by the obvious plight of the stranger, she remembered her Bible, asked him in, gave him hot tea, and attended to his frozen feet. She then clapped him into bed to ward off the pneumonia that had undoubtedly ridden in on his shoulder.

During the next few days, between changes of hot bricks in the bed and the restorative of nourishing food, Jocelyn began to thaw out physically and vocally. According to him, that ill March wind had blown nothing less than a full-fledged graduate of Cambridge into the Hutchings household and "Cambridge" was not to be confused with Cambridge, Massachusetts. His genteel manners and elegant speech were proof that he was no mere Yankee stray. Word spread up and down the road of the Hutchings' high-toned visitor. Folks came to call. And Annie began to re-appraise her Yankee suitors who could offer her, at best, a continuation of the same sparse living which she had accepted in boredom to date.

To the amazement of all, Jocelyn revealed further that he had been brought up, as prospective heir, in the household of a wealthy uncle, a landed Baronet, no less. As heir presumptive, to prove his loyalty to the crown, and for the honor of his rich uncle, he had served with British forces in the field against warring Zulus. Here, through bravery, he had risen to the rank of Petty Officer.

At the end of the campaign he had returned to England and the welcoming arms of his uncle, victorious and unscathed. On the first available Sunday, he had accompanied the Baronet to church, where the old gentleman had offered prayers of gratitude to the Almighty for sparing his nephew from those grisly, ebon-shafted spears. Indeed the old man was so emotionally overcome that he suffered a jolt of apoplexy right in church and expired.

Next, skulduggery. For just as Jocelyn was about to take over, a cousin appeared, a few weeks older, and laid claim. Barristers, skeptical at first, made careful investigation and ruled that the dark horse was the winner. Shattered and penniless, Jocelyn, chagrined to have had ermine slip through his fingers, fled to the West Indies.

After a few months, Mrs. Hutchings realized that here, right under her own roof, a match might be in the making between her daughter and her star boarder. It would be a link-up of dazzling brilliance—far beyond anything which might develop with local boys up and down the road. Annie was regarded by her neighbors as a smart and intelligent young girl. She was reassured by the enthusiasm of the local minister of her church. Charles had joined the congregation, and the Reverend noted that it was his habit to sign the local guest books with this forthright statement in a flourishing hand: "Charles Jocelyn. Trust in God and be not Daunted."

They were married. To prepare his bride for the formal and sophisticated life in England that seemed to lie ahead, her husband prescribed a course of reading which would broaden her mind and give her social perspective.

In his early married years Jocelyn, according to a neighbor, "was not one to work around the place." He was devoting all of his time to the development of strategy which would bring him finally into his temporarily frustrated birthright. He stuck to his story, embroidered it here and there, and his reputation spread.

Then came an incredible break which put those who had begun to doubt him squarely in their places. A newly-arrived Britisher was said to have recognized Charles as a boyhood playmate back home. Furthermore, he passed along the electrifying news that the Baronet incumbent was not long for this world. Word breezed up and down the road that Charles and Annie would shortly be shipping out in triumph. To make it stick, at home Charles played mail-order Pygmalion. He ordered a course of sprouts from the city which, with study, would fit Annie for the high station she was about to occupy. Annie pitched in and Ma Hutchings, with a Queen Mother complex, held the book —the old-fashioned "Emily Post"—with daily quizzing.

He smelled a rat—Lizzie Hutchings' cultured

Give Charles credit for thinking things through. "He could look you right in the eye and with that polished palaver make you believe that Castine Light was Bishop's Rock." With the estate about to fall in his lap, he whispered the word about that he had already received advance payments. He began to indulge himself in trips on the Boston boat, rooms at the Hotel Touraine, and new clothes for Annie.

At this point my interest in the dark doings draws much closer to home. For Charles became involved with Jonas Turner. And Jonas Turner lived for 80 years under the roof of the very house which shelters me as I write. Jonas was an odd man. Very odd. He never married. In his later days he lived in this eighteenth-century farm house under the eye of Abby, his sister-in-law. Abby's husband, Oren, had been inconsiderate enough to toss a halter over a beam in the carriage house, mount a cracker box, and hasten his exit from North Castine. Jonas overcame his fraternal grief by a constant communing with the spirits. Every move he made, every daily decision was guided by instructions from the spirit world. It was his habit, when walking the roads, to stop dead, spit, stamp three times, and jerk around in his tracks. Such a maneuver exorcised the evil spirits creeping up at his shoulder.

When Abby died, Jonas was left to shift for himself with spirit friends, a stew pot on the stove and a fiddle for company. Daytime he did well enough. But nights, alone, were hard to take. He made arrangements to rent a room up the road in the Hutchings house where he could be safe in the company of Eliakin, Lizzie, Annie and Charles. He took his valuables along in a small trunk, installing it beneath his bed. Presently he became aware of a grave shortage —namely, a thousand dollars in bonds and cash, a third of the sum in what was apparently not-so-safe deposit. Lizzie Hutchings, who had now

and again joined Jonas in seances, suggested that an ectoplasmic hand had probably extracted the funds for celestial loan to a needy old spirit friend. Jonas, despite his faith, knew for certain that hard cash will never orbit of its own accord. He smelled a rat—Lizzie Hutchings' cultured pearl of a son-in-law.

True to his gentlemanly instincts, Charles, when confronted with plain talk from Jonas, confessed in an elegant manner. Jonas, after consulting a spiritual adviser, forgave him but found a new hiding place for his strong box. When the story became known, as such things inevitably do in the country, there was indignation up and down the road. Despite Jonas' forgiveness, the High Sheriff was summoned. He followed Charles' trail to Bucksport where he had disposed of Jonas' bonds. True to his public trust, he drove the Baronet pretender off to the lockup at Ellsworth.

After serving his sentence, Charles talked himself into Annie's good graces and opened a new chapter of their married life in Bucksport. Here was a new field altogether elysian in its broader opportunities. Ever the cultured and educated man, Charles conducted important ichthyological research at the Government Fish Hatchery at Orland. "He would sink a bottle sixty feet into the lake to get a sample of water. He'd analyze it and then dissect out a fish's stomach and see just what he was feed'n on. Why, some cancer experts came all the way from Buffalo to see if they could learn anything from what he was up to."

But then a resumption of those sprees on the Boston boat with a suite at the Touraine happened to coincide with shortages in a building and loan society. Charles had been handling the cash. The Judge decided that six years at Thomaston would be about right.

Ah, those Cambridge graduates who came to a fork in the road!   END

pearl of a son-in-law.

The Oddities of Mr. Small

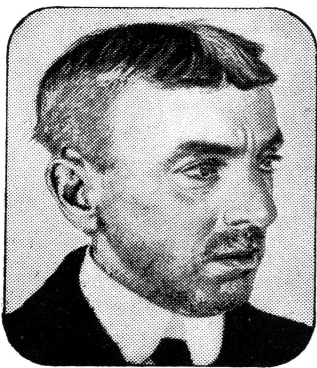

Frederick J. Small, fiftyish, undersized, with grey hair and a limp, looked mean enough to bite.

WHEN FREDERICK J. SMALL MOVED WITH HIS wife to Mountainview, New Hampshire, in 1914, he soon gained a reputation as an odd one. Gray-haired, fiftyish, undersized, he walked with a limp and looked mean enough to bite.

But he could be affable when he felt like it. His affability was best when he had had a nip or two at the local bar. Then he could become sociable, delivering judgments on everything from President Wilson to the Boston Red Sox.

Small, however, was seldom affable to his wife, Florence, who was three inches taller than he, years younger and outweighed him by some 25 pounds. It was his custom to address her in snarls. Florence, somehow, could never do anything right. He seldom called her by her given name, usually referring to her as "Stupid," or "Numbskull." Being a peaceable sort, she tried to placate him, which only seemed to increase his anger.

The Smalls, who came from Massachusetts, had a cottage on the south shore of Lake Ossipee, a mile from the village, a neat place except that the cellar took in water when the lake was high. Small didn't work. He said he was an investor, and talked knowingly of U.S. Steel, Pennsylvania Railroad and other stocks. Once a month or so he would go down to Boston and come back telling of the smart deals he had made with his broker, and how easy it was to beat the stock market if you knew how.

The rest of the time he just fiddled around the cottage, berating Florence, or he went fishing, or tinkered. Mechanically he was very clever. He had a workshop at the end of the cottage where he turned out bookcases and other specimens of carpentry, but above all he liked to experiment with electricity. He bought dry-cell batteries and wire and delighted in sending electrical impulses that would activate a buzzer at the other end of the house—a real feat in 1914.

When he went fishing, he naturally had Florence do the rowing for him, and complained angrily about her clumsiness. Florence must by W. A. Swanberg

best of all to experiment with electricity . . .

have been relieved when he bought an outboard motor, which he could take apart and put together again better than most mechanics. The Smalls occasionally fraternized with summer-resident neighbors on the lakeshore, but not very successfully because of Small's temper. One night a couple named Emerson, who rented a nearby cottage, came to play hearts with them. Things went fairly well until Florence dealt Small the Queen, which sent him into such a paroxysm of rage that he shouted imprecations at her and she retired sobbing into the kitchen. The Emersons decided to call it an evening. As they walked home, they heard a scream from the Small place. Emerson thought of going back, but reflected that it was best not to interfere in domestic quarrels.

While a few henpecked husbands in the area envied Small his iron rule, it could not be said that he was popular. Yet in time he became accepted as a local eccentric. Early in 1916 he insured his cottage for $2000 and the contents for another $1000. He suddenly became very insurance-minded, deciding to insure his life and that of his wife jointly for $20,000. He called in Edwin Conner, principal of the Center Ossipee school, who was also agent for the John Hancock Mutual of Boston. Conner was only too happy to handle the deal. However, in making out the application, which had to be signed by both husband and wife, Small signed not only his own name but his wife's, too, in his own hand.

Conner explained that this would not do. Mrs. Small had to sign her own name. Small grumbled about this, but finally had his wife affix her own signature, and the transaction was completed. Small seemed to like Conner, telling him he had a couple of friends in Boston who needed insurance, and he thought he could steer Conner into some more business.

By the middle of September, the summer residents had departed, and the Smalls were alone in their part of the lakeshore. Small arranged to

go with Conner on the afternoon of September 28 to Boston, where he would attend to his own stocks and steer the insurance man to a sale or two. They would meet at the station and catch the 4:07 train. That morning, Charles Sceggel, the Mountainview grocer, delivered an order to the Small home—five gallons of kerosene and some staples. He spoke cordially to Mrs. Small and went his way. At 1:30, Small, who had no car, telephoned John Kennett of the Central House in Mountainview, asking him to pick him up and drive him to the station, a chore Kennett had performed before. Kennett arrived in plenty of time, to find Small waiting outside with his topcoat and bag.

Small nodded to him, then strode to the door of his house, opened it and shouted, "Well, goodbye!"

He then got in with Kennett and they drove to the station, Kennett reflecting that Small must be in unusually good spirits to be so thoughtful as to bid his wife farewell.

Small met Conner at the station and they boarded the 4:07 together, reaching North Station in Boston at 8 P.M. They registered at Young's Hotel, where Small took the trouble to send his wife a postcard. Then he and Conner went to a movie, planning their business for the morrow.

Meanwhile, at Mountainview, around 10 o'clock someone saw flames leaping high into the sky on the lakeshore. A swarm of citizens hurried out there with the town's lone fire apparatus. They found Small's home ablaze from end to end. The firemen had never experienced such heat. The house seemed more like a blast furnace than burning wood, and it was impossible to get within 100 feet of it. Luckily there were no other houses nearby, but trees at a considerable distance were shrivelled by the heat. The firemen could do little but watch the blaze and wonder where Mrs. Small was, realizing that if she was inside she was long past any help.

In Boston, Small and Conner got back to the

hotel at 12:30 to find that Small had received an urgent telephone call from Mr. Ferren, the proprietor of the Central House in Mountainview. Small called Ferren back. Bystanders heard his voice rise in apprehension.

"My house—burned down?" he cried. "Where is my wife? . . . Oh—my poor darling!"

He turned a stricken face to Conner, asking him to take the wire and verify the message. Conner talked to Ferren, who repeated the tidings and advised that Small come home immediately. Small was weeping bitterly when Conner took him up to their room, where both of them packed their bags. Since there was no train at that hour, they rented a Packard and driver from the hotel. Small had a bottle of rye in his bag, which he opened, taking an occasional nip to steady his nerves as they rode northward through the night.

"Florence kissed me goodbye when I left," he groaned. "Who would have thought that was the last time I'd ever see her on this earth?"

Eventually he got his grief under control. He reasoned that the fire must have started from sparks popping from the fireplace. Florence liked to sit in front of the fireplace and read in the evening, he said. Once he turned to Conner.

"You don't think there'll be any difficulty about the insurance, do you?" he asked.

They reached Mountainview at 4:30 in the morning. Small said miserably that he did not want to see the ruins just yet. He went to the Central House, where he had ham and eggs for breakfast. At 5:30 he telephoned the agent of the company that had insured his house, arousing him from bed to report its total loss. At about 6:30, when it was light, he went out to the cottage with Conner and others. It had burned to the ground and was still smouldering. In the cellar was about a foot of water that had seeped in from the lake. Small looked around for a time, shaking his head.

"Just think," he said. "Only yesterday afternoon, when I left for Boston, Florence came out the door and kissed me goodbye. She asked me to get some lace for her. Kennett was waiting in his car. He saw her."

Saying he did not have the heart to stay, he soon returned to the Central House, where he took a room.

Florence, Frederick Small's third and last wife.

A little later, Sheriff Chandler arrived with a local physician and several citizens to examine the ruins. Putting on rubber boots, they sloshed around in the cellar to see what they could find. One of the first things they found was the body of Florence Small. Obviously, the floors had burned through, allowing the body to fall into the water-filled cellar.

A townsman hurried back to the village to inform Small.

"We've found the—er—body, Mr. Small," he said. "What do you wish done with it?"

Small started. "What!" he exclaimed. "Is there enough left to be buried?"

"Yes. You see, it fell into the water in the cellar."

Small seemed much upset. He got up and paced the floor. Naturally, all this was a great shock to him.

"Well, I want the best coffin money can buy," he said at last. "Nothing is too good for Florence."

Back at the cottage, the investigators were examining the body. Parts of the arms and legs had been burned away, but the head and torso were intact.

Surprisingly, there was a noose of thin rope tied tightly around the neck. There was a bullet hole in the head. There were eight wounds on the skull.

Mrs. Small had been bludgeoned, strangled and shot. Whoever had done this had been efficiently intent on making death certain.

The searchers also found several lengths of copper wire, some dry-cell batteries and a blackened alarm clock. Small's mistreatment of his wife was well known, as was his mechanical ingenuity. It would have been easy for him to kill his wife, then leave for Boston after arranging a timing device that would touch off the fire hours after he left. Since he had insured Mrs. Small for $20,000, and his house and effects for $3000, he stood to gain $23,000 minus the premiums he had paid. The way he treated Florence, some felt that he would have murdered her for 23 cents.

However, there was one hitch in this neat theory. This was Small's story, told to several villagers, that he had kissed his wife goodbye as he left, and that Kennett had seen this. Obviously, if Florence Small was alive and well when her spouse left for Boston, he was innocent.

Sheriff Chandler sought out Kennett.

"Tell me what you saw when you picked up Small," he suggested.

"Well, not much," Kennett said. "Small was waiting for me. He said goodbye to his wife, then got in and we left."

"He said goodbye to her. Did you *see* her?"

Kennett pondered. "No, not exactly. Small went to the door and hollered 'Goodbye' inside."

"So you didn't see her. Did you hear her say anything?"

"No-o, I didn't. Of course, maybe she said goodbye and I didn't hear her."

The sheriff, however, had other ideas. He believed that Mrs. Small lay dead when her husband departed, and that the alarm-clock device was ticking away. He believed that the five gallons of kerosene Grocer Sceggel had brought that morning had been sprinkled around where it would do the most good. Small had seemed almighty anxious to prove his departure and his presence in Boston at the time the fire started. He had had Conner with him as a witness. He had even written his wife a postcard, something he did not ordinarily bother to do.

Sheriff Chandler went to the village and arrested Small.

"You fellows must be out of your heads!" the widower stormed. "Why, Kennett saw my wife when I left. He'll tell you that."

Nobody bothered to inform him just then that Kennett, a prosaic sort, had not been influenced by the power of suggestion. The sheriff searched Small's bag, which he had taken to Boston with him. In it he had put important papers, such as the deed to his house and a careful inventory of its contents, as if he thought it unsafe to leave them at home. Small now changed his mind about the best being none too good for Florence, buying her a forty-dollar coffin, the cheapest he could get.

Further investigation at the murder scene disclosed that part of the stove, found in the cellar, had been melted. This could not have been done by the heat from a wood blaze. A slag-like substance was also found in the cellar, which, on analysis, proved to be residue left by thermite, a welding agent used in garages and railroad shops that produces an intense heat of more than 5000 degrees Fahrenheit. This explained the fierce heat that had melted the stove and kept the firemen at a distance.

Although Small had never been really popular, his stock went down considerably when these facts came to light, so much so that the sheriff thought it a good precaution to put a special guard at the jail in Ossipee, just in case the citizens might plan an unofficial necktie party.

Small, loudly proclaiming his innocence, went on trial at Ossipee in December. Although the evidence against him was entirely circumstantial, the jury found him guilty. The necktie party he got at Concord Prison on January 15, 1918, was an official one, supervised by the State of New Hampshire.

The sheriff, generally praised for his solution of the mystery, modestly gave the credit to Lake Ossipee. He pointed out that had not a portion of the lake trickled into the Small cellar, the body would certainly have been incinerated, there would have been no evidence of murder, and Small would have collected a nice piece of insurance.   END

3.
FIRE!
FIRE!

Boston's Most Terrible Night

Never was there such a combination of misfortunes as during the night of November 9, 1872.

by Polly Stone Buck

SATURDAYS, FOR SOME STRANGE REASON, SEEM far more unlucky than Fridays. It was on a Saturday night that the steamship *Portland* sailed to her doom;* it was a Saturday when the submarine S-4 was rammed and sank off Provincetown (see p. 10); and November 9, 1872, which saw the beginning of the Great Boston Fire that turned 65 acres in the heart of the city's business district into a charred wasteland, killed nine firefighters, injured unnumbered firemen and citizens, and caused a property and merchandise loss of more than $75 million, was a Saturday too.

The fire started in the three-storied Klous Building, numbers 83, 85, and 87 Summer Street, where three firms rented floors: Tebbetts, Baldwin and Davis wholesale dry goods; Damon, Temple and Company, neckties; and Alex. K. Young and Company, manufacturers of hoopskirts and bustles—all storing combustible materials, all ready food for the licking flames. The beginning was apparently somewhere in the basement; then, creating their own draft, flames were sucked up the elevator shaft as up a giant chimney, burning the pitchy sprucewood sheathing of the shaft as they went; and since the elevator was open on all sides, the flames leaped out at each floor into the chambers, all of which were piled with potential fuel, such as hoopskirt frames and empty packing cases.

*See *Yankees Under Steam*, Yankee Inc., 1970, p. 104.

Because it was a business district and everyone who worked there had gone home, there were no passersby and few people in the streets. The two top floors were burning fiercely before anyone saw the flames. Then cries of "Fire!" quickly gathered a crowd, who gazed in fascinated horror and repeatedly asked each other, "Oh, why don't the engines come?" But no one made any motion toward turning in an alarm, each believing that surely this had already been done. Even the watchman employed for that and adjacent buildings, Charles Andrew Bodge, came running with the rest and looked on at the fire but did absolutely nothing about an alarm. He testified later that he "heard someone in the crowd say that someone had already gone to do it."

There were no telephones, then, remember! A fire alarm had to be given at one of the callboxes. These boxes were located about the city but kept locked to prevent false alarms by pranksters. (In vain had the Fire Department protested this arrangement with the City Fathers, pleading that it would be better to have four false alarms turned in than a delay in reaching one real one!) The policeman on the beat had a key to the box, but he might be blocks away, patrolling at the other end of his beat. Some responsible citizens, apt to be in their shops long hours, such as apothecaries, also were entrusted with keys. On every call-box was posted a notice telling where a key was to be found, but valuable time was lost locating an alarm-box in the

eft: The Great Boston Fire—from an actual photograph of Washington Street, looking towards the Old South Church.

first place, reading the notice, getting to where the key was, and then back to the box.

The alarm was finally given by John Page, the policeman on the beat, from box 52 on the corner of Lincoln and Bedford Streets. Because of tall buildings in between, he had not seen the flames and smoke. His account was: "I was chasing some rough boys half way up Summer Street. When I got to the corner, sure enough, fire appeared to be coming out of the building. The box 52 was right on the corner where I stood. As quick as I could put my hand in my pocket and take out the key, I gave the alarm."

But alas, that wasn't quick enough! When the alarm began to ring, it was 7:24 P.M. Twenty-five minutes had already passed since the fire had been seen from across the harbor in East Boston, and in those minutes the building where it originated was practically consumed. One elderly bystander remarked later, "I've been going to fires since I was a boy, and I never in all my life saw one where the alarm was so long in being given!"

Over in East Boston, the first engine company to see the billowing smoke did not wait for the tardy alarm. East Boston companies were not even supposed to cross to Boston fires on the first alarm—only if a fourth alarm was sounded—but on this night, the captain used his own judgment. Albert Damon, one of the volunteer firemen with that company, later told their story:

"Saturday, November 9, was warm and sunny like a late May day. The call members of the East Boston Engine Company followed their usual custom and gathered at the fire house to talk. The rear of the building overhung the harbor, and gave us a clear view of the city of Boston, a mile or so away. As we sat talking, one of us called the attention of the others to a great mushroom cloud of smoke rising from a district near Trinity Church. We watched it for some minutes, but no alarm sounded. Finally our Captain said to me, 'Al, we're going over; hold the ferry!'

"The ferry ran on the hour and half hour. I ran to the ferry slip only two or three hundred yards away and told the Captain to hold the boat for five minutes. Soon I could hear the engine coming, hauled by ropes by a great crowd

of firemen, bar loafers, and riff-raff of the town. We got onto the ferry about 7:05, crossed in a few minutes, and by watching the smoke, quickly found ourselves on lower Summer Street. As we did so, the bells in City Hall and the churches began tapping out the first strokes of what became a famous box: 52.

"As we swung into Summer Street, we could look ahead and see a most terrible sight. A great crowd filled the entire street, which would usually be deserted on Saturday night. The building at the corner of Summer and Kingston Streets was a raging furnace. It was of granite construction, and as the flames shot from the windows, great pieces of the granite chipped off by the heat showered all over the street, felling many of the onlookers. The moment the fire struck granite, it began to crumble and fall off, all the way from pieces as big as your fist to blocks weighing as much as a hundred and fifty pounds. The windows were covered with metal shutters which melted and ran down in streams, to which was added the molten lead and zinc from the mansard roof. Whole shingles and pieces of the roof a yard square were coming down like a heavy hailstorm, and burning cinders were flying like flakes in a driving snowstorm."

There never was such a combination of misfortunes anywhere as there was during that terrible night in Boston! *Everything* went wrong—the delay in sending the alarm was only the beginning. There was an epidemic of horse distemper and lung fever in the area, and most of the horses which usually drew the fire engines were sick and could not be used. Milton Fire Company No. 16 did use four horses, weak and convalescent, on an engine ordinarily drawn by two; Dorchester No. 17 also used convalescent horses, and the effort killed them. Most of the companies knew that it was impossible to bring their sick horses out. Even if there had been healthy extra horses, they would have been afraid, sensitive to flying cinders and shouting in the streets, and impossible to control.

When the horses had become sick, the Board of Fire Engineers had wisely organized 500 men to act as handpower for the engines. They were to be paid $1.00 for going to a fire, and

View from Washington Street showing nearly the entire area damaged by the fire.
Extreme left—Milk Street; extreme right—Summer Street. See maps below.

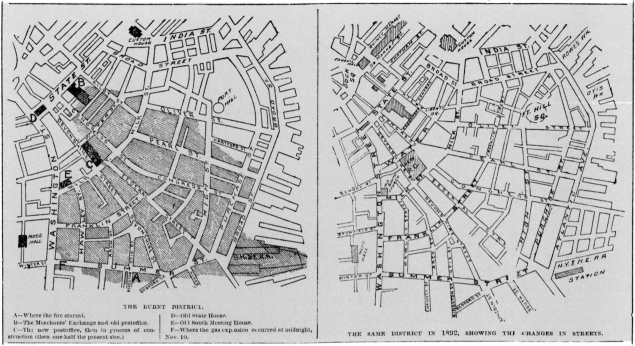

THE BURNT DISTRICT.

A—Where the fire started.
B—The Merchants' Exchange and old postoffice.
C—The new postoffice, then in process of construction (then one-half the present size.)
D—Old State House.
E—Old South Meeting House.
F—Where the gas explosion occurred at midnight, Nov. 10.

THE SAME DISTRICT IN 1892, SHOWING THE CHANGES IN STREETS.

25 cents for every hour they worked. There were now plenty of volunteers, and on this Saturday night, as soon as the 50- to 80-foot-long drag-ropes were brought out, 50 to 100 men immediately took a handhold along the rope and brought their engine at a steady trot to the fire. The East Boston company to which Albert Damon belonged had come this way.

Once the alarm was given, more engines began to arrive, pulled by excited men. The swaying crowds of people now jamming the streets greeted them with lusty cheers, but the pressure of the throng interfered with the firemen at every turn. ("The crowd broke your ribs at Franklin and Summer Street," one fireman told the Commission.) The roar of the flames, the noise of the mob of spectators, the frantic excitement of store owners trying to get to their goods to save them, all created a scene of mad confusion. A fireman said later, "The engines had to break a way through the crowd by force.

We had to drive them out of the way with sticks. We didn't strike anyone, but we had to threaten to if they didn't get out of the way, and I did strike the tall hat of one gentleman. We couldn't get a connection with the hydrant because of the crowd, I had a stick in each hand and talked pretty loud. We had hard work to drive the people back, and lost about eight minutes doing it."

To pick up Fireman Albert Damon's story of his company: "We attached our engine to a hydrant on Bedford Street and managed to get a line inside the burning building, but we were driven out of it after only a few minutes by the heat and flames; already several other adjacent buildings were on fire, especially those with mansard roofs. At that time only one engine from Boston had arrived. Engine No. 20 from Ward 16, which had to come five miles, did not arrive until five minutes to nine. Steamer No. 19, from the same Ward, did not get there until

City of Boston officials at the time of the fire.

9:30. Apparatus was coming in not only from all over Boston, but from Roxbury, West Roxbury, Malden, Everett, Medford, Wakefield, Brookline, Newton, and other places."

Chief Engineer Damrell of the Boston Fire Department, realizing at once that a conflagration was on his hands, at 8:10 gave orders to telegraph every town and city within 50 miles. The wires were down at places on the Worcester road, so a special train was sent to Worcester to tell them to bring all men and apparatus possible from all towns on that road. The apparatus from Worcester arrived after midnight; later a fire engine came from Portsmouth, New Hampshire (which did a spectacular job), and others from Providence and Newport in Rhode Island. They came from 21 Massachusetts towns, from Manchester, New Hampshire, and from Norwich and New Haven in Connecticut.

Mr. Damon's narrative continues: "Then if ever the complete lack of planning ahead and common sense was evident, for with over fifty steam engines on the ground and over seventy-five hand engines, only a comparative few could be used: their hose and hydrant couplings differed from those used by the Boston Department, there were no reducers, no standardized threads on couplings and hose! One fire engine from Charlestown, for instance, had to wait for reducing couplings to be brought before they could make any hose connection, and in the meantime, it just stood there in the street, idle, watching the fire."

Even once hitched up to a hydrant, troubles were far from over. Everything that could possibly have gone wrong did so! It was a good 30 minutes from the time the alarm was sounded until any water was thrown on the blaze, for the water situation was another of the catastrophes of that unlucky night. There was a paucity of both water and hydrants. Some engines had to get so far away to find a hydrant that they were playing through 600 or 700 feet of hose. When more than one hose was attached to a hydrant, the pressure immediately fell so low as to render the stream useless. As more and more engines arrived from all over Boston, the water pressure fell more and more. Some engines had to stop in order to give the others water. Half the time the hoses were playing air. There was never enough water for a stream to reach beyond the third story, and soon not even that high. The burning buildings were often five and seven stories high, and were catching and beginning to burn always at the top. The small streams of water were broken into ineffectual spray by the wind before they even reached the third floor, or from the intense heat became steam and went off into vapor.

There were no fire escapes on the buildings, so the men would have been trapped if they had gone on the roofs where they might have turned the water down on the fire from above. They were criticized for not taking the hoses up through the buildings, but this was impossible without making many turnings, which would have burst the hose. Also, there wasn't a hose

MAYOR
WM GASTON

CHIEF FIRE DEPT
J S DAMRELL.

in Boston that would stand being carried to the top of a 100-foot building without bursting.

There was criticism later from the citizens, not only about this but that what water there was was wasted. If the intense heat of the fire drove the engines away and the firemen had to move their hose, they left the hydrants open. Thirty-six hydrants were found running the day after the fire. The Chief Engineer exonerated his men by saying that if the water was not shut off, it was because the men stayed as long as it was in their power to stay, and finally had to "get up and get" as quickly as they could.

Another of the many mischances that plagued the firemen was the lack of fuel for the steamers. Each engine ordinarily carried one-quarter ton of English cannel coal, enough to make steam for 45 minutes to an hour, which was usually enough for the duration of a fire. If the supply was exhausted, the engine gave a signal for more fuel by blowing three sharp, peculiar whistles. A coal cart always went along to a fire loaded with about two tons, and would supply the engines that whistled. On this night, the coal cart, a light express wagon drawn by five or six men, made at least a dozen rounds, going repeatedly to the wharf for other loads, but it could not keep up with the constant cry for more coal. The engines exhausted their supplies in 10 to 20 minutes; the whistles were shrieking continuously.

Albert Damon said, "We had anchored down our whistle when we first arrived. This was the signal for more coal, but although we kept it screaming for eight hours, we never saw an ounce of coal from any Boston coal cart. We borrowed coal from several buildings on Atlantic Avenue, and then used boxes."

Firemen with engines out of coal realized that the coal wagon would not get to them, so they entered nearby houses seeking fuel. Any people who had coal or firewood gave it freely; but for the most part the firemen resorted to dry-goods boxes and packing cases. They even broke down fences, tore off shutters and blinds from houses in the path of the fire, dragged out counters from stores, and hacked them to length. This was about as good fuel as the coal would have been, but it required three firemen to keep one engine supplied.

Meanwhile, Boston's citizens stood in crowds in the streets, appalled at the rapidity with which the fire spread, for they had regarded the granite of which the buildings were made as fireproof. After the Chicago fire of 1871, the English underwriters sent representatives to this country to make a survey of conditions in all large cities. Their finding was that Boston was a prospective Chicago, and the very area that was actually burned in this fire a potential location for a terrible conflagration. Now the merchants of Boston ridiculed this, for almost all the buildings were new, heavily constructed of Quincy granite, and considered fireproof! Many merchants even carried no insurance, because they felt the buildings were so nearly indestructible.

But the conducting power of granite is con-

73

Franklin Street
before the fire.

Franklin Street
after the fire.

siderable, and when the entire combustible center of a five-story building was a roaring furnace, its heat was so intense that it would melt everything before it. Adjacent buildings were literally roasted, and burst into flame of themselves. Although the weather was calm, with only a slight wind of five to nine miles an hour, because of the narrowness of the streets, and the height of the buildings, the draft of air created on the windward side soon assumed the character of a brisk 16-to-18-mile-an-hour wind, which swept 15-foot flames across the streets to ignite the wooden parts and trimmings of buildings opposite.

Once under way, the fire swept along like a tornado. Albert Damon said, "From the first it was a hopeless fight. There was no direction from anyone in authority. The chief dashed from one spot to the other with no more idea of what he was doing than a hen with its head cut off. We ourselves probably were in error in attempting to fight the fire in the building where it originated. It would doubtless have been better to have surrounded the building, and kept water turned on adjoining buildings until danger from the original building had passed. However, we chased the fire from place to place

rather than outline a natural place to stop it, draw back, prepare for its advance and then hold it at that place."

Mr. Damon again: "Chief Clark of the London Fire Brigade, who visited America after the Chicago fire, had called attention at that time to the lack of any training in fire fighting in Boston. He said that while most of the chiefs were intelligent and zealous in their work, not one had the slightest professional knowledge of fire fighting. It was the opinion in those days that the only way to learn the business of a fireman was to go to fires. As well tell a surgeon that the way to learn how to perform an operation was to go to the operating room and pitch in!

"Early Sunday morning, our own engine was out of commission, all wooden gauge cocks had been burned off, wheels charred, and every one of us had been burned by flames or melted lead or struck down by flying debris. We were forced to abandon our engine, so we attached ourselves to a small hand engine hauled over the road from Wakefield, Massachusetts. This engine strangely enough had hose that fitted Boston hydrants.

"Gradually we were forced back onto Milk Street, where the new Boston Post Office and

The Beebe Block,
Winthrop Square.

Winthrop Square reduced
to rubble by the fire.

Federal Building were under construction. A great wooden scaffolding covered the south side of its full height. We were nearly exhausted, but the great crowd reinforced with gin and whiskey were in a holiday mood, yelling and cheering as if they were at a carnival, and when we called on them for help to man the hand-engine, the whole mass moved forward. By this time, the fire had seized on the buildings across from the new Federal Building, and the scaffolding was afire in a dozen places. But when the ancient hand-engine started, a feeble stream crept gradually up the side of the building. Higher and higher it went, as the crowd roared encouragement to the volunteers, and finally the stream over-topped the building and put out every flame. As the volunteers grew tired, others took their places, and probably in the next four hours, almost a thousand men 'worked the brakes' on that old Wakefield hand tub. And incidentally, with the exception of the steam engine from Portsmouth, it gave the most powerful stream I saw that night.

"The whole nation is indebted to that Portsmouth engine. Here's why: About three on Sunday morning, as I was walking to a doctor's office on Washington Street to have my burns dressed, I heard a great cheering down the street near the Transcript Building. Pushing through the crowd, I found an engine from Portsmouth, New Hampshire. They had a line on the Old South Church steeple, which was almost afire. There were several Boston engines there also, but no stream could reach the steeple except that of the Portsmouth firemen. The engine was under such terrific pressure that its vibration shook the whole neighborhood, but it did the job, and although the fire crossed Washington Street to the west, and crossed Milk Street to the north, the old landmark was saved for posterity, and we have Portsmouth to thank for it."

Old South was saved, but great Trinity Church was burned. Its famous preacher, Phillips Brooks, stood silently in the crowd in the street beside his friend, Charles Eliot, President of Harvard College, and watched its fiery destruction.

Great excitement prevailed down at City Hall. The United States mail was packed and ready to move out if necessary; records of Registry of Deeds and Registry of Probate were to be carried by teams to the reservoir as a safe place, but the flames did not reach City Hall. Councilmen and other prominent citizens were bluster-

Though many of the steamers remained idle for lack of fuel, many thousand tons of coal were stored on the great docks forming one boundary of the burned district. These huge coal heaps took fire and burned with a steady intensity for days after the conflagration had been extinguished.

ing around in Mayor Gaston's office, bombarding him with wild suggestions as to how to handle the fire.

Almost everyone was demanding that a path around the fire be cleared by the explosion of gunpowder, which had been done at the Chicago fire, and if the requests of the many citizens who eagerly volunteered to handle the powder had all been granted, the whole city of Boston would have been blown up!

The main idea behind the use of powder was to bring the whole building down, as the minute the walls were flat, they would be more easily drenched with water. But when the powder was tried, none of the buildings fell flat! The fuse often didn't ignite the powder; the fire itself often did the trick. In no case did the powder level a building and tumble the walls and roof into the cellars in fragments, as it was meant to. The explosions blew out windows and doors, making conduits through which flames, burning cinders, and heated air could enter from the neighboring buildings.

By 2 o'clock Sunday morning, pilfering had begun in the burning district. There was a huge, excited crowd and they were seeing quantities of goods destroyed by fire or dumped on the sidewalks to be ruined by water. Store doors and windows were out, and what else could be expected than looting? The military were called out to aid the police in controlling the voracious mobs.

Some businessmen asked to be appointed special police officers in order to guard their property from looters; others, with the best intentions in the world, added to the demoralization of the crowd by inviting people in to help themselves. Merchants brought out great stacks of shoes, hats, etc., and set them in the streets. Piled helter-skelter, the goods only impeded the firemen. Mr. Peck, at Peck's Fur Store on Devonshire Street, told citizens to take what they could.

When a Jordan Marsh executive brought out a case of blankets and began giving them to the firemen, saying they deserved them, a man from an insurance company protested. The storekeeper said, "I might as well give them away as have them burned up; they belong to me!"

"No they do not!" the agent told him. "They belong to the insurance company. You are making thieves out of the Boston Fire Department." As the crowd became more demoralized, they began breaking into stores that were still intact. A policeman reported, "Three of them would bump against the door and keep butting their backsides against it until they broke it." A ribbon shop, a cigar store, and Goodyear's Rubber Store were among those broken into.

Some firemen, after fighting valiantly for hours, joined in the looting on Sunday. Out-of-towners, who felt no responsibility for Boston goods, were right in there helping themselves; firemen from Charlestown, Bedford, and Newton Center were identified, and even a few Boston firemen were seen taking goods. The regular firemen also got a good deal of blame for looting which they did not deserve, for on the ladder carriages were always a few extra fire hats and coats to replace those lost by firemen in their work. Firemen later said that the men with firemen's caps and badges who were breaking into the warehouses, loading themselves up with goods, and bearing them off in all directions were citizens who had stolen uniforms from the ladder carriages.

In all, the police locked up 450 people for pilfering. Three hundred more had been arrested, but were let go when they convinced police headquarters that the things were given to them. The Chief Constable of the Commonwealth reported that later in the week, when the excitement of the fire had abated somewhat, the police procured search warrants and recovered a large amount of stolen goods.

Then, as though there had not been enough shame and disaster that night, there was the whiskey. Albert Damon said, "From seven on Saturday night until five on Sunday night, I neither saw food or had a drink of anything except straight whiskey. This last was brought out by the police and militia about two on Sunday morning to bolster up the exhausted firemen, who had been working steadily, soaking wet, and often with burns or other injuries from falling debris. It was served in full-sized tumblers, and it quickly produced results. By four in the morning, almost all the police, firemen, and onlookers were a little or a lot drunk, sometimes to the point of insensibility. Men lay in gutters, on steps of stores, under hose carts, anywhere. Some of those who died in the fire may have been too drunk to move on when the fire reached them. As someone else would trip and fall, hoots, catcalls, and jeers would go up from the crowd. A kind of reckless, Mardi Gras feeling was in the air: people were surging around, and stores were being broken open and ransacked."

Whiskey was flowing entirely too freely to suit the authorities. Monday morning, the liquor and beer shops were ordered closed; six men who refused to close their places were arrested.

"By the middle of Sunday morning, it was evident that the fire was slackening. It had already been checked to the west, had burned to the harbor on the east so could go no farther, and only on the north side did it still seem vigorous."

One interesting thing that occurred Sunday night was that a flock of wild ducks or geese passed at a great height overhead. The light from the flames reflected from their plumage made them appear as fireballs passing rapidly through the sky. Many who saw them were terrified, thinking them meteors, and perhaps a heavenly message.

When the fire was finally out on Monday, the desolation left behind was appalling. Within about 20 hours, the most valuable portion of the city had been wiped out. Two churches and 68 dwelling and lodging houses were burned, but most of the 547 buildings destroyed were important business houses, crowded from cellar to garret with valuable merchandise. From a financial point of view, it was fortunate for the merchants that the fire did not occur six months later, for the English insurance companies were on the point of cancelling $4½ million of their Boston insurance!

There were many things which happened that night of which no city could be proud, but almost everyone had only praise for the individual fireman. Each worked gallantly, displayed great bravery, and constantly exposed himself, sometimes recklessly and unnecessarily, to danger.

The fire in Chicago the year before, and the one following the San Francisco earthquake, in 1906, were the two greatest conflagrations the nation has ever known, and their statistics in every category far overtop Boston's, but this is one time when we do not hanker to be the biggest and the best: Boston's fire of 1872 was quite big enough for us!   END

". . . no doubt that an arsonist was at work. . ."

by W. A. Swanberg

Crazy Like A Fox

Willard Spaulding said that Ducey had progressed from arson to murder, just as he'd expected . . .

SOME MEN HAVE AN ABSENT-MINDED HABIT OF scratching their heads, tugging at an ear or twiddling their thumbs. Willard Spaulding, a 47-year-old bachelor merchant of West Peabody, Massachusetts, had his own distinctive gesture. When deeply engrossed, he would take the end of his nose between thumb and forefinger and wiggle it gently.

Spaulding, a self-righteous sort who was one of the pillars of the town, called on Police Chief Ed Wiggin in October of 1897 and fixed him with a disapproving eye.

"It's high time," he said, "that you were catching that firebug."

His tone clearly indicated that Wiggin was delinquent in his duty. The trouble was, he had good reason to be exercised—a series of fires which had devastated mansions and cottages ringing nearby Lake Suntaug, causing a loss so far estimated at more than $200,000. First to go up in smoke was the impressive residence of General Francis Appleton, from which volunteer fire-fighters were lucky to salvage some antique furniture and a priceless old grandfather clock. After that, as the weeks wore on, came a veritable parade of disaster. The colonial mansion of George S. Silsbee burned to the ground. The lakefront showplace of David P. Ives succumbed to flames with all its contents, as did the expensive home of Henry Saltonstall.

All of the fires took place at night when the homes were vacant, the owners being wealthy Bostonians who lived at Lake Suntaug only in summer. Traces of kerosene were found in several of the ruins, leaving no doubt that an arsonist was at work—a cunning criminal who touched off each building in several places at once. Two smaller houses had likewise burned,

and all in all Chief Wiggin had been losing more sleep than was good for him. Now here was Willard Spaulding, complaining because he couldn't perform miracles.

"You just tell me who's setting the fires," Wiggin said acidly, "and I'll arrest him."

Spaulding grasped his nose and wiggled it. "I can tell you," he said. "Tom Ducey."

The chief scoffed at this. The firebug, he pointed out, demonstrated considerable craftiness, whereas Tom Ducey was the town half-wit, of whom there was widespread doubt that he was smart enough to come in out of the rain. Suspecting him of such finesse was like accusing a three-year-old of turning out counterfeit $20 bills.

Ducey, an 18-year-old orphan, lived with an uncle, Patrick Geary, who owned a small farm on Lake Suntaug beyond the Appleton place. While Tom had been cheated when the brains were handed out, he had done very well in the muscle department, and he faithfully performed farm chores for Geary. He had never learned the complicated business of forming words, speaking instead with a weird mixture of grunts, facial contortions and gestures that only one person in the world understood—Annie Geary, the farmer's 19-year-old daughter. Tom regarded Annie with dog-like devotion, and until Spaulding got his queer notion the townspeople generally considered the boy odd but harmless.

Spaulding, however, was filled with dark suspicion. Hadn't Tom been seen prowling by night along the heights above the lake, right in the neighborhood of the fires? That young fellow had a lot more shrewdness than people gave him credit for, he insisted, and his warped brain was just the sort that would take delight in setting big, beautiful fires. Spaulding, always apt to become impatient with anyone who disagreed with him, stalked out angrily when Chief Wiggin still couldn't see Tom as a suspect.

It was no wonder that the town was in a ferment, with nobody knowing whose house would go next. While Spaulding was a hard man to please, it had to be admitted that he was a bear for action. He had formed the Citizens' Emergency Committee, a sort of vigilante organization that selected members to patrol the town and lakeshore each night. The fires had not stopped, it was true, but Spaulding vowed there would have been twice as many but for these sentinels.

In view of all this, General Appleton was regarded as being in a ticklish spot. After his place had burned down, and before it was known that a firebug was responsible, the general had contractors busy on a new 19-room home only a stone's throw from the ruins of the old. When it became clear that an incendiary was at large, Chief Wiggin advised him to hire a full-time watchman. Appleton thought it over and decided that the citizens' patrol was enough. Work progressed until by the fall of 1897 the new mansion was completed except for interior finishing.

That winter, possibly because of the citizens' vigilance, there were only a few minor fires—a haystack, an unused barn and a small cottage on the east side of the lake. Occasionally the pickets saw grinning Tom Ducey loping along the lake road in the dead of night. Some, impressed by Spaulding's talk, felt that the unfortunate young man might not know any better than to touch off fires just for the childish glee of watching the flames, while others argued that the arsonist's methodical cleverness ruled Tom out.

In the spring, furniture was moved into the new Appleton place to ready it for summer occupancy. Among the items was the big grandfather clock, a treasured heirloom that had been in the family for generations and bore the Appleton monogram on its pendulum.

On the night of April 7, it happened. A citizen watchman saw flickering light in one of the Appleton windows. The alarm was sounded, firemen came on the run and Chief Wiggin was routed out of bed. The blaze was already well advanced, having been started with kerosene in several places. Willard Spaulding was at the scene, and before the flames took over entirely, he, Wiggin and several others went inside to save what they could. They carried out a dozen pieces of furniture before the heat drove them away. The grandfather clock and a valuable Chippendale chair, however, were already gone, obviously looted by the firebug. Tom Ducey, jumping in excitement, watched the firemen at their hopeless task. By morning, the second Appleton mansion was a ruin like the first.

"The responsibility is yours," Spaulding gritted to Wiggin. "You should have jailed that maniac long ago."

The chief still couldn't agree. That day, Spaulding forced his hand by getting a search warrant from Justice of the Peace Amos Merrill. Wiggin went along with Spaulding and several townsmen to the Geary place, where Patrick Geary stoutly defended his feeble-minded nephew. There was kerosene here, of course—everybody used kerosene—but Tom Ducey's clothing did not smell of it. A search of the farm failed to turn up the missing clock and chair. Pretty Annie Geary was indignant.

"Tom is as innocent as a baby," she said. "He couldn't hide such a thing from me."

He always had a queer habit of awakening in the middle of the night, she explained, going abroad for an hour or two, then returning to bed. Furthermore, she was sure that from things he had seen on his nocturnal jaunts, he knew in his dim way who had been setting the fires.

"From what I've got out of him so far," she went on meaningly, "you may be in for a surprise. But I can't rush him. Let me work on him another day or two, and I'll have something to tell you."

That was all Annie would say. The callers left, Spaulding tweaking his nose in his characteristic gesture as he growled that Tom ought to be jailed, evidence or no evidence.

Two days later, Tom Ducey staggered into the Geary farmhouse, weeping and gibbering, a stain of blood on his shoe. He led Patrick Geary outside, where they found Annie's body on the lake shore. She had been bludgeoned to death, and when the news got around, the village was in a panic. Willard Spaulding said that Ducey had progressed from arson to murder, just as he expected, to which the sorrowing Geary snapped that Tom had worshipped the ground Annie stood on, and merely picked up the bloodstain when he found the body. State Detective George C. Neal arrived from Boston next day at the urgent request of Chief Wiggin, who had never before had a murder case on his hands.

Neal found that townspeople unthinkingly had trampled the murder scene, destroying any clues that might have been there. To be sure, Tom Ducey had to be regarded as a suspect. After a long talk with Wiggin, Neal also recognized a contrary possibility—that Tom and Annie were innocent victims of a ghastly plot. Annie may have signed her own death warrant when she said publicly that Tom knew the arsonist's identity and would disclose it to her if given time. Since she alone could understand Tom's grunt-and-gesture language, her murder effectively shielded the guilty man at the same time as it cast suspicion on Tom. Although all this sounded like a stage "mellerdrammer," Neal did not discard the idea.

During a long stay in Peabody, he went to painstaking effort to win Tom Ducey's confidence. Daily he called at the Geary farm, delighted Tom by giving him chocolate, and took him for long walks among the ruined houses around Lake Suntaug. He discovered friendly, winning qualities in the boy Spaulding termed a "bloodthirsty idiot," and became convinced that Tom was silently grieving over the death of Annie, the only person who ever understood him.

Neal observed that Tom grew excited whenever they passed the Appleton ruin and went into a demonstration that at first was meaningless. He swung his arms back and forth in a rhythmic motion, at the same time making similarly rhythmic throaty sounds. It was some time before Neal gathered that he might be trying to represent a clock.

The state detective inquired of Wiggin whether a clock had been stolen from the Appleton place. Yes indeed—a valuable grandfather clock! This was a minor triumph for Neal—his first establishment of communication with the boy who could not talk. He felt sure that Tom must

have seen the man who carried away that clock. The problem was to get him to identify the thief.

The pair made more trips to the Appleton place, where Tom always went into the same act. Neal got to be fairly eloquent with gestures himself. By patient effort he made Tom understand that he knew the clock was stolen and wanted to know *who* stole it.

Tom pondered that for a while before he executed another pantomime. He struck a self-important pose, then took his nose between his thumb and forefinger and wiggled it.

Puzzled, Neal went once more to Chief Wiggin. "Is there someone in town with a big nose, or a crooked or broken nose?" he inquired.

He described Tom's gestures. Wiggin's jaw sagged.

"There's only one man he can mean," he said. "That's Willard Spaulding, our most noted stuffed shirt."

There was some discussion about annoying such a leading citizen, but Wiggin for one had no tender regard for him. A warrant was secured. Spaulding was outraged when they arrived to search his place. His indignation played out when they found the Appleton clock and chair in his carriage house. He burst into tears.

"I set the fires," he blubbered. "I couldn't help it—did it for a thrill."

The scandal all but paralyzed the town. Prosperous, upstanding Willard Spaulding, setting fires and stealing things he didn't need! Normal folk can never understand the manic firebug to whom flames are a drug, but the big question was, did Spaulding also murder Annie Geary?

He denied it, of course, and the only witness against him, Tom Ducey, couldn't speak a language understood in courtrooms. The state had to settle for charges of arson and burglary when Spaulding was tried in Salem. He drew 12 years—a sentence both Neal and Wiggin felt lenient for a man they believed a killer.

Spaulding was a wasted wreck when he was released from Charlestown in 1911. Just before he died two years later, he summoned a clergyman, gasped out the name of Annie Geary, and expired before he could say another word. When George Neal, still a state detective, heard of that, he had a good idea about what the dying man had tried to say.

END

"E. V." at the Salem Fire

Despite the valiant efforts of the small band, three million dollars went up in

IN THE EARLY PART OF THE YEAR 1914, I WAS A young engineer in the Boston office of The Insurance Company, working on plans of sprinkler systems and water mains for factories we covered. There were always three or four of us young fellows in the drafting room; we had plenty of fun as we worked, making wise cracks, discussing what we had done the night before, making plans for some dance or party on the weekend.

A happy ship, although we had to remember we were working for a week's pay. If the work did not get turned out, we heard from "E. V. F." He was vice president in charge of engineering, and his duties included seeing to it that we young shrubs toed the mark.

No one ever referred to him except as "E. V. F.," or "E. V.," nor did he ever sign anything within the organization except by initials. We used to say he never would waste time unnecessarily writing out his name.

This boss of ours was a man who believed in efficiency, practiced efficiency, and taught efficiency. He never raised his voice; indeed, there was no need. He enunciated well, his clear-eyed gaze completely held his listener, and he was so earnest that one listened with extra attention.

When one of us was called to his office, the problem was explained with complete clarity by E. V., his outlines written in varicolored pencil before him on his desk. If one of us got too gay in the drafting room, there was a brief word from E. V., spoken quietly and in a kindly way.

One day we all took an old friend to lunch, had a few beers, and returned at one o'clock, cackling and laughing like so many sailors on shore leave. E. V. put a little more effort into getting across certain points. There was a faint flush on his cheeks, his gaze was even more level, his remarks more pointed, yet he raised his voice not at all. He was a small man, in his forties, always immaculately and conservatively dressed, and always in the manner a real gentleman achieves without visible effort.

We juniors asked each other what it would take to make him shout or swear. We wondered whether he had ever had on a soiled shirt. Had he ever had dirty hands, even at age nine? Had he ever done anything in his life except appear at the office on time with his briefcase that contained engineering problems taken home for evening work? We concluded that E. V. had never known adventure, or any activity except the calm, precise, efficient routine of his office

Salem after the Fire
~ 1914 ~

smoke with the Naumkeag Mills.

existence; the complete command of every factor in his daily work that had carried him to the post of vice president before he was fifty.

So we were more than a little sorry for our boss who followed his never-varying routine without even so much of an error as a spot upon his necktie or a problem not already worked out on those sheets of his. We knew we would never hear him swear or see him with a few drinks aboard or see him run or hear him shout or learn that any unusual experience had come to him.

After lunch one day in June, 1914, he sent for me to work with him on a problem of water pressure and size of pipe for the sprinkler system for one of the large cotton mills insured by us. We covered a considerable number of mills; indeed, it was the company's principal line of insurance, so we were frequently working with the design of sprinkler systems.

We had been at it a while when his telephone rang. To this day I can recall nearly every word I heard him speak. Characteristically, there was no wasted conversation.

"How many buildings are involved?"

A pause as he listened and then he asked: "Can't you be more exact?"

I could hear the crackle of this man's loud talk over the telephone; I heard the phrase "out of town help" and "moving right our way." There was considerable bad language sprinkled into his remarks, and then I heard, "It's completely out of hand."

E. V. never changed expression, even at the man's vast oaths—and profanity was something he never tolerated.

"Now stay calm," he said. "Try to keep your mill fire department from running home. We'll be down there to help you as soon as we can."

I wondered what was going on, but E. V. wasted no words in explanation. He put in a call to Boston Fire Department Headquarters. When he got them, he shot one question: "Has your apparatus started for Salem yet?"

There was talk, but E. V. slammed down the receiver, snatched his hat, took me by the arm, hustled me into the drafting room, and snapped out an order.

"Every man take his hat and follow me. On the double."

Through the offices we went. Even E. V. was running now. "Come on, Teague," he barked as we went past an office door. "Come on, Brown. Hats." And two more men joined our group.

Out on Broad Street, he flagged down a taxi

Salem, Massachusetts—June, 1914: flames gutted a large part of the industrial district . . . *Courtesy Robert E. Ashley.*

... and the residential section, too. *Courtesy Robert E. Ashley.*

and crammed us all in. "Charlestown yards of the Boston & Maine Railroad. As fast as you can."

We reached the railroad yards in time to help manhandle three Boston steamers and their hose wagons onto flat cars. The horses were led away, a locomotive coupled onto the head end, and we whistled off, rumbled along the sidetrack, and out onto the main line.

The engineer knew where he was headed. The line was clear, he had rights over all other trains, his throttle was way out, and that short train of ours rolled through Chelsea and Revere as fast as the Boston & Maine's swiftest limited. People heard our whistle as we approached the crossings, for at that speed, even with the gates down, our engineer gave two long and two short. The people turned to wave and cheer, for they knew where we were going; one look at the towering cloud of smoke in the sky to the northeast told the story, and it gave people a lift to see this trainload of shining, nickel-plated steamers and bright-red hose wagons on the way to help.

Rolling through Lynn, our eyes never left that enormous cloud of smoke. Less than five miles ahead a whole city was burning—a conflagration of the first magnitude, completely out of hand, the sort of thing we had read about in the textbooks but had never seen.

As the train left Lynn and speeded through Swampscott, E. V. stood on the rolling, pitching flat car, his gaze straight ahead like a general viewing the battlefield, making up his mind how to use his troops. He called us around him.

"We'll be in Salem freight yards in a few minutes. Point number one: we do not stay to help get the Boston apparatus off the flat cars. There will be plenty of volunteers as soon as this train stops.

"Point number two: our company carries the insurance on the Naumkeag Steam Cotton Company. Three million dollars. Our party goes directly to the Naumkeag on Salem harbor

the instant this train stops. You will see people moving out their furniture. Do not stop to help. You will see fire engines from every city and town in this part of the country working. Do not stop to help. Just follow me to the Naumkeag. Three million dollars. Any questions?"

There were none. Seldom were there any questions when E. V. spoke. Never did I hear him speak vaguely or obscurely. When the train stopped, it was as he said. A hundred volunteers were ready to help; the Boston firemen had the ramps in place, ropes rigged, and a hose wagon going down the slope to the ground before we were out of the freight yard.

Everywhere people were getting their belongings out of the houses. The sky was darkened by the solid pall of smoke above us; glowing red brands bigger than a half dollar came down on the district in a constant shower. These brands landed on wooden shingle roofs, collected in the valleys formed by roof and gable, and lay there glowing. The roofs started to burn. We saw a Lynn engine company go to work on one of these roof fires. Their steamer had used up all its coal, but a group of high school boys smashed down a fence, brought the pickets to the engine's stoker, and he kept up a head of steam with wood.

A Salem chemical engine managed to extinguish another roof fire; they used the last of the chemical in the tanks, rolled up their hose, and prepared to return to their station to reload with water and the soda and sulphuric acid that gives a chemical stream its driving force.

"I wouldn't bet more than a dime this building will be here when we come back with full tanks," said a fireman, as they started off through the never-ending rain of burning brands. On to the Naumkeag we hurried through streets full of confusion, sparks falling everywhere, the thick pungent smell of wood smoke in our nostrils. Behind us we saw, little more than a quarter of a mile distant, the rolling flames, the churning, billowing clouds of smoke obscuring the sky.

Our party did not reach the Naumkeag any too soon. The mills, a group of a dozen buildings, had an excellent fire brigade under ordinary circumstances. However, this day the chief could not hold his men. From the rooftops of the mill buildings, every man could see where the fire was; he knew when it was approaching his home, and then away he went on the dead run, to protect his family. Nor could he be blamed.

This left the mill fire brigade with only out-of-town employees, so our party's arrival was very important. The city water pressure, with fire engines from more than 20 communities drafting from the mains, was gradually weakening here at the Naumkeag. This E. V. had foreseen. His first act was to see to it that two stationary steam pumps that took suction from the South River, a branch of Salem Harbor, were properly manned. Here was a water source not dependent on the city's system.

Then he walked slowly along the 1500 feet where the group of mill buildings adjoined the city of Salem. He ordered Brown and me to go with him.

The air was hot, glowing embers falling in a hellish red blizzard. The dense cloud of rolling smoke, glowing red at the base, showing flame here and there, was only a few hundred yards beyond the closely-built, three- and four-story wooden tenements that came almost to the boundary line of the mill property. We moved over a little, looking right up one of the streets of this tenement district. The street was a solid mass of flame; as we looked, another building was involved, fire swirled around it, and soon blazing clapboards and piazza railings were dropping off. We saw no firemen.

"No one can stand in front of the intense heat of a conflagration," remarked E. V. "The heat melts glass. It bends the rails of the street car tracks. It makes granite explode because the different kinds of rock in granite expand at different rates under heat. When you walk through the burned district in a day or two, you will notice that all the curbstones and granite steps will have rounded edges."

And that is precisely what I saw later. E. V. told us these things as though he was a profes-

sor and we his students on a field trip. His voice was calm; he seemed to lack only a blackboard and pointer. He continued:

"Now, as I said, the heat generated by a conflagration is so intense no one can stand in front of it. See? No firemen. They are working at the sides of the fire trying to narrow it down, or at least keep it from spreading sideways."

"But we are standing in front of it," I said.

"Quite true, my boy," replied E. V. calmly. "So we really do have a problem. To meet it, we have those two fine mill pumps to supply the sprinklers and give us some good hose streams. Now we will lay some lines and hit it as it comes through these clusters of tenement houses."

We from the insurance company and the men of the Naumkeag fire brigade manned the lines and waited until the fire was in the last of the tenements—those right in front of us. The stationary pumps gave us wonderful pressure; we threw streams like battering rams that tore into the blazing buildings, blackening the burning areas wherever they struck.

One of the thrills in this business I have been in all these years is handling a long, powerful, straight stream from a good engine, see it hit, rip off shingles and clapboards, and knock the fire down. This was one of those times.

We moved back and forth along the fire front with our lines. The heat set off the outside sprinklers on the cornices of the mill behind us, a curtain of water came down the side of the building. Then, although I could scarcely believe it, the curtain of water turned to steam from the intense heat. How we stood the temperature where we were I shall never know.

Even with heat that turned the water from the cornice sprinklers to steam, the windows of the mill building held. And the big streams from our hose lines, supplied by those two 1000-gallon pumps working to their limit, were batting down the fire here and there in the tenements. Behind us stood E. V., directing us, watching every detail, telling us where to point our big streams, when to move them.

Then happened one of those things that seem like a bad dream. The streams from two of our big hose lines lost their strength; they dwindled to weak dribbles arching out in front of us and splashing uselessly on the ground. No longer could we reach the blazing wooden tenement houses. The other two streams, still powerful, continued to strike the burning buildings, yet two streams could cover but half the area.

I have said E. V. never swore. If ever there was a time to swear, this was it. But he did not. He tapped me on the shoulder, "Follow me."

He did not run, but he walked so fast I was put to it to keep up. We reached the engine room where one of the pumps had stopped, while the other continued. The failure was due to a sheared-off pin in the cross head. We went to work on it, we pounded, and we struggled to get a new pin in, as E. V. stood there telling us exactly what to do. Twenty minutes later the pump was again running.

But one cannot afford to give 20 minutes to an antagonist like the Salem Fire. While the pump was out of action, the pressure in the sprinklers dropped to ten pounds, the head increased terrifically without those two big streams. The outside water curtain, now mostly steam, weakened and nearly stopped; the window glass cracked and dropped out; sprinkler heads inside the building opened, further decreasing the pressure.

Soon that mill building, a four-story structure, was burning all over. We retreated, at E. V.'s order. I could guess how he felt, but never a word of complaint did he speak.

At 9:30 P.M. the chief of the mill brigade decided the lives of his men were in danger, so he ordered them to retreat over the last remaining exit, a bridge over the South River. The bridge was burning as they scampered over it. That left only us from the insurance company, doing what we could and that not much. Yet it was a satisfaction to be turning those big streams into the mill buildings, several of which were now ablaze from one end to the other. Our pumps were still supplying the sprinkler system, but too many sprinkler heads were now open in the several buildings that were burning.

About this time, I got to thinking about that burning bridge over which we had seen the last of the mill fire brigade departing, on the double. The bridge was now practically destroyed. How were we to escape? Here we were, with an inferno in front of us, and Salem Har-

bor behind us. Did E. V. stop to think about us in his eagerness to fight fire? The answer to my wondering was not long in coming. At about 10:15 P.M. every building except two concrete storehouses was hopelessly involved. He called each of us by name; he had us leave the streams with nozzles wedged between timbers so they still shot at the fire, then he motioned for us to follow him.

"We leave the boilers with fireboxes full. We leave the pumps running. Our streams and the sprinklers will be fighting on without us. In my opinion it is no longer safe here."

He led us to the edge of the bulkhead at the harbor's edge. Below us we saw a dory tied to one of the uprights. Apparently this was a regular landing place, for a ladder was nailed to the side of the plank bulkhead.

"I was afraid something like this might happen, so I thought I'd see about a dory. All right, boys, down you go."

There he stood, staring at the fiercely burning Naumkeag Mills, as we climbed down the ladder, one by one. Reluctantly, he turned and came down the ladder, the last to leave, in the true tradition of a sea captain. And we, without really planning it, had left the seat in the stern sheets for our commander.

"Give way, men," he ordered, and we bent our backs to the oars.

He had us row to Derby Wharf, across the harbor, a place out of the path of the conflagration. There we made fast our dory and went ashore. On the wharf he beckoned to us to gather around him. "In a few days we'll have a get-together, write our report, and try to see if there was anything we could have done that we failed to do. You may as well go home now, although I'm afraid public transportation is somewhat disrupted. We were defeated, but I am proud of you, every one of you. I'm proud of how you fought."

E. V. paused, almost as if to consult a notebook to see what more.

"Oh, yes. One more thing. In view of the circumstances, it is all right if you do not happen to be on time tomorrow morning at the office."

That was the end of our lost battle at the Naumkeag. Exhausted, I wandered up the wharf to Derby Street, which was out of the path of the fire. On a street corner I found a drugstore with an elderly clerk on duty. I persuaded him to make me the grand-daddy of all chocolate ice cream sodas, and with that inside me, I began to feel a return of strength. I decided to go have a look at the Salem Fire from a new angle.

When I reached the area of active fire fighting, I saw what E. V. meant when he told us that the principal effort of the firemen was to keep a conflagration from spreading sideways and to try to narrow it down. At this point a steamer from Beverly was working hard, pistons flashing, flywheel spinning, rocking on her springs, a straight column of spark-flecked black smoke flushing from her stack. Her two lines of hose led to a driveway between a couple of pitched-roof, two-and-a-half-story dwellings, one fiercely burning, the other just beginning to catch.

One crew of men, on the sidewalk, had a strong stream on the house not yet really involved. They hit first the roof, then the walls, keeping the house wet, dousing any part that started to burn and keeping a spray of water deflected onto another crew of men halfway down the driveway. This second crew had a strong line on the house already burning, their

stream ripped into the fire, tore off boards, blackened burning places where it struck. The heat where they stood was terrific, yet they maintained their position because of the spray the other crew kept on them. Here was one part of the fight to keep the fire from spreading sideways.

Watching, I envied those men in the driveway with their strong engine line that hit the fire like a sledge hammer. Never have I gotten over my love for working with a strong stream on a tough fire. I do not recall deciding to go in there and help—I was simply there.

One of the men was a Beverly fireman; the other two were civilians with borrowed fire helmets reversed so the broad tail of the helmet shielded their faces from the heat. These civilians were soaked and dirty, and the smaller of the two had holes, half-dollar size, burned here and there in his coat by red-hot embers. I thought I might help. I reached for the handle of the playpipe.

"Don't you want me to relieve you, sir?" I asked.

The man turned to look at me, tipping back the tail of his helmet. It was E. V., face streaked with soot, dirty shirt, still in the battle.

"Now see here," he said, calmly but incisively. "Didn't I tell you to go home?"   END

The Naumkeag Mills, where three million dollars went up in smoke. *Courtesy Essex Institute, Salem, Mass.*

The *Hindenburg* Tragedy

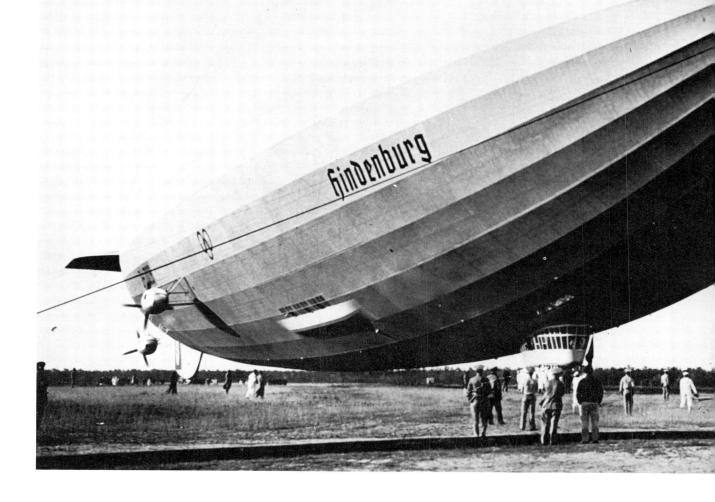

A few minutes before, an impressive landing. Now a scene of misery, a ghastly holocaust!

by Robert W. Hirschman

"UP SHIP!" SLOWLY, CALMLY, STEADILY, THE huge, silvery hulk rose—quiet as a balloon which had just slipped loose. The complete silence was almost awesome. There was no roar of propellors, no racing of motors—only the smooth, continuous lifting as 97 passengers and crew ascended into the land of the lighter-than-air craft.

The eleventh flight of the *Hindenburg* on May 3, 1937, from Frankfurt/Main, Germany,

The great German airship, *Hindenburg* at rest (left) and in the air over Boston (right).

to Lakehurst, New Jersey, was not as unusual as it might have been the previous year. In 1936, the Hindenburg, previously known only as LZ-129, successor to the *Graf Zeppelin* which had just finished nine years of service, had begun the first commercial air service across the North Atlantic. Nevertheless, there was something of a "first-nighter" crowd on hand whenever the *Hindenburg* upped ship—the *Hindenburg* which was always on schedule in any weather.

Except for the hushed whispers of the group on the ground which were nearly audible within the rising ship, the passengers heard nothing. Then, faintly, there was a sharp staccato from each of the four 1100-horsepower engines, a small shower of sparks from the exhaust, a mild crescendo of whirling propellors and then a low, steady hum.

The Queen of the Air, the largest airship ever built, circled the field and headed towards its

Above: A crew member washes up aboard the zeppelin in the well-appointed washroom. Note interior girders visible through window. *United Press International Photo.*

Below: The aerial dining room and promenade photographed just after the *Hindenburg's* (then known as LZ-129) first successful flight—a three-hour cruise over Lake Constance. *United Press International Photo.*

Hindenburg officers in the control gondola of the airship. *United Press International Photo.*

destination, 3895 miles across the Atlantic. The passengers stayed at the windows for a long time, watching the panorama fade away like a gigantic movie setting disappearing into the background. They could see the lights twinkling here and there across the countryside of Germany and later, France; now and then, the ship's powerful beam spotlighted a tiny toy farm.

It was raining when the *Hindenburg* left the new Rhein-Main World Airport, although Captain Max Pruss, commanding the ship on this first of twelve runs for the 1937 season, did not mind at all. In fact, he preferred foggy weather because the clouds seemed to give the air a silky smoothness which it did not have when the air was clear and yet bumpy. The weather, however, usually determined the course of the ship, and shortly after setting out, Captain Pruss

called Captain Lehmann to the control gondola to discuss this matter. Captain Ernest Lehmann, now serving as an advisor, had been the commander of the *Hindenburg* until this year, and had sometimes gone as far north as Greenland or south in the vicinity of the Azores if the weather had not been satisfactory.

Meanwhile, the passengers were becoming acquainted with each other, signing souvenir passenger lists, and learning shipboard routine from Mrs. Imhof, the first airline stewardess. Businessmen, students, professional men and women, representing five nationalities—all were fascinated by this giant airship.

John Pannes, an official of the Hamburg American-North German Lloyd Steamship organization of New York City, and a friend, Otto Clemens, admired the strength and sta-

bility of this remarkable zeppelin. Pannes, who was returning from Germany with his wife, explored his neat, well-furnished cabin, exactly like the other 49 two-passenger cabins along A deck.

Down on B deck, in the smoking salon, Ferdinand Lammot, a student returning from Paris to Washington, was amused by the tricky little ash trays which automatically doused all stubs. Although the ship was fireproof, Lammot noticed that the walls were made of asbestos and remembered that he was not allowed to have a cigarette lighter or any matches with him.

A group of passengers were gathered around the cocktail bar, where Max, the genial bartender who had had experience aboard several luxury liners, provided the perfect nightcap.

He liked to tell the story of one dirigible passenger who stood a fountain pen upright on the bar to see if it would stay there through the evening and found, to his surprise, that it was still erect at the end of the voyage.

In the combination reading-writing room, Captain Anton Witteman of the *Graf Zeppelin*, an observer on this trip, was talking to another group. He was explaining the construction of the *Hindenburg*, how it was stabilized by its 36 long girders and 15 wire-braced main transverse frames. The *Hindenburg* was built of duralumin, an aluminum alloy as strong and hard as soft steel, and it was twice the size of the *Graf Zeppelin*.

"But wasn't it designed to be inflated with helium?" asked George Hirschfeld, a member

The *Hindenburg* explodes as it approaches the mooring mast at Lakehurst, New Jersey (opposite page) . . . and crashes to the ground, all compartments afire, the flames rising some 500 feet into the sky (left) . . . to become a twisted mass of burning wreckage on the field (below). *All photos courtesy Wide World Photos.*

of the Chamber for Industry and Trade of Bremen.

"Yes, but helium is about ten per cent less efficient than hydrogen. With hydrogen, we can get a much greater lift from the ship than with helium."

"Is it as safe, though? What was the experience of the zeppelins during the war?" asked Ernest Anders, a tea merchant from Dresden.

Captain Witteman answered, "During the war, we used hydrogen exclusively, and even though many of the ships were shot full of holes, none of them was ever in any serious trouble. You see, the ship is divided into various gas compartments and if one should be punctured, it would not affect the rest of the ship at all."

Both Captain Witteman and the passengers knew also that helium was unattainable; the United States, under the provisions of its Helium Act of 1927, virtually monopolized all the helium known to exist.

Mr. Nelson Morris, returning from Paris where he had been visiting with his wife, the French actress, Blanche Bilboa, still wondered whether hydrogen was safe because of its inflammability.

"Of course, it is perfectly safe," the captain assured the group. "Germany has been using it without any difficulty for more than a third of a century. Our airships have been struck by lightning numerous times, but lightning cannot enter—it's impossible. Already the *Hindenburg* has flown 209,481 miles without a single mishap."

Soon all the lights were going out in the cabins of this populated cloud as it moved on through the night, steadily, speedily, always so smooth—a sort of Utopian adventure.

* * * * *

Newfoundland, Nova Scotia, Boston, Providence. The giant ship passed over these successive spots, although headwinds had delayed its schedule considerably. Captain Pruss had realized that they would not reach Lakehurst by Thursday morning, so he had cut down his speed from the average 84 miles per hour and planned to land at dusk.

When they reached New York City, Captain Pruss lowered the airship so that sightseers could

The skeleton of the once mighty dirigible lies crumpled and broken on the Lakehurst field. *Courtesy Wide World Photos.*

get a good view. At 3:12 P.M. on May 6, they passed over Times Square. Amateur photographers perched at vantage points on top of the Empire State Building to get pictures. Plans were underway to use this building as a central midtown dirigible terminal, the skyscraper tower to be used as the mooring mast. A roar of steamship and other harbor whistles greeted the zeppelin. At Ebbets Field, where the Dodgers were playing the Pittsburgh Pirates, the fans momentarily took their minds off the game and gazed up in the sky at this twentieth-century marvel.

At 4:15, the *Hindenburg* appeared over the field at Lakehurst, but after circling the reservation, Captain Pruss decided not to make a landing. A thunderstorm was in progress and it seemed advisable to let this pass, so the ship headed towards the coast again and disappeared.

* * * * *

At Lakehurst, the ground crew of approximately 200 members, under the leadership of Commander Charles E. Rosendahl, was all ready for action. The *Hindenburg* was scheduled to leave at midnight that same day. Standing at one side were many railroad cars filled with more than 10,000 gallons of fuel waiting to be pumped aboard.

Tickets for the return trip had been sold for months. More and more people wanted to try this new method of traveling where there could be no seasickness and the trans-Atlantic trip could be made in just a little more than two days. Ten Americans, planning to take the return trip, were going to attend the coronation of King George VI, which was to take place six days later in London; others were going to the Paris Exposition. Dr. Hugo D. Keil was planning to take a vacation in Germany; his trunks had already been sent by ship.

There was an air of excitement aboard the ship. Passengers were packing and collecting their papers for their passport examination. In the reading room, Mrs. Doehner was crocheting while her three children were playing games. Others were playing bridge or signing postcards.

In the air-conditioned dining room, waiters were serving roast goose in the usual excellent *Hindenburg* manner. No canned food was ever served aboard the ship; dry-ice refrigeration and an adequate storage insured a supply of only the freshest foods, as well as choicest wines, liquors, and beer. From their seats at the table, the passengers could easily watch the landing operations.

A light rain was falling, and the ground was well soaked when the *Hindenburg* reappeared over the field, flying in from the coast at an altitude of about 500 feet. This was too high to land, and the ship circled the field and came back at an altitude of 200 feet, heading slightly westward against the wind.

At 7:21, the dirigible dropped two landing lines which were being coupled to ground equipment. A light gust of wind pushed the ship slightly to the starboard side, and the port rope tightened under the load. But this was not unusual; this often happened.

Clifford L. Osbun of Chicago sat next to the window in the dining room, watching the landing crew down below. His bags were packed, and soon he would be walking down the gangplank to solid ground. Mr. Osbun, father of three daughters, was concluding a three-month tour for his company which had taken him to South America, England, and Germany. He had planned to be in Chicago the next day, not expecting that the *Hindenburg* would have been delayed nearly 12 hours.

He saw the fuel cars being brought over to the landing area. Bags of mail were waiting to be put aboard; provisions were piled up along the side of the platform.

The ship was nearing the ground. Passengers in the dining room were waving to friends and relatives on the ground. Spectators gazed in awe at this monstrous balloon descending upon them.

Suddenly, Mr. Osbun noticed a look of shock on the observers' faces. People were running in every direction. What was it?

Standing beside a WLS sound truck, Herb Morrison had just a minute before been describing the arrival of the *Hindenburg*:

"The ship is sliding majestically towards us like some great feather. These giant flagships standing here, the American Airlines flagships, are waiting to take the passengers on flights to all points in the United States, when they get the ship moored."

Funeral services for the 28 German victims of the *Hindenburg* disaster were held on the Hamburg-American pier May 11, just prior to their last voyage home. *Courtesy Wide World Photos.*

Morrison's voice flowed on easily, describing the scene.

"It is practically standing still now. They have dropped ropes out of the nose of the ship. The rain has slacked up a little bit. The back motors of the ship are just enough to keep it from . ."

Suddenly Morrison seemed gagged into shocked silence.

"It's bursting into fl . .

"Get this, Scotty; get this, Scotty. It's flashing; it's flashing terrible. Get out of the way please. It's burn . . it's bursting into flames and falling on the mooring mast.

"Oh—the flames! This is one of the worst catastrophes in the world—oh—the flames—four to five hundred feet into the sky.

"It's a terrific crash, ladies and gentlemen—oh—the smoke and the flames—and the plane is crashing to the ground. It's not tied to the mooring mast.

"Oh, the humanity, and all the passengers . . ."*

What Morrison had seen was a spot of red on top of the ship, a puff of smoke, then the enveloping mass of flame.

The onlookers gasped, "The hydrogen will explode." What could they do? They shrank back; they froze.

"Oh, my God! Everyone will be burned. This is horrible." White hydrogen flames flared above the ship.

The stern slumped to the ground. The forward section pointed skyward, the flames shooting through it.

Someone jumped from the forward end, nearly 300 feet above the ground.

A voice shouted, "Run for your lives. Run! Run!"

A mass of red flames and black smoke, the forward section began to settle—silently, steadily.

The ship was now only 35 feet from the ground. A dozen people were jumping. The flames crackled; the covering flaked off.

The fire crept forward. The outer fabric of the ship disappeared. The ribs stood out like the outline of a skeleton. Masses of flame were whirling around in the wind.

More people jumped through the windows or hatchways. One man jumped and started to run. Someone else jumped and landed on his back, knocking him down.

Horrified spectators fainted. A woman was sobbing, "Oh, my son, my poor son."

The ship crumbled and sagged to the ground with a crash of red hot girders. A man staggered out, his hair flaming, his clothes gone.

The inferno blazed. An old woman had come through a hatchway just before the crash and was running forward to safety, carrying a little suitcase. The stunned crowd rushed forward to help, only to be driven back by the flames.

The stench of scorched flesh filled the air.

---

*The direct quotes in this section are a transcription of actual remarks made by Morrison as recorded on Columbia record ML 4095.

Passengers, crew, hair burning, clothes burning, groped through the flames and smoke. Mrs. Rosendahl ran forward screaming; she thought her husband had been struck by the falling ship.

Captain Lehmann staggered away, "I can't understand it, I can't understand it."

Morris had snapped the red hot metal, fought his way clear. Franz Werner, a cabin boy, jumped through a hatch. The flames were choking him when a water tank burst over him; he stumbled his way through an opening to safety.

Mrs. Doehner had thrown her children through the windows; Mr. Doehner was missing. Pannes, frantically searching for his wife, never came out.

Sections of the ship continued to explode. A fiery furnace—the heat was unbearable!

A man collapsed—George Shahs, the German acrobatic dancer, who had survived the 300-foot leap to the ground.

Another man ran into the hangar. His face was black although he seemed to be all right otherwise. He was shouting, "I must call my mother; I must call my mother." It was Herbert O'Laughlin of Chicago.

Reporters raced for phones. Photographers took pictures madly.

Survivors staggered around, unable to speak although they could make gestures.

Rescuers swarmed to the field. Ambulance sirens blared.

The blaze continued. Lakehurst had become a veritable hell.

A few minutes before, a magnificent, impressive landing. Now, a scene of misery, a ghastly holocaust!

* * * * *

The disaster had been terrifying. Thirty-six people, including Captain Lehmann, had burned to death or had died later as the result of burns and injuries. Had the fall of the ship taken any longer, everyone would have been killed.

The whole world was shocked. At first, several people thought this was a case of sabotage. Italian newspapers carried the story on an inside page, so that they would not offend Germany.

Inquiry was placed in the hands of the Department of Commerce with the Army, Navy, U.S. Senate and state of New Jersey cooperating. A committee of German experts, headed by Dr. Hugo Eckener, the world's No. 1 zeppelinist, who was the builder and first commander of the *Hindenburg*, left immediately for the United States.

Although it was difficult to determine the exact nature of the catastrophe, it was generally thought that the ignition of the hydrogen was attributable to a discharge of atmospheric electricity in the vicinity of some sort of hydrogen leak, although this cause is questionable. Had the ship been filled with helium, the committee maintained, there would have been no possibility of a disaster.

Two days after the tragedy, the Senate Committee on Foreign Affairs approved the Sheppard-Hill Helium Bill, which had been submitted on February 17 of that year. Congress subsequently passed the Helium Act of 1937 which allowed countries operating civilian transport airships between this country and foreign ports to purchase helium from the United States, with the approval of the President and of the Army, Navy, and Interior Departments.

An empire had fallen; the Queen lay crumpled, burned, and broken on the fields of New Jersey. The *Graf Zeppelin* cancelled all further trips. With flags at half mast at the Zeppelin works in Friedrichshaven, work continued, nevertheless, on the LZ-130, a sister ship of the *Hindenburg*, which was completed in 1938. A widow of one of the crew members of the *Hindenburg* sent her gold wedding ring to be used towards building a new and better dirigible. Contributions were made by many German communities to continue airship activities.

But because the Department of the Interior turned down the helium export plan—not on the ground that it would affect our national supply but for security reasons—Germany did not get any helium, nor did the United States build any airships. Was the story of transoceanic zeppelin travel brought to a close by the last and final flight of the *Hindenburg*, the 129th zeppelin? Or will the energy crisis of the '70s bring back these gigantic and majestic airships as a way of travel once again?*   END

---

*The New London *Day* reported in February, 1974, that the Soviet Union planned construction of a nuclear-powered dirigible, capable of carrying 180 tons of freight and 1800 passengers. Ed.

The circus tent, moments before the entire top burst into flames, spilling "balls of fire" into the arena and on the seats. *Courtesy* The Hartford Courant.

Circus Fire

That crying clown was one of the saddest sights I'd ever seen.

by Mary Louise Kitsen

THE DAY STARTED OUT DECEPTIVELY.

I awoke that morning to a beautiful summer day. The date was July 6, 1944, and as I looked out of my bedroom window, I could see that this was to be summer at its best. The sun made everything sparkle, and the sky had never seemed bluer. My mood was a happy one anyway. For I loved the circus. And this was circus day. I grinned just thinking about it. My best friend and I had made plans to take the bus from Southington, the small town where we lived, to our capitol city, Hartford, Connecticut, where the circus was playing.

"Eat a good breakfast," advised my grandmother. "You have a big day ahead." I laughed because my grandmother found a different reason for eating a hearty breakfast every single day. She really believed in starting the day with a full stomach. I can recall thinking about many things as I ate that morning. Perhaps it will seem odd that anyone could remember what happened on a morning so long ago. But this was to be a day to be remembered well for a lifetime. And what thoughts ran through my head that day? The circus was on my mind, of course. Also, I felt quite grown-up about going with my friend and not with my family. Always before, this had been a family event. However, six days earlier I had turned fifteen, and after all, everyone knows that fifteen is practically the gateway to womanhood.

But things started going wrong early . . . The first bad thing that happened was a telephone call. I was just finishing breakfast when it came. My friend was ill, her mother said; evidently something she had eaten the night before had not agreed with her. She couldn't go.

All morning long I changed my mind back and forth about what I'd do. I'd think about staying home—it didn't seem as though it would

99

be as much fun without my friend along. Then I'd remember how much I loved the circus and decide to go anyway. I'd consider calling another friend, but then I wondered if that might look like "second choice," which wouldn't do! Maybe I could talk my family into going that night. That was a good idea. No, it wasn't! I remember how nervous the high acts made my mother and how she had expressed her relief that I was old enough to go to the circus alone. What a morning!

Finally, almost at the last possible moment, I decided to go. My decision came so late that I had to run to make it to the bus on time. The bus rounded the curve in the road just as I reached the stop. The next bus would have been too late. I considered myself lucky. But I wasn't. Missing that bus would have been lucky.

Once in the tent, I decided I was glad I'd come. For one thing, I was seated next to a young man with a little boy and a smaller girl. The mother was home with a new baby. I didn't feel alone with the children there. What fun it was to watch their happy grins and listen to their squeals of delight.

The lions had just left the big tent of the Barnum and Bailey Circus, and the Wallenda Family had climbed to the top of the arena ready to start their high wire act. Unlike my mother, I loved the high acts. The flyers, the pole swayers, the high wire groups—I loved

Opposite page: The entire Big Top was a fiery mass of flames and smoke. *Left:* Young survivors sadly view the site of the tragedy that took the lives of 169 people and injured 500 others—many critically. *Below:* The fire left nothing but charred remnants of the stands. *All photos courtesy* The Hartford Courant.

them all, and my eyes were glued to the Wallendas. Through my concentration, I heard a voice shouting something. I didn't understand what it said, but that didn't worry me. I figured it was someone with the circus calling to the Wallenda troupe. Then I heard a scream, followed immediately by another scream. The voice called out again. This time there was no mistaking what the voice said.

"FIRE, FIRE!"

The Wallendas started sliding down a pole or a rope or some such—I cannot be sure. My eyes darted about. At the opposite end of the tent, flames could be seen, and they were spreading quickly. Panic took over. The audience wanted out; people were rushing toward the exits, pushing each other as most of them headed downward to the ground of the tent. The noise was unbelievable—shouts, screams, sobs, and that awful sound the flames made. As for me, I sat rooted. Somehow I remembered my family telling me that you should always take a moment to think in an emergency. But I couldn't think.

Then I felt someone shaking my arm. "Come on, come on!" It was the young father. I got to my feet, and he put his little girl in my arms. Then he picked his small son up. "Just follow me. Come on, come on!" I moved behind him, wondering how I could stay close. People were actually pushing each other down in their blind panic, their fear taking over. And no

101

wonder. Most of them had the dearest possession of their lives with them, their children!

Nearly everyone else was heading downward. The young father headed upward! "Where are you going?" I yelled. Then dense smoke made me choke on the words.

"Just come on," he answered, "trust me." I turned for a second and glanced down. Balls of flames were dropping down into the ring area and on some of the seats! I looked up. Nearly the entire Big Top was a flaming mass. Suddenly up did seem like a good idea. We were all coughing now. Because we had sat for a few seconds, most of the people around us had already started down. Going up was not too hard, but it seemed to me that in the end we would probably die.

By the time we reached the top, the flames and smoke were rolling quickly toward us, obscuring everything below. The young father pulled on the weakened tent, and it fell away. Oh, did the air feel good. My chest hurt terribly from the smoke, and it must have been even harder on the two tots. Then I looked down. We were so high! So high!

The noise was frightful. Added to the sounds from the start of the fire were sirens, moans, and a roar as the fire engulfed so much of the huge tent. The terrible smell was even worse now.

"Someone break the fall of these children," yelled the young father. He was hoarse from the smoke, and no one heard him. He yelled again. This time a man in a clown's suit carrying a pail of water toward the tent heard him. The clown dropped the bucket and ran to a spot beneath us. He closed his eyes for just a second, and somehow I knew he was saying a prayer.

The father tossed his little boy down, and the clown managed to catch him. He stood the boy beside him and put his little hand on his suit closing it tight. I took a deep breath and tossed the little girl. The clown caught her too, and her brother took her hand when the clown stood her up.

The father shook me. "Jump," he said. I looked down and froze. "Jump!" he said. I took a deep breath and jumped. Both the clown and I went down under the impact, but we weren't hurt. The clown scrambled back to his feet and motioned to a policeman who had just come into sight. The two of them broke the fall of the father. I can see that clown in my mind today. He was crying. The tears had made his painted face all streaked. That crying clown was one of the saddest sights I've ever seen.

Suddenly it seemed that there were people all over the spot where we were. I saw the young father pick up his children, one under each arm, and look around. I knew he was looking for me, but someone pushed me and then some other people cut in front of me. I never saw that little family again. At least they were safe.

A policeman touched my arm and asked if I was hurt. I said I wasn't, so he told me to walk away from the fire and find a phone and call my home. I walked away. Fire trucks and ambulances kept speeding by. People were rushing toward the scene. I looked back just once. The entire tent seemed to be a ball of flames from where I was. It made an eerie glow through the thick smoke. Oh, that awful smoke . . . that smell! I didn't look back again.

A woman stopped me and asked me if I was all right. I remember wondering how she knew I was from the fire. You know, I actually didn't realize then that I was covered with black soot! That seems funny, but I really didn't know that my face, my arms and my dress were all blackened. I said I was all right and she started on toward the fire, but then she ran back. I remember telling her that I wanted to call home, and she took me to a nearby drugstore. The man in the drugstore sat me in a chair and called for me. My grandmother had remained by the phone. My folks had heard a bulletin on the radio and were already heading for Hartford, calling home every few miles in case I had called.

One hundred and sixty-nine souls perished in that tent. The sister-in-law of a neighbor was one. The Murphy family of Plainville was almost wiped out . . . Red, the father, his wife and a small son. Little Patty Murphy was critically burned and was the last victim released from the hospital. Something like 500 people were injured. And all that happened to me was that I was covered with soot and frightened badly. I was a very lucky girl.   END

4.
MYSTERIES AND GORE GALORE

What Happened to Lucy Keyes?

Her bones may still lie hidden away somewhere on the easterly side of Mount Wachusett—no one knows for sure . . .

by Albert B. Southwick

MOUNT WACHUSETT SHOULDERS UP INTO THE SKY of central Massachusetts with a majesty that cannot be denied. It dominates the town of Princeton and the whole surrounding region. In the bright sunshine Wachusett is a friendly mountain.

Yet, for more than two centuries, the Mount Wachusett region has been haunted by a memory of a lost child and a demented woman.

From father to child, from generation to generation, the tale has been passed down—all except the ending.

No one knows the ending. Knows for sure, that is. Some think the Lucy Keyes case was solved by a strange deathbed confession of guilt, 50 years after the event. But no one knows for sure.

It was in May, 1751, that Robert Keyes and his family moved from Shrewsbury to the easterly side of Wachusett, where he bought a tract of 200 acres.

The Keyes family seems to have made out fairly well in the next few years. Gradually the land was cleared, as the stubborn forest gave way to the axe and plow. A cabin was built. Things went along happily until April 14, 1755.

On that fateful day, Patty and Anna Keyes, aged nine and seven, were sent by their mother to Wachusett Pond, a mile through the woods, to get some sand for household tasks. Lucy, being only four, was told to stay at home. She was playing outside when her mother went into the house. She was never seen again.

Robert Keyes was plowing in a nearby field when he heard his wife's frantic calls for Lucy. He ran to the house immediately and began

105

the search. Shortly afterward, the two older girls returned from the pond. They had not seen Lucy. Thinking that the little girl had wandered off after her sisters and become lost in the dark forest, Robert Keyes ran off toward the pond. But no trace of Lucy was to be found. He rushed back to the house, desperate, saddled his horse and rode off to the nearest neighbors, four miles away.

The word spread rapidly through the sparsely settled region. By the next day volunteer searchers had come from Shrewsbury, 17 miles away, Lancaster, 12 miles to the east, and Rutland, eight miles distant. On the day following, there were people from 30 miles around offering to help find Lucy.

Thus began one of the greatest man hunts in colonial history. For days, scores of men, women and youths combed the region. Finally, in desperation, Keyes organized the searchers in a great ring around the base of Mount Wachusett. Keeping contact by continual shouting through the dense forest, they climbed slowly to the summit—but no Lucy was found.

Day and night the search went on. One night, around a camp fire, the seekers heard an eerie howling in the forest.

"Are those dogs?" asked one man uneasily.

"I think they are wolves," said another.

Could it have been wolves that did away with Lucy Keyes? No evidence, no shred of clothing, no blood-stained leaves were ever discovered.

Did Lucy drown in Wachusett Pond? The pond was dragged thoroughly. No body ever rose to the surface.

Gradually the mother became partially deranged with grief. Consumed with feelings of guilt, torn by her heartache for her missing little girl, she refused to believe that her daughter would not come back. For years after the tragedy she would wander down the path where Lucy was last seen, calling her name and entreating her to "come home to supper." Her wild, piteous cry, heard frequently by neighbors on the slopes of the mountain, became a legend in itself, and enhanced the legend of Lucy's disappearance. Those who saw her and heard her never forgot it.

Robert Keyes retained his sanity, but the loss of the little girl, his favorite, was a cross he bore to the end of his life. After weeks of search produced no sign of Lucy, he became convinced that she had been spirited away by Indians. It was a plausible explanation. Although there were no tribes permanently settled in the region in 1755, stealthy bands of savages were sometimes seen passing along the mountain trails, on their way to Canada or New York.

Driven by a remorseless wish to know what had happened to his daughter, Robert Keyes began to track down every rumor he heard. A white child was reported living with Indians in New Hampshire. Keyes made the long, expensive journey, only to find that the rumor came from Canada. He sent letters and advertised in the papers, but to no avail.

Ten years after the tragedy, weary and impoverished, Keyes wrote to the General Court in Boston, praying for a measure of relief for the expenses he had incurred during the search for his daughter.

"The cost he hath been put to (the petition was in the third person, after the prevailing custom) in Searching for said Child being about 100 pounds lawful money, that he is not able to bear it being in a new plantation . . ."

But his petition for another tract of land on the slope of Wachusett was turned down for reasons unknown.

Robert Keyes lived on until 1795, dying in straitened circumstances, according to legend. His wife had preceded him by a few years. The gravestone in the old burying ground on Meeting House Hill in Princeton marks the end of that part of the tragedy.

But what about Lucy? Was her fate to rest forever among the things unfathomable by human mind?

For more than a century, that was the case. The legend of Lucy Keyes grew dusty in the memory. She was only a little girl who had somehow been lost on the mountain once upon a time.

Then, in 1859, quite by chance, came a startling story that tore open the whole controversy once again. If true, it gives the answer to the famous tragedy.

Princeton celebrated its centennial in 1859, and one of its speakers was Prof. Erastus Everett, of Brooklyn, New York. He made a casual reference to the Lucy Keyes legend and then passed on to other matters in his oration.

Word of his talk somehow reached an old lady out in Kansas. She said she had lived in Princeton as a girl, and that she remembered hearing, third hand, about the deathbed confession of a man named Littlejohn, who had been a neighbor of the Keyes family in 1755.

As Professor Everett read the letter, the dead past leaped to life. He was carried back to those desperate days when the whole region had turned out to help comb the mountain wilderness in search of the lost little girl. He could almost hear the hounds baying in the dusk, and hear the anxious shouts, and see the flickering campfires in the forest.

For, allegedly, this man Littlejohn lay raving on his deathbed in Deerfield, New York, when he demanded that a minister be summoned. The minister arrived just in time to hear the dying man, his soul consumed with dread of the eternal fire, tell how he had murdered Lucy Keyes so many years before.

There had been bad blood between Littlejohn and Robert Keyes, according to the story. Furious over a boundary dispute, he had come across the little girl in the forest on that fateful day. In a fit of rage, he struck her on the head with a heavy stick. He hid the body in a hollow tree.

Littlejohn was one of the first to join the searching party. He succeeded in keeping the others away from the scene until nightfall. Then, under cover of darkness, he took the tiny corpse, buried it in a big hole under a stump, and lit a fire on the top to destroy the scent.

As the days and weeks went on, Littlejohn began to feel the burning sense of guilt that was to curse him for the rest of his life. Every time he walked through the woods, he seemed to see the little girl running before him, her little hand on her head, crying for her father. And, as the months went by and Littlejohn heard the grief-stricken mother calling for her Lucy to please come home, he decided he could not stand it any longer. He moved away, but was never able to blot the terrible deed from his mind. Now, with the torment of Hell about to engulf him, he threw himself on the sweet mercy of Jesus.

Then, having delivered himself of this hair-raising confession, Littlejohn fell back, dead.

Francis Everett Blake, who was to write the definitive history of Princeton, became intrigued with the Lucy Keyes legend at the turn of the present century. An amateur historian, he spent many an hour pouring over the case. Noting that the letter from Kansas, which told of a third-hand experience, had been generally accepted as the truth, he decided to investigate further.

He found discrepancies in the Littlejohn story. The only man by that name that Blake could track down was a Tilly Littlejohn, who did not, according to the records, live in Princeton in 1755, but moved there later.

Assuming that the records could have been wrong, Blake traced the career of Tilly Littlejohn, and found that he had never moved to Deerfield, New York, where the confession was supposed to have taken place. There were other inconsistencies in the story.

On the other hand, the account had been related by persons who seemed thoroughly reliable. There seemed to be no possible motive for fabrication.

There the matter rests. The bones of Lucy Keyes may still be hidden away somewhere on the easterly side of Mount Wachusett. No one knows.   END

by Lloyd W. Fowles

The Strange Case of the *Mary Celeste*

Enduring Puzzle of the Sea

Waterspout? Mutiny? Violence? Explosion? *Why* **was the half-brig abandoned in running condition with sails set?**

Giberalta, Dec. 14th, 1872

Dear Wife: I write you these few lines to let you know that I arrived here safe and well, and hope you are the same. We left New York the 15th Nov. and had a very hard passage of 26 days, we had nothing but westerly gales till we got to the western isles and then we had a very moderate passage.

From there I must inform you of our good luck in Lat. 38.20 and Long. 17.15 W. We fell in with the brig Mary Celeste of New York abandoned, we went on board and found that the crew had left her and had left everything behind, the Capt. had his wife and child and eight men in all and they must left in a hurry for they left all there clothes behind and I do not think they took a change. When we boarded her she had only 3½ ft. of water in the hole and had been left 10 days, her fore sail and upper top sail were blowed from the yard and the lower top sail was hanging by the four corners and the decks were swept clean but the hull was new, and strong. I think she was hove down and they got scared and left in a hurry. I took two men out of the brig and brought her in here with only two men and myself and I had a hard time of it. I would not like to undertake it again, I had very fine

weather for the first two or three days and then we had it hot and heavy. I made the land all right and it was blowing a gale at the time and I got drove through the gut and 40 miles to leaward.

The Brig only got in one day before me, my men were all but done out when I got in here and I think it will be a week before I can do anything for I never was so tired in my life, I can hardly tell what I am maid of but I do not care as long as I got in safe . . .

I still remain your most affectionate husband,

Oliver Deveau

These opening paragraphs by the Chief Mate of the brigantine, *Dei Gratia*, to his wife in Nova Scotia formed the most forthright and direct statement made about the abandoned vessel—barring the testimony in the admiralty court (which had its own peculiar deviations). The concluding parts of the letter contain one sentence that must have brought satisfaction and high hopes to the wife and mother in Nova Scotia: "I shall be well paid, for the *Mary Celeste* belongs to New York and was loaded with alcohol bound for Genoa Italy and her cargo is worth eighty thousand dollars beside

Left: Captain Benjamin Spooner Briggs, lost master of the *Mary Celeste. Below:* This scale model of the *Mary Celeste* created by A. G. Law is rigged as the ship was when found, sails torn, hatches open, and the ship's boat missing. *Courtesy A. G. Law and Charles Edey Fay.*

the vessel, we do not know how it will be settled yet." However, any hope of handsome remuneration was fated to be unfulfilled—just another instance of the many unlucky circumstances surrounding this vessel.

More than a century has passed since the abandoned half-brig *Mary Celeste*, under her master, Benjamin Spooner Briggs of Marion, Massachusetts, was found between the Azores and coast of Portugal with no one on board. Although every detail has been subject to intense scrutiny and many theories advanced (all attacked by proponents of other solutions), the origin of this unsolved sea mystery is briefly told and told best by "the man who was there."

On December 18, 1872, in the Vice Admiralty Court at Gibraltar the case of "The Queen in Her Office of Admiralty against the Ship or Vessel Supposed to be Called *Mary Celeste* and her Cargo Proceeded against as Derelict" opened, and Chief Mate Oliver Deveau was the star witness. Mr. Deveau told the story that has since become the basis for theories, fantasies, speculations and lies.

His story recounts the manner in which the *Mary Celeste* was sighted, "apparently in distress," boarded, searched, and a decision reached by Captain David R. Morehouse, master of the *Dei Gratia,* for his mate and two seamen to sail the ship to Gibraltar as a salvage operation.

Briefly told, the ship was in running condition and on the starboard tack, the hatches had been removed, two sails (the jib and fore topmast staysail) were set, two others blown away, one (lower fore topsail) hanging loose, and the remaining sails furled. Due to an accident, while the cargo was being loaded at New York, the original lifeboat had been smashed and a replacement (not fitting the davits) had been "lashed to the main hatch." When Deveau boarded the vessel, this boat was found missing. The last entry on the log slate indicated that on November 25 the island of Saint Mary (Santa Maria) had been sighted. In the opinion of Mr. Deveau "there seemed to be everything left behind in the cabin as if left in a great hurry" and again, "My idea is that the crew got alarmed and by the sounding rod being found lying alongside the pumps, that they had sounded the pumps and found perhaps a quantity of water in the pumps at the moment, and, thinking she would go down, abandoned her."

The Court and especially Solly Flood, the Queen's Proctor in Her Office of Admiralty, were not satisfied or pleased with results of the hearing and so they were resumed in January and March, 1873. At the latter hearing Mate Deveau was questioned about certain features which had aroused the suspicions of the Queen's Proctor. Due to the confusion of ropes and the main staysail hanging loose over the forward house, the Mate had never mentioned the broken peak halyard which became a more important detail as the hearing progressed. Neither was the Mate able to account for axe cuts in the rail, alleged blood stains on the deck and on a sword found under the Captain's berth. In his closing words of testimony he reiterated his basic belief to the court for the last time: "It did not occur to me that there had been any act of violence—there was nothing to induce one to believe or show that there had been any violence."

The high hopes of the three sailors who performed the titanic task of sailing a strange ship over 600 miles in seven days, enduring a heavy storm as well as subsequently an unfriendly court, were never realized. Sometime in early April, 1873, after the court had fulfilled its determination to "take time to consider the Decree for Restitution," a judgment was given. The sum of £1700 was awarded to the master and crew of the *Dei Gratia*. Mr. Charles Edey Fay, who has written the authoritative study of this mercantile mystery, feels that the award was inadequate because "it was no negligible feat of seamanship for three men to bring in the *Mary Celeste*." The crew of the *Dei Gratia* had been reduced by a third when Deveau and his two seamen left for the abandoned ship, and the compensation was considerably less than normally awarded. No wonder the owners, captain, mate and seamen of the *Dei Gratia* rightfully felt defrauded.

During the century just past, whenever the mystery of the *Mary Celeste* has been considered, three questions were generally asked: What happened? Who were the people involved, and, of course, what is the solution? Mate Oliver Deveau was one of two main characters for he led the boarding crew of three from the *Dei Gratia* which brought the derelict into Gibraltar. The other important figure must necessarily be the master of the half-brig *Mary Celeste*, Captain Benjamin Spooner Briggs of Marion, Massachusetts. Whatever decisions he made or what befell him must have been at the bottom of the mystery and therefore many of the legends have grown up around this man.

That Captain Briggs came from a seafaring family and knew his trade is a well substantiated fact. As one son in a family of five boys and one girl, children of a sea captain, he learned the mystery of sailing ships from his youth. Three of his brothers, Nathan, Oliver and Zenas, died at sea; while his sister, Maria, was drowned in a shipwreck off Cape Fear. The family's life was intertwined with marine tragedies and to have lost five of their six children to the demands of the sea was a heavy burden to the parents.

On this particular voyage, originating in New York, November 7, 1872, Captain Briggs had decided to take his wife, Sarah, and their small daughter, Sophia Matilda, with him. The quarters were cramped, but the custom of the Captain's wife, and perhaps a child, periodically accompanying the master of a vessel was often practiced. Furthermore, the ship which was now one-third (eight twenty-fourths) owned by the

Captain was in fine shape due to a recent over-haul. The first mate, Albert Richardson from Stockton Springs, Maine, had sailed with Captain Briggs before, and the remainder of the crew (one second mate, a cook and four seamen) were all capable hands. The Captain looked forward to an agreeable voyage in spite of the season of the year as he wrote to his mother. "Our vessel is in beautiful trim and I hope we shall have a fine passage." One other matter which later became an important factor in the analysis of the mystery of the tragic ship was the nature of the cargo. This consisted of 1700 barrels of alcohol, insured for $37,000 and shipped by the firm of J. H. Winchester & Co. from New York to Genoa. There was nothing out of the ordinary or that could lead to disaster when the *Mary Celeste* left New York on her ill-fated passage, for it was a normal mercantile shipment in the hands of capable mariners.

What has happened in the century since the *Mary Celeste* was found derelict and Captain Briggs, his wife, child and crew disappeared to explain this event which seems to defy solution? Aside from the personal effects of Captain Briggs and his wife, which were returned to his home in Massachusetts, nothing has been found. This fact in itself has caused the growth of tales which range from the fictitious to the fabulous but which are all unsupported.

Three men, however, as conscientious researchers during their lifetimes, studied every available aspect of the catastrophe and wrote books, pamphlets or articles which bear the stamp of authenticity and scholarship. Mr. Charles Edey Fay of Lake Worth, Florida, in 1942 wrote *Mary Celeste, The Odyssey of an Abandoned Ship* and with this book all known material pertaining to the "wandering, ghost-like" ship was collected into a scholarly and readable book. The nephew of Captain Briggs, Mr. J. Franklin Briggs of New Bedford, Massa-

These monuments in Marion, Massachusetts, bear mute and timeless witness to the marine tragedies that beset the Briggs family. *Photos by Robert A. Benson.*

111

chusetts, who was the author of *In The Wake of the Mary Celeste*, made his lifetime avocation the pursuit of material relating to the ships and personnel involved. Dr. Oliver Cobb of Easthampton, Massachusetts, cousin of the Briggses, also maintained a lifelong interest in the *Mary Celeste* and its captain, whose family he described in his nostalgic *Rose Cottage*.

These three men have, so it is believed at present, exhaustively stated or restated the case of the *Mary Celeste*. How anything else can be added it is difficult to perceive. What, therefore, have these students concerned with every phase of the mystery—the ships (both *Dei Gratia* and *Mary Celeste*), the routes, the weather, the court proceedings, the finances, the correspondence, the possible solutions and the personnel—concluded?

Mr. Charles Edey Fay lists and explains ten "theories and attempted solutions," the only one of which he supports is that of Dr. Oliver Cobb. His theory accounts for almost every factor and is based on the belief that some of the barrels of alcohol leaked causing loud rumblings or an explosion in the hold. Captain Briggs feared for his wife and small daughter, so all people aboard left the vessel in the small boat using the peak halyard as a tow-line. When this parted, the small boat either capsized or was left behind to the mercies of the wind and sea. Several facts militate against this conclusion of Dr. Cobb.

In the first place, although some barrels had leaked, there was no sign of any explosion in the hold, and it is not believed by modern-day chemists that alcohol would create a condition such as Dr. Cobb describes, causing all hands to abandon the ship. No other vessel carrying al-alcohol—such as the *Dei Gratia*—and following the same route ever experienced such a condition as that which Dr. Cobb pictured. However, Mr. Fay and Dr. Cobb are in substantial agreement about this possibility, while Mr. Briggs—a thorough and diligent scholar—maintained that the solution would never be known.

One theory, surprisingly overlooked, is contained in an article entitled *Sinbad's Genie and the Mary Celeste* written by Dr. James H. Kimball, former meteorologist of New York. The whole work is an extensive analysis of waterspouts—their history, locations, occurrence in the area sailed by the *Mary Celeste*, amount of water in the cabins and below the decks of the vessel, and the *modus operandi* of these phenomena.

Near the beginning of his explanation, Dr. Kimball wrote, "Some catastrophic situation must be envisaged before one can believe that the Captain would judge an overloaded lifeboat in a rough sea as providing a greater measure of safety for his family and crew than did his own vessel, which he had ample reason to think to be sound." The author's contention is that the vessel was struck by a waterspout.

He envisions the following situation: "A fully developed spout is observed approaching from the southwest. It bears down on the vessel so rapidly that nothing can be done to mitigate the onslaught. The whole ship's company gathers in a terrified huddle. The southerly blast to the right of the center of the vortex strikes the vessel, causing it to lurch violently to port; as it is being righted, the tube passes over; its circling wind from the north careens the ship to starboard, the deckload of water shipped when the *Mary Celeste* careened sweeps across the deck. Passage of the waterspout's vortex over the vessel would require but a few seconds, the twinkling of an eye, in that moment the entire ship's company and the boat they hoped would save them are swept into the sea which buries its secrets with the dead."

Theories of what happened to the vessel and crew will undoubtedly continue to be written, and they deserve consideration inasmuch as they represent logical efforts to account for all known and substantiated facts. Mr. Fay states what every explorer of sea mysteries knows so well. "Now submissively bearing Man's far-flung commerce, and now with insatiable ferocity devouring his proudest creations, it is the Sea, which, holding within her vast treasure-house the secrets of her multitudinous dead—'unknelled, uncoffined and unknown'—defies his challenge and intrigues his imagination."

Only the family monument in the Marion cemetery which bears the names of Captain Benjamin Spooner Briggs, Sarah Elizabeth Cobb Briggs, and Sophia Matilda Briggs—lost at sea—remains as a permanent marker of this devoted family whose lives represent the seafaring tradition of their country.   END

George Welden, Whalingperson

Something let go inside of George; the heavy oar struck the officer a slashing blow on the head . . .

by Chester Scott Howland

WAR NEWS WAS FRONT-PAGE MATERIAL DURING the second year of the Civil War. Doubtless few folks noted in the shipping information that appeared daily in the *New Bedford Mercury* that the bark *America* sailed from Holmes' Hole, Martha's Vineyard Island, September 10, 1862. Fewer still would have been interested enough to read the crew list. And if they had, no one would have known George Welden, foremast hand. But, six months later, the readers of the *New Bedford Standard* were shocked upon turning away from the good or bad Civil War news to see a small drawing (reproduced

above) by a staff artist reconstructing the very moment when the officers of the *America* made the discovery that one member of their whaling crew was deadlier than the male.

The drawing showed a fully-clothed girl in a seaman's outfit, tied up, *back* to the mast, in preparation for a flogging. The bewhiskered whalers around her are aghast with their discovery—the flogger has let the cat slip from his nerveless fingers and his mouth hangs open. An officer who looks very much like a second-generation Josef Stalin is gesticulating with both hands in manly horror. Another officer is

113

gazing on with mouth agape. The lady herself is fastening glazed eyes upon the horizon and apparently gritting her teeth. It is altogether an uncomfortable moment for one and all.

In real life, it was just a little bit different. The "seaman" had been ordered flogged. Of course, this always means on the bare back. Second Mate Casmire had ripped off the clothing down to the waist. What he saw occasioned words which are not on record, but it can be reported with happiness that the flogging did not progress.

It's all quite a story, and it goes like this:

In the fall of 1862, the whaler *America* was recruiting men for a four-year cruise. She would sail from Edgartown to the Indian Ocean with a crew of 40, which means she was a big ship. Captain Luce was in command.

One of the sturdy youngsters who signed the whaleship's papers was an 18-year-old who gave the name of George Welden.

Not to be mysterious, George was no man, and from this point on we'll refer to George Welden as "she." What the real name was, nobody seems to know, which is too bad, because it would be interesting to know more about her. She had lots of spunk, scampered up the ropes like a monkey, and handled herself like a veteran.

Of course, she had to crop her hair and bind her breasts quite tightly. But she had a low voice anyhow and didn't speak much. Nobody even thought to be suspicious.

When the chief mate, before dawn on the sailing day, sang out, "Stand by to cast off," George took her place with those shipmates of the forecastle who handled the port bow hawser and hauled in true sailor fashion. The vessel was soon out in the stream and under weigh before a strong fair wind. Cuttyhunk, the last seaward tip of land, lay well astern by sun up. As the island fell out of sight, George was busy in the foretop shaking out the topsail, 80 feet above the foamy whitecaps breaking about the ship's sides. A careless confidence in the rigging indicated that the girl had sailed on ships before.

When the vessel lay to for an hour or more the next day and lowered the boats to allow the men to get the feel of the oars, George Welden was tub-oarsman in the second mate's boat. Mr. Casmire, the officer, was an impetuous but capable whaleman who in his younger days had sailed out of Dundee on the Scotch whaleships.

Welden proved willing and able and stood out among the men before the mast, always alert to every responsibility. Her fair skin burned quickly as the *America* cruised through southern latitudes. When whales were sighted, she pulled a strong oar, and when they were killed and "cut in" along the ship's side, she made fast to the huge blanket pieces of oil-saturated blubber, held by the crew from washing off the whale's body into the sea by a "monkey rope" tied around her waist.

As the weeks passed, the ship sailed deep down into the South Atlantic. One morning, cruising in latitude 46 and longitude 56.20, George and another member of her watch standing the masthead lookout "raised" a large sperm whale a mile from the ship, spouting regularly and moving slowly off the starboard beam. The boats were lowered in chase as usual, but that whale was Welden's undoing, and before the day closed it was discovered that George Welden was a woman.

Though the men rowed desperately all day, they were not able to get within harpooning distance. The sun was baking hot, and its blinding glare on the water made the men's eyes sticky and feverish. Their hands were like glue because of broken blisters. With each stroke George had a tearing pain in her back that almost strangled her. There had been no such chase as this during the voyage.

At two o'clock a large whale broke water a hundred yards from the mate's boat. The oarsmen closed the distance, each with a grim face dripping sweat, and in silence. The whale lay sogging in his own suds.

The second mate, handling the great steering oar, snapped out an order to his harpooner, "Stand up there and get your irons ready." With a sharp, "Aye, aye, sir," the harpooner immediately shipped his oar and stood poised in the bow ready for darting.

"Now at him—a few more strong strokes—bear down men—bear down I tell you. Lay on to him—pull—pull—spring on those oars." The men rallied for the last surge that would place the boat into position.

All but George—she faltered. The unceasing

Captain Luce's entry in the *America's* log book, Friday, January 9, 1863.

efforts of the past hours had taken their toll, and now there was no reserve left in her exhausted muscles. Her oar was weak just when the strength of every oar was needed. She had never been tested so crucially. She was proud and hurt and her nerves were aflame with the tension of the excruciating ordeal. Mate Casmire, keenly sensitive to everything going on in the boat, felt a sag in the speed of the spurt and barked out, ugly in desperation, "Welden —bear down, bear down—do you hear me? Are you quittin'—have you no thought for the rest of the men—you—you—." He never concluded his implication.

Something let go inside George. She could not stand such an accusation after she had pulled the eyes out of her head trying to keep up. With an exhausted cry, she jumped to her feet and swung her heavy 15-foot oar so that it struck the officer a slashing blow on the side of his face. He sprawled headlong overboard into the sea.

Mate Casmire was painfully but not seriously hurt; recovering quickly, he climbed back into the boat. In a rage he ordered the men to make for the ship.

The whale, startled by the splash, lifted his flukes and disappeared. In an hour the vessel was sighted and, as soon as the boat was hoisted in the davits and secured, Mr. Casmire reported the act of insubordination to Captain Luce who immediately called all hands to witness the flogging.

"Welden," he said in a hard voice, "striking an officer is mutiny aboard this or any other ship. You are to be punished."

There was an inarticulate grumbling among some members of the assembled crew, but the captain paid no attention to it, and addressing, the chief mate continued, saying, "Mr. Cottle, trice him thumbs up to the rigging and Mr. Casmire, you bare his back for a dozen lashes; my orders are to lay them on heavy! We propose to have order on this craft."

George was handled roughly and a surge of blood showed crimson on her face when Mr. Cottle spread-eagled her to the mizzen shrouds. Then Mr. Casmire removed her shirt, exposing her breasts which were bound tightly to her body. Her face paled, bloodless, and she sagged, unconscious, held upright in the rigging by the cords about her thumbs. The uplifted rope's end never reached its target.

Later that day Captain Luce made the following entry in the log book:

"Bark *America* in the South. Friday January 9, 1863. Commences with light breeze from the west. The boats in chase of whales. At three P.M. the boats came aboard. This day found George Welden to be a woman the first I ever suspected of such a thing. Later part breezes from the south by west. Took in sail. Steering east-southeast. Three sails in sight."

It is believed that Captain Luce kept George in close confinement until a South American port was reached, and that, unbeknownst to the crew at large, he left her there in the custody of the local authorities. There the trail of her life's journey ends.

Who George Welden really was, *why* she chose to go to sea aboard a whaleship, and *how* her story ended remains a mystery. Perhaps some day, someone who knew her will fill in the blanks for us.   END

The Sinking of the *John Dwight*
Mystery off Cuttyhunk

by Everett S. Allen

One of the grimmest marine disasters ever in Massachusetts waters . . .

IT WAS 7:25 A.M., APRIL 6, 1923. THE SKIPPER OF the Coast Guard station on Cuttyhunk scanned what he could see of Vineyard Sound through wind-blown fog.

"Something there," he said to his No. 1 rated man, training his binoculars on the sound's western entrance.

It was an old pogie steamer, her single mast well forward.

The skipper passed the glasses to No. 1. "What do you make of that thing in her rigging?"

"Looks like a blanket, or an oilskin coat. Maybe a signal. The boat's out of the davits and I think there are lines trailing. Believe she's in trouble . . ."

"I think so, too," said the skipper. "Keep an eye on her. We'll launch the lifeboat and go to her."

Even as he left on the run, No. 1 yelled, "She's sinking!" and they could see steam spurt from her starboard side and the stern settling rapidly.

The unknown steamer was going under in the fog-shrouded sound, an area swept by boiling tides, in approximately 100 feet of water.

That was the official introduction to one of the grimmest marine disasters ever to occur in the heavily-trafficked waters of Massachusetts.

About the time the Cuttyhunk Station was alerted to trouble afloat, the Coast Guard station skipper at Gay Head, on Martha's Vineyard just across the sound, heard a steamer's whistle coming out of the fog. He couldn't see anything, but he described it as a "long, drawn-out whistle" that slowly died away. It wasn't necessarily a signal of distress, but it made him feel, sea-wise from a long career of aiding vessels in trouble, that something was wrong out there.

Real sailors don't ignore hunches. He ordered the station lifeboat launched, and prepared to go see whether anything was amiss. But both the Cuttyhunk and Gay Head boats were delayed by unavoidable circumstances from reaching the *Dwight* for long enough to have permitted anyone who might have scuttled the steamer to slip away in the fog.

The Cuttyhunk crew could not get through Canapitsit Channel, the normal route, and had to go an additional eight miles around Nashawena Island. The Gay Head station boat had been under way only a short time when engine trouble developed, and the crew had to row most of the distance to the *Dwight*.

One factor did help, however; the fog was lifting rapidly, and soon the *Dwight's* general location was revealed. Even though she had gone to the bottom, floating barrels betrayed the spot where she had sunk.

The Gay Head crew reached the scene first, and when the Cuttyhunk boat showed up was already busy picking up the barrels, each of which contained 120 half-pint bottles of ale, individually packed in straw. Several other small boats, fishermen, soon came into the area and picked up some of the barrels, too.

To the trained eyes of the Coast Guardsmen, one thing was immediately wrong. The sun was well up by now, the fog had been dispelled. Visibility was excellent; a white lobster pot buoy could be seen a mile away without binoculars. Yet there was no sign of any person from the sunken steamer, either dead or alive. There were no bodies, no life jackets, no wreckage, and no lifeboats of any kind.

Thus it was obvious from the beginning that the sinking of the *John Dwight* was not just another marine disaster. It also caused authorities to believe from the first that the steamer went to the bottom by design and not by accident.

If there had been any doubts about the unusual character of the *Dwight's* sinking, they were dispelled 24 hours later when all the signs of a sunken vessel finally showed up. At 7:30 the next morning, horrified searchers fished seven dead men in life jackets out of the waters of the sound. Nor were they ordinary victims of marine tragedy; each had been murdered. Bloody and battered, their skulls were bashed in, and their faces mutilated to prevent identification.

The body of an eighth man—one Harry King —the only one ever identified, drifted ashore in a small boat near Gay Head. The back of King's head had been beaten in. Inexplicably, there was a cheese knife in the boat with him. Soon after, a large gray hatch cover was picked up, and a wooden cradle, evidently designed to hold a small boat on a vessel's deck. On Naushon Island, across the sound from the Vineyard, other searchers found a lifeboat and two vessel's name boards, each of the latter bearing the legend: "John Dwight."

Investigating authorities, baffled by the tardy appearance of all of these evidences of tragedy, would have given much to know where they were—bodies and all—24 hours earlier, when painstaking Coast Guard crews were searching the waters over a wide area without finding a single thing to indicate what had happened.

Another strange fact emerged as the inquiry proceeded. The steamer *Dorchester*, which passed through the sound about five minutes before the *Dwight* sank, had observed a small boat, possibly a lifeboat, containing three men. It was apparently heading for the Vineyard and was about 150 yards from shore when seen.

These three men were the only living persons seen by anyone in the vicinity at the time the steamer went to the bottom. Who they were, where they came from, and where they were going has never been explained.

But inquiry did produce, through a combination of fact and theory, a picture of circumstances leading up to the *Dwight's* dramatic end.

The steamer *John Dwight* was a former naval vessel converted to civilian use. Five or six weeks before her last trip, she was overhauled and repaired in Newport, Rhode Island. She had left that port a few days before the sinking. Those responsible for her gave fictitious names and addresses to port officials, which made void all of the ship's papers and rendered her virtually a pirate on the high seas.

The steamer apparently had a crew of 15. Her skipper was Captain John King, although there were two persons aboard bearing the title "Captain," the other being Malcolm J. Carmichael, who probably served as navigator. Harry King, the only dead man identified, was from Brooklyn, and was the son of Captain King.

The *Dwight* had been acquired to carry a cargo of liquor from the "mother ship" of a fleet of rum carriers, stationed off the northeast coast, to some mainland distributing point. She may possibly have been accompanied by another vessel working on the same deal.

The "mother ship" contact had been made, the liquor was taken aboard the *Dwight*—and the barrels of ale stowed below and on deck. Eleven of these latter were picked up by the Gay Head lifesaving crew.

Investigators at this point were reliably informed of a circumstance which came to dominate the entire affair of the *Dwight*—and still does. Aboard the steamer at the time of the sinking was a large sum of money—$250,000 was the amount most often mentioned.

Why?

Some of the informants said the cash had been pooled by the 15 men aboard to swing a big liquor deal involving Canadian and Boston rum-running interests. Others who knew something of the illegal liquor trade said someone from the *Dwight*, perhaps Carmichael, had made a business arrangement in New London, possibly involving the rum cargo aboard, for which he received $100,000. In Newport, Captain King was reported to have transacted some kind of a deal to deliver liquor, for which he was paid an additional sum of $150,000.

The only money every known to have been recovered was $50 in the pocket of one of the dead men.

The Vineyard sheriff, who examined all of

Terry Rioux, left, and Bradford W. Luther, Jr., of the Fairhaven Whalers Skin-Diving Club, with the ship's binnacle and empty ale bottles recovered from the *John Dwight*.   *Courtesy Ed Rosa.*

the bodies found, said they bore evidence of a "wicked, free-for-all fight," and there were major cuts and bruises about their faces which obviously came from repeated blows of a solid, heavy instrument. But they never found out who the "young and clean-shaven" murdered men were.

Investigating officials thought there might be a possibility divers could answer these questions, but it was not to be. The sound, at any season, is a tough place for divers and was especially so for the available gear of that day. The current runs hard; the slack-water period between tide changes is brief. Also, northeasterly winds at the time of the sinking had left the water chilly, as the divers soon found out. They couldn't stay down long.

They did get down to the wreck, however, both then and later, and about all they discovered was that the hold was full of bottled ale which soon was rendered worthless by sea water. No bodies and no money were found. The engine room was a mass of wreckage, as if a bomb had been exploded there. On the floor in the engine room was what one diver described as a sword or cutlass, but it was not recovered.

At the end of May, 1923, the Attorney General said the inquiry was complete as far as the Commonwealth of Massachusetts was concerned, "without having developed sufficient evidence to warrant any criminal proceeding."

Federal agents in July, 1923, exploded four TNT bombs in the *Dwight's* hull and then ceased watch over the spot, satisfied that nothing was left to be salvaged by liquor-seekers.

The sinking of the rum-running steamer *John Dwight* posed four questions that neither federal, state nor local law-enforcement authorities ever have been able to answer:

Who murdered more than half the *Dwight's* crew?

Who scuttled the steamer loaded with ale, and why?

What happened to $250,000 in cash?

What happened to the remainder of the crew?

There may be men still living who know the answers to these questions, but they are not likely to tell. The case remains as much of a mystery today as it was 24 hours after it happened.   END

The White Slipper

Soon the pile of rubbish began to heave and pulsate, taking of itself the form and shape of a skeleton . . .

by Arthur W. Blackman

I WAS ONE OF THE PIONEER BICYCLE RIDERS IN this country, starting in with the first type of machine, the kind with the very large wheel in front. The early ones came from England, and it so happens that the one I owned was one of the first seven ever imported. If I remember correctly, it was a "Hallamshire" and had roller bearings.

Naturally, the early riders were drawn together by a common interest and many lifelong friendships were thus formed. In those days, on the rare occasions that two riders met on the road, they generally dismounted and usually in the center of a curious crowd of onlookers introduced themselves, and then each proceeded to enlarge upon the outstanding virtues of his own particular make of machine.

Early in the game (about 1877 or 1878), I heard of a young man by the name of Arthur Foster who lived in Andover, Massachusetts, who also owned a bicycle, so I opened up a correspondence with him, to the end that I was invited to ride up and spend a weekend with him.

Now, Andover was 25 miles away from Cambridge, and the road to it led through what was then strange untravelled territory to me, and as I had never ridden my bicycle such a long distance, the trip loomed up as quite an adventure (and it certainly proved to be so).

In a brand-new brown corduroy bicycle suit, with cap to match, I ventured forth one Saturday afternoon, with my toothbrush and nightie in a bundle tied onto the handlebars. I wended my way, with the aid of a road map, through Winchester, Stoneham, and Reading, into the wilds of Wilmington, over rough, country carriage roads that were narrow, winding, and exceedingly dusty. When I arrived at this point, the rumbling of distant thunder warned me of the threatened danger to my new corduroys, and the angry-looking black clouds rolling toward me from directly ahead seemed to confirm it, so I craned my neck in every direction for a place of shelter as I nervously sped along. Alas and alack, there was nothing in sight but *more* road and plenty of wilderness.

Finally, rounding a curve, I nearly bumped into a two-horse farm wagon headed in my direction. Hailing the farmer who drove it, I asked if there was a farmhouse near, where I might put up for the night. He shook his head slowly, hesitated and then said: "Well, there used to be a place where the old stagecoaches stopped, off to your left a piece. I hear tell that an old couple still live there. You might try there. You'll find a wood road off to your left, about a mile or so ahead. Take that, and go a piece till you come to a fork, then take the right turn and you'll land plumb in their dooryard. You may have to open a gate or two as that road is closed now and ain't used much. I don't know no one else round here. I live down Reading way."

It grew rapidly darker overhead as I raced along, and the thunder claps were not much behind the blinding lightning flashes. When I could no longer safely ride in the ruts of the wood road, I got off and pushed my wheel and finally arrived at the dooryard gate, breathless, but still dry.

I saw before me a large two-story, colonial-

Enormous rats swarmed crazily around the room, each carrying a brownish-grey object in its mouth.

type weatherbeaten house, surmounted by a huge cupola. On one of the seats, built into the wide, deep porch, sat a fat little man smoking a pipe. To the left of the house extended a long carriage house with three arched doorways, filled in by heavy strap-hinged doors. This in turn was joined further to the left to a big tumbledown barn. Panting for breath, as the first sprinkles spattered about me, I asked the astonished little man if I could come in out of the rain. "Sure, young fellow," he said. "Put your contraption in that first coach house and come up here."

As I opened one of the big doors and pushed my bicycle under cover, I had a glimpse in the dark interior of a huge yellow strap-slung stagecoach covered with cobwebs and dust.

The storm broke loose in all its fury as I slammed the door to and scampered for the shelter of the covered porch. After consulting with his "old woman," as he called her, he decided that I could spend the night there, for

Illustration by Abbott Cheever

121

the roads were by this time impassable, for bicycles at least.

In due course of time supper was announced, and we went in. I can see that wonderful old room now, in my mind's eye. It extended across the whole front part of the house, had a sanded floor, a low ceiling crisscrossed with heavy, rough, smoke-stained beams, and side walls paneled in some dark-colored wood. In the far right corner was a lattice-work cage which my host said was the old bar. In the center of the left side was an enormous fireplace, it and the chimney extending three feet or more out into the room, while two high-backed settles faced each other in front on either side of it. A rectangular tavern table stood between these settles in front of the yawning fireplace, in which dying embers glowed.

As we slid into our places opposite each other, his wife set before us a big brown earthenware dish rounded up with a deliciously crisp-looking pie crust, whereupon he discoursed as follows: "My friend, in my grandfather's time long ago, this was an inn. All stagecoaches from Lowell and points further north on their way to Boston changed horses here. It was especially noted for its pork pies and flip. So, every Saturday night, for old times' sake, my old woman makes me a pork pie, and sometimes I also mix me a glass of flip. If you would like, we will have one tonight. What do you say?"

It is true that I had never drunk a flip, or even *heard* of one; nevertheless, I felt called upon to say: "Sure thing." It may have been that the look and smell of that appetizing pie had something to do with my temerity.

The little man arose from his seat and from a cupboard on his side of the chimney, produced two large, tall, but very thin glasses and a small tin can. His wife brought him two yellow pitchers, two bottles of ale, and four eggs. He first emptied the ale into one pitcher and set it on the hearth to simmer. In the other he broke the eggs, put in two wine glasses of rum and a tablespoon of a powder from the can. This powder, he explained, was called "spicemix" and made from equal parts of nutmeg, grated ginger, and fried lemon peel, pounded and rubbed in a mortar. Then with a long-handled wooden spoon, he beat up the egg concoction to a froth, emptied it into the pitcher of simmering ale and

poured the united contents back and forth many times from one pitcher to the other, holding one well above the other, to get a cream-like effect. He then filled the flip glasses, sprinkled some nutmeg on top, and plunged into each the cherry-red loggerhead which had been nestling all this time in the glowing embers of the dying fire.

Having finished off two generous portions of the wonderful pork pie and about a pint of flip, I did not even hesitate when he passed me a long churchwarden pipe. In a sort of reckless daze, feeling a little drowsy and in a very contented frame of mind, I asked the old man if he would tell me some of the traditions associated with the inn—ghost stories, romances, or adventures. He said that it had been nothing but an ordinary inn with "no ghosts that I ever heard tell of." However, when I pressed him further, he recalled *one* strange thing that had happened long ago. His recollection of it was as follows:

"In my grandfather's time, one dark and stormy night something like this, a chaise drove up to the door, from which alighted a young couple who sought lodging. In the middle of the night my grandmother was awakened by a frightful piercing scream that gave her an awful shock. She woke up my grandfather, who laughed at her, and told her that she had merely had a bad dream. They listened a while and, as no further sound was heard, she was convinced that he was right and soon fell asleep again.

"However, in the morning, as she was preparing breakfast, the young man, half-clothed, rushed downstairs very much excited and dashed into the kitchen, shouting: 'Where is my wife?'

"A diligent search failed to find any trace of her except her clothing and one shoe.

"Of course," continued the old man, "I never really believed that yarn, but you wanted a story, and that is the only one I ever heard about this place."

About this time I began to feel a little queer, and my head began to spin, so I suggested retiring.

The fat little landlord led the way up the narrow stairway to a hexagon-shaped hallway on the second floor. The storm having passed, the moonlight streamed down from the windows in the cupola above, and aided the feeble light of the single candle in bringing to my startled gaze the strange sight of the six green panelled doors which alone practically formed the sides of this unusual hall. As he led the way into the first room at the left of the stairway, I made a hasty note of the furnishings.

In the far corner stood a tall four-poster bedstead. Close by its head was a window, through which the moon sent a shaft of light to the fireplace. Directly opposite the bed stood a hooded highboy and nearby a deep wing chair and a small table. To the right of the fireplace, I noticed a door (possibly to a closet). The floor arrangement, as I remember it, was about like the following diagram:

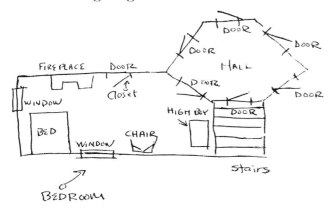

After undressing and climbing into the high bed, I sank down a foot or more into a sea of feathers and relaxed. Believe me when I say that it felt good to lie there quietly and look at the moonbeams pouring through the window.

Whether or not I fell asleep I do not really know, but I *do* know I suddenly became aware that from a hole in the corner of the closet (?) door there emerged an enormous rat. It was followed by another, and then another, and still others—until an endless stream of them poured forth and raced around the room in an orgy of delirious glee.

Each and every rat carried in its mouth a brownish-grey object. After they circled around and around for what seemed minutes to me, they swarmed in the center of the room, directly in the path of the moonlight, and deposited their burdens in a heap and then renewed their crazy antics.

Soon, the pile of rubbish (for that's what it appeared like to me) began of itself to heave and

pulsate and to take the form and shape of a skeleton. In desperate terror, I reached down and grabbed one of my shoes and threw it into the midst of the quaking horror. Then I burrowed down into the feather bed once more, pulled the bedclothes over my head, and held my breath. When I was finally obliged to come up for air, and ventured to peek out, nothing was visible but the silvery moonbeams as before.

Assuming that I had been visited by one monstrous nightmare as the result of mixing pork pie, flip, tobacco, and a ghost story, I finally calmed down, rolled over, and went to sleep.

In the morning, as I sat on the bed partly dressed and reached down for my second shoe, I could not find it. After vainly searching for it under the bed, I spied it, to my astonishment, by the closet door—and right beside it lay a dead rat with a broken back. Believe it or not, in its mouth was a white kid slipper. Hastily tucking this in my pocket as evidence that my weird experience had been real, and not a dream after all, I made a hasty exit in search of the breakfast table.

As I nonchalantly paid the landlord the enormous sum of 75 cents as his asking fee, I asked him if the room which I had occupied happened to be the bridal suite referred to in his tale of the lady who so mysteriously disappeared. With a surprised look he answered: "Yes!"

I have always regretted that I did not open that closet door. If I had, perhaps I might have solved the problem, then and there. Again, perhaps I might not have ever returned myself. Who knows?

Several years later, having told my experience to the assembled members of my Bicycle Club, in Cambridge, I was challenged to lead them to this mysterious inn. I accepted the challenge. I took them as far as Wilmington, where all traces of any wood roads leading off to the left seemed to be lost. We made inquiries at a nearby farm and were told that the old back-road inn had burned to the ground the year before.

I was never able to convince my fellow club members of the truth of my story, though I showed them the white kid slipper in evidence.

Pasted inside of the slipper was a small, stained, printed labèl reading: "Thomas F. Woodbury & Son. Dealers in Trunks, Bags, Saddlery, and Shoes. Corn-Hill, Boston."　END

The Phantom P-40 from Mindanao

by Curtis B. Norris

The haunting and true story of a battered, bullet-riddled American plane bearing the wrong insigne, coming from the wrong direction, with empty wheel wells and a dying pilot . . .

ON DECEMBER 8, 1942, I WAS A STUDENT IN PEMbroke (Massachusetts) High School, and World War II was thundering along in a not-very-promising manner. My biggest problem that day was the prospect of a four-mile walk home due to hell-raising on the school bus.

On this same date,* over the Chinese coast 10,000 miles away, someone else from Massachusetts was enduring a graver problem. This other fellow was an unusually courageous P-40 pilot, in a "home-made" pursuit plane, completing a 1300-mile escape from the Japanese-held Philippines.

No story has so affected my writing career. I have researched the episode for three decades

and many gaps remain, including the identity of the pilot. Perhaps his family is still alive, silent and unaware of his unique ordeal. Maybe some of his old drugstore crowd are still around, unaware of the exploits of this fellow Bay Stater who once joked and laughed with them. More likely, the central figure in one of the most daring and saddest exploits of World War II will never be known. This brave and innovative U.S. Army Air Corps lieutenant deserves better than a whimsical brush-off by fate. No one more deserved this nation's highest tributes, or better demonstrated the utter futility of war.

Our story begins on an overcast December day in 1942, just off the China coast. The Chinese Warning Net, maintained by our wartime allies, picked up reports of an unidentified P-40 pursuit plane entering the mainland from the direction of Formosa. No friendly plane should have

---

*Author's note: All times and dates in this story are based on Pacific Time—approximately 12 hours later. For instance, when it is 12:00 noon in Boston, it is 1:00 A.M. in Manila (that is, 1:00 A.M. on the morning of the following day).

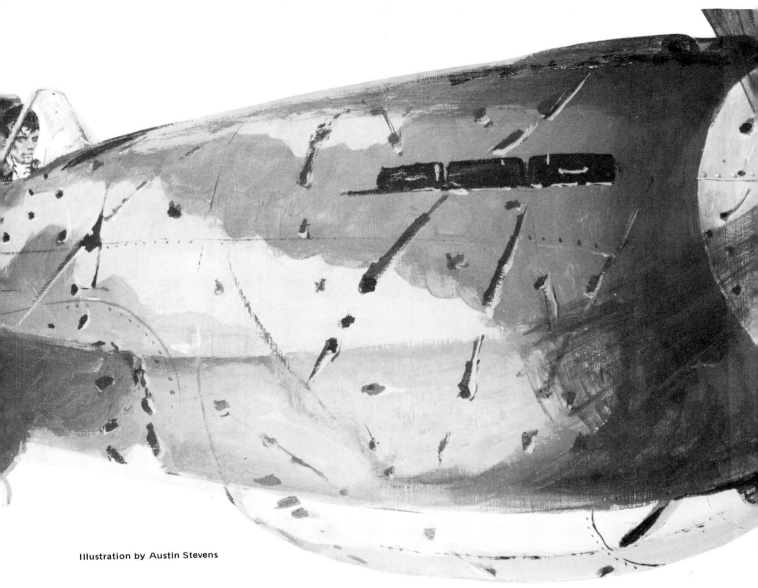

Illustration by Austin Stevens

been approaching from the direction of Japanese territory. Besides, this aircraft bore old Army Air Corps identification, and a Japanese trick was feared.

Americans of the China Task Force, located at a field in Kienow, China, were alerted, and two P-40 pilots were sent to check the mystery aircraft. They found the plane, flying above what we then called in the Far East "a ragged overcast"—long streamers of gray clouds hanging ghost-like into neatly terraced valleys below.

The strange plane's markings were the same as those used on our ships at the time of Pearl Harbor, exactly one year before. Her insigne had a blue background with a white star and red center. The Army Air Corps hadn't used that insigne for a year because the red circle had often been mistaken for the Japanese "meatball." The aircraft, filled with bullet holes, was

a flying sieve. The two China Air Task Force P-40s flashed recognition signals—but there was no response.

Reluctantly, they opened fire on the old ship. She shuddered and flew on. One of the intercepting pilots, identified as Johnny Hampshire by Colonel Robert L. Scott, Jr. in his recollection of the incident, flew under the battered plane and discovered the wheel wells were empty. Enemy bullets could not have done that. This P-40 never did have wheels.

Hampshire jabbed at the rudder pedals and absently moved the stick over to ease his ship from under to the right side of the flying wreck. He discovered the canopy had been shot away. Behind the broken glass of the windshield was the form of the pilot, his head slumped down on his chest. Hampshire was more puzzled than ever and called over his radio to the other P-40 pilot (a man identified by Scott as Costello).

"What the hell is this?" Costello shook his head. It was too much. His throat was dry and the words wouldn't come. Hampshire then called the field at Kienow. "I don't know what's going on up here. We have intercepted the plane and fired upon it, but there's something we don't understand. It's a P-40 with old markings and it's headed straight for the field. I don't think he'll make it. It's shot to pieces."

Low and trailing now, Hampshire gently fed his engine more power and gingerly eased the stick to the left and slightly back. Now he could see the pilot, his long dark hair and bloody face. Then something strange happened. The mystery pilot seemed to sense the presence of the other Americans, and Hampshire insisted he turned his head, weakly signaled with his hand and dropped it.

Costello doubted this—he thought the pilot had been dead long before they had intercepted his ship. Perhaps this happened, but maybe it was merely the way each of the China Task Force pilots wanted to remember the experience.

The three P-40s then entered one of the long gray overcasts, and this was the last time either of the two China Task Force pilots saw the mystery P-40 in the air. A few seconds later, the stranger struck the soft earth of a rice paddy, skidded a few feet, and flipped over. There was the flash of an explosion, and a cloud of black smoke puffed from the wreckage.

Hampshire marked the spot in his mind as carefully as he could, then flew back to Kienow with Costello. Over the field he checked to see if any enemy planes were reported in the area, on the chance the strange P-40 had been a decoy. The reply was negative, and the two pilots landed. They grabbed the base doctor, climbed into an alcohol-burning truck, and searched throughout the night for the wreckage. No luck.

The next morning, word came to the station master, Captain Chow, from the Chinese Warning Net of the exact location of the wrecked ship. Hampshire, Costello, the doctor and two engineering men hurried to the site, high on one of the eastern China hills which jut damply into the ever-present clouds.

As Colonel Scott later recalled, "The P-40 had really been shot to hell. From the spinner of her prop, through the wings, through the cockpit, and through the tail, it was riddled with bullet holes—bullets which had come from above and below, from behind and in front, proving that enemy planes as well as enemy ground fire had sieved the ship. None of the men could understand how any pilot had lived to fly the ship as far as they later learned it had come.

"The plane had struck the ground in a landing position, and then had nosed over and burned. As Hampshire had reported, it had no wheels, no landing gear. Apparently it was assembled without the gear and had taken off in some way they couldn't fathom."

The pilot was dead and the fire hadn't left much in the way of identification. The doctor tried unsuccessfully to take fingerprints. The unknown pilot's leather jacket had not burned entirely, and here the clues were found that would lead to a partial reconstruction of the flight.

Several letters were found in the jacket, parts still legible, along with a notebook diary. The unburned letters were mailed, and it is rumored some were sent to Massachusetts. But were they from the pilot? No one knows. The recipients could tell, if they would speak up today.

The partially-destroyed diary gave the Americans enough facts to explain where the ship had come from and what its mission had been. Other details emerged from a close examination of the P-40 itself. The facts make up the material for an updated Beau Geste-style mystery.

The phantom ship had come from the Philippine Islands, leaving there on the anniversary of the Japanese attack on the Philippines, December 8, 1941. Months after all organized American resistance had ceased in the Islands, what better day to mount a surprise attack on the triumphant Japanese?

The mystery of this pilot and his flight has intrigued me since I first read of it in a 1943 issue of *Time* magazine. I was a product of the days when the American Volunteer Group (Flying Tigers) was waging a dramatic sky battle against the Japanese (from the late '30s through 1942), and I must have sketched a thousand shark-faced P-40s, the most romantic machine, I thought, contrived by man.

By 1945 I was in the old Army Air Corps, attached to an air field on Bataan. This had been familiar stamping ground for the mystery pilot and his buddies, until all were swept away by Japanese conquest. The flight of the unknown P-40 was pretty well known among our group and caused much speculation. That was when I started researching, and I questioned everyone I came across who had served in, or knew people from, the old P-40 squadrons. Several were American prisoners released from Japanese camps who had served in the pre-war P-40 groups.

I have tried all sorts of ways to determine the identity of the pilot. Over the years I've advertised in such magazines as *Air Classics* and *Aerospace Historian*. Letters have been sent to the Pentagon and to the departments of Army, Air Force and Navy. The responses were sympathetic and often produced leads—all dead-ended.

The American Defenders of Bataan and Corregidor, Inc. (ADBC) have been especially helpful. Comprised of a mere handful of survivors of the 70,000 American and Filipino troops who surrendered in April and May of 1942, these men know firsthand the pathos of struggle and defeat. An ad in their newspaper, *Quan*, brought responses from several P-40 veterans of the Philippine campaign, including the late J. Walter Foy, former commandant of the ADBC, Oscar L. Look, South Addison, Maine, and John C. Morrow, of Orlando, Florida. But their collective and heartfelt sympathy for a fallen buddy could not produce a name for the mystery pilot.

In reply to my inquiry in *Aerospace Historian*, Edward J. Cserny of Long Island, New York, informed me in May of 1971 that Colonel Robert L. Scott, Jr. had written of the incident in his book, *Damned to Glory*. This was the first time I had heard of the book, and it seemed to provide the break I was searching for. I was unable to obtain a copy then, but Mr. Cserny sent me four reproduced pages which added a little to my existing knowledge. For instance, I now knew the pilot had been intercepted by other P-40 pilots who were attached to the AVG.

I wrote to Colonel Scott in May, 1971, thinking he could tell me further details now that World War II restrictions were over, but did not receive a reply to that letter. He did reply, however, to my second letter sent early in 1973. (See "Postscript," p.129.)

While I was editor of the *Wareham* (Massachusetts) *Courier*, I ran an editorial about the P-40, ostensibly to point out the futility of war but actually hoping to reach someone who might have knowledge of the incident. The editorial was accepted at face value—as a statement deploring war. I heard nothing further from the very state that allegedly had produced the plane's pilot.

I next obtained the name of the man who designed and developed the P-40 fighter plane. Incredibly, Dr. Donovan R. Berlin is still alive and active as an executive in Ft. Worth, Texas. I asked if he had heard of the 1942 flight, and questioned the range possibilities. This was in December of 1972, and I have not yet received a reply from him (July, 1973).

A query to Charles G. Worman, Acting Chief, Research Division, Air Force Museum, gave me the complete data sheets for the P-40B model, which I turned over to Leslie B. Sutherland of Norton, Massachusetts, for analysis. (Les is a former P-40 pilot, now a Vice President of New England Merchants Bank in Boston.)

P-40 pilots must have been carefully screened and well-chosen men for, in addition to Les Sutherland, those I have met have made a distinct mark on New England commerce and business. Clarke Simonds is the Senior Vice President of G. H. Walker & Co., Inc., of Providence, Rhode Island, and a well-known civic leader. John C. A. Watkins is the publisher of the Providence *Journal Bulletin*, one of the most influential newspapers in the country.

Although I wrote a number of former P-40 pilots, none could offer any clues to the mystery, but in February, 1973, I finally obtained a copy of *Damned to Glory*, 29 years after its publication. And I found it within a stone's throw of my office at Brown University, in the University's Rockefeller Library. So near! I literally grabbed that book and devoured the 74 pages Colonel Scott devoted to that long-ago flight. He prefaces his speculations, which occupy 62 pages of the account, with the following two paragraphs:

> I want to emphasize that though the American-made ship described in the

story was actually shot down in China, the place names which appeared in the diary have been altered wherever necessary, for the sake of military security. Active resistance goes on in many of the islands, especially in those jungle mountains of Mindanao, and information must not be furnished to the Japanese. But I feel that some version of the story of this extraordinary and heroic flight ought to be told.

The pilot of the plane was never identified. As I worked out what might have been his story, he became identical in my mind with another flyer, now dead, whom I once knew well; he was the sort of pilot who would have tried to carry out a mission of this sort. I have changed his name too, but some of the incidents that I have added to the narrative were true of him.

R.L.S.

As I read through Scott's account—part fact, part speculation, and the whole diluted by security considerations—it was obvious that my main problem was still unresolved. There were no clues here to help identify the pilot, although Scott's account of the escape flight is fascinating.

On April 7, 1942, the mystery pilot left Bataan and flew south to Mindanao, flying a P-40E. While there he met and joined a group of 11 mechanics. When Bataan fell on April 9, they lost contact with the scattered American forces.

This small group refused to surrender. They gathered up all the wrecked P-40s they could find and transported the parts to a location in the middle of the island. They wanted one serviceable P-40 at all times, which they used for scattered attacks just to prove the Army Air Corps was still alive in the Philippines.

In May, after Corregidor fell, they heard that Brigadier General William F. Sharp had called for all Americans to surrender. These Air Corps men had no intention of doing so. They continued their short attack flights after the surrender—once travelling 400 miles to Manila and back. However, these token raids ended when the surviving P-40 was damaged during a wheels-up landing. The partially lowered gear, damaged by gunfire, was destroyed, the propeller bent, and the fuselage buckled.

At the bottom of a nearby cliff the men found a wrecked P-40 with good engine parts; four miles west—across the Syre National Highway

—the group found a second wreck with a salvageable fuselage. A party of 40 Moros went to the scene, bringing back the 1500-pound Allison engine and the 2000-pound fuselage over a difficult four-mile trek. On June 26, they laid the fuselage where the fighter would be assembled. As they worked, the group was joined by others until by late July they had a crew of 19 Americans and seven Filipinos.

In August, the good wing was removed from the crash-landed P-40 and attached to the salvaged fuselage. A tripod and gin pole was rigged to swing the engine into place onto the engine mount.

To increase the internal fuel supply, the radio and dynamotor were removed from the baggage compartment, along with everything else. A fuel tank of 50-gallon capacity was mounted just aft the fuselage tank and ran into the engine by gravity feed, giving the pilot about 200 gallons of gasoline in internal tanks.

The prop was straightened by use of a homemade piledriver, a heavy wooden mallet, and finally by laying pieces of hardwood over the blade, which was placed over a tree stump, and belting the wood with a sledge-hammer. The propeller repairs were completed on Labor Day, 1942, but the wheel assemblies were the big problem.

They could locate no spare parts, and the men couldn't repair the items damaged in the crash. So they came up with the idea of detachable bamboo skids. After much planning, the group dug the earth out from under the fuselage. Using four long lengths of three-inch bamboo, they extended those makeshift skids from the "knee" in each wing which housed the retractable landing gear back to the tail post. The skids were cross-braced, and two guy wires were used to space the skids and to limit sidewards movement during takeoff. The skids would be released after takeoff by jerking a control wire that disengaged the rear of the skids from the tail post. As the spring tension of the four flexed skids straightened out, wind pressure would pull the skids from the wing "knees."

The skids were greased with engine oil to lower resistance when the plane later took off over a swath cut through the Cogon grass.

A 75-gallon external belly tank, its leaks repaired in a makeshift manner, raised the total gas supply to 275 gallons. The fuel was drained from the unruptured tanks of a B-17 that had crash-landed nearby, then filtered through 10 thicknesses of cloth. The men figured on a flight of 1250-1300 miles and counted on favorable winds and a low cruise speed of 180 m.p.h.

Each of the men remaining behind gave the pilot letters to mail to loved ones when he reached the safety of China. Those letters which survived the crash were sent home. Potentially, any one of these 19 or 20 messages, if still in existence, could tell the story in detail.

The rest of the story we already know: the successful takeoff, the arrival over Formosa five hours later (confirmed by Japanese records), and then, after seven hours in the sky, the fateful meeting with Costello and Hampshire.

I firmly believe there was such a flight as that recorded on December 8, 1942, from Mindanao to China. I am as determined now as I was in 1945 to rescue this Massachusetts P-40 pilot's name from obscurity. Were those his letters which survived the crash? Or the letters of the crew that had to remain behind? The answer may lie in the Bay State—in that box on the bureau, in that attic trunk, in the heart of a friend or sweetheart. For such a man as this must have made an impact on those who knew him in the days of swing bands and Model "A" convertibles. Someone has to remember this pilot from the era of white silk scarves. And he deserves better than a forgotten Chinese grave.

END

POSTSCRIPT

A letter to Curtis Norris from Robert L. Scott, Jr., B/Gen. USAF (Ret.) and author of *God is My Co-Pilot.*

Feb. 13, 1973

Dear Mr. Norris: Over a month ago I received a letter from you about a P-40 I helped to shoot down over Eastern China, way back in 1942. I remember it well—it was over Kienow, China— and it was a P-40, an old B-Tomahawk, and it had faded American markings. But it would not identify itself and had approached from enemy territory, and so we shot it down.

I did not invent the story—I certify. But I also learned as time went on that the truth has many faces. What really is the truth? It was definitely an American P-40, made in Buffalo, New York, and it did come from out of the Pacific. Even after we had called and called on our old radio frequency (3105 kc), there came no reply. We flew up beside it, one of us on either side. It kept going right straight on the course we had originally seen it in the approach. We first fired tracers "across its bows." It kept right on—and so we then fired into it, my shots aimed at where

the wing on the right joined the fuselage. I think I knew even then that the pilot was dead. I kept thinking about it for all the rest of that year.

I did not get to land beside the wreckage—as I may have indicated in my story "Ghost Ship" —but the Chinese guerillas did bring in all they found, they said, and even told how they had buried the pilot at the scene of the crash, there close to Kienow.

Of course I have added much of my own deduction to fill in the gaps, but I did not write the story until even after I had written God is My Co-Pilot *when I first came back to the U.S.A. in February 1943 . . .*

Later on I did talk to others in Mindanao who had not only escaped Luzon with the pilot, but also those who helped him assemble the one flyable plane out of the cannibalized parts of eight or ten. The diary was one of those things which had to be sent in to Military Intelligence (G-2), as even my photographs had to be. As usual, you not only never get those things back and when you inquire about them they are never available again—they just disappear.

5.
TERROR AT SEA

Double Trouble

by Wm. Edward Mason

The day the Coast Guard really had its hands full . . .

EVENTS DURING TWO AWFUL DAYS IN THE WINTER of 1952, when two huge tankers broke in two within 40 miles of each other off Cape Cod, rate high on the list of notable disasters which have befallen seafarers in the treacherous waters of the North Atlantic. Etched deeply into the official records of the Coast Guard service is the account of the loss of the tankers *Fort Mercer* and *Pendleton*. It is one of the strangest stories of the present century.

The first inkling of the drama that was about to unfold during those memorable 48 hours came at 12:03 A.M. on February 18. The Coast Guard headquarters in Boston received a radioed SOS from the heavily laden Delaware oil tanker *Fort Mercer* reporting "Our hull is splitting" and giving its position as 32 miles off Chatham Light. The radio operator said that one tank was leaking and a plate on the starboard side had split.

A howling full northeast gale was raging at the time, a storm that had roared up the eastern seaboard, bringing with it blinding snow to cover all New England. In many places the winds, which for two days gusted to 65 miles an hour, piled snow six feet deep. Snow fell for two days—the 18th and 19th.

A short time after the first SOS came in, a message on the *Mercer's* ship-to-shore telephone from the vessel's skipper, Captain Frederick C. Paetzel, reported the tanker's plight as "Pretty bad. We're just standing still. It's very rough." The captain then described the vessel as being battered by waves that reached 68 feet up into the rigging.

Within minutes, the Coast Guard cutter *McCulloch* steamed out of Boston in the face of the terrible storm and headed across Massa-

A howling full northeast gale broke two huge tankers, *Pendleton* and *Fort Mercer,* apart in the sea. The stern half of the latter is shown left. *U.S. Coast Guard Photo.*

133

Above: A Coast Guard cutter attaches lines rigged with life rafts to the *Mercer's* stern.

Below: The cutter *Yakutat* moves in close to the bow to float a string of rafts. *U.S. Coast Guard Photos.*

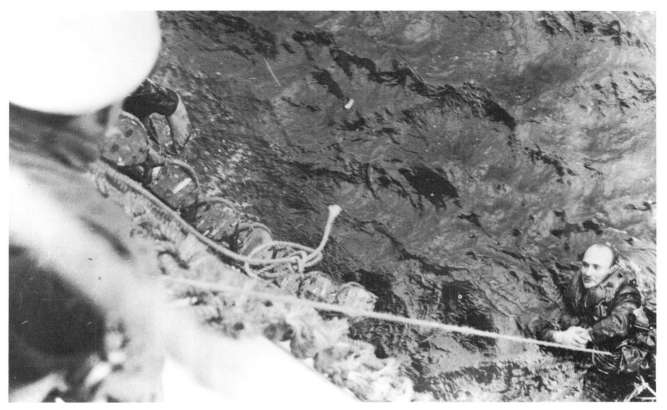

Exhausted and nearly frozen, a sailor is hauled aboard the *Yakutat. U.S. Coast Guard Photo.*

chusetts Bay. Alert to emergencies at all times, the Coast Guard ordered the cutters *Eastwind* and *Unimak* to abandon a search they were making at the time for a fishing trawler named *Paolina* to go to the aid of the stricken *Mercer*. Meanwhile, the cutter *Yakutat* was dispatched from Provincetown and was soon joined in the race against death by motor lifeboats from the Chatham and Brant Point stations. Amphibious planes were also ordered out from the Quonset Point, Rhode Island, naval base.

Thus got underway what the Coast Guard described as one of the greatest rescue feats in its history.

Flying through stormy skies, the pilot of one of the planes, Lieutenant George W. Wagner, came upon an almost unbelievable sight. While searching for a ship described to him as painted brown, he discovered one that had broken in two, but it was painted white! Dropping low over the treacherous waves, Lieutenant Wagner barely made out the name of the vessel painted on its bow. It was *Pendleton*, yet he had been searching for the *Mercer*. Rescue crews in min-

utes realized they had two wrecks on their hands instead of one.

About the time Lieutenant Wagner was flying over the broken *Pendleton*, rescue vessels and planes had located the two parts of the *Mercer*. They determined that the 43 members of the crew were on the separated sections of the shattered vessel—34 on the stern and 9 on the plunging bow.

Despite the peril they faced in the churning seas and darkness of night as the storm still raged, crews of the assembled craft moved closer to the stricken tanker. All the ships were being tossed about like corks by the tremendous waves, and at times would nearly disappear from sight in the deep troughs.

By the time the cutters arrived on the scene, the radio of the *Mercer* had been rendered inoperative by the onrush of water into the forward house and soon two lifeboats were swept away. The crewmen on the forward section, battling to escape the crashing waves, made their way to the forecastle by climbing a line improvised from signal flags.

135

Captain Paetzel and Purser Edward Power, Jr., jumped from the bow and were picked out of the sea by this Coast Guard surf boat. *U.S. Coast Guard Photo.*

First casualty was the radio operator, John V. O'Reilly, who lost his hold on the makeshift line and was swept into the sea.

By maneuvering with the utmost skill and seamanship, the *Yakutat* moved in close enough to float a string of life rafts from the windward. Three crewmen jumped from the *Mercer* and tried to reach the rafts but were lost in the boiling sea. The rescue attempt was then temporarily abandoned.

A let-up in the storm at daybreak on the 19th allowed the *Yakutat* to send a boat in close to the bow section. The shivering, soaked, and hungry crewmen were advised over the bullhorn on the cutter to jump so they could be picked up.

The master of the *Mercer*, Captain Paetzel, in poor physical condition, was urged to jump first; he was saved one minute after leaping into the water. Minutes later the purser, Edward Power, Jr., was similarly saved. The rescue work

was then interrupted again because the wind had increased, causing the surfboat to ship water.

Deciding against great odds to make another try, the guardsmen in the surfboat drifted a life raft toward the tanker section, after shooting a line across its deck. The remaining crewmen managed to jump, were taken aboard the raft, and back to the *Yakutat*.

Twenty minutes after the last man was taken off, the bow section capsized and disappeared. The stern section was later salvaged, towed to Newport, Rhode Island, and finally to New York. Five men had died out of the 43 who were aboard.

The Coast Guard vessels remained in the vicinity all the next day, searching for bodies without success, and then were ordered to proceed to Portland, Maine, with the survivors, arriving there late the afternoon of the 19th.

Right: The *Mercer* bow goes under—just 20 minutes after the last survivors were taken from it. *U.S. Coast Guard Photo.*

The *Pendleton* bow section tossing in heavy seas off Chatham after the tanker broke in two. *U.S. Coast Guard Photo.*

Now back to the *Pendleton,* and the second phase of the dual rescue.

Radar of the Chatham station picked up the two broken sections of the *Pendleton* sighted earlier from the air. Why had not the *Pendleton* sent out news of its plight, the Coast Guard wondered. It developed that the ship broke apart so suddenly under the pounding of the sea that the radio operator had no time to send an SOS. It was made further impossible to do so because the radio room was located in the stern and the power plant situated near the bow. The power lines had snapped when the vessel broke apart.

Neither section of the broken *Pendleton* ap-

proached near enough to the beach to enable rescue operations to be carried out with beach apparatus. The two floating sections were drifting rapidly southward. Realizing that the only way to save those on the *Pendleton* was by using a motor lifeboat, a craft put out from Chatham in charge of Bernard C. Webber at 6 P.M. Webber lashed himself to the wheel as the craft struggled through the gigantic waves for an hour before reaching the stern section.

By repeatedly maneuvering the lifeboat into position at the bottom of a Jacob's ladder, the Chatham heroes were able to save 32 of the 33 men on the stern. They jumped one at a time into the sea and were picked up. The only man

Pendleton's stern the day after the storm. Its rusting hulk still lies off Chatham. *U.S. Coast Guard Photo.*

lost in this part of the mass rescue operation was ironically the largest of the entire crew—George D. Myers, ordinary seaman, died because he was too big . . . he weighed 350 pounds.

Last to leave the floating wreck, Myers, who had helped all the others down the ladder, jumped into the sea himself. He bobbed to the surface close to the tossing wreck and was crushed against its side as a giant wave hurled the lifeboat into the hulk. Several of the men in the lifeboat got a grip on Myers and tried to pull him into the craft, but because of his tremendous weight and the violent tossing of the lifeboat, all attempts to save him failed and he disappeared. His body was never found.

The lifeboat then took the survivors to Chatham. Nine men died in all, including the captain, John J. Fitzgerald of Boston.

Five days later salvage workers got aboard the stern section and found one man dead in the forecastle. Search failed to locate any more bodies. Coast Guard records list the names of the men who were lost but account for the manner in which only one died—Myers' tragic end. The other eight were presumed to have been swept overboard before rescue efforts began.

The bow section of the *Pendleton* sank 6.7 miles from Chatham Light. What remains of the stern can still be seen partly buried in the sand near Monomoy Beach. END

Nightmare Steamboat

Embittered passengers of the *Narragansett* agreed that the crew hastened to

EARLY FRIDAY EVENING, JUNE 11, 1880, THE Reverend O. G. Buddington hurried to a New York pier to catch the steamer *Narragansett* for Stonington, Connecticut. He was too late; he arrived just in time to see her pulling out into the harbor, and thus fortunately escaped one of the worst catastrophes in the history of Long Island Sound, involving, strangely enough, two vessels of the same line.

Balmy days in early June had turned the city's thoughts to summer weekends in the country, and to the night steamboats of the Providence and Stonington Line which connected New York City and Stonington, providing comfortable staterooms where passengers could enjoy a refreshing sleep before reaching their destination in the morning. The vessels were a much-used but still dangerous means of travel. Rival-

ry between competing lines often forced captains to abandon caution to meet schedules, and safety arrangements were casual. One writer commented that the relatively small loss of life from steamboat disasters was due to the American public's good luck rather than company vigilance.

More passengers than usual boarded the sleek wooden *Narragansett* for the Stonington run that beautiful Friday, among them business men and vacationing families. The steamer's regular captain and first engineer were not aboard; they were in Hartford, witnesses in a company lawsuit. Temporarily in command, Captain William S. Young followed the well-traveled course on the Sound, proud of the 13-year-old steamer sparkling with new paint from her recent rebuilding. The purser hadn't yet

Steamer leaving Stonington for New York.

by Carol W. Kimball

save themselves, taking all the undamaged lifeboats . . .

listed the exact number of passengers, but they carried at least 300, with all staterooms and berths full and latecomers sleeping on extra mattresses and benches. Counting the 50 boat employees, about 350 were aboard as they steamed eastward.

At 7:10 that night, another steamer of the line, the *Stonington*, Captain George F. Nye, cast off her moorings at Stonington village for a New York trip. Steaming westward over smooth water she ran into thick fog, causing her 400 passengers to retire early. By 11 P.M. all was quiet on board.

"When the two floating palaces were plowing through the water of Long Island Sound that Friday night, only the eye of God saw that they were coming into collision," lamented the Reverend T. Dewitt Talmage in his next sermon.

Their courses were about to converge three miles west of Cornfield Point, near Saybrook.

On the *Narragansett*, Mrs. Roswell Fish and her elderly mother couldn't sleep; after 11 o'clock the boat's fog whistle sounded constantly. Shortly after 11:30 P.M. Captain Young heard a steamer whistle but couldn't place her exactly through heavy fog and mist. Confident that he was on course, he slowed to 12 knots, expecting to pass Cornfield Lightship. Suddenly the bow watch shouted a warning as lights appeared to starboard. Without reducing speed the Captain signaled to pass to port; too late he ordered the engines reversed. Young, steering a northeast course, had crossed the track of the *Stonington* heading due west.

The *Stonington*, also traveling at 12 knots, plowed into her sister ship with a fearful crash,

tearing a huge hole in the starboard side of the wooden hull.

The *Narragansett* leaned over and immediately began to sink. All lights went out. Mrs. Fish hurried into the gangway, finding water up to her ankles. The sea raced over the lower deck like water over a mill dam. In five minutes five feet of water filled the main saloon. And then the steamer caught fire.

How it started no one knew. Perhaps the impact of the crash broke open the fireroom doors, allowing flames to escape; perhaps the main gas pipe burst. The engineer who discovered the blaze in the boiler room turned the hose on it, but left his post. When he returned the fire was out of control, as flames erupted to envelope the stricken vessel.

With the double dangers of collision and fire, the *Narragansett's* passengers panicked, looking to ship's officers for assistance. But Captain Young thought otherwise. Mrs. Fish, reaching the deck where men fought over life preservers, heard the Captain say, "We'll have the boats lowered, and everybody must look out for himself the best he can."

Embittered passengers agreed that the crew hastened to save themselves, taking all undamaged lifeboats. Significantly only two employees failed to reach safety—an engineer and a fireman who burned to death.

Passengers were left to shift for themselves as the *Narragansett* filled with suffocating smoke and steam. Their only course was to jump overboard. Some sank immediately. Others grabbed floating objects for support. About 40 found safety on a life raft from the hurricane deck, launched and managed by Henry Duroy, a sailor from the U.S.S. *Tennessee*.

Back on the *Stonington*, sleepers roused by the crash rushed frantically from their bunks in all stages of undress, believing the steamer to be sinking. On deck they pushed, shoved and battled for life preservers while officers tried to tell them there was no danger in spite of the large hole in the bow.

No one knew what they had struck until light from the burning vessel pierced the fog, revealing the wreck of the *Narragansett* from

the *Stonington's* own line. Then they saw the water black with struggling humans, trying to reach safety by clinging grimly to life preservers, mattresses, chairs, doors—anything that floated. As shrieks and cries of distress filled the mild night air, the eerie light of flames through the mist silhouetted figures rushing hysterically about the burning steamer or leaping desperately into the water. A man and wife embraced and jumped, never to be seen again.

Flames crackled and blazing timbers fell hissing into the Sound; smoke was stifling in the calm foggy night. Fire made the deck scorching hot; within ten minutes the steamer was destroyed to the water's edge. Witnesses never forgot the horror of the scene.

Still the *Stonington's* crew made no effort to

The steamer *Narragansett,* 1633 tons, on Palmer's Marine Railways in Noank, Connecticut — January, 1880, five months before her nightmare New York-Stonington run. *From the collection of Robert S. Palmer.*

lower rescue boats. Concerned passengers managed to launch two lifeboats, but with plugs left out so they filled with water. When that was remedied, it developed that many of the volunteers couldn't row. But in spite of handicaps they saved a number of lives.

Providentially, the rival Norwich Line's steamer *City of New York* observed distress signals near Cornfield Point and responded at full speed. Reaching the crowded *Stonington,* they took off 100 of the rescued, relieving the leaking vessel. Then the *New York's* crew efficiently lowered five boats and began hauling victims to safety.

Narragansett survivors told grim tales. F. M. Howard, awakened by splintering wood when the crash burst open his stateroom door, raced on deck, grabbed some life preservers, and jumped. On the way he saw a man put a pistol to his head and deliberately shoot himself. Mr. Sandharne of Boston also saw the suicide. He hurried on deck without stopping to dress and plunged into the sea. Looking back he saw the *Narragansett* a sheet of flame to the water's surface.

Henry L. Higgins of Westeden, Maine, was lying fully clothed on a bench when the crash knocked him to the deck. As screaming men, women and children ran in all directions, he dived into the water and swam for his life.

The Reverend Solomon Gale, asleep in his cabin on the *Narragansett,* awakened at the crash, thinking they had reached Stonington and struck the dock. With his wife he waded

The steamer *Stonington*, bound for New York, rammed her sister ship, *Narragansett*, in the fog. *From a lithograph in the collection of the Marine Historical Association, Inc., Mystic Seaport, Mystic, Ct.*

through waist-deep water and leaped. Suction from the sinking vessel kept them near the wreck until he managed to push away.

A lifeboat propelled by an old broom passed many of the drowning, carrying *Narragansett* waiters with an officer in charge and refusing to take on anyone else for fear the boat would sink.

G. W. Johnson of New London floated for an hour on a starch box, suffering head injuries and losing his diamond stud before the *City of New York* picked him up. Mrs. Fish and her aged mother floated even longer. The old lady was unconscious when taken into a boat, but revived aboard the *Stonington*.

When at last no more struggling forms were seen, the *City of New York* went on her way with nearly 200 survivors, some scalded and half-naked, all drenched and exhausted. At 10:30 A.M. she arrived at Pier 40 in the North River, looking like a hospital, her decks and cabins crammed with victims wrapped in undergarments and blankets.

Leaving Captain Young and his mates to patrol, the *Stonington* returned to her home port

with 50 survivors. Most of the women wore only nightclothes, and some men were minus even this.

As news of the tragedy spread, reporters besieged the company's Stonington office for details, but learned only that the passenger list was missing and the exact number lost unknown.

Next day, with canvas covering the 20-foot hole in her bow, the *Stonington* went to New York to be hoisted into dry dock at the foot of Pike Street. Large crowds gathered to view her upper deck still strewn with torn, soiled and drenched clothing.

As survivors' stories circulated, an aroused public directed a storm of criticism at the management of the Stonington Line, condemning the conduct of employees on both vessels. Actor Clarance R. Leonard of Booth's Theater, a passenger on the *Narragansett*, was outspoken against the officers. At least 30 passengers, and perhaps as many as 50, lost their lives in contrast to two company men missing. Complaints included lack of organization on the *Stonington* and the delay in lowering boats, traveling at 12

knots through heavy fog, poorly disciplined crews and substandard equipment. Because the tradition of women and children first had been ignored, a shocking number of children were lost, among them two Stilson youngsters trapped below deck and three Dix children lost with their nurse. Two small bodies washed ashore at Niantic—a little girl in a red plaid dress and a sandy-haired boy.

On June 20 Captain William S. Young attended church in Jersey City and heard Pastor Harcourt's sermon denounce the *Narragansett's* officers as cowards. Young stood up and stated clearly, "Anyone who made such a charge is a liar." Church members escorted him to the police station to be locked up for disorderly conduct.

Captain T. A. Scott, master diver, investigated the wreck, which was grounded on the west end of Sand Shoal, her hog frames, walking beam and mast above water. The hull lay below the surface, its tremendous hole choked with freight and debris. After recovering 16 bodies and salvaging part of the $40,000 cargo, Scott raised the vessel and towed her away on July 1.

Just a week later, July 8, the *Stonington* re-sumed her regular nightly run. But the sea continued to cast up dead bodies for weeks, some never identified.

After a hearing in August, U.S. Steamboat Inspectors revoked Captain Young's license and refused renewal for Captain Nye's expired license. The Stonington Line was held in violation of regulations concerning the number of licensed officers on the *Narragansett* and the number of watchmen on deck. Captain Young was fined $100 for failure to complete the required passenger list.

The *Narragansett* went back into service Thanksgiving night, her boiler and engine room newly cased in iron and her hull strengthened. Public indignation had increased respect for safety measures. Her boat crews drilled every Saturday, boasting they could unhook, lower, and man the lifeboats in three and one half minutes. Her Captain Jesse Mott claimed to know the Sound like a compass, and had never lost a life.

But it is a safe bet that few of those who survived the horrors of June 11, 1880, ever cared to board the *Narragansett* again.   END

145

The extreme clipper *Hornet* is consumed in a furnace of flames as her crew watches in the longboat and two quarter boats. Contemporary engraving from *Harper's Weekly,* September 29, 1866. *Courtesy Chrispix Archives.*

Fire in the Doldrums

The charred hulk of the clipper *Hornet* slid down into the waters of the Pacific; this marked the start of a remarkable 4,000-mile voyage . . .

by Sheldon Christian

THE EXTREME CLIPPER *Hornet*, WITH CAPT. Josiah A. Mitchell of Freeport, Maine, in command, was slowly working her way up through the doldrums, off the Pacific coast of South America. Strict orders respecting safety precautions had been observed by the crew, as well they might, for she was New York-to-San Francisco-bound with a combustible cargo that included 45 barrels and 2000 cases of oil, and 6195 boxes of candles. On this particular morning of May 3, 1866, however, a seaman who went down into the "booby-hatch" to get some varnish carried, contrary to regulations, an open lantern. Suddenly the fumes from the cask of

varnish exploded. Instantly flames were belching from the open hatch to the deck. It was a particularly bad time for a fire at sea, because the ship was becalmed and the nearest land more than a thousand miles away.

The probing flames reached up and ignited the loosely clewed-up crossjack and, even while the cry of "Fire" was being heard aft, spread with shocking rapidity. Efforts were at once made to extinguish the blaze, but from the beginning the fire was out of hand. It spread faster than it could be checked. One of Captain Mitchell's first cares was to bring up four men who were ill. When it was seen that the ship was doomed, he ordered provisions and equipment gathered and placed in the ship's longboat and two quarter boats. So little time was available, however, that when it came time to abandon ship, the longboat and one of the quarter boats were damaged in being lowered away.

Once off the stove-hot ship, the men rested on their oars, watching with fascination as the flames, rising mast-high amid black clouds of swirling smoke, consumed the ship that had been their home upon the deep. The trauma was cushioned by the conviction that, with such a gigantic flare burning, some passing vessel would be sure to see it and pick them up. All

147

107 and 113 Days to San Francisco

COLEMAN'S CALIFORNIA LINE

FOR

SAN FRANCISCO.

The Well-Known and Celebrated New-York Built Clipper Ship

HORNET

MITCHELL, Commander.

Is again loading in our Line for San Francisco,

At Pier 11 East River,

AND WILL HAVE PROMPT DISPATCH.

For balance of Freight, apply to

WM. T. COLEMAN & CO.,

161 PEARL ST. near Wall St.

Agents in San Francisco, Messrs. WM. T. COLEMAN & CO.

Ship sailing card announcing what was to be the ill-fated *Hornet's* last voyage around the Horn. *Courtesy American Antiquarian Society.*

the following night, the men stood by, spectators at the pyre of their burning ship, but no vessel appeared. At five o'clock the next morning, the charred hulk of the beautiful clipper suddenly slid down into the waters of the Pacific. Still the men waited about. Finally it was obvious that no one had seen the light of her burning.

Thirty-one men were crowded into the three boats. Captain Mitchell was in command of the longboat. With him aft were the ship's two pas-sengers; amidships and forward were 11 other crewmen. The second boat held the first mate and eight men, while the third carried the second mate, with seven men. They had managed to take off the ship food and water sufficient only for 10 days' voyaging. Their first hope was that they would be picked up. But if not, then clearly it behooved them to bend every effort to reach land as quickly as possible.

Captain Mitchell did some ciphering. About a thousand miles to the east of them lay the Ga-

148

lápagos Islands. Somewhere a thousand miles to the northward lay the Revilla Gigedos. And to the northeast, about a thousand miles, lay Acapulco, Mexico. But half the distance of the route to Acapulco lay through the doldrums, through which their boats were not rigged to sail to advantage, closehauled when necessary. With short provisions, it did not look as though they would ever make it to Acapulco. The Galápagos route was rejected for similar reasons. The northward course, then, seemed the only one to hold promise, and so they headed north, the longboat towing the others. They had 400-500 miles of doldrums to try to cover.

Each boat was equipped with a compass, a copy of Bowditch's Navigator, a nautical almanac, and a quadrant. The captain's and first mate's boats also had chronometers, by which they would be enabled to determine their longitude.

The ship's passengers were brothers, Samuel and Henry Ferguson, of Stamford, Connecticut. Samuel, 28, a graduate of Trinity College, Hartford, was in advanced stages of consumption, and was taking the sea voyage in the desperate hope that he might regain his health. Henry, 18, was a student at the same college. The two kept diaries. Captain Mitchell also kept a "log." From these entries we learn the story as it unfolded.

A rooster had come with them from the burning ship, and although the men had soon begun to feel the pinch of hunger, no man lifted a finger to take the bird's life. His crowing cheered them every dawn.

When the first Sunday came, Samuel Ferguson remembered that it was Sacrament Sunday back home, and was comforted by the thought that prayers were being offered for them by his friends, even though they could not know of their present situation.

Henry was a young man of few words. He wrote, "May 4, 5, 6, doldrums. May 7, 8, 9, doldrums. May 10, 11, 12, doldrums. Tells it all. Never saw, never felt, never heard, never experienced such heat, such darkness, such lightning and thunder, and wind and rain, in my life before."

Of May 17—a nightmare of rain, squalls, thunder, and lightning—Captain Mitchell wrote, "Most awful night I ever witnessed."

By the 19th, Captain Mitchell had come to the conclusion that they would never reach land if the longboat had to continue to tow the two quarter boats. The first mate agreed. The second mate, whose men had improvidently consumed their allowances of food and water and thereby reduced the rations available to the rest, was all for his men's joining those in the already crowded longboat. The first mate generously volunteered to give the second mate his quarter boat, which was in better condition, and take the second mate's himself; and with some redistributing of the men in each, the first mate thereupon went off in the second mate's boat. This left the second mate and his group still being towed, for they would not hear of going it alone. After a few days, the men were gladdened by the cry, "Sail ho!"

Their troubles, they thought, were over, but the sail proved to be the first mate and his quarter boat crossing courses with theirs. It was a bitter disappointment, but before the first mate departed with his group, never again to see them, one of his men, a Mr. Cox, was taken aboard the longboat. This was a great stroke of luck, for it was to be Mr. Cox who alerted the captain to the possibility that cannibalism might rear its ugly head among the starvation-crazed men.

It was at this time, too, that Captain Mitchell felt obliged to make the hard decision that the men in the remaining quarter boat go it alone. Otherwise, he felt convinced, none of them would survive. The second mate did not accept the decision graciously—there were, indeed, some mighty hard words spoken—but the second mate nevertheless had to cast off, and each crew was on its own.

As day succeeded blistering day, the rations in the longboat were further reduced; nevertheless, Samuel wrote, "All are wonderfully well and strong, comparatively speaking." Even the men who had been ill had recovered and the Fergusons began the practice of reading aloud to the men each day from their pocket prayer books.

Captain Mitchell decided to change their course to west by north. This proved to be a bit of luck. The "Isles" they thought they might find were shown in Bowditch, although in one edition they were marked "doubtful." But the men were in no position to insist on certainties.

Eventually, the rooster, which had been sustained for 19 days by the small offerings of the men, made one last effort to crow, then fell over dead. He had helped keep up their spirits while alive. Now his scrawny carcass contributed to their physical survival. From time to time, they were also aided by a bonito, a flying fish, or a booby that practically offered itself to them.

The simple minds of some of the seamen had begun to warp under the strain. This was when it seemed remarkable that Cox should have been added to their number, because while his place was forward with the men, his understanding and his sympathy were aft with the Captain. One day he passed word to the Fergusons in writing that there was disquieting talk among the crew. They were wondering if Captain Mitchell was steering the right course. The way they saw it, it was he who was really to blame for their predicament. Why hadn't he let them continue to fight the fire? Maybe if they had, they wouldn't be where they were now.

Officers nearly always stand up better under such circumstances than common seamen. Noticing that the officers seemed better nourished and more cheerful than they themselves were, the men suspected this was because the captain was secretly giving the officers a larger share of food and water than he was allowing them. Some of the men had even come to believe that the captain was sitting on a million dollars in gold, and when the right moment came, planned to kill the two passengers and the others so he could have it all to himself. And an even more ugly thought worked itself up to the surface: if one of them died, would it be wrong to save life by eating his flesh?

Cox was asked how he stood on this. He courageously said that, for his part, he would sooner die. It was his act of secretly informing Henry Ferguson that alerted the group aft to their possible danger. Henry told his brother Samuel to keep an eye on his pistol and cartridges. If the men got hold of these, they would gain the upper hand, and they would all be lost.

They were heading west now, but they never did find those "doubtful" Isles in Bowditch, even though they sailed right over the spot where they should have been.

The castaways had been at sea in their open boat for 33 days and already had sailed more than 2000 miles. All were getting weaker. Their only hope was to make a landfall in the Sandwich Islands—yet these were still some 1200 miles away, and the last fragments of food were practically gone. Their water supply, supplemented by rains, was holding out, but they had taken to eating the greasy cloth from a ham bone, the rind, and the bone itself, strips and scrapings of leather boots, and scrapings from wooden food containers impregnated with moisture from food.

On June 14, the 42nd day, the haggard men saw a magnificent rainbow. "Cheer up, boys," Captain Mitchell assured them, "it's a prophecy —it's the bow of promise." And so it was.

The next day—the 43rd from the time they had abandoned the burning *Hornet*—the welcome cry of "Land ho!" was raised. But all at once, after having covered so many perilous miles of sea for so many trying nights and days, they found themselves in a more hazardous plight than at almost any time during the whole passage. As they approached the land, the sail was let go, and came rattling down the mast. Too late they saw that they were drifting toward a dangerous reef. Efforts were at once made to hoist the sail to bring the boat under control, but the men were too weak to manage it. They could not even pull an oar.

At this moment, two splendid Kanakas, seeing their situation, sprung into the surf, swam out to meet the strange boat, and climbed aboard to lend a hand. Through the narrow channel in the reef, the Kanakas piloted the all-but-helpless men to the shore. They were at Lapahoehoe, Hawaii!

The opening to which the boat had sailed was the only ingress to this particular coast where they could have put foot on shore, because for miles the land rose precipitously out of deep water. Their landing place also happened to be the only place in that vicinity that was inhabited. Their luck had held to the end.

Thus ended this amazing voyage during which 15 men, under their leader, Captain Mitchell, starting from a point some 1250 miles south of Cape St. Lucas, off the coast of South America, navigated an open longboat, with rations for only 10 days, across 3360 miles as the crow flies (but actually 4000 as they sailed), experiencing every kind of weather as they

Captain Josiah Mitchell, of the *Hornet,* whom Mark Twain characterized as a "New Englander of the best sea-going stock of the old capable times." *Courtesy Chrispix Archive.*

voyaged. Of the men in the two quarter boats, no trace was ever seen.

The story of the *Hornet* and her crew was given to the world by Mark Twain, then an emerging author. He happened to be convalescing in a hotel at Honolulu when he heard of the arrival of the survivors. Thanks to an influential friend, he was brought to the hospital where the shipwrecked men were being cared for. His friend took the trouble to ask the men about their experience, as Twain listened and made notes. Other correspondents were also getting the story, but they were satisfied with scant reports that stated the bald facts. Twain went without supper, worked for several hours just organizing his extensive notes, then stayed up all night pounding out his story. The next morning, as he approached the dock from which the ship for San Francisco would be leaving, he saw she had already cast off forward. He just managed to throw his heavy envelope, bulging with manuscript, onto the deck as she pulled away. While all the stories were carried to the States by the same ship, Twain's account was the only detailed one. His employers telegraphed it to the New York papers, which published it at length.

Mark Twain enjoyed his *Hornet* triumph, but he was hungering for larger recognition of a "literary" sort. To get that, one had to have one's story published in a magazine. During his voyage back to San Francisco, the ship was becalmed for extended periods. Also on the boat were Captain Mitchell and the other survivors— happily for Twain, who used the occasion to advantage by getting permission to copy pertinent entries from Captain Mitchell's log and the diaries kept by the Fergusons. From these he wrote a new story about their struggle for survival, and that December, 1866, when the story appeared in a magazine, the young writer made his real "literary debut." His debut, however, was not without an element of minor tragedy. He must have scrawled his name without due care, because it appeared in the magazine as "Mike Swain." Or perhaps, he remarked later, it may even have been "McSwain."

But there was never any doubt about the name of Freeport's Captain Josiah Mitchell, whose Yankee character, navigational acumen, and unshakeable faith, so evidently assisted by Providence, enabled him to bring every one of the 14 men in his care safely across 4,000 miles of South Pacific Ocean to a secure landfall in Hawaii.

END

151

by Carol W. Kimball

The Lone Fatality

In contrast to the Providence and Stonington Line (see p. 140), the Fall River Line emphasized passenger safety; it lost only one passenger in its entire history.

MRS. ROSIE BROWN, ASSISTANT STEWARDESS ON the *Plymouth* of the old Fall River Line, never forgot the night of March 20, 1903. New York was fogbound when they left for their regular run, and Rosie was apprehensive although she had worked on the water for many years and was not easily alarmed. But that night she had a real premonition of danger. When the passengers settled down, her sense of foreboding was so strong she did not go to bed herself. Shortly after midnight, her worst fears were realized— a shadowy steamer emerged dead ahead in murky fog; a moment later, the *Plymouth* shuddered and shook from a terrible grinding crash.

Officials of the Fall River Steamship Line never forgot that night either. With steamers sailing Long Island Sound from 1847 until the company went out of business in 1937, only one passenger on their vessels lost his life through accident, and it happened the night of Rosie Brown's premonition. A passenger was killed when two Fall River boats—the spacious steel passenger steamer *Plymouth* and the sturdy wooden sidewheel freighter *City of Taunton*— collided.

It was the old story of dangerous fog, but with a happier ending. Five unlucky crewmen perished along with the passenger, but everyone else was saved. And for a lighter touch, a company of United States Marines emerged on the *Plymouth's* deck before the echoes of the crash subsided, coolly assembling with as much precision as if to be reviewed.

The 3700-ton *Plymouth*, carrying over 500 passengers plus a full freight cargo, left New York at 5:04 P.M. Thursday, March 19, with wind moderate from the south and thick weather all the way. Although Second Pilot Hambley was at the middle window, fog prompted Captain Elisha Davis, better known as "Danger" Davis, to stay in the pilot house throughout the trip. The captain sat at the starboard window on his special stool and peered into the mist. Bronzed, gray-bearded, and no longer young, Captain Davis was small in stature but a mighty man on the Sound. His nickname came from his habit of bringing his vessel safely through peasoup fogs or heavy blizzards when no other steamer dared leave the harbor. "Danger" knew every bit of the Sound like his own back yard. But this time his luck ran out.

Earlier that evening, the *City of Taunton*, under Captain John S. Bibber, left Fall River for New York, jammed with freight. After Newport she ran into thick fog and proceeded cautiously at reduced speed down the Sound. Some 70 feet shorter than the majestic 366-foot *Plymouth*, she was a profitable carrier for the company. Captain Bibber, at sea since 1880, had a fine record on the New Bedford, Providence and Fall River Lines; he had recently substituted for "Danger" Davis on the *Plymouth*.

Shortly before midnight, some distance east of Plum Island, Bibber heard a steamer whistle off his port bow. He stopped and blew three whistles, then started slowly ahead. When he

Above: The proud Sound steamer *Plymouth* of the Fall River Line as she looked in her prime with all flags flying. *Courtesy, the Mariners Museum, Newport News, Va. (Elwin M. Eldredge Collection.)*

Below: The wooden side-wheel freighter *City of Taunton,* less elegant, but trim and efficient, was also well known in the Sound. *Courtesy, the Mariners Museum, Newport News, Va. (Sedgewick Collection.)*

Plymouth tied up at New London, Connecticut, March 20, 1903, showing the gaping hole torn in her side by the collision in the Race. *Courtesy, the Public Library of New London.*

found the other vessel was still coming on, he ordered the engines stopped and backed full speed. He saw a starboard sidelight winking off his port bow.

The *Plymouth* had passed Gull Light and was right in the middle of the Race, where the current swirls and rushes like a mill stream, when Pilot Hambley heard the freighter's whistles. Quickly he too rang STOP and BACK FULL SPEED. Abruptly off the *Plymouth's* starboard bow a headlight flashed. In spite of attempts to slow down, nothing could keep the vessels apart. The *Taunton's* bow struck the *Plymouth* with terrific force, slicing through the forward hull just aft the gilt letters FALL RIVER LINE. The blow completely demolished staterooms 200 through 207, opening a huge space to the waters of the Sound and exposing a tangled mass of mattresses, boards, blankets, clothing, valises, splintered furniture, and detached paneling, crisscrossed with twisted bars of iron.

In the fog the *Plymouth's* men could not make out the other vessel; they had no idea who she was. Captain Davis did not know for several hours that he had collided with another Fall River steamer.

On the *Plymouth*, a momentary hush followed the crash. Then shouts of terror and surprise and cries of the wounded mingled with the noise of rushing water and escaping steam. The sea poured into the *Plymouth*, filling the forward section, but, thanks to her water-tight compartments, she did not go down. Captain Davis ordered the bulkhead doors closed at once to prevent the entire hull from flooding. "Our forward bulkheads saved us," he said later.

In minutes everything was under control. There was no panic. Officers quieted anxious passengers while Stewardess Brown circulated the welcome news that there was no danger of sinking; they would make for the nearest port.

Seventy-five Marines were aboard the *Plymouth* that night, fresh from duty in the Philippines. Commanded by Lieutenant William C. Hardlee, they were bound for new posts at Boston and Portsmouth and had turned in for the night in the second starboard cabin. The men were peacefully sleeping when the *Taunton* struck, throwing some from their berths and bruising others with falling timbers. The sleepy trumpeter thought it was a terrible explosion.

On the company's long rail journey from the west coast, trains had often stopped suddenly, throwing the men from their bunks. When this crash came, Lieutenant Hardlee dreamed he was back on a train. Then he heard the passengers' cries and came wide awake as water surged in. Leaping from his berth, he ordered the troops to the upper deck, but before they could get out they were knee-deep in water. Shoes, socks, and clothing disappeared; knapsacks were lost in the flooded cabin. Hardlee waded in water up to his waist before he had accounted for all his men.

Once on deck, the Marines lined up precisely and flawlessly as though on parade, although somewhat less than trim in appearance. This crack military display in the face of disaster did much to reassure the passengers. Said Mrs. Faye of Baltimore admiringly, "Of course they were Marines, you know, and knew exactly what to do." Lack of panic on board the *Plymouth* was due in part to the cool discipline of Company B, Second Regiment, United States Marine Corps.

Meanwhile, the crew methodically inspected damage and treated casualties. Four were injured, one seriously. The shattered cabins yielded one significant corpse, the first passenger killed on the Fall River Line since it began in 1847. The victim, dead of a skull fracture, was believed to be Jonathan W. Thompson of Reading, Pennsylvania. However, the next day Fall River officials heard from Mr. Thompson —who had been very surprised to read his death notice! The mix-up occurred because Thompson's card was found on the body. The dead man was later identified as G. H. Marsten of Paterson, New Jersey, occupant of Cabin 203.

Also dead was the 67-year-old watchman, John McCarthy, veteran of 45 years on the line. On his midnight rounds when the *Taunton* rammed the steamer, he was trapped between two wooden partitions and decapitated.

In addition, four kitchen workers who slept in the forward lower cabin were missing and presumed dead.

Many had tales of hairbreadth escapes. Mrs. Faye, the Marines' admirer, was assigned to Cabin 200, which had disappeared. She escaped because a friend invited her to the main saloon just as she was about to retire.

After the collision, Mr. and Mrs. Robert Sinclair were imprisoned in the bridal stateroom when the door jammed. To release them, a husky cabin boy demolished the wall with a fire axe.

M. H. Zack and wife had retired early, after a hard day in New York. Their cabin was crushed like an eggshell; they were tossed to the floor and showered with wreckage, but not badly hurt.

As soon as possible, Captain Davis turned the *Plymouth* toward New London, Connecticut, some seven or eight miles away. With her gaping wound she moved slowly; soon the Norwich Line steamer *Maine* overtook her and offered to help. Captain Davis declined, instead dispatching the *Maine* to alert the New London hospital, asking for ambulances and doctors to stand by at the pier.

At 3 A.M. the crippled *Plymouth* limped into the Fishers Island Navigation Company dock. The gangplank was thrown ashore, and the most seriously injured landed. First fireman Patrick Daley, his right arm crushed off at the shoulder, was rushed to the hospital by ambulance; passengers J. S. Creger, with a sprained ankle, and David Samuelson, with a badly wrenched knee, also required hospitalization. Michael Kilduff's crushed right foot was treated at the pier.

Still there was no word of the other vessel. As the *Plymouth* lay shuddering in the Race, Captain Davis had heard a distress signal as the unknown backed away, then nothing further.

Captain Bibber, on the *City of Taunton*, thought the crash occurred about 12:05 A.M. The freighter's bow was carried away; at once her forward compartment filled with water. Their only hope, the protective bulkhead, leaked badly. Bibber ordered his crew to fill the cracks with blankets, and with makeshift calking they shored up the bulkhead. Then for nearly two hours the *Taunton* wallowed in the Race. Fortunately she did not go down. At 1:55 A.M., along came the freight propeller *Nashua*; she hove to and offered assistance. The *Nashua* eventually towed the *Taunton*, stern first, all the way to New London, slowly probing her way through ever-present fog. In the harbor, tug *Harriet* aided the stricken steamer to the Norwich Line wharf. At 5:55 A.M. the *City of Taunton* arrived, and "Danger" Davis learned that he had met another Fall River vessel in the fog.

The old river town of New London awoke to find two damaged steamers in the harbor. Crowds flocked to inspect the victims—a gruesome sight. On the *Plymouth's* lower deck lay Patrick Daley's severed arm. Debris filled her open side. Photographers snapped pictures while the police tried to keep order. One young woman with camera and tripod haughtily requested an officer to disperse the crowds so she could take a better picture of the *Plymouth*, adding, "Please have the boat crew come out and pose on the pier. I want them in front of the steamer."

The sad task of locating bodies in the hold began at daylight. Capt. T. A. Scott sent an experienced diver; an air pump was set up at the head of the gangway leading to the submerged forward cabin. At 9 o'clock the diver located the first body—John Williams, the baker, who was killed in his bunk. Other bodies were recovered soon. Pantryman John Cleman had a water-soaked $1500 insurance policy in his pocket made out to his mother.

At six o'clock a special train arrived to take the 500 passengers to Boston. A thankful crowd boarded the cars at Union Station as Captain Davis cordially shook hands with all. Each departing passenger expressed sympathy for the popular captain's troubles and paid tribute to his seamanship. The survivors arrived in Boston before noon, tired but little the worse for their experience. To the irrepressible Marines the whole affair was a lark. They left the coaches in military formation, although some wore makeshift footgear of oilcloth or burlap.

Back in New London, an army of freight handlers swarmed about for two days, removing huge piles of freight from the *City of Taunton* and the *Plymouth*. At 6:10 A.M. Sunday, the *Plymouth* left New London for repairs, under her own steam but convoyed by a tug. Although her bulkheads had been shored before leaving, there was some worry when she struck choppy seas, but at top speed of six miles an hour the groaning, straining bulkheads held. Early Mon-

City of Taunton, minus her bow, hauled out at Palmer Yard, Noank, Connecticut. *Courtesy, the Mariners Museum, Newport News, Va. (Elwin M. Eldredge Collection.)*

day morning she reached the Fletcher Iron Works dry dock at Hoboken, New Jersey.

The *City of Taunton* was repaired at the Palmer Shipyard at Noank, Connecticut, with G. A. Slade, Superintendent of the Stonington Line Shops, in charge. Slade connected 100 electric lights to the steamer's dynamo so repairs could go on day and night. In a few weeks the double shifts of workmen had the *Taunton*

ready—she was planked, sealed, and all traces of her accident had vanished. She returned to her route where she was urgently needed.

The *Plymouth*, too, went back to work, serving for many more years on the Sound. But in company records the night of March 20, 1903, remained unique—the first and only time a passenger lost his life by accident on the Fall River Line.   END

Suicide of a Submarine

An awful tragedy was taking place on the floor of the ocean a few hundred feet below . . .

**by Admiral Philip Andrews
(as told to Lowell Ames Norris)**

Admiral Philip Andrews

ON THE MORNING OF SEPTEMBER 6, 1918, THREE American sub-chasers were out hunting submarines, and had lowered their listening devices about 150 miles east of Lands End. It was a quiet morning, about half-past eleven. Two boats reported to Ensign Ashley D. Adams, in command of the unit, that they had detected the presence in the immediate vicinity of an enemy submarine.

It was so close at hand that two of the chasers put on speed and dropped depth charges over the site of the "fix." The "fix" is the spot, incidentally, that the instruments of the three boats determine as the spot where the submarine is located. Apparently, little or no damage was done by the first explosion, as no oil or wreckage came to the surface. The units carried on. Stopping every now and then to listen, they continued to stalk their prey for several

hours. Finally, it was determined that the submarine lay only a few hundred yards ahead. Barrages were laid and more depth charges shot from the three "Y" guns. Not content with this, the entire plotted section was strewn with explosives.

Gradually the force of these died away. Again the listening tubes were lowered. Minute after minute passed and nothing was heard. It began to look like a false alarm. Then one of the crew at the listening tube held up a hand for silence. From below the surface had come the sound of a slowly turning propeller, a propeller that did not seem to be attempting a slow, well-ordered retreat, but labored, as though each revolution was made with difficulty. And there was that peculiar grating, squeaking sound associated with damaged machinery.

Another long period of silence, interspersed

by the moaning of a ghost ship whose wrecked timbers lay hundreds of feet below the surface, and then—the propeller of the unseen submarine was clearly heard again. A few fitful revolutions—silence—more revolutions—and then a longer silence. A slight wake was noticed on the surface such as is commonly left by a submarine when submerged. Crippled, and perhaps blinded, the submarine was attempting a getaway, but her progress was slow, painfully slow. Charge after charge was dropped in the path of her wake; more bombs and more bombs were cast. A black cylindrical object suddenly rose from the water and shot high in the air. What this was has never been determined, but the crews of three ships saw it.

Only one avenue of escape was left, and the submarine sought to take advantage of it. It stumbled along, seeking shallow water not over 300 feet deep. There it could lie in comparative safety on the floor of the ocean, playing 'possum, in the hope that the sub-chasers would think the submarine had eluded them and return to port. Under ordinary conditions a submarine could stay in such a position for two or three days, but this craft—well, the Americans wondered.

The submarine seemed to be slowly sinking, although, judging from the sounds brought through the listening tubes, it still was struggling desperately to rise to the surface. There were long, agonized creaks, squeaks and groans from the badly strained machinery, a series of uneven jolts as the submarine reached the ocean floor. There she rested, struggling, twisting, turning in the slimy mud, but to no avail. It was useless. Overhead not a single movement of her struggles escaped the delicate wire antennae of the listening instruments.

Gradually it became apparent to the auditors that an awful tragedy was taking place on the floor of the ocean a few hundred feet below them. Men, enclosed in thin steel walls, were fighting desperately for life. Trapped in their steel casket with the danger of their air supply becoming exhausted, possibly groping in the darkness of that hideous prison with oily sweat dripping from the walls, these men faced death. There came a sharp, metallic tapping. Frantic hands were hammering in a desperate attempt to make needed repairs. From time to time came other sounds which revealed without sight the harrowing details of that terrible struggle for life.

It was growing late. Two chasers were sent to Penzance for more ammunition. A radio call was put in for a destroyer. The position of the imprisoned submarine was marked by a lighted buoy, while the third chaser stood by in case the boat rose to the surface to give fight or surrender. The listeners at the tubes, standing through the long hours, reported intermittent noises from below that grew fainter and fainter as time went on.

A fog shut down soon after darkness. The lights on the buoy were extinguished by heavy seas. Presently the buoy itself disappeared. It had been sucked under by the tide. The seas grew heavier and the light boats pitched and tossed. The location of the submarine was lost. About three o'clock in the morning a British destroyer came alongside in response to the earlier call. There they stayed. There they waited . . . hoping, watching, praying, wishing for action. None came. Nothing happened.

Daybreak arrived. The exhausted listeners on the chasers again attempted to relocate the submarine. Position was shifted time after time, without results. Still they persisted. They knew intuitively that the submarine was still in the vicinity. They were determined to locate it. They must locate it. The day wore on. It grew high noon, afternoon. The sun began to sink slowly toward the west.

It was five o'clock. One of the listeners, ears still glued to the instrument, suddenly started. His face grew pale under the tan.

"My God!" he gasped. "Listen!"

The others gathered round him. On the chaser and on the destroyer they listened too. There could be no mistaking the sound. It was the sharp crack of a revolver. It reverberated again and again. Once—twice—three times the shots rang out—up to 25—and the average German submarine carried that number of men.

"The poor devils," gasped somebody. "They've shot themselves." There were a few instants of breathless silence. Nobody spoke. Under those sullen, heaving waters another incident of the war had come to a close.   END

159

Fathoms Deep the

SOS—COLLISION—SEND IMMEDIATE ASSISTANCE
the dramatic story of the mighty doomed liner, *Andrea Doria.*

The stricken Italian liner, *Andrea Doria,* on the morning of July 26, 1956, just before her

As DARKNESS FELL ON A FOG-ENSHROUDED SEA off Nantucket Island on the night of July 25, 1956, in an area known as the Times Square of the North Atlantic, the 697-foot Italian luxury liner *Andrea Doria* moved rapidly through the glass-like surface of the ocean. Although there had been an offshore fog for three days, the giant liner was still expected to arrive on schedule in New York early the next morning. Aboard the pride of the Italian Line were more than 1700 people.

The last glimmer of daylight disappeared, and the early evening hours passed. Flushed with the excitement of approaching their homeland again, returning passengers, including important personalities of society and the business world, celebrated with political leaders, screen stars, physicians, newsmen, as well as immigrants.

Some miles to the eastward, similar gatherings were taking place aboard another vessel, outward-bound. Passengers of the 12,165-ton Swedish-American liner *Stockholm*, which had left New York for Europe at 11:30 that same morning, were filled with anticipation for the coming journey. Their first night out on the ocean, they were trying their sea legs. Back in New York Harbor that morning, the smaller, 510-foot

Treasure Lies

by Edward Rowe Snow

final plunge. Note the lifeboats still in their davits on the port side. *U. S. Coast Guard Photo.*

Stockholm had waited briefly as the mammoth 44,500-ton transatlantic veteran, the *Ile de France*, took the lead down the bay.

By eleven o'clock that fateful night the *Andrea Doria, Stockholm* and *Ile de France* were in the general vicinity of Nantucket Lightship. In relatively easy range were the *Pvt. W. H. Thomas*, the *Cape Ann* and the destroyer escort *Edward H. Allen.*

Many activities were in progress aboard the *Andrea Doria*. In one of the four spacious theaters a moving picture, "Foxfire," was being shown. In the luxurious Belvedere Lounge on the boat deck an orchestra entertained dancers.

Below, tiers of baggage already crowded the passageways, ready for the next day's exodus. Throughout the ship scores of weary voyagers were sound asleep in their cabins.

. For three full days foggy weather had covered the entire sea area from Newfoundland down to Martha's Vineyard. Most mariners were attempting to make up for lost time. Nearer and nearer to each other came the *Stockholm* and the *Andrea Doria*. Suddenly, through the mist, many on the decks of the Italian vessel stared in horror at the chilling sight of another vessel's lights surging toward them. A moment later, with a terrifying crash of snapping girders and bulkheads, the *Stockholm* plowed into the starboard side of the *Doria* immediately abaft her flying bridge.

The two vessels held together in their unnatural union for a split second. Then they seemed to leap apart in a dazzling shower of sparks. The *Stockholm's* sharp bow, which had been rebuilt for use as an icebreaker, had punched a fatal hole in the Italian liner. The jagged gash torn into the *Doria's* side was 40 feet wide and 30 feet deep. It extended more than 50 feet above and at least 15 feet below the water line.

All over the *Doria* the collision caught the passengers and crew, and tossed them about mercilessly. The shock dropped the dancers to the deck and ripped the card tables away from the players. In the bar, patrons were sprinkled with cascades of flying glass, and those in the auditorium watching the motion picture were jumbled together in heaps. Hundreds of passengers, asleep in beds and bunks, were hurled about in their cabins, while far below in the bowels of the ship, crew members, recovering from the crash, soberly prepared for whatever might lie ahead. Out in the corridors, smoke and dust from the collision began to settle over the masses of baggage that had been flung about into hopeless confusion.

Captain Piero Calamai, master of the *Andrea Doria*, quickly discovered the seriousness of the wound which the *Stockholm* had dealt to his beloved craft and ordered his radio operator to send out an appeal for help.

At approximately 11:22 P.M. Eastern Daylight Time, a distress message flashed through the air: SOS . . . COLLISION . . . SEND IMMEDIATE ASSISTANCE.

The stricken Italian craft, with tons of water pouring into her gaping wound every second, almost at once began to list on her starboard side. Soon the cant of the deck approximated 25 degrees. Moments later it was 35 degrees!

Within the next two hours eight crowded lifeboats were released. The officers appealed by radio for additional boats, for with the port deck at the precarious angle of 45 degrees none could be launched from that side. To add to the problems, the angle of the ship brought the water from the *Doria's* swimming pools flowing across the deck to stream into the sea.

While the mighty liner was gradually submerging beneath them, little groups of frightened passengers gathered together and clung to one another in various parts of the giant ship; some told jokes as others took turns praying.

Several craft which had been in the vicinity were arriving to lend assistance to the stricken vessel with lifeboats and motor tenders. Captain Gunnar Nordenson of the *Stockholm*, having examined his own ship and found her seaworthy, also sent across lifeboats for rescue work.

The fog lifted to reveal for the first time the beautiful 793-foot French liner *Ile de France* sliding into full view. Every light on the ship proved a comforting sight to the frightened people still aboard the *Andrea Doria*, which, even at this time, appeared to some to be capable of staying afloat indefinitely.

The *Doria* had actually released ten of her own lifeboats, and the *Ile de France* began taking off the survivors at once. The *Pvt. W. H. Thomas* and the *Cape Ann* were soon removing their share of the passengers. Later the *Edward H. Allen* joined in the rescue work.

These efforts continued through the night. The tanker *Hopkins*, sailing from Revere, Massachusetts, picked up one man, Robert L. Hudson, whom it found hanging to the debarkation net. The *Stockholm* took off 570 people and the *Cape Ann*, 129. The *Thomas* picked up 165 survivors, the *Ile de France*, 758, and the *Edward H. Allen*, 77, from the sinking Italian liner. It is a tribute to those involved that all but 45 were saved.

Although it is an overwhelming thought, it is possible, and even probable, that some of the last people were still alive when the *Andrea Doria* reached the bottom, about 240 feet below the surface of the ocean. Caught in staterooms sealed up by the crash, they may have lived for days at the bottom of the sea breathing the air imprisoned with them.

Captain Calamai and the last Italian crewman left the *Doria* by 7:00 that morning. Flying above the stricken ship, an hour and a quarter later, one could notice the change in her posi-

Though *Stockholm's* ice-breaker bow looked like crumpled tinfoil after ramming the *Doria,* the Swedish liner was still seaworthy. *U. S. Coast Guard Photo.*

tion. The sea was lapping around the *Doria's* starboard rail, and the port propeller could easily be seen above the surface.

With the coming of dawn, helicopters and airplanes were literally swarming around the disaster area. At ten o'clock Bob Cadigan of the Nantucket Flying Service passed low over the scene and found the decks of the *Doria* awash. Shortly afterward six lifeboats ripped loose and came to the surface. Giant geysers spurted forth from the amidships section, rising 70 and 80 feet. The great vessel was by then down by the bow. At the last moment, her stern appeared to rise slightly above the surface of the sea, as if making a final effort to stay afloat. The port propeller broke water along its entire shaft, and there was foam ten feet deep by her stern. Then, at 10:09 A.M., she simply slid over and went under, leaving the lifeboats and other wreckage swirling around on the surface and masses of green, bubbling water everywhere.

Hundreds of individual episodes of heroism and tragedy were enacted that fateful night. Mr. and Mrs. Tullio di Sandro were aboard the Italian ship with their four-and-a-half-year-old daughter, Norma. When a lifeboat from the *Stockholm* maneuvered immediately below the dangerously canted liner, Mr. di Sandro became panic-stricken from fear that the *Doria* was about to sink. Shouting down to a member of the lifeboat crew, he dropped his little daughter over the side to the sailor. To everyone's horror, her body turned in the air and her head struck the lifeboat. Mr. and Mrs. di Sandro were unable to follow their daughter into the lifeboat, and the unconscious girl was taken to the *Stockholm* and later flown ashore in a helicopter, without the parents' knowledge.

Landing at Nantucket Airport, Norma was first examined by physicians of the Cottage Hospital. Her condition was so serious that she was rushed by Coast Guard airplane to Boston's Logan Airport, and from there to the Brighton Marine Hospital nearby.

Meanwhile her desperate parents were taken aboard the *Ile de France* and taken to New York. There the frantic couple learned that a young child with a ram's horn charm bracelet, which they knew Norma was wearing, was a patient at the Marine Hospital. They arrived in Brighton at 3:30 the next morning, but little Norma never regained consciousness and died 18 hours later.

When the two vessels came together, actress Ruth Roman rushed into her stateroom to tell her sleeping three-year-old son to get ready for "a picnic," but she became separated from her child during the confusion. After many agonizing hours, they had a joyous reunion at a New York pier.

Colonel Walter Carlin of Brooklyn, prominent in political circles, discovered in shocked surprise, on returning from the washroom after the collision, that not only had his wife vanished but their cabin had disappeared as well! Mrs. Carlin had been instantly killed in the crash.

The most unbelievable story of the entire disaster was that of 14-year-old Linda Morgan, who with her family shared two staterooms on the Italian liner. The *Stockholm* smashed into the very rooms in which they were sleeping. Missing after the collision, Linda was officially listed as dead. What actually happened was no less than a miracle.

Aboard the Swedish liner *Stockholm* was 36-year-old crewman Bernabe Garcia, who had gone to bed at 9:45 that night. When the crash came, he had just dozed off from his reading of Strindberg's *Röda Rummet*. Stumbling to his feet, he felt the strong pull of reversing engines as he made his way toward a babel of voices forward.

In the darkness he noticed how the bow of the *Stockholm* had been crumpled by the collision. Then he heard a voice and began to walk around the sound, a confused cry that ended in a sob. Ahead of him, there was a mass of debris, but he fought his way through it. Finally he discovered the head and shoulders of a girl buried to her waist in wreckage.

Garcia cried out for aid. When no one came, he attempted to pull the child from the rubble without injuring her. Then, suddenly, the girl spoke.

"¿Donde está Mama?"

Instinctively the Spaniard answered her. "Was your mama here? I am a native of Cadiz."

"She was here with me. What has happened?"

Garcia then explained to the girl that, at the moment of the collision, in some unexplainable way she had been scooped up by the *Stockholm's* bow from her bed on the *Andrea Doria*, and that she was caught in the debris on the Swedish vessel. He managed to work the Morgan girl free within a few minutes. Carrying her aft, he handed Linda over to a Danish gentleman, who took her to the ship's sick bay. Meanwhile,

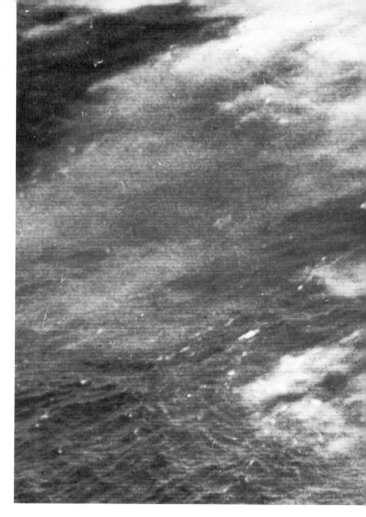

Garcia scrambled back to the bow wreckage in an attempt to discover Linda's mother.

He sighted the remains of a blond woman, but a moment later, before he could reach it, the body slipped off into the sea with several broken fragments of the bow. Without question the woman had been killed instantly at the moment of collision, but it turned out that she was not Linda's mother. Linda's stepfather, Camille M. Cianfarra, Madrid correspondent of *The New York Times*, and Linda's stepsister Joan, were killed but the mother, although injured, was still alive aboard the *Doria*.

Another terrifying incident involved Dr. Thure C. Peterson, a chiropractor of Upper Montclair, New Jersey, and his wife Martha. The *Stockholm's* bow plowed right through their cabin, pinning Mrs. Peterson by the spine and legs to the broken wreckage of the deck, after which the ship backed away again.

Struggling through the wreckage, Dr. Peter-

The death throes of the *Andrea Doria. Courtesy Wide World Photos.*

son discovered not only his wife but also Mrs. Cianfarra, both cruelly pinioned by the twisted steel girders. After attempting in vain to rescue his wife, with the aid of a crewman named Gino, Peterson was able only to lift Mrs. Cianfarra free from the debris.

As the initial glow of the false dawn came, Dr. Peterson noticed for the first time that he was working on a tiny triangle of twisted metal, which was suspended high above the water like an island in the sky. At any minute the entire mass might slip off into the sea. The moment that he had freed Mrs. Cianfarra, Dr. Peterson again attempted to cut away the steel which had caught his wife, but was still unable to do so. Searching for something which might push the wreckage free from her body, Peterson found a jack. Together he and Gino wedged the heavy tool under the wreckage and the mass began to move. But at that very moment Mrs. Peterson spoke to her husband.

"I'm going," she said quietly. A moment later she was dead.

* * * * *

When the *Andrea Doria* was completed in 1951, it was maintained by her builders, as the builders of the *Titanic* had claimed two generations before, that the hull had been specially constructed not only to prevent her from ever sinking but to give her more stability in case of collision. The *Doria's* hull was subdivided into 11 watertight compartments which extended the entire length of the ship. Bulkheads parallel with her engine rooms were also designed to lessen the effect of a crash at sea. Her builders were certain that she was unsinkable.

However, if the *Andrea Doria* had been built according to the standards set up by the 1948 Convention on the Safety of Human Life at Sea, at the time of the collision she should have retained stability even with two compartments open to the water. Therefore, either the con-

165

vention standards were inadequate, or the *Andrea Doria's* builders did not adhere to the standards. American standards would have required her watertight doors to have automatic sealing bulkheads controlled by electric magnets. This system keeps water out of connecting compartments.

Right of way on the high seas is a complicated problem. The *Stockholm* appeared from the north of the *Andrea Doria* to strike the starboard side of the Italian vessel. However, as neither craft was attempting knowingly to cross the path of the other, it is extremely difficult to decide to the satisfaction of all concerned which was the privileged craft on that fatal night.

The *Stockholm* was accused of being north of the usual eastbound lanes. Unfortunately, neither the Italian Line nor the Swedish-American Line ever agreed to join with the other nations in the North Atlantic Track Agreement. This agreement merely suggests that the westbound lane, Track Charlie, should be taken while proceeding toward New York, and another course to the south should be followed eastward.

In the 19th century the average speed of liners in good weather or in fog was not over 11 knots, but the record-breaking voyage of the *United States* in 1952 was at the unprecedented rate of 35.59 knots. When ships collide at speeds exceeding 20 knots, they will be much more likely to sink.

In this instance, for example, the accident took place at 11:22 P.M. the night of July 25. As the *Andrea Doria* was scheduled to dock almost 200 miles away by 9:30 the next morning, she would have had to maintain an average speed of over 22 knots to reach the Ambrose Lightship by 7:00 the next morning. We have no proof, but it is reasonable to believe that she must have been going close to 22 knots that night, and she may have been exceeding that speed just before the crash, fog or no fog.

Although radar is a blessing to humanity, man has come into the habit of relying too much on this navigational aid. Strangely enough, if it had not been for radar, the two craft might not have noticed each other at all in the fog and probably would have sailed along without collision, passing by each other miles apart.

In January, 1957, the Italian and Swedish-American Lines mutually agreed to abandon court action to fix the blame for the collision. On February 15, 1957, the last day for filing, the total number of claims was announced as 1565, involving more than $116,000,000. Both vessels were partly covered by insurance.

Millions of dollars' worth of cargo and valuables including a $200,000 experimental Chrysler car, a fortune in jewelry and an estimated $2,000,000 in cash went down with the ship, as well as priceless Italian paintings and sculpture that adorned her interior. A real King Solomon's mine of treasure!

So far, the several attempts at salvaging the *Andrea Doria* have yielded very little. To give you some idea of the difficulties involved in recovering anything from the wreck of the great luxury liner, it took a team of four divers eight days in 1964 just to salvage the life-size bronze statue of Andrea Doria, which was hacked off at the ankles from its pedestal in the first class lounge on the promenade deck.

Frederic Dumas, veteran French diver and co-author (with Jacques Cousteau) of *The Silent World*, who visited the liner 240 feet below the surface a month after she sank and brought an ashtray back up with him, said that because of the "murky water, wild currents and aggressive sharks . . . she will never be salvaged."

The most recent attempt to wrest some of the *Doria's* riches from Davy Jones was during the summer of 1973, with divers utilizing an underwater habitat called *Mother* in order to minimize the hazard at that depth of nitrogen narcosis. However, dangers from the deteriorating hulk were such that after 23 days the team of surface and habitat-launched divers succeeded in recovering only a few silver platters and a bottle of French perfume, although they were able to cut a four-foot square hole in the hull with an underwater acetylene torch.

Scheme after scheme has been evolved to enter or even to re-float the liner for salvage, but she remains buried deep in the mud, stubbornly guarding her treasure and policed by whole regiments of fearsome sharks. I agree with Dumas that the *Andrea Doria* will never be salvaged. END

Left: It took four divers eight days in 1964 to salvage this life-size bronze statue of the Italian admiral for whom the ship was named.

Below: Frederic Dumas (center), veteran French diver and co-author (with Jacques Cousteau) of *The Silent World* before his visit to the *Doria* 240 feet below.

Bottom: Diver John Clark of the 1973 expedition examining port side davit of the *Doria* as photographed underwater by Jack McKenny of *Skin Diver* Magazine on his 24th dive to the lost liner.

6.
NARROW ESCAPES AND BRAVE RESCUES

The Frozen Couple of Owl's Head

It took ten strong men to move the great ice cake containing the two lovers and hand it down to others waiting below, waist-deep in the freezing surf . . .

by Edward Rowe Snow

ONE OF THE MOST INCREDIBLE INCIDENTS IN THE entire history of the New England shore occurred in 1850 near the famed Owl's Head Light, located a few miles from what is now Rockland, Maine.

A terrible gale which began on December 22, 1850, sent no less than five vessels ashore in the area between Rockland Harbor and Spruce Head. Ice built up along the shore, forming a hard white sheathing over a foot thick which covered wrecks and rocky ledges up and down the Maine coast.

A small packet owned by Henry Butters of Haverhill, Massachusetts, was anchored off Jameson's Point just before the storm began. The captain had gone ashore, leaving the schooner in the care of his mate, Richard B. Ingraham. One seaman, Roger Elliott, and a single passenger, Miss Lydia Dyer, were also

aboard. Lydia Dyer, Ingraham's fiancée, was aboard with the owner's permission to make the trip to Boston scheduled to start early in the morning.

That night, the gale increased by the hour. Lydia went below and retired about nine o'clock. By eleven the craft was in great danger from the waves. Suddenly, a few moments before midnight, both cables snapped, and the schooner began a journey across the bay toward Owl's Head.

Clearing the promontory at Owl's Head, the schooner smashed ashore on the cruel ledges a short distance to the southward. The jagged boulders soon pierced her hull, and she settled in a rocky cradle a few hundred yards below the high tide mark.

The moment the schooner crashed on the ledges, Lydia Dyer sprang from her bunk, grabbed a comforter and a large blanket, and rushed up on deck.

Ingraham quickly wrapped the bedclothes around the girl to protect her from the driving surf and icy snow then hitting the vessel. Desperate in his anxiety to help her, he guided Lydia to a relatively sheltered part of the deck close to the taffrail. There they crouched, trying to obtain some protection from the storm.

Elliott joined them shortly afterwards, and the three huddled together. The tide soon turned, starting to come in. The spray and surf dashed with increasing fury against the helpless trio, drenching them thoroughly. As the hours passed, their clothing began to stiffen, freezing to their bodies. Standing by the taffrail, Richard Ingraham realized that there was little chance of their living through the night unless he could arrange some better shelter at once. The wind was still rising, and the tide was almost high.

"Lydia," Dick said to his sweetheart, "I don't have to tell you that we are in great danger, but I've thought of a plan which may save our lives."

"I'll do whatever you say," Lydia answered.

Dick continued. "Put the blanket down as close as you can get it to the taffrail and then lie down on it and pull it around yourself."

Lydia did as directed, and when she had pulled the blanket around her back, Dick placed himself beside her, pulled his own blanket around both of them and wrapped his arms firmly around her wet, icy body. Then Elliot crawled in beside Dick, forced himself as close as he could and pulled the old comforter around him. Although he believed that Ingraham was right in suggesting that they all huddle together for the night to keep alive, Elliott took the precaution of making sure his sheath knife was handy to chip the ice away so that they could breathe.

When at last the schooner broke in two, Elliott freed himself, climbed down through the break to the rocks and began his journey toward civilization. But the rocks were icy and extremely slippery. His stiffened clothing was an enormous hindrance, too. He stumbled and staggered over the rocks, falling down at almost every step. Finally, it was too much of a temptation to stop and rest before he went on.

Elliott relaxed against a giant boulder and fell into a deep sleep. It was a sleep from which he might never have awakened, but luck was with him, for the tide was turning. Soon it began to come in, and a giant wave splashed over the sleeping man. The icy wave revived him—and saved his life.

Elliott tried to scramble to his feet, but the effort was too sudden. He toppled over backwards, hitting his head as he fell. The shock, however, helped to bring him to his senses, and he got up again, this time more slowly and deliberately. Eventually, after agonizing minutes of tortured walking, he reached the high tide mark, where giant snowdrifts blocked his way.

Foot by foot, yard by yard, Elliott broke a path through the drifts until he finally reached a road. Of course he had no way of knowing where the nearest house was located or in what direction he should turn. The tracks of a pung with the hoofmarks of a horse decided his course. He would follow the tracks until he reached help. Turning to the right, he started along the road which actually led to Owl's Head Light.

Now upright, now falling, Elliott made slow but steady progress. He did not know how much longer he could continue in his weakened condition. Then through the cold morning air he heard the sound of bells. He looked up and thought he saw a sleigh coming toward him along the road. A minute later he realized it was a pung drawing closer to him. With a half-cry, Elliott collapsed in the road.

The driver of the pung was Keeper William Masters of Owl's Head Light. Masters soon got Elliott onto the pung and drove toward the lighthouse, where he took the freezing man inside and cut his stiffened clothing from his body. A drink of hot rum was forced down his throat, and he was put to bed and covered with heavy blankets, comforters and quilts. But even in his semi-conscious condition, Elliott remembered that there was a message he should give to the lighthouse keeper immediately. With a tremendous effort he opened his eyes and tried to get up.

"Take it easy there," admonished Masters.

"You've had a hard time of it. Just lie back and go to sleep." Elliott was not to be denied, however, and opened his mouth to speak.

"Others—on the wreck," he gasped faintly. "Please—get them."

"All right," Masters assured him. "We'll leave at once. Now you go to sleep."

A moment later Elliott was so deeply asleep that he didn't hear the lighthouse bell signalling every able-bodied man in the surrounding countryside to leave his home and aid in rescue work. Soon, Masters' pung with a dozen men aboard was following Elliott's tracks back to the shore. The wreck out on the rocks was quickly sighted.

By now the tide was well on the way in. It was quite a task to reach the broken vessel, but the men waded out, hip-deep in the icy brine, and clambered aboard. They began to hack away at the two bodies frozen in the ice by the taffrail and soon had the block of ice severed from the deck. They worked fast because of the rising tide. Ten strong men moved the heavy cake containing the two lovers over to the break in the deck and handed it down to others waiting below in waist-deep surf. The men of Owl's Head then carried their icy burden ashore in

the bitter cold and loaded it onto the pung.

"They're both dead, all right," exclaimed one of the men.

"I'm afraid so," answered Masters, "but we've got to try to bring them back to life."

The huge ice cake was brought into the kitchen of the nearest house, and by careful chipping and thawing, the ice was completely removed from the blankets which covered the bodies. Cold water applications were then administered, with the water as near freezing as possible. The temperature of the water was slowly raised until eventually it was approximately 55 degrees. The next step was to move the hands and feet of the victims, slowly at first, and then at a more rapid rate. Their bodies were massaged, first carefully and then vigorously for half an hour.

Lydia was the first to show signs of life, stirring slightly after two hours of constant attention. Ingraham took almost a full hour longer to respond to the treatment, but he finally moved uneasily and opened his eyes.

"What is all this? Where are we?" he asked, and they told him the whole story. He looked across at Lydia, and she smiled at him faintly.

Then, after Lydia and Ingraham were covered with extra blankets and fed hot drinks,

From left: Lydia Dyer; Richard B. Ingraham; their savior, Roger Elliott, as he looked circa 1862.

they fell asleep. The following day they were well enough to eat, but it was several months before they could get up and walk around. Spring arrived before their recovery was complete.

The state of Richard's finances prevented his marrying Lydia at once, but as soon as he was able to raise a sufficient sum, the pair married, and four children were born to the happy couple in the next seven years.

I am deeply indebted to one of their descendants, Mrs. Louise Thompson Squires of Whitestone, New York, for many of the details of this story. She first heard the story of Lydia and Richard from her mother, who learned it from hers.

Incidentally, Roger Elliott was the only one of the three who did not recover fully from his terrifying experience, and there are those who believe that in some way his exposure to the air was responsible.

Nevertheless, if he hadn't kept the knife cutting through the freezing ice, he would not have been able to free himself and get ashore to notify the lighthouse keeper that two others were still aboard the schooner.

The episode of the frozen couple of Maine was discussed for years afterwards around the fireplaces up and down the Maine coast, but today only a handful of people are aware of the details of this truly remarkable account.

END

Rocky promontory and light at Owl's Head, Maine.

LOST!
150 yards from home.

I remember thinking, "This is how I am going to die—frozen to death." Everything seemed distant, cold, and futile.

by Jim Newton

ALL OF MY LIFE I HAD READ OF LOST HUNTERS, mountain climbers, skiers, and hikers becoming trapped in blinding snowstorms, with the wind howling at below-zero temperatures, and drifts piling eight and ten feet high in an hour or two.

But I never dreamed that I would become a victim of such a situation, within a half mile of my home in the hills of Sutton, New Hampshire.

Looking back, I know now that I placed too much faith in the physical strength of my youth and overestimated my courage in the face of whatever elements Mother Nature could toss at me.

It was a cold, sunny Saturday afternoon, with more than a foot of snow already on the ground, the second day of the 1946 deer season. I was bundled to the nines for the below-zero temperature—from leather boots covering two pairs of wool hunting socks, to a red wool hunting cap with ear flaps, and from insulated underwear to hunting gloves.

I walked out the back door of our small bungalow about two o'clock in the afternoon, shouting over my shoulder to my wife that I would be back by four. The 30-30 rifle had three shells in it, more than enough for two hours of hunting.

The wind began to howl; the snow was coming fast . . .

I headed for the wood road winding up the hill behind the house, leading to the abandoned apple orchard at the top of the hill. There was a bright sun, a small patch of dark clouds moving toward the orchard, and a sharp wind at my back as I made my way up the road.

I stopped halfway up the hill to admire the scenery, to look down on the small New England town I loved, and to listen to the crackings and snappings in the woods on both sides of the road. Removing one glove, I dropped my hand in the coat pocket, pulled out a cigarette and a book of matches, and just stood there counting blessings.

Flicking the cigarette into the snow drift along the road, I pulled off my glasses and held them up toward the sun, making sure that my vision would be perfect, should a careless deer cross my scope.

I moved slowly up the hill, planning only to walk through the orchard, take a stand in the rear of the long-forsaken field, and return home in a few hours.

The stone fence parted at the opening to the orchard, and as I walked through the gate I saw a large set of fresh deer tracks leading back through the trees, toward the high granite rock where I usually took my stand.

Moving slowly and listening, I followed the tracks, and that old feeling began to sweep over me; the feeling any man gets when he knows there is a deer within rifle shot. The tracks wove in and out among the trees, suddenly following the stone fence that separated the orchard from the pine woods, and I didn't notice that the wind was getting stronger, the sun was now clouded, and a light snow had started to blow.

The tracks led out of the orchard, to the foot of the large granite rock I used for my stand. Then the huge prints in the snow cut a sharp right, down the hill that was cleared for the utility lines serving the village.

I must have been tasting the venison, counting the points on the rack. Whatever I was thinking about, it was not the weather. The steep, cleared right-of-way offered a crystal view of the outskirts of the village, a half mile down the hill. The deer tracks followed the edge of the woods, bordering the right-of-way.

The hilltop vantage point also made me a clear target for the wind that was now starting to howl, as it hammered its increasing snow load into my face and body. I looked up for a second, mentally measuring the snow in the clouds that now covered the sky, and assured myself that I had plenty of time to follow the tracks down toward the village. If I didn't see my prey as I walked, I would continue on home. There was a path down the power line right-of-way, a narrow path between the giant boulders in the snow-covered gully, but the path was covered with snow, leaving only slight dips between the peaks of the rocks.

I started down the hill, following what I thought was the path, and had moved a hundred feet or more before I noticed that it was getting quite dark. The driving snow had started to cake on my glasses, and was too long falling away with a swipe of my glove.

Another hundred feet and I had lost the deer tracks. The snow had removed my venison-steak meanderings. The wind howled through the giant pines on my right as I paused to get my bearings and to decide my next move. Should I continue down the right-of-way, or climb back to where I had been and return home via the orchard?

Turning around, the two hundred feet of steep hill behind me gave me a quick decision. I would have a cigarette, and continue on down the right-of-way. It was shorter, and it was all down hill.

My snow-covered gloves had become iced to the sleeves of my coat, the visibility had narrowed to the next utility pole, and my glasses were covered with solid snow. My eyebrows and eyelids supported a bar of ice from one side of the face to the other.

I knew I had exhausted all my strength

"Don't panic," I kept saying to myself, first in a whisper and then almost in a frantic shout. I moved carefully down through the rocks, stepping into drifts waist high but remembering to hold my rifle high to prevent clogging the gun barrel. The visibility decreased, and the wind blew across that gully as I had never seen it blow before.

Then, I slipped. I must have stepped over the edge of one large rock and into the narrow opening before the next boulder. I remember going down, I remember cracking my head against the rock, and I remember thinking, "This is how I am going to die, frozen to death."

In that few short seconds before unconsciousness, I thought of my wife, the two small children she would have to raise alone, and I thought of my lying there beneath a blanket of snow that wouldn't reveal me for weeks or months. Then there was darkness, complete, total darkness.

How long I was unconscious I will never know. It couldn't have been too long, but my feet were numb and my arms were heavy. There was a small dark patch fading in the snow—a disappearing blood spot from the light cut on my head.

The rifle was sticking straight up out of the snow, barrel pointing toward the sky. For a moment I lay there, wondering whether I should just close my eyes and sleep it all away, or whether I should make another effort. In the numbness, the coldness, the pain, it was difficult. But the breaking-point had not yet arrived. There was still one more spark of self-preservation.

I struggled to my feet, and stumbled on, falling, rising, scratching, praying. How much longer I went on I don't remember. The wind had almost stopped, the snow fell softly, and from between the dark clouds there came a ray of light.

I was almost entirely coated with ice and snow. My body ached with bruises from falls against the granite rocks, and beneath my clothes I could feel other, bleeding cuts, stifled by the freezing snow.

It was the ray of light from between the dark clouds that provided a mere shadow of my distance from rescue, from paved road and the village. I fell over the top of a gaping boulder, and stretched out in the cold with my chin resting in the snow. I knew that I had exhausted all of my strength.

There was a small building at the edge of the road—a house with a woodshed just a few feet behind it. I couldn't think who lived there; I had lost my sense of direction. Everything seemed distant, cold, and futile. Just 150 yards from safety, from life, from home.

They say I fired the rifle at the woodshed. I don't remember. It must have been an unconscious act, the final straw of self-preservation.

Rob Partridge had gone from his house to the woodshed to get some logs for his stove, or so they said. And the rifle shot didn't miss him by much. He looked up toward the direction of the firing point, saw me, and came up to investigate. "Carried to safety by a Partridge" was how the townfolk jokingly described my rescue. He was the best bird in all the land as far as I was concerned.

They thawed me out in the shed where they kept the town road-scrapers, and took me home at exactly four o'clock, the time I had given the wife for my return. The two kids were playing in the living room; my family had not known of my narrow escape. They had no reason to be concerned—Daddy had always told them, "Don't start worrying about me until an hour after dark."

Outside, the snow had stopped, the sun was out in full glory, an hour away from touching the tree tops on its descent behind the hills.

I know now how it feels to be a lost hunter, trapped by a blinding snow, just minutes from a freezing death.   END

Newport's Forgotten Heroine

NEWPORT, RHODE ISLAND, RESIDENTS WHO HAP-pened to look out their windows early on the morning of March 29, 1869, saw a wall of ominous black clouds forming above the Sakonnet River to the northeast. A light rain fanned by a stiff breeze had already begun to fall. Muttering bitter imprecations against the changeable weather, they closed them hurriedly as if to silence the steadily mounting wind. By mid-afternoon, the rain was coming down in blinding torrents. People gazed skyward and nodded, making a mental note: Newport was in for a nor'easter. It was an apt forecast. But what they didn't foresee was that the storm about to strike the city would create one of the strangest, most enigmatic public idols in the nation's history.

By 5 P.M., the wind had increased to gale force. Whipping through the harbor, it churned the sea into huge, angry waves which battered the shoreline with malignant fury. The storm, more of a winter hurricane, was now directly over the city.

At that moment, Sergeant James Adams and Private John McLaughlin hired a 14-year-old boy to take them by boat to nearby Fort Adams. After a day's leave in Newport, the two artillerymen had decided to forego the dreary three-mile hike, preferring the somewhat shorter, yet riskier, trip by sea. After assurances from the youth that he was an expert sailor even in the foulest weather, they set out in a small, unseaworthy sailing skiff. At a point a half-mile

by Norris Randolph

"My God, Jim! We've been saved by—by a woman!"

Above: Ida Walley Zoradia Lewis, lifesaver and lighthouse keeper at the height of her unwelcome but richly deserved fame. *Courtesy Providence Journal Bulletin.*

Left: Lime Rock Island off Newport, Rhode Island (later the Ida Lewis Yacht Club), as it appeared in 1869.

from the fort, a sudden gust struck the tiny sail. The startled skipper jammed the tiller in the wrong direction. The boat, out of control, heeled over and capsized. Bobbing to the surface, the trio clung helplessly to the keel and began a long fight against exhaustion as the freezing water tore at their fingers, threatening at any moment to drag them under. After 30 minutes of struggling, the youth lost his hold, clutched frantically at McLaughlin's shoulder, screamed, then disappeared. Close to death, the weary soldiers were about to sink when suddenly they saw a nondescript skiff being put out from neighboring Lime Rock Lighthouse. With sure, rapid strokes the slight figure at the oars battled through the mountainous breakers.

Coughing and sputtering, the nearly unconscious pair were laboriously wrestled over the stern. McLaughlin, however, had enough strength left to nudge Adams who lay prone beside him in the bottom of the boat, "My God, Jim! We've been saved by—by a woman!"

To this remarkable woman, Ida Walley Zoradia Lewis, the rescue of the water-logged soldiers was merely a duplication of similar miracles she had wrought before and would continue to perform for 48 years. Perhaps the greatest saltwater heroine who ever lived, she saved 18 people from drowning from 1858 to 1906. Some say she cheated the sea of more than 40 victims during her lifetime. The discrepancy can be attributed to a personality which, if it wasn't inscrutable, was certainly retiring. Loath to talk about herself or her rescues, she would do so only grudgingly and then after a lot of urging. Ida shunned publicity on her barren outpost in Brenton Cove. Yet her name, soon to resound in every corner of the land, would symbolize courage and daring, fearlessness and bravery.

Ida was born February 25, 1842, the daughter of Hosea Lewis, a coastal pilot from Hingham, Massachusetts, and Zoradia Walley Lewis of Block Island. The family moved to Lime Rock, an island 250 yards from Newport's mainland, when Ida was a young girl. Her father, keeper of the light, was shortly stricken with paralysis. Her mother also in poor health, Ida took charge of the household. Daily she would row to Newport for groceries and transport her brothers and sisters to school. The boathandling experience gave her the forearms of a blacksmith and the hands of a good shortstop necessary for the life-saving exploits to come.

Handsome rather than pretty, of average height, with blue eyes and brown hair, Ida possessed an indomitable spirit which made her react instantly to danger even when relatively young. Her first trial, at 16, occurred during a sudden squall just before sunset on a September afternoon in 1858. Four boys were cruising near Lime Rock when one climbed the mast and started rocking the sailing skiff. It promptly upset. Ida spotted them floundering in the chilly water and saved all four just as their boat went under. Ida, though, considered the matter unimportant, according to her official biographer, George D. Brewerton.

Most of the rescues were typical. Using the stern technique taught by her father to prevent the skiff from overturning, she would grab the drowning person by the arm, give a backward heave on an oar, and pull the victim in. If the victim were in bad shape, she would take them to the lighthouse for dry clothes and a warm drink. The lighthouse, currently the Ida Lewis Yacht Club, is the only club of its kind named for a woman in the United States.

The second call for assistance came on a cold, windy February day in 1866. Three drunken soldiers from Fort Adams had stolen a skiff for the return trip to the post. Six hundred yards from the lighthouse, one of the bleary mariners deliberately shoved his foot through the thin planking of the hull. When picked up he had his "hat in his teeth and a whiskey bottle in each pocket," said Ida dryly. His companions either drowned or went permanently AWOL.

By 1867 at the age of 25, the "Heroine of Lime Rock" had made ten rescues in nine years, with only brief notices in the local press. As far as Ida was concerned, they weren't brief enough.

That day in March, 1869, that was to make her famous for the rescue of Sergeant Adams and Private McLaughlin, she was warming her feet prosaically in front of the kitchen stove, recovering from a nasty cold. Outside, she could hear the March storm as it beat against the lighthouse, "a very solid building, square, whitewashed and altogether Uncle Sam-ish in its exterior finish and decoration," situated on its solitary acre of rock. Mrs. Lewis, filling the lamp with oil, heard the soldiers' cries of distress and immediately alerted Ida. Without shoes, coat or hat, she leaped into her skiff and subsequently rowed to renown.

New York newspapers, *Harper's Weekly* and *Frank Leslie's Illustrated* quickly spread the story. Ida's reputation for valor and fortitude rapidly circulated from Maine to California. Editorial writers, taking a cue from abroad, called her the "Grace Darling of America." Grace, the daughter of a lighthouse keeper on the English coast, had helped her reluctant father save five persons from the steamer *Forfarshire* wrecked off the Farne Islands in 1838.

At home in the Lime Rock Lighthouse with her parents, Ida Lewis gazes out upon Newport Harbor.

Regardless of Wordsworth's poem immortalizing the event, there were those on this side of the Atlantic who claimed Grace should be remembered, instead, as the "Ida Lewis of England."

Visited on her lonely perch by statesmen, industrialists, military and naval leaders and destined to be honored by Congress, Ida nevertheless remained deaf to the hosannas of praise. In fact, she was probably annoyed by all the fuss. A Washington politician wrote requesting a lock of hair. He had to be content with three strands. An Indiana man asked for autographs to sell at a fair benefiting widows and orphans of the Grand Army of the Republic. These are just two examples of the hundreds of letters she received. The more commercial marketed Ida Lewis hats and scarfs. The Ida Lewis waltz became a favorite. Marriage proposals poured in. A West Point cadet sent his father to plead his case in vain. The cadet, said Ida, "was a young thing and too adolescent to be lovable." Besides, she was already engaged to William H. Wilson, a Connecticut yacht captain.

With her popularity at full throttle, Ida was offered $1,500 a month to go on the stage. She refused—the Yankee in her said no. But if she wouldn't go to the people, they would come to her. In the year 1869 she welcomed 9,000 unsought visitors. Even those famous in their own right came to marvel at this feminine St. Luke. Admiral George Dewey, General William T. Sherman, Susan B. Anthony and Vice President Schuyler Colfax arrived to shake her hand. President Ulysses S. Grant, on a Newport tour, invited her over for a chat. Whatever these luminaries said has been forgotten by history.

The honors she so richly deserved now descended on her in abundance. Several societies struck off medals, including the Massachusetts Humane Society, which presented the award for the first time to an outsider. These were exhibited at the Chicago World's Fair in 1893. The Federal Government established a special citation for lifesavers and made Ida the first recipient. Andrew Carnegie put her on his pension list, which meant $30 a month. In 1879, Congress appointed Ida the official lighthouse keeper—her parents being dead—at the munificent sum of $750 a year. Her bed was placed so that she could be sure the light was always burning. "It is my child," she would say, "and I know when it needs me even if I sleep."

A generally warmhearted person, there were two types of people she particularly disliked: the practical jokers who would yell, "Help!" in the middle of the night, and the tourist guides who pointed her out and announced, "There's Ida Lewis. She's 100 years old," when she wasn't quite 70.

In 1911, a minor government employee admonished Ida, virtually forgotten except by a few friends, on trifling mistakes in her reports. On October 19, it was incorrectly disclosed that the lighthouse would be abolished and Ida relieved of duty. Two days later the accumulated worry resulted in a stroke. Never regaining consciousness she died on October 24 at 69.

More than 1400 people viewed the body in Thames Street Methodist Church which was inadequate to accommodate the large crowd gathered for the funeral. Throughout Newport, flags were flown at half staff. In the family plot in the Farewell Street cemetery, a tombstone with an anchor and crossed oars marks her grave.

In a sense, Ida wrote her own epitaph. In an interview just before she died, she told a reporter: "If there were some people out there who needed help, I would get into my boat and go to them even if I knew I couldn't get back. Wouldn't you?"   END

An Avalanche at Willey's Slide

I always thought avalanches roared—but this one whispered. It engulfed me, pushed my feet out from under me, and enveloped me in darkness . . .

by Robert D. Hall, Jr.

IN CRAWFORD NOTCH, NEW HAMPSHIRE, THERE occurred a chilling event in 1826 which Nathaniel Hawthorne recounted in his *Twice-Told Tales*. In that year a great landslide came down from the mountain behind the home of the Willey family. Hearing the roar of the mighty avalanche of mud and rock, the entire family rushed from their house to what they thought was safer ground. But all were crushed beneath the rubble. When would-be rescuers arrived at the site the next day, they found the house intact and without damage. A huge boulder that stood just behind the house had temporarily diverted the slide into two streams that circled the Willeys' homestead, then flowed together again farther on, burying every member of the family.

The scar from that great avalanche of nearly 150 years ago is still borne by the mountain, and today it is known as Willey's Slide. It is a vertical concave wall of rock that rises nearly 1000 feet above the timberline and in winter is coated with a mantle of blue ice, several feet thick. Because the center of the slide area is almost perpendicular, the great snowfalls that come to this part of the country every winter do not cling to the ice. Rather, the snow masses on the top of the mountain, at both sides of the ice wall, and at the base.

It was to this place that I came to climb on the ice in February of 1972.

I had just finished strapping on my crampons and was getting ready to leave the bivouac area in the snow to the left of the ice wall when the avalanche hit me. The other climbers were already out on the ice face, getting the feel of their crampons. I didn't hear anything except the warning shout:

"S L I D E !"

I always thought avalanches roared . . . but this one whispered.

My hand moved instinctively towards my ice axe which I had stuck in the snow next to me. Simultaneously, I glanced up and saw the avalanche wave break against the prow of the granite boulder I stood beside. At first I thought I could stand up against that hissing

Ice climbing at Crawford Notch, New Hampshire.
Photo by F. A. Bavendam

white breaker, so I braced my back against it. (I hadn't been able to reach my ice axe in time.)

The force that hit me was incredible. It engulfed me . . . pushed my feet out from under me . . . plucked me from beside the boulder . . . and carried me down the mountainside. I was immediately enveloped in darkness. Yet, incredibly, so it seemed, I was able to breathe normally. (Later, I found out that avalanche victims can breathe in light, dry snow which traps air around it. It is only heavy, wet snow which suffocates its victims.)

I remembered to try to bend my knees. Instructors from the Appalachian Mountain Club, from whom I had learned my mountaineering skills, had taught me to keep my crampons up in the event of a slide. This was to prevent the crampons from catching on an obstacle and breaking your leg. But I couldn't bend my knees. The snow that encased me was too heavy and my momentum too fast. I couldn't even perform the recommended swimming motions one is supposed to use to get out of an avalanche. Instead, the snow and the speed were actually forcing my legs down and out . . . straight . . . like two wooden matchsticks.

Suddenly, my left leg hit something and I felt my bones snap. I was held against the pressure of the sliding snow, spun around sideways, and pulled up to the surface. I lay there in daylight again, looking up at the sky as a few last trails of snow slid across my face.

Somewhere beneath the snow, my left leg ached.

"Is everybody all right?"

"Who got caught?"

"Anybody missing?"

There were about 15 climbers out on the ice and they had all started down and were heading toward me. I found my voice.

"I'm over here . . . and I think I've got a broken leg."

Cautiously they approached me. The snow which had buried me could start sliding again. So they terraced it by digging a platform around me and bracing it with snowshoes. Equipment stuck out of the snow all over the area. Snowshoes . . . knapsacks . . . clothing . . . all the things the climbers had left in the "safe" bivouac area. Now, like me, these things were buried and had to be dug out.

An Appalachian Mountain Club member took charge of the rescue operations. (Fortunately for me, he was leading a group of climbers on Willey's Slide that day.) He asked me to describe the locations of my arms and legs. Since all of the climbers were wearing crampons, it was imperative that they knew where my limbs were so they wouldn't inadvertently step on me with their spear-like crampon points.

I told the leader that both my arms were beside my body and that my right leg was extended straight out from my hip, but I could not pinpoint the exact location of my left leg. It just seemed to be twisted under me somewhere off to the side.

A group of climbers dug around me with their hands and snowshoes and in a short time had uncovered my entire body from the snow blanket which had been over me. My arms and right leg were located where I had indicated. But my left leg had been buried about two feet below my hips. It was bent at the knee, then the lower leg and foot took a peculiar twist which terminated where my crampon was caught in the branch of a fir tree.

I couldn't see my left leg because of my position in the snow. I only knew that it was broken and I was beginning to feel a throbbing pain.

The A.M.C. leader sent two men down the mountain to the parking area with instructions to bring up the Stokes litter and the first aid kit which were kept there for emergencies. Down and back would take about an hour. In the meantime, I needed something for the pain

down and out straight—like two wooden matchsticks . . .

in my leg. Someone had a small first aid kit in his pack and gave me the painkiller that was in it. That helped.

I was lying on the cold snow and getting colder by the minute. It had also started to snow, and I was being coated with white again. Some of the climbers took off their down jackets and covered me with them. Nevertheless, I couldn't get warm or stop shivering. Because of the position of my broken leg they didn't dare move me without a splint on it, so they were not able to put anything under me. I just shivered!

While the climbers waited for the litter to be brought up, they probed for and gathered up their scattered equipment. The leader stuck an ice axe in the snow next to my left foot as a marker to warn the climbers away from it. Because of the falling snow, my left leg was covered with white and difficult to see.

Once in a while someone would come over and offer me a piece of orange or a drink of water. In an effort to keep me warm and to keep the falling snow off me, the leader had one of the climbers lie next to me and then covered us with a large poncho. The hope was that his body heat would help warm me. It didn't.

The litter bearers finally arrived. The leader immediately took the first aid kit and began to minister to my leg. I could not see what he was doing, but I could feel his competent hands at work. He cut off my gaiter so he could unstrap the crampon. Then he cut the lacings on my boot and removed it. As he worked, I felt only a few brief flashes of pain. Then he wrapped an inflatable splint around my leg, zippered it up, and began to inflate it. As he blew into the valve, I could feel my leg relax into a normal position.

Next, they put some down jackets on the bottom of the metal litter that was to be my transport down the mountain and to the hospital. Then four men lined up on each side of me and, at a command from the leader, lifted me from the snow and lowered me into the litter.

I had practiced mountain-rescue routine with the Appalachian Mountain Club several times in the past so I followed their movements with interest. (Strap the head so it cannot move. Tie down each foot. Secure the arms and legs. Tie in the torso. Make certain the whole body is immobile; in the event the litter is dropped, the victim won't fall out.) In practice, after the victim has been trussed in, the litter is turned on end to prove the strength of the ties. Mercifully, the climbers didn't test their ties by turning *my* litter on end.

Instead, they organized themselves into three teams of four men each. One team got on each side of the litter and lifted it. A team went in front to guide the litter and break the trail. When a carrying team tired, they put the litter down and shifted position with the lead team. The usual trip down the mountain from Willey's Slide took about 15 or 20 minutes. Hampered as they were by the weight of the litter and their lack of snowshoes, this trip took over an hour.

They finally got me down the mountain and out to Route 302. Here a van outfitted as a camper was waiting for us. The climbers opened the door and slid the litter in. I thanked them all as best I could. Then the leader got in front with the driver and another climber got in back with me. He immediately went to work to get me as comfortable as possible, covering me with blankets to replace the down jackets that had covered me on the trip down the mountain, then brewing hot chocolate on a small portable camp stove. Gradually I got warmer and stopped shivering.

The van owner had tied nylon slings to the roof struts of his van. As we drove towards the Memorial Hospital in North Conway, those slings rocked rhythmically back and forth just like subway hanger straps. I was getting drowsy. Soon I would be safe in the hospital. I had survived an avalanche on Willey's Slide.　　END

The Romance of Molly Finney

IT WAS A BEAUTIFUL WARM DAY ON THE COAST OF Maine in June, 1756. Casco Bay was always at its best in June, or so it seemed to Molly Finney. She watched the gathering shadows before she went inside to join her sister's family. She had lived with her sister and her brother-in-law, Thomas Mean, ever since her parents had died in the epidemic three years before.

Molly was a pretty girl, lithe and dark-complexioned, and knew her prettiness too, as maidens often do. But she was unspoiled by the attentions of admiring young men she met at the trading post, or at the blockhouse in nearby Freeport. Her cheeks still blushed with modesty at their glances.

The Means were her family now. Never would she willfully bring them worry, and she loved their three children as though they were her own. As she sat by the fire that night, the family talk turned to the possibility of an Indian raid. Everyone was a little more anxious than usual for there had been reports of Indians in the neighborhood. Already some of the settlers had removed their families to the blockhouse as a precaution.

But Thomas lived near enough to the place of refuge so he felt he could wait to move his family until such time as an Indian had actually been seen in the vicinity of his house. He had worked hard to clear some land of timber and his log cabin was strong and comfortable. The vegetable garden showed good promise and the grain was lush and green. It was hard to think of leaving it now when everything needed attention.

Molly studied his face as he stared into the flames. He wasn't listening to what the others were saying, yet it was unusual for him to remain so quiet. Molly hadn't been told about the messenger who had stopped by during the day with word that redskins had been seen near his house. Thomas had thought it better not to alarm his family. As darkness gathered, however, he began to wonder whether after all he should have moved his family to the blockhouse before dark.

"Mother," Thomas said to his wife at last, "have everything ready to load up tomorrow morning. We must be off before sunrise." He hesitated. "I almost wish we had gone today."

Later, Thomas bolted each door and nailed the windows shut. Then he put out the fire and barricaded the fireplace against any unwelcome guest. Soon the cabin was quiet except for the heavy breathing of the sleepers.

It was nearly midnight when five or six dark forms crept toward the cabin, weapons in hand. Quietly they worked the bolt from one of the doors and crept inside the cabin. One of the children, Alice, was the first to waken. With a scream at the sight of the Indians in the cabin, she leaped from her bed and escaped through the open door into the dense bushes outside. At first a savage started to follow her. Then he decided to remain with the others.

Thomas was hardly aware of what was happening when he was dragged from his bed into the night air outside. The other members of the family heard the shot which ended his misery. Molly rushed from her room clad only in her night clothes and made a frantic dash for freedom. But one of the savages saw her and brought her back. She was to be taken to Quebec in captivity.

Mrs. Mean clasped her baby boy in her arms and attempted to bolt the door to the adjoining room where she sought refuge. But a ball from the Indian's rifle came crashing through the open crack and found its target in the infant's body. Laying the baby upon the bed, she suc-

**It was nearly midnight when
six dark forms crept towards
the cabin, weapons in hand . . .**

by Louise Hale Johnson

ceeded in barricading the door before the Indian could reload his rifle. Quickly she called upon friends and neighbors as though they were in the room with her, giving the impression that the house was well fortified.

"Martin, shoot from the back window," she called. "Thompson, fire from your window. Kerns and Brown, hurry and lock the door so they can't get out."

Martin did fire, wounding an Indian. Frightened, the savages took refuge in the woods, taking Molly with them. At dawn there were only Martin, Mrs. Mean, and the two children to make the trip to the blockhouse.

With a blanket which one of the Indians had thrown over her shoulders for protection from the night air, Molly was marched to the northwest.

They had traveled for several weeks and were in sight of Quebec, when one day Molly overheard the Indians talking in their broken English about selling her as a servant-slave. She had heard many stories of the Indian practice of capturing white women and girls to sell as servants to the French. (The men were more valuable dead. Their scalps brought a heavy bounty.) She froze with terror at the thought of being sold to be a servant. But even that would be better than being held captive by the Indians.

The party had halted in the center of the city but a short time when a bowed old Frenchman shuffled up to the chief. He pointed to Molly, and she saw the chief nod his head. The old man looked her over carefully before he offered a price for her. His offer was accepted and, taking her by the hand, he led her away. Molly stumbled over the stony path in her ill-fitting moccasins.

Her owner proved to be a wealthy old man, with much land to be farmed. At first Molly was put in the fields to weed and prune, but later she was switched to kitchen work, much to her relief. Not only was she a good cook, but she enjoyed cooking. If she must spend the rest of her life as a slave, this was what she would have chosen to do.

In September, 1757, an English trading vessel, the *Rose*, nosed her way along the Atlantic coast and down the St. Lawrence River. Aided by the winds, she found her way to the wharf at Quebec, a pretty sight in full sail. She was a beautiful cruiser, fitted for long journeys and rough seas. Captain McLellan was in command, and he had long been anxious to visit the famous French city of Quebec in Canada.

He explained to his crewmen that Quebec had much to offer for trade in Indian wares and other articles of merchandise. But he didn't explain to them that recently, when the ship had been docked at the town of Freeport, Maine, a woman by the name of Mrs. Mean had sought him out. She told him she was making a habit of talking about her sister's capture to every sea captain who came to town. A while ago an Indian had arrived at Freeport with the news of Molly's captivity in Quebec. Surely, Mrs. Mean had said to Captain McLellan, there must be someone, somewhere, who would help her find her sister.

Captain McLellan had listened to her story with interest. When he looked into her sad face, his heart was filled with compassion.

"Mrs. Mean," he said, taking her frail hand in his, "if it can be done, I shall go to Quebec and try to find your sister. If I can find her, I shall bring her home to you."

Once the *Rose* was docked at Quebec, Captain McLellan made his way to the hotel. If Molly's whereabouts were known to anyone, surely this would be at the hotel. The landlord

187

waited while the captain signed the register.

"By the way," Captain McLellan asked as he laid down the quill, "Would you happen to have heard of an English girl in these parts named Molly Finney?"

"Feeney? Feeney?" the landlord asked in broken English. "Oh, yez—she iz a servant of a wealthy Frenchman. His name is Monsieur Lemoine. Oh yez—he bought her from ze Indians, over a year ago. I understand she iz a beautiful girl, but no one ever sees her." The landlord was enjoying the feeling of importance which possession of the information gave him. "There iz a young man in town who would like to see her, but Monsieur keeps her locked up in ze house. Never iz she allowed to leave it. Do you know her?"

"I have heard of her. I'd like to meet her some day."

"Oh no! That you cannot do. She isn't allowed to go out of ze house unless a member of the family iz with her, and that has only been once or twice since she went there. At night ze old tyrant locks her door on the outside and keeps ze key.

"I am told she iz not only very beautiful, but that she iz also shy and timid. She has not been about in ze world. But why are you so interested?" he asked.

"Just curiosity." The captain turned away to go to his room for the night. Then he looked back at the landlord. "By the way," he said, "Where did you say this Monsieur Lemoine lives?"

The landlord pointed down the street. "Right down there, but take my advice. Don't go there."

The next morning Molly was alone in the kitchen. The soft knock at the half-open door startled her. She looked up to see a stranger dressed in the uniform of an English sea captain. Without speaking, he stepped into the kitchen. Molly jumped back and was about to cry out for help, when he cautioned her to silence.

"Sh—not a word." Removing his cap, he bowed low. Molly noted his fine features and the warm smile about his mouth. She liked his gallant manners.

"Are you Molly Finney?" he asked softly.

Molly nodded, unable to speak.

"Do not be frightened." His voice was calm and reassuring. "I am commander of the ship which came into port last night. I have a message for you." He took a paper from his inside pocket. "Read it carefully. You will find directions inside."

Then he left as quietly as he had entered. Her heart pounding, Molly watched him hurrying down the street. Now her thinking was more clear. She went into the pantry and closed the door so no one could see as she read the note.

> Miss Molly Finney—
> Your sister, Mrs. Mean, of Freeport, Maine, has sent me to your rescue. I am captain of the Rose, an English trader, and I can carry you home to your relatives if it is possible to get you out of the house. Let me know if it is possible for me to talk with you. I will pass this door this afternoon at five o'clock. Have your answer ready at that time. Your friend, William McLellan.

Quickly she stuffed the letter into her pocket. She tried not to seem excited or gay until her first chance to go to her room alone. Then, hiding in the closet, she hurried to write her answer.

> Captain Wm. McLellan—
> I cannot express my gratitude for your kindness. Monsieur Lemoine is constantly watching me. Do not pass the house too often, or he will be suspicious. If you will come beneath the second story window overlooking the alley tonight at midnight, I will come to the window and perhaps you can talk. Do not speak above a whisper. Gratefully, Molly Finney.

That evening as the clock struck five, Molly looked out of the kitchen door. The captain was walking slowly past the house. At precisely the same moment, Molly took the broom from behind the kitchen door and hastened out to sweep the leaves from the sidewalk. She swept in his direction without looking up. Among the leaves was a tiny piece of white paper which rested at the captain's feet. He stooped to pick it up. Without looking at Molly, he stuffed it into his pocket and sauntered down the street. Finishing her sweeping, she returned to the kitchen.

When Molly's work for the day was finished and she was once more back in her room, she opened the window on the alley. Then she sat inside to wait for the hour of ten. For that was the time each night when her master came to lock her in her room. For the first time since she had been his slave, she was happy to hear the sound of his shuffling feet. In his high squeaking voice he called.

"Molly! You in ze room?"

"Yes, sir," Molly answered in a sleepy voice, "I'm here."

Molly waited for the sound of the key turning in the lock. Then putting her ear to the door, she listened to the sound of disappearing footsteps and for the closing of a door. With cheeks burning from excitement, she moved her chair nearer to the window and waited. At the stroke of midnight there was a dark figure moving along the fence by the alley. It stopped beneath her window.

"Molly?" She heard the soft whisper.

"I'm here."

"Is there anyone in the room below you?"

"No. That's the kitchen. I'm alone, locked in."

"Good. Can you fasten a rope to something?"

Molly looked back into the room. "Yes. The bedpost. It's a big heavy bed."

"Fine. I brought a rope. Catch it and tie it securely." Molly reached out and caught the coiled rope.

"When you are ready, slide down easy. I'll be here to catch you."

Molly fastened the rope about the bedstead, climbed to the window ledge, and slid to the ground. Without a word, the captain took her hand and led her to the wharf. There a yawl was waiting, manned by two crewmen who held well-padded oars. They slid over the water to where the *Rose* was riding at anchor.

The sail to Freeport was a smooth run. On both sides of the St. Lawrence River was scenery such as Molly had never seen. Trees, hills, valleys, inlets. She went from one side of the boat to the other, lest she should miss some of the beauty about her. At last, anchor was dropped in Casco Bay.

When Molly had been reunited with her family and friends, her heart was filled with misgivings. Each time Captain McLellan came to the cabin she was sure he had come to say good-by. For there was nothing now to keep him and his skillful crew from heading back to sea and adventure.

As they sat alone in the twilight outside the cabin door one evening, she noticed the tinge of gray which was beginning to show at the sides of his head of wavy black hair. It made him even more handsome. How, she thought, was she going to be able to bid him farewell when the time came, as come it must? His kindness, his gentleness, she could never forget. The captain met her gaze. He covered her hand with his and felt the shiver which rushed through her body.

"Molly," he said, "I've been sailing the seas most of my life, until it seems to me the sea is such a lonely place." With his handkerchief, he wiped his brow.

Molly felt her cheeks turning crimson. "I didn't think the sea was lonely when we came from Quebec to Casco Bay. It was a beautiful trip, and I shall never forget it."

"That's just it. This last trip was different. For the first time in a long while, I wasn't lonely either." He took her face between his hands and looked into her eyes. "Do you suppose it could be because you were aboard?"

Molly smiled at his faltering words.

"Hang it all, Molly," he blurted out. "All of the trips would be beautiful if you were aboard —even the storms would be easier to ride out. Won't you be the captain's wife and help him guide the vessel, always?"

In answer, Molly put her hot cheek against his face.

When the *Rose* lifted anchor and headed out to sea a few days later, Molly stood upon the deck, radiant and laughing as she waved farewell to those on shore. Beside her, tall and proud to be her husband, stood the captain, his strong arm about her shoulders.

The people of Freeport still like to tell about the younger generations of McLellans and Means, some of whom loved to roam the seas seeking fortune and adventure, and the others who returned to the region about Freeport to settle and make their way through life in Maine's hills and vales. END

7.
BANKS, BURGLARS AND BURIALS

The End of Mr. XYZ
The Bookworm Burglar
Northampton's Million-Dollar Heist
Stockbridge Loved Him
All about the Concord Bank Robbery

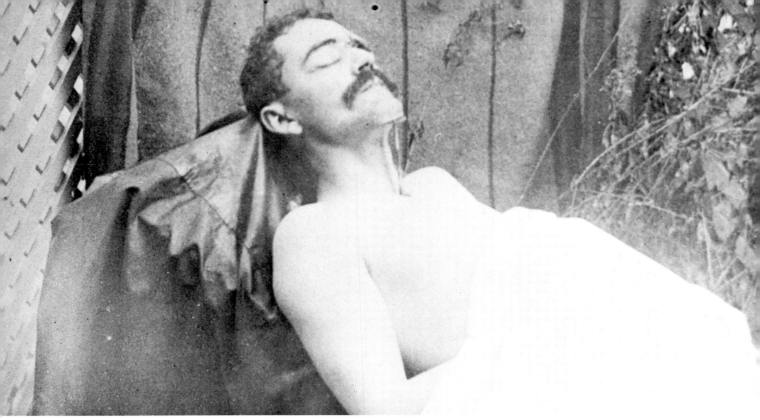

Above: "Mr. XYZ" laid out in La Place's Undertaking Rooms after the attempted burglary. *Courtesy Henry Josten.*

Below: The old Deep River Savings Bank. Night Guard Tyler aimed his Winchester through the far window on the left side of the photo. *Courtesy Deep River Savings Bank.*

by Allegra Batchelor

The End of Mr. XYZ

A robber lay dead under the north window, deserted by his pals. He was young, with dark curly hair and a dark moustache.

IF YOU HAPPEN TO BE A DIGNITARY IN THE BUSY village of Deep River, on the banks of the Connecticut—or if your credentials are in order—the Secretary of the Deep River Savings Bank will give you an amiable tour of his handsome establishment. Your tour will end in the Directors' Room. You will see, hanging in lone grandeur against the richly paneled wall, a Winchester Model 97 shotgun—polished and well oiled. The story goes back to the winter of 1899 and a lonely grave in beautiful Fountain Hill Cemetery.

On January 2nd of that year, bank president Asa Shailer was opening his morning's mail . . . a routine job done with deliberation. Then Shailer opened a letter that sent him into quick action. The letter was from the Protective Committee of the American Bankers Association, New York City. Marked "confidential," it read:

> We are today in receipt of information obtained confidentially by our detective agency, showing that a band of burglars is being organized to operate on banks in Connecticut. Your bank and the Deep River National Bank are mentioned as institutions upon which attack is contemplated. As a member of the Association we extend you the information as we have received it, and for such precautionary action as you may think best.

Shailer called an emergency session of his Board.

"Precautionary action" was taken. Bank officials secretly dispatched a man to the Winchester Arms Company in New Haven to purchase a weapon. A night guard was set up. Tapped for the job was one Harry D. Tyler, something of a local hero. Two years previous-

ly, Tyler had captured a midnight thief in the village general store after the intruder had knocked him down with a chair. Word got around that the bank was being guarded. Bank officials were noncommittal and outwardly unconcerned. Villagers wondered. But nothing disturbed the peace of Deep River.

Four weeks later came a second communication from the Bankers Association:

> Referring to our confidential letter of January 31, in which we mentioned that a band of burglars was being organized to operate in Connecticut, we beg to add for your information that our detective agency has been further advised that these burglars are contemplating an attack at Deep River when the moon has waned and the nights have grown darker.

Nerves grew more taut. Tyler was admonished to maintain the highest vigilance. The moon waned and the nights grew darker. Nothing happened. Winter passed into spring. Summer came. The old elms lining Main Street took on the brilliance of fall, then lost their leaves to November.

Deep River Savings Bank, which had opened October 31, 1851, with deposits of $27.00, had by 1899 deposits of $1,343,213.19, with a surplus of $64,095.56. The Directors were aware of their responsibility. They also were mindful of previous bank burglaries in their village. Twenty-one years earlier, for example, in February of 1878, notorious bank bandit Jimmie Hope and three of his pals made a midnight entry into a sister bank. They were after the $6,000 payroll of the local ivory factory which had come down from New York that day. Fortunately, bolts

193

Above: The bank as it looks today.

Right: Harry Tyler's Winchester Model 97 shotgun still hangs in the Directors' Room of the Deep River Savings Bank.

jammed on the safe and they had to leave without their booty. Hope, who had eluded all the big-time law enforcers, had the ignominious experience of being picked up by a local constable a few days later. They lodged him in Haddam jail and held him for a long time. He conducted his own defense at the trial, mocking the court. Because they had no evidence on him —none, that is, except for his notorious reputation and the fact that he was well equipped with burglary tools—they had to let him go.

So "precautionary measures" were retained. Tyler stayed on. Villagers began to accept the bank guard as just another step in "progress."

December 13th. The early morning moonlight was hazed with fog. Shortly after one o'clock, William Stevens' dog barked. Stevens' house was about 20 rods north of the bank. From his post in the darkened Directors' Room, Tyler looked out of the window. He saw four men, near Main and High Streets, walking single file, lock step toward the bank. But Tyler was not concerned. He thought some of the young fellows of the village were planning a practical joke on him.

There were no outside shutters on the bank windows. A light was kept burning in the counting room and at the entrance of the vault at all times. The Directors' Room, across the back of the building, was kept in darkness. There were two windows in the Directors' Room—one on the north and one on the south. Inner shutters on these windows made it possible for a man to look out without being seen, but impossible for anyone to see in from the outside. From a certain point in this room, a man could look through a hall and directly out of a window in the counting room to Main Street.

As Tyler told it later that day, he took up a position in the darkened room where he had a view in the three directions. He didn't have long to wait. In a moment he saw one of the four men tiptoe up the front steps and peer into the window in the counting room. In another moment his alert eyes spotted a second man trying to peer through the window on the south. As he started noiselessly toward the south window, he heard someone at the window on the north. Wheeling, he slid to the north window

194

and, looking through the inner shutters, saw two men trying to pry the window up. The man nearest the window was using both hands. The other man, directly behind the first, was using his left hand and holding a revolver in his right. This was no joke.

Quickly retreating about ten feet, Tyler took aim, and just as he heard the window give a crack as though it were giving way, he fired, immediately stepping against the wall to avoid return fire from any of the three directions.

There followed the quietest silence he had ever heard. For a nerve-strung ten minutes he waited. Then moving cautiously toward the window he looked out through the hole torn in the shutter and glass to see a man lying on his back on the ground.

Tyler made his way to the phone and began to ring all those who had telephones to the bank. Finally, he heard an answer from hotel-keeper William Mitchell, who promised to go immediately for help.

For an anxious hour Tyler waited alone in the darkened room, keeping a constant lookout through first one window, then another. Finally the phone rang. It was Henry Wooster, bank treasurer, who lived directly across Main Street. The posse had met there. Over the wire they worked out a strategy. They would spread out, guns ready, in case any of the robbers were in hiding. Tyler volunteered to crawl out on his belly, gun ready, and investigate the layout. There was no stir, no sign of life, and they came together at the north window where the robber, deserted by his pals, lay dead.

He was a young man, around thirty, rather good-looking, about five feet four, with dark curly hair and a dark moustache. He was dressed in a dark suit and coat. He lay where he had fallen backward, with his arms thrown back and one knee slightly drawn up. Tyler's Winchester riot gun had put several bullet holes in his forehead; his left eye was gouged out; blood and brains oozed from the left side of his head.

A quick search was made for identification. In his pocket was found a copy of the *Springfield Republican*, a Waltham silver watch with gold-plated chain, six Morse steel twist drills, a safety fuse and soap preparation for tamping the fuse in, dynamite cartridges—and a dollar bill and two dimes. One hope of a clue was found in a money-order receipt which had been issued nine days earlier from a Springfield post office.

Sticking in the window were two new 18-inch ship's carpenter chisels with which the robbers had been attempting to pry up the window. Strangely enough, the chisels were later found to have been stolen from Harry Tyler's own boathouse.

The body was taken to LaPlace's Undertaking Rooms. As news of the affair spread, the village overflowed with the excited and curious. So great was the jam trying to see the body that doors to the undertaking rooms had to be locked several times during the day. But the dead man was a stranger to all, and the crowd turned its interest to the guard. Tyler was a hero.

Deputy Sheriff William Smith of Saybrook summoned a coroner's jury, but had to hold up until one of the jurors got down from Middletown on the 3:15. There was no delay in the jury's findings. The still-unidentified man "had been shot and killed while trying to make entry into the bank. He was a professional burglar as evidenced by the tools on his person. Tyler was justified." Tyler was also rewarded—with a $500 check from grateful bank officials.

The three who got away left no clues. M. D. Hollister, prosperous Glastonbury farmer, reported that a tired-looking fellow stopped by his place the day after the attempted robbery, looking for a job. And Dr. Webb, of Madison, reported that early the morning of the robbery, his man, Willard, saw two men in a buggy driving west and running their horse, which was all in a foam. But nothing resulted from either "tip."

The money order receipt in the bandit's pocket revealed that one P. E. King of Worcester had sent money to a T. J. Farley at Albany. Farley, a bartender, was located in a dive called "The Skates" in the tenderloin district of Albany. He said that P. E. King had been a brakeman on the Boston and Albany Railroad, and he had loaned him money. But no trace of King could be found.

Justice, not sentiment, prompted the search to learn the identity of the dead bandit. The Connecticut Yankee, at the turn of the century,

was not bothered with a sob-sister complex. Communications pouring into the Deep River Bank revealed the stern Yankee traits of moral wrath, understatement, brevity, an eye to business, and the prudence of always "having God on your side."

The National Council of Congregational Churches sent a grim message: "When the rascals learn that it is sure death to attempt to crack one of our banks, we need not worry about our deposits."

The Newton Theological Institute of Newton Center, Massachusetts sent word that "it is a pleasure to know that there is one place of a kind where 'thieves do not break through nor steal'."

From other banks throughout the area came such messages as:

"You have a very serviceable watchman."

"Congratulations on the salutary lesson taught to others in that line of business."

"Pleased to learn there is one less bandit in the State."

"Congratulations on having held on to your surplus."

"When they face a loaded shotgun it makes them thoughtful."

And the New Haven Savings Bank didn't forget God. They sent "praise for kind Providence for providing the moonlight for an accurate aim on the fiendish intruders."

But justice was tempered with mercy and a place was allocated for the remains, overlooking the Connecticut River in Fountain Hill Cemetery, whose founders were substantially the same as the founders of the Savings Bank.

So the lawless one went to an unidentified grave. Two men and three women were in the funeral procession when his body was transported in an ordinary business wagon from the cemetery vault to a spot on the hillside overlooking the Cove.

Shortly thereafter, Tyler received an unsigned letter requesting that he put a marker over the grave inscribed with the letters "X Y Z." Generously, he complied, erecting a plain board slab with the requested lettering scratched on it. Years later this board was replaced with a stone marker, flush with the ground, and bearing the same "X Y Z" inscription. Today the stone is erect, stands a foot above the ground, and these letters are chiseled on both the top and the front. A bouquet of artificial flowers is on the grave.

It is said that for over 40 years a lone woman made an annual pilgrimage to the handsome bandit's grave. Getting off one of the Valley railroad trains, she would walk the tracks from the Deep River station and enter the cemetery from the back to place her flowers in remembrance of the man known as "X Y Z." She was never intercepted.

Local skeptics are inclined to scoff at the "every year" legend. But even the most skeptical do admit that at various times for several years an unknown woman, dressed in black, left her floral token of compassion or love at the grave of the unidentified robber.

Today, up-to-date "precautions" are taken at the handsome modern home of the Deep River Savings Bank, with cameras and alarms wired right into the police barracks. But hanging on the wall of the Directors' Room—a symbol of the alertness and sense of responsibility of bank officials—is the Winchester shotgun which stopped a burglary and sent a bandit to an X Y Z grave, back in 1899. END

Final resting place of the still unidentified bandit XYZ.

The Bookworm Burglar

**Upright Clarence Adams was a mousy,
studious fellow who doted on books—particularly books on
murder and crime, detective work, black magic, necromancy
and other such bloodcurdling lore . . .**

In Chester, Vermont, bearded bachelor Clarence A. Adams was respectability personified. Owner of a prosperous farm on the outskirts, he bought lollipops for the kids and served the town variously as assessor, selectman, member of the legislature and chief trustee of the library. This last job was his perennially, for he was a mousy, studious fellow who doted on books. While he kept the local library stocked with upstanding works, he had a choice collection of his own that was considered a mite racy in the eighties.

The upright Adams owned some 700 books devoted to murder and other misdoings, detective work, black magic, hypnotism, necromancy and such suspect arts. Now and then he would pop off to Boston, to return with a sedate set of Emerson or Wordsworth for the Chester library, and a bloodcurdling account of Jack-the-Ripper or Burke and Hare for his own delectation. Townspeople had to chuckle about that—such a mild fellow steeping himself in gore!

In 1886 the normally placid town began to be afflicted with what later became known as the Sixteen-Year Crime Wave. Once or twice a month a store or factory would be looted. Now and then a nocturnal wayfarer would be held up. Several times the grocery of Elijah Peck was entered, the swag each time being nothing more than a cheese or a sack of flour. J. E. Pollard's clothing store occasionally lost a suit of clothes, size 38. The Acme Bakery repeatedly found all their crullers gone, making it plain that the culprit liked to munch. A regular victim was C. H. Waterman, whose feed store was invaded again and again, with the loss of a couple bags of grain each time.

Although this was petty thievery, the merchants got almighty tired of it, as did the police. Mysteriously, in no case was there any evidence of forcible entry, making it appear that the marauder had a ghostly ability to wriggle through keyholes. Not until almost two years later was it discovered that he was a slick man with a screwdriver. He simply unscrewed the entire lock, entered, then replaced the lock carefully before leaving. Waterman installed a patent lock with no screws showing, with the result that the door was jimmied and the lock ruined. After that he fell back on regular locks.

Clarence Adams, a friend of all the victims, owned the works of Poe, Gaboriau and a recent writer about a detective named Sherlock Holmes. He considered himself something of an amateur sleuth, and after each robbery he would visit the scene with his notebook and get under the policemen's feet as he searched for clues. People snickered at the innocent Adams in the role of investigator, but it had to be admitted that he had as much success as the authorities, which was none at all. Years passed. Occasionally a tramp would be jailed, but the depredations continued.

In 1895 Pollard's store was entered for the eighth time, this time with the loss of $200 worth of clothing. Enraged, Pollard offered a $50 reward, with Adams helping him distribute the posters. Four nights later, three masked men entered Pollard's house and, as if irritated by his reward offer, robbed him and his wife of some

$42.00 and some jewelry. The sheriff and the local police were catching Hail Columbia. They tried setting traps, to no avail. Waterman's feed store was still being raided. On Adams' advice he hired a night watchman, which stopped the robberies but cost him more than the trivial loot he saved. After two months he fired the watchman—and the very next night three bags of feed were stolen.

It seemed that the thief must be an insider who knew what was going on in town. People began to look at each other suspiciously. Adams, much concerned, conferred with the sheriff about hiring a private detective from Boston, but the plan was dropped for lack of funds. There were several intervals of three or four months when the robberies ceased, causing the townsfolk to hope that the plague was over—a vain hope, blasted when the depredations resumed with fresh energy. By 1902, when Waterman's feed store was entered feloniously for the twenty-fourth time, Waterman was hopping mad.

Giving up on the police, in July of 1902, Waterman devised a trap. Each night when he closed up, he left his shotgun propped and aimed at the back door, the one invariably entered, with an elaborate string arrangement that would pull the trigger and blaze away at any skulker entering. He kept this a secret. It was a fussy job that had to be done just right, and it took him a half-hour each evening. After two weeks of this with no success, he was about to quit. However, on the morning of July 30 he was pleased to see that the door had been entered and there was a stain of blood on the floor.

The ghost had been hit, all right, but not so badly but what he was able to get away. The trail of blood petered out in the alley. Waterman hot-footed it to the police and told them to look for a man carrying a load of birdshot.

It happened that Clarence Adams was to close a deal for a parcel of land at the bank at ten that morning. When he did not show up, a boy was sent for him. The boy found Adams in bed with a wounded leg. Although he said he had fallen off a ladder, the news got around and the police made some deductions. Adams wore about a size 38 suit. He was fond of crullers. A check of the records disclosed that there had been no robberies when Adams was away in Montpelier at sessions of the legislature. A search of the Adams barn clinched the case, for much of the loot was found in the loft.

Arrested, Adams admitted his guilt as a doctor picked birdshot out of his leg. The scandal in Chester was considerable. Meek Clarence Adams, stealing the town blind for 16 years while he was nurturing the young and holding positions of public trust! Newspapers all over New England headlined the story. The fact that he was prosperous and actually had made no use of most of his booty added piquancy to the mystery. His uncle, solid Samuel Adams, demanded why he had stolen things he did not need.

"I got a thrill out of it, Sam," he said sadly. "You have no idea what sport it was, robbing those places. And to listen to the police and other folks trying to figure it out—well, that was rich."

Life had been dull for him until he took up night-raiding, he admitted. The idea entered his mind from the criminal exploits he had read about in his own library. One of his well-thumbed books, it was noted, was "Dr. Jekyll and Mr. Hyde." His good friends Waterman, Pollard and the rest couldn't see the joke. Put on trial three weeks later, Adams confessed all the one-man jobs. However, he denied knowledge of the three-man robbery at the Pollard home and several similar crimes, making it apparent that he was shielding his accomplices. He got ten years at the state prison at Windsor,

while his several relatives in Chester tried to hold their heads up and explain that Clarence always was a little odd.

In fact, his oddities were not yet finished. At the prison, where he was regarded as a harmless freak, Warden Oakes naturally put him in charge of the library and allowed him to bring his own collection of books. He became friendly with another inmate, a physician we shall call Henry Jepson, who had been imprisoned for performing an illegal operation. The two began reading up on hypnosis. The state saved money in a canny Yankee way by letting Dr. Jepson handle routine sickness among the convicts, calling in a Windsor physician, Dr. John Brewster, only once weekly.

On February 21, 1904, when Brewster called, he found Adams, now 53 years old, bedded in the infirmary complaining of a severe cold. He ministered to the patient, then left him in the care of Doc Jepson. Two days later Adams was moaning piteously, so sure he was going to die that he made his will. On the 26th, Jepson reported that Adams had died of pneumonia and made out a death certificate, which Dr. Brewster signed without investigation. In his will, Adams wanted no truck with undertakers, asking that "my dear friend Jepson" prepare the body for burial and then hand it over to another friend, Elias Dunn, for interment.

These instructions were followed. Jepson prepared the body, Dunn called for it, and it was carted to Chester for a brief ceremony attended by only a few of the Adams clan, who were still irked by the scandal Clarence had caused. Then Dunn took the body to the family graveyard at Cavendish, north of Chester, where it was placed in a vault to wait burial in the spring.

In April, a traveling salesman returned from Canada to say flatly that he had seen Clarence Adams walking down a street in Halifax. Another report had him very much alive in St. John, New Brunswick. These and other rumors bothered Uncle Samuel Adams. In May he ordered the sexton to make sure that Clarence's body was in the coffin before it was buried. The sexton took a hasty peek, saw that there was indeed a somewhat deteriorated body in the coffin, and it was duly buried in the Adams plot.

Later that year a new crop of rumors had it that Clarence was enjoying excellent health in Canada. A newspaperman had a saloon conversation with a former Windsor convict who had been friendly with both Adams and Dr. Jepson there. After a few drinks, the ex-con said of course Adams was still alive because he had never died.

According to this worthy, Adams and Jepson had studied hypnosis and catalepsy until they became proficient at it. Adams had merely faked illness, after which Jepson had put him into a state of hypnosis in which he breathed so lightly that he appeared dead. The "body" was then taken to the vault in a coffin well drilled with holes to permit the entrance of air. Adams' friend Elias Dunn was actually an old criminal pal who, like Jepson, had been paid $1000 by Adams for the deception. Dunn had secretly bought a real corpse—one intended for the medical school at nearby Dartmouth College. Using the old screwdriver system, he had returned to the vault, removed the lock, freed Adams from the coffin and put the corpse in it. He had then hustled Adams by carriage to the station at Claremont, New Hampshire, where the book-lover grabbed a train for Canada.

There was quite a stir about this. Jepson, still a guest at the prison, said the tale was pure poppycock, that Adams was dead as a doornail. Dr. Brewster, however, admitted that he had signed the death certificate after no more than a glance at the body. The sexton said he *thought* it was Adams' body in the coffin, but it developed that his vision was so poor as to be nearly extinct. Elias Dunn had vanished, and the Adams relatives did not know him.

The ex-convict who told the story suffered a change of heart after sobering and said it was only the liquor talking. Some said, however, that he was more likely to be truthful when intoxicated. There was talk of exhuming the body, but the Adams family was opposed to this and the tempest finally subsided.

Still, now and then rumors continued to drift in that Adams had been seen vigorously alive in various Canadian cities. For years Vermonters argued the matter pro and con, agreeing only on one point—dead or alive, Clarence Adams was a queer'un.   END

Northampton's Million-Dollar Heist

America's Most Daring Bank Robbery

A woman stuck her head out of the window and screamed, "Run to the bank! Robbers have carried off my husband!"

by Robert N. Linscott

Pictures courtesy Daily Hampshire Gazette, Northampton, Mass.

EARLY IN THE MORNING OF JANUARY 26, 1876, more than a million dollars in cash and securities was stolen from the "burglar-proof" vault of the Northampton (Massachusetts) National Bank. Not even the celebrated Brink's case, three-quarters of a century later, equalled it in skillful planning and in sheer melodrama. "It was," in the words of a bank examiner, "the most daring and successful bank robbery in American history."

Northampton lies on the Connecticut River in a region famous for its institutions of learning, and it is appropriate that a schoolhouse should have been the scene of the first act of the drama. Here, on the day preceding the robbery, a boy by the name of Clark was sent with a lantern into the windowless attic to mend a broken ventilator. As he was starting down the ladder, he noticed on the floor two pieces of the scrip of the period, one worth a quarter, the other a dime. That afternoon he climbed back to look for more.

Throwing his light into the far corners, he found, not money, but evidence that the attic had recently been inhabited. Eight blankets were lying on the floor, and with them were a pint of whiskey, 33 feet of new rope, pulley-blocks, a bitstock with bits of assorted sizes, a copy of the *New York Sun* dated December 22, a pair of men's drawers with one leg cut off, and

Scene of the crime, 1876.

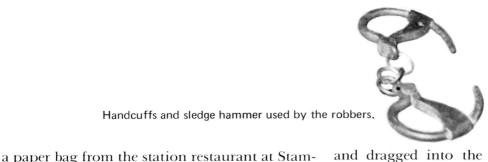

Handcuffs and sledge hammer used by the robbers.

a paper bag from the station restaurant at Stamford, Connecticut, containing a cooked chicken (far gone in decay), two apples, and a large assortment of beef and chicken sandwiches (very mouldy).

The find was reported to the teacher, who dismissed the school and sent for D. S. Potter, a Deputy Sheriff. Potter, as it happened, had been puzzling for nearly a month over another odd discovery. A woman, on her way to an early morning train, had found, across the street from the schoolhouse, a valise containing 48 large screws with rings, two pounds of heavy spikes, 100 feet of Manila rope, and a new pair of handcuffs. This strange assortment, plus the cache in the schoolhouse attic, seemed to indicate that Northampton had been entertaining some very queer visitors. But who? For what purpose?

The answer came at 6:35 the next morning. At the office of Potter's colleague, Deputy Sheriff Ansel Wright, a panting messenger arrived with the news that something strange had happened at the Whittelsey house; a woman had stuck her head out the window and screamed "Run to the bank! Robbers have carried off my husband."

Something very strange indeed had happened at the Whittelsey house. John Whittelsey, cashier of the Northampton National Bank, lived, as befitted his position, in a large and dignified home set on Northampton's elm-shaded main street, two-thirds of a mile from the bank. Seven persons—all adults—occupied the house, sleeping in five bedrooms on the second floor: Mr. Whittelsey and Mr. Cutler, a printer on the local paper; their wives; Mrs. Whittelsey's niece, Miss White; an invalid, Miss Benton; and a "kitchen girl," Kate Nugent. All were home and sleeping soundly when, shortly before two o'clock, Mr. Whittelsey was aroused by the pressure of hands on his throat and by a voice that said: "Be quiet and no harm will come to you." At the same moment the other bedrooms were broken into (three of the doors smashed with sledge hammers) and the occupants were seized and dragged into the Whittelsey bedroom, a hand over each mouth to stifle cries.

By the dim illumination of dark lanterns, the startled prisoners could see seven invaders, one for each member of the household; the first indication of the careful attention to detail with which the enterprise had been planned. Six wore overalls, with jackets to match, and masks (cut from the leg of a pair of men's drawers) pulled over their heads, with slits to see through. The seventh, the dandy of the party, sported a linen duster, a cambric mask and kid gloves. Five had sledge hammers; all wore rubbers and carried dark lanterns.

The sudden awakening to the sight of masked men and the crash of sledge hammers produced panic and hysteria. Only Mrs. Whittelsey remained calm. Realizing at once the purpose of the invasion, she slipped her watch under the bureau and told the leader he was wasting time, her husband's keys would not open the bank vault without other keys not in his possession. To this the bandit replied: "We have them."

The printer and the five women were then ordered to dress, one of the men returning to their rooms to gather up their clothing. Next, each was gagged with an ingenious contrivance made of a rubber ball the size of an egg and perforated for breathing, with an iron rod running through it, and strings at either end to tie behind the head.

Now that the household was cowed and under control, the invaders became more courteous. When the women protested that the gag strings pulled their hair, the leader gently adjusted them. And while they were dressing he had his men fetch extra stockings so that the ropes with which they were to be bound would not chafe their ankles. However, when told that one of the prisoners was ill, he brusquely replied, "There's always someone sick on these occasions." Throughout the proceedings a minimum of words was used, the leader directing his men by hisses, raps, and gestures as though every move had been rehearsed. When it was necessary for the robbers to address one another, numbers were used instead of names, the leader being "Number One."

The final step was to handcuff the women and the printer, take them into three bedrooms (two to a room) and fasten them to the beds with leather straps and rings. In addition, the wrists of each couple were tied together with ropes passed under the bed. The straps, the gags, the ropes, the handcuffs, all were taken from a carpet bag that one of the men had carried in.

With everyone thus disposed of there was a lull during which Mr. Whittelsey's gold watch and his key to the bank door were fished from his pockets, all the clocks in the house were stopped, and the bureau drawers were ransacked although nothing was taken from them. All this time, Mr. Whittelsey had been lying, prone and handcuffed, on his bed. Now, at about 3:30 A.M., his handcuffs were removed, and he was told to get dressed as he was to be taken to the bank and forced to open the vault. Instead, he was dragged downstairs and placed in a chair in the sitting room. One man stood with a pistol pointed at his head, another sat at a table with pencil and paper. The latter demanded the numbers of the combinations, of which there were three: one for the vault, one for the safe within the vault, and one for the securities box within the safe.

At first he attempted to mislead them by giving false numbers, a ruse that was quickly discovered when he was ordered to repeat them. "Talk fast," the leader said—and he could not remember them correctly. Thereupon, he was jabbed in the chest with the pencil and pummeled until, "after much suffering," as he later reported, he gave the right numbers, and repeated them until the leader was satisfied he had given them correctly. He was then gagged, blindfolded and strapped to a bed in a downstairs room.

Shortly after four o'clock, the prisoners heard three sharp raps, followed by two more, a signal, as they later discovered, that the coast was clear

and the bank unguarded. For the crucial fact the robber scouts had learned was this: the watchman for the bank and the town's two policemen on night duty all went home promptly at four o'clock every morning, not only in summer when dawn was near, but in winter when it was still two hours or more away. Before learning this, the robbers had planned to overpower the watchman and police and put them in the town lock-up. Now, in darkest January, force was no longer necessary. The thrifty town fathers and bank officials had solved the problem for them.

At the signal, three of the robbers departed, carrying the Whittelsey family's half-bushel market basket, the only property taken from the house except the watch and bank key. At 5:45, the three remaining robbers (one had left earlier to act as scout at the bank) slipped away to catch the six-o'clock train for New York. They left behind them five masks, five sledge hammers, five dark lanterns, five pairs of handcuffs, five gags, five gimlets, ten leather straps, two pairs of rubbers, and one pair of gloves with the fingers cut off.

By 6:30 the indomitable Mrs. Whittelsey had worked her mouth and feet loose, thrust her head out of a window, and cried the alarm to men on their way to work. (Unknown to her, Mr. Whittelsey was still lying, bound and gagged, in the room below.) The men ran to the bank and finding all quiet, kept on running to the police station, which was empty, and then to the office of Deputy Sheriff Wright, who had risen early that morning to catch a train. Wright ran, in turn, to the Mansion House, the town's leading hotel, to summon J. L. Warriner, Vice President of the bank.

Warriner and the Deputy Sheriff reached the bank at 6:45 and were soon joined by the unfortunate Mr. Whittelsey, still wearing his handcuffs, as he continued to do until they were filed off. At the bank all appeared to be in order. There were no signs of nocturnal visitors except for a small jimmy lying on the floor. However, when Mr. Warriner attempted to open the

vault, the dial fell off and could not be operated.

The new vault door and lock—a "Dexter Double Dial Combination with Herring Patent for Disconnecting the Dial from the Spindle"—was an innovation of which the bank was very proud, so proud, in fact, that Mr. Warriner had posted a notice extolling its burglar-proof features! And so, maintaining at least an outward show of confidence, he assured the gathering crowd that the contents would be found intact, meanwhile telegraphing the New York manufacturer, Herring and Company, to rush their men to the scene.

At nine that evening William D. Edson, a Herring salesman, arrived with a locksmith. Aided by a local machinist, the locksmith put the dial back in place, and after trying 31 combinations, hit on the right one. Mr. Warriner then stepped forward and swung the great door

open. The vault, the safe within the vault, and the box within the safe, all were empty. Twelve thousand dollars in cash and over a million in stocks and bonds had vanished.

In cold fact the riches had been moved only a few hundred feet.

A reward of $25,000 was offered by the bank for information leading to the apprehension of the robbers. Police in all neighboring cities were alerted. Mr. Williams, one of the bank directors, left for New York to be on hand for any developments. A list of the missing securities was issued, which indicated a loss of $800,000 (the amount was later raised to a million and a quarter) of which $111,250 belonged to the bank; the balance to about 80 depositors, mostly in registered bonds which could not be disposed of by the robbers. And a bank examiner announced that the bank was safe and sound

in spite of its loss.

During the day clues and bits of information came to light. It was discovered that seven railroad tickets from Northampton to New York had been bought a month before the robbery, four of which had been turned in on the six-o'clock train that morning. The remaining three members of the band must have gone by some other method of transportation, and the method was soon discovered. Two weeks before, a "sandy-complexioned man of medium size and agreeable appearance" had called at Burr's Livery Stable in Springfield (17 miles south of Northampton) and hired a carriage and a pair of horses to be ready that evening. He failed to show up, but returned two days before the robbery and took the rig for the day. When he brought it back, he engaged it for the next night, asking that it be ready promptly at six as he

"was going to a surprise party." The following night (January 25), he turned up half an hour late, paid in advance, asked to have the side curtains put up, as it was raining, and drove away. He brought the team back early the next morning (the horses were dripping with sweat as though they had been driven at top speed) and rushed off, presumably to catch the New York train.

A curious footnote to this incident was the discovery next day, beside the road from Northampton to Springfield, of a linen duster and a cambric mask which the Whittelseys were positive had been worn by the robber chief, and a carpet bag containing a pint of sweet oil, an empty whiskey bottle, a pair of men's rubbers (extra large) and a piece of wrapping paper. Indeed the most curious feature of a case that abounded in oddities was the prodigality with which these skillful criminals strewed their belongings and left behind them every possible clue that might lead to their apprehension.

Putting together this evidence with the evidence found in the schoolhouse, the police decided that at least two of the robbers had spent several days in Northampton about a month before the robbery, hiding by night in the schoolhouse attic, and by day studying the lay of the land and the customs of the community. They then returned to New York to perfect their plans. It also appeared that all the robbers had come from New York—four the whole way by train, three by train to Springfield and by carriage the rest of the way—and that all had returned as they came—the leaders probably carrying the plunder. Except for the last, the surmises proved to be correct.

On February 6 the *Springfield Union* printed a dispatch, credited to a New York detective, which stated that the treasure had been buried in Northampton and that the robbers were on their way back to dig it up. Police were alerted, special deputies patroled the streets, but no robbers were seen. The report, as it later developed, was true in part. What had happened was this. The robbers had worked with such speed that within half an hour of their arrival at the bank they had ransacked the vault and departed, carrying the loot in a pillow case and bag. (They had overestimated the bulkiness of the loot; the half bushel market basket stolen from the Whittelsey house was not needed.) To take it at once to New York was risky, since they were known to the police as bank robbers, and might anticipate a search when news of this—the biggest of all bank robberies—hit the headlines. And so, instead, they carried it to a graveyard near their schoolhouse hideout, and stuffed it into the vault.

A few days before the *Union* published its story, they had returned by night and taken the cash and securities from their semipublic hiding place. However, as the case was still too hot and the trains were too closely watched to venture on bringing home the loot, they carried it to the schoolhouse, ripped out a bench along the wall, shoved the bags under it, and nailed the bench back in place. Here, right in a classroom, the million dollars remained for several weeks while the case was cooling; then, in a final trip, the treasure was brought back to New York.

The prodigious size of the haul astonished and delighted the robbers. To be sure, most of it was in non-negotiable securities, but they were convinced the bank would pay handsomely to get them back, and meanwhile would refrain from prosecuting as the chance of recovery would be gone once arrests were made. And so, late in February, they sent two of the stolen bonds to the bank with this proposal:

> "When you are satisfied with the detective skill you can make a proposition to us, the holders, and if you are liberal we may be able to do business with you. If you entertain such ideas please insert a personal in the *New York Herald*. Address to XXX and sign Rufus to which due attention will be paid. To satisfy you we do hold papers we send you a couple of pieces.

The bank had already engaged the services of the Pinkerton ("We Never Sleep") Detective Agency which had put its men to work shadowing suspects, and began a mole-like operation which did not emerge to the surface for many months. Now, with the ransom letter at hand, they were ready to negotiate for the return of the bonds.

One possible lead had already been suggested. On the day after the robbery, a clerk at the bank had approached his superiors with a startling theory. Two years before when the new door and locks had been installed, on the vault, the work had been supervised by Edson, the same Herring salesman who had been present when the looted vault was opened. Two months prior to the break, Edson had returned to Northampton to see how the new door and locks were working. Told that the keys were a little tight, he had taken them into the director's room and filed them down for a more exact fit. During his visit he had supper with Mr. Warriner, and counseled him to be more cautious in entrusting the lock combination to employees; the entire combination should be given only to the cashier. Impressed by Edson's thoughtfulness in making the suggestion, Mr. Warriner complied. And so, said the clerk (the same who had been deprived of a share in the combination), is it not likely that Edson, who had an opportunity to make impressions of the keys, and through whose suggestion the combination could be extorted from one man instead of two, is an accomplice of the robbers?

Mr. Warriner thought not. Mr. Williams was not so sure, and finally asked Edson if he was in a position to act as intermediary for the return of the bonds. After considerable hedging and evading, Edson admitted that he was, and negotiations cautiously got under way. For the bank clerk was right. Edson had indeed been an accomplice, and now was both angry and frightened. He was angry because his associates had refused to give him more than $1200 until the securities were disposed of. And he was frightened because one of his underworld friends had said to him: "There isn't an old knuck-moll (female thief) in New York who doesn't know all about the Northampton robbery," and he feared that his part in the plot would come to light. If the negotiations went through his hands he would know how much was paid and thus eliminate the chance of a double-cross. And if all else failed he could turn state's evidence with the possibility of a reward and the probability of avoiding jail.

After months of fruitless negotiations, Edson finally arranged a personal interview between Mr. Williams, the bank director, and Connors, a New York thief who was acting as mouthpiece for Robert Scott and James Dunlap, the two men who had organized the raid on the bank. The robbers had at first expected to be paid at least $300,000 for the return of the securities. Now Connors reduced their demand to $150,000. Williams refused.

With this, the bank abandoned hope of recovering the securities, the Pinkertons arrested Scott and Dunlap, and Edson dictated a full confession.

Twice Scott and Dunlap stood trial in Northampton—once for robbing the bank and once for breaking into the cashier's house and stealing his watch. (Later the watch was found under the station platform in Springfield.) From the testimony and from a contemporary story in the *New York Sun* (probably based on the Pinkerton records), it appears that the prologue to the drama was a visit by Scott and Dunlap to Edson at his New York home in 1873, soon after he had been hired as a salesman by Herring and Company. In the course of the conversation, the pair confided to him that they were professional men of the highest standing. Their profession was bank robbery. The last job had netted them $200,000 from a Kentucky bank and had baffled the country's shrewdest detectives. The money had gone for wine, women and horses, and now they were on the prowl for other "weak" banks they could break.

However, the practice of their profession was growing more difficult. Alarmed by the superior skill of safe-breakers over safe-makers, the banks were installing new and better locks and taking more elaborate precautions. Obviously the time had arrived for the safe-breakers to seek an ally within the enemy camp. And so they had come to propose a partnership. If Edson would work with them, they would split the take and make him a millionaire.

This was their siren song. Edson, a man with a shady past—he had been arrested for bigamy and had gone through an odorous bankruptcy—enthusiastically succumbed.

During the next three years, Edson had advised his confederates on nine jobs, of which only two had brought him financial rewards: $7600 for a break in Quincy, Illinois, and $850 from Pittston, Pennsylvania. Then the chance to make impressions of the Northampton vault keys had brought him his golden opportunity.

Edson's testimony at the trial was damning but insufficient since the judge ruled that the defendants could not be found guilty on his evidence alone. Conviction, therefore, depended on proof of identity; the defense admitting the robberies but denying that Scott and Dunlap had committed them. And although the two robber leaders had been closely observed by the Whittelsey household, their masks had made identification difficult. Also, alibi witnesses had been brought from New York.

In the end, the case turned on a shrug, a beard and a woman. Mr. and Mrs. Whittelsey were positive that the robber leader had a habit of shrugging his shoulders and they had observed the same shrug when watching him since the arrest. The alibi witnesses swore that Scott had a beard at the time of the robbery, but the Springfield stableman swore that the person who hired his team was beardless. And Mrs. Scott, who might have testified to her husband's alibi and who was present in the court, failed to take the stand: a failure which made a deep impression on the jurors. So, in spite of beard and alibis, the two defendants were found guilty and sentenced to 20 years in prison. They took their sentence calmly, tipped their jailors lavishly, and smiled cheerfully to the crowds that escorted them to the station en route to jail.

Five years after entering prison, Scott—in hope of getting time off—ordered Red Leary, Number Four man in the gang, who was then holding the securities, to return them to the bank under threat of exposure. This he did, the bank recovering about $700,000, most of which belonged to their depositors. Scott's gesture was in vain as he died in the Charleston State Prison before his term was up. Dunlap was finally released, with time off for good behavior. Connors was arrested, escaped, was rearrested and held for the Grand Jury, but was never indicted. No trace of Red Leary could be found, and no other member of the gang was ever identified. Edson, who evaded prison by informing, but who never, so far as is known, received a reward, changed his name and thereafter "led a pure life." What happened to the cash and negotiable securities—a fortune in itself—was never revealed.

END

207

Stockbridge Loved Him

Mrs. Buckley came after the Burglar with a wildly swinging axe. The gentleman

IT WAS PRECISELY THE 15TH OF JUNE. THE OLD blue china on the walls of the Stockbridge Inn was dusted. The livestock belonging to the livery stable was brought in from pasture. The drugstore sent to the city for a large supply of chocolate candies. Mrs. Haag's pretty housemaid, Laura, woke before the cock had crowed—to see a tall man by her bedside with a pistol in his hand.

He was exquisitely dressed in morning clothes: light, striped pants and a four-button cutaway. A costly hemstitched handkerchief masked the lower half of his face. Silk handkerchiefs shielded his hands, too—even his feet were muffled in expensive fabric. Good breeding showed only in his well-groomed hair and musical, mesmeric voice, at the sound of which she almost swooned.

There could be no mistake. It was indeed the Stockbridge Burglar, opening his 1893 season in this pious resort. And *she* was his first victim!

She could hardly speak when he asked her where the silver was. She offered him her own watch, which was silver but didn't run. He rejected this, and followed her directions to the pantry where he made his selections from the family sterling, indulged in a morning glass of sherry—and took his leave. He went by the front door, didn't replace his derby till he'd left her presence. Such niceties could only mark the true, the polished gentleman intruder. The Stockbridge Burglar! And he'd chosen their house *first of all*!

If news hadn't travelled fast, she would have spread it. By mid-morning everyone in Stockbridge knew the Burglar was back. It was like the return of the swallows or the blossoming of the orchards. In alerting its reporters for the busy weeks ahead, the *Berkshire News* saluted the gentleman's return by noting that he should be regarded as "no ordinary or common individual, but as quite a refined person well advanced in the higher classes of his profession.

"He is, it would seem (the *News* continued), a sort of pet in the village, a kind of serious night-bloomer that should be cultivated, if not perpetuated. It will not be long before the cottagers of Stockbridge will, in extending invitations to their city friends, add the special inducement of his visiting the house while they are there."

Indeed, the Burglar's scheduled recrudescence brought a sense of All's Right with the World. Spinsters took from their cedar chests the laciest of night clothes. Sheriff Day and Constable Pease polished their revolvers. Husbands cautioned anticipatory wives, and locked the family jewelery in the safe. Town fathers checked the street lamps.

The Burglar didn't rush the season. He took time to refresh his memory of village customs and traditions. Two days after his arrival, Mrs. John Swann drew a large sum from the Housatonic Bank. An armed guard saw her home. He insisted on leaving his revolver with her, for she was alone with an eager visitor from out of town named Lillian Stetson. That night she awoke to find the Burglar standing by her bed.

"I have a pistol," she informed him.

"Oh, have you," he said, raising "his conspicuously-arched eyebrows" (the reports made much of this arched-eyebrows business).

For proof, she took it from beneath her pillow. He asked to examine it, then held the pistol to her temple, and requested the money she'd withdrawn that afternoon. More for a witness than for help, Mrs. Swann called Lillian from the other room. The Burglar robbed them both. In addition to the money, he relieved Miss Stetson of her rings, though allowing her to keep one valuable piece when she claimed it was a memento of her mother.

The night was young. The Burglar moved down the street to the home of wealthy lawyer

by Samuel Carter III

was obliged to take the axe and apply it to her rear—as a lesson in manners.

David Dudley Field. Mr. Field was absent, Mrs. Field asleep. As he reached under her pillow for a bracelet that he evidently knew was there, the lady threw her arms around his neck. She clasped him so violently he begged her not to harm herself. She screamed for the valet. The valet arrived in his pajamas. Finding himself in mixed company, he correctly withdrew to don a dressing gown. He then returned with a Civil War cavalry pistol and blasted the lock off the front door by which the Burglar had departed.

The next day the town council reinstated its annual advertisement in the local paper, offering a $500 award for the Burglar's capture and conviction. This brought to $1,350 the award money that had been accumulating through the seasons. A description was broadcast, picked up by the venerable *New York Times*. His clothing was "that of a gentleman, of mixed material, and of fashionable cut, fitting his figure to a nicety." His eyes "were dark and mild and soft in expression, his ears small and shapely, his tall figure erect and carried with dignity and ease." He was also reported as making his rounds in "an upholstered carriage with two fast horses." This seems unlikely. He did, it is true, once "borrow" a carriage from William Palmer's livery stable—perhaps in anticipation of a strenuous night—but as a rule he disdained such ostentation.

This flattering description, along with details eagerly provided by the victims, made every tall and handsome man in Stockbridge suspect. In the Congregational Church, Mrs. Swann observed a tall and handsome stranger who distinctly arched his eyebrows. She slipped out and reported this to Selectman F. H. Aymar, who rounded up the Constables and had the man arrested. The suspect turned out to be a Brooklyn gentleman named John B. King, who had just moved to Stockbridge for its cultured, peaceful atmosphere. Mr. King became the butt of so many jokes at the Casino that he finally left town for good.

Imagination soared, as in the days of Salem witchcraft. Someone remarked that the new Dr. Crandall, just starting practice on the green, resembled the former Mr. King. Since Mr. King, in turn, had looked like the Burglar, Dr. Crandall automatically became a suspect (his hands were "small and delicate" too, like the Burglar's). The young doctor tried to laugh off the insinuations. But when he found he couldn't step outdoors at night, even to light his pipe, without getting shot at, he, too, thought of leaving town.

Two robberies an evening seemed to be the Burglar's schedule, and he never worked on Sundays. His was a talent sensitive to strain. The following night he canvassed the home of J. C. Carter and found two silver watches. Mr. Carter surprised him in the act and protested that the watches were of sentimental value. It was a ploy that often worked. The Burglar offered to sell them back to Carter at a reasonable price. Carter told him he regarded them as priceless. Reluctantly, the Burglar returned the watches and pronounced the matter closed.

Mr. Carter, however, knew his duty. Saddling the horse, he raced to town like a 19th-century Paul Revere. On the way he passed the Burglar; they waved to one another. Reporting the abortive crime to Sheriff Day, the latter asked Carter —a well-conditioned gentleman—why he hadn't overcome the Burglar by force. Carter properly replied that this "would not have been in accord with the dignified manner in which affairs are conducted at Stockbridge."

For his second appearance of the evening, the Burglar chose the home of Mrs. Rose Burns, a prosperous widow in the village. Here he met some action. Mrs. Burns shouted to an Amazonian neighbor, Mrs. Buckley, who came after the Burglar with a wildly-swinging axe. The gentleman was obliged to take the axe, and—as a lesson in manners—apply it to her rear. Since she wore a bustle, it was later debated whether or not this constituted an unsporting use of force.

The confusion aroused neighbors. A farmer and groom from the adjoining Teichman estate came to the rescue, armed with pistols. They held the Burglar at bay while he explained that he had stopped by merely to ask the best way to the village green. They told him about a short-cut, and he took it.

But again, the groom and farmer knew their duty. Like Carter, they raced to town and sounded the alarm. This time, a posse of a hundred men was rounded up to comb the country-side. They met with some success. In the Crown-inshield barn they found a cache of vintage wines and rare imported cheeses. The butler confirmed that they'd been stolen from the house—and by the Burglar, who had sampled their champagne the night before. How did he know it was the Burglar? Not, perhaps, a thirsty servant? Because he'd heard the champagne cork pop. Only a gentleman would pop a cork; Stockbridge servants were trained to open bottles noiselessly.

By now there was a run on the supply of pistols in Great Barrington. In Stockbridge, iron grills were put around the street lamps to protect them—light being considered a deterrent. The Reverend Dr. Henry Field closed up his house and left town altogether. Dogs, it was noted, kept to the center of the streets at night. Sheriff Day assured the citizens he was about to take the Burglar, dead or alive. That night the Sheriff's house was robbed.

Meanwhile, in nearby and less-fashionable Pittsfield, an epidemic of breaking and entering occurred. The press accused the Burglar of moonlighting in his spare time. Stockbridge indignantly denied the charge. Their Burglar was no sneak-thief! He favored only the best Stockbridge homes, made his entrances and exits by the front door. He never hurried or lost composure, except when the Constables came after him.

The comic-opera aspects of the situation yielded to a growing apprehension. The Barrington weekly reported that the town was now in terror, and "every home is an arsenal." The *News* no longer referred lightly to gentlemanly peccadilloes, but called them "a series of the most desperate burglaries ever perpetrated in Western Massachusetts."

It was even suggested that the Burglar sometimes overstepped the boundaries of good taste! Accosting Herbert Basset with a pistol, on the latter's evening stroll around the green, he demanded money—an approach that was thought to be beneath him. Finding that Basset had only 50 cents in his possession, the Burglar ordered him to bend down. He then booted Basset in the rear, with the command to: "Get on home!" Basset did—to put iron bars across his windows and employ a bodyguard.

With women, however, he continued to observe "the politeness of a born gentleman." Many expressed the wish to meet him under better circumstances, "after he got caught." He was known to have gallantly returned a brooch and pendant that the owners had received as keepsakes. Occasionally he would settle for a gastronomic delicacy or a bottle of imported wine. He never resorted to violence and did his best, for their sakes, to discourage violence in his victims. One woman desperately tried to save a $1,500 diamond-studded watch by jumping on his back. He carried her upstairs in that position—and gently dumped her into bed.

As the season drew to a close, only a handful of distinguished homes remained unburglarized—like mighty oaks in a wind-levelled forest. Their owners didn't know whether to feel fortunate or slighted. Only Charles Southmayd stooped to the indignity of showing his alarm. He barred his windows and double-bolted his doors. He allowed no one—but *no one*—inside. This was hardly cricket. More to the point, it proved ineffectual. A loud knocking woke him late one night. A voice called: "Mr. Southmayd, quick! Your home's on fire!" He bounded downstairs and flung open his door to the Burglar. The latter was miffed at Southmayd's crude security precautions. He not only stole his jewelry; he went off with Southmayd's pants.

There remained one social fortress—nay, a shrine!—in the Burglar's short, remaining path: the Sedgwick Mansion, as sacred to Stockbridge as its town memorials. The family itself was

Main Street, Stockbridge, in the Burglar's heyday.

so above the normal level that even the crickets in the field chirped: "Sedgwick, Sedgwick, Sedgwick." Was the Burgular dazzled by this awesome target? Did he recognize the limits of his daring? No. He was simply saving it for last.

As the season closed, the Sedgwicks, following their custom, entertained some 50 members of the Stockbridge aristocracy. There were flickering candles, a string quartet, crisp linen napery, and hand-cut crystal. And there was the Burglar. The footman discovered him in the pantry, making his selections from the wine and the cigars. He chose six bottles, some imported cheese and bread, and borrowed a silver knife to cut the bread with. The footman confessed that he was too astounded to report the incident till later. When he finally did, the guests organized a posse and searched the premises. They found the knife. And the cigar box. And the empty bottles . . .

But the Burglar was on his way. This was October, and his time was running out. Inspired by the wine, he hit full stride and robbed

six houses in that single interval of dusk to dawn, returning to the Sedgwicks for a light snack in the early morning. It was a fitting swan song for the season. Stockbridge felt comfortable about it. The Burglar had not missed the Sedgwicks!

It would indeed be suitable to let this last-act triumph be his curtain call. Throughout the long hot summer, his performance had been flawless. Not a breach in decorum, not a break in tradition. But the Constables (good Massachusetts men, for sure, but not quite "Stockbridge" in the fullest sense) remained dissatisfied. Like the heroes of the Penny Magazines, they felt they had to get their man. They arrested a stone-cutter on the estate of Joseph Choate. The accused reportedly confessed—who wouldn't? There were many who said he was a rank imposter. Even today, few truly-Stockbridge people have accepted him. But in a way the outcome was a double blessing. The Constables at long last had their man. And Stockbridge forever had its legend.   END

211

Diary of a Crime

by the Bank Robber, Langdon W. Moore

ORIGINAL IN ROGUES' GALLERY, BOSTON.

Obtained by fraud and falsehood, Feb. 21, 1880; since copyrighted without my knowledge or consent, and sent among the nations of the earth.

Above: Langdon Moore, criminal (remarks beneath the photo are his own).

Right: Langdon W. Moore, author. (Both photos are from his book.)

I was one of that kind which is just honest enough not to be suspected of crime . . .

Bank Robbery

**by Langdon W. Moore
(with a biographical note
by Alton Hall Blackington)**

ON THE TWENTY-FIFTH DAY OF SEPTEMBER, IN
the year 1865, the town of Concord, Massachusetts, was thrown into a state of wild excitement.
Its two banks had been boldly entered and
robbed at midday; the perpetrators of the crime
had succeeded in effecting an escape, and one of
the most daring and mysterious robberies ever
known became a matter of criminal history.

The descent was not a sudden move, but the
culmination of five months' steady work, by
which keys were fitted to ten locks. It should be
borne in mind that at that time I was one of that
kind which is just honest enough not to be suspected of crime, and my family and neighbors in
Natick, Massachusetts, firmly believed me to be
what I represented myself, a respectable New
York business man.

At noon one Monday I stopped in Concord
and was satisfied from all I saw that by hard,
persistent work the bank could be cleaned out
completely.

Harry Howard at the time lived in Boston and
was already a trusty friend. I told him of the
Concord discovery and invited him to assist; a
day or two after his arrival we went over to Concord and visited the bank.

When night came, we began the examination
of the vault door. To open this door was the
hardest part of the job, for it was of unusual
make and had five different keyholes. I went to
Boston, and, after hunting all over the city,
stumbled over something of the same sort in a
safe-maker's shop. Pretending I was an insurance agent and in need of protection for some
private papers, the agent fully explained the
working of the locks to me. I told him I would
probably buy something more modern, and left
without purchasing.

I then returned home to Natick, and for three
nights a week for six weeks we worked from
midnight until three o'clock in the morning.
Then we succeeded in opening that outside
vault door.

On the 21st of September, I decided that I

would finish the job that day, cost what it might.
Rising from a sick bed, I joined Howard, who
harnessed a sorrel mare into an old-fashioned
phaeton of mine, believed in the neighborhood
to be his exclusive property; I entered the carriage entirely unobserved and sat back out of
sight, so that when the rig passed down the
street on this expedition, it excited no comment.

It was just before noon that we drove quietly
into Concord and up to the old church near the
bank, where I got out. Passersby saw me reading inscriptions on the old gravestones. Howard drove to the grocery store on the other side
of the street, a few rods above the bank. He sat
there in the wagon looking over some blank
deeds which he held in such a position that
passersby would not be able to recognize him
at any future time. When the cashier had left
the bank, I left the churchyard and walked
down the sidewalk to the bank door, which I
opened with the key we had spent so many
nights making.

I entered and was closing the door behind
me when I heard a child's voice say, "Let me
in."

I knew it was now or never, and that if I did
not use a little tact, the child might mention
the fact that a strange man had entered the bank
during the cashier's absence, thus causing my
arrest and wrecking the whole plan. I satisfied
her by telling her that the directors were in
session, and asked her to come back at two
o'clock. She ran off to her playmates under the
big elm on the other side of the street.

I bolted the door behind me, admitted myself
to the banking-room, and locked the second
door on the inside. The vault was then unlocked. The outside door gave way to the gentle
persuasion of the five keys; two more keys provided an open sesame for the inner door; another key removed the plate from over the key-
hole; and access to the burglar-box was gained
with the key which I had located in the cashier's
hiding place for it, on the shelf of the vault.

213

Diary of a Crime

The contents of the box were soon transferred to a meal-bag which I carried under my vest. Locking the now empty box and keeping the key, I locked the two vault doors. I then leisurely left the room, unbolted the front door and passed out, closing it after me.

Howard was on the watch for me. As soon as he saw me come out, he untied his horse from the hitching-post and drove around the church, stopping to water his horse in order to let me walk ahead of him, so that when the phaeton overtook me, I could step into it without attracting attention. In the meantime I had passed slowly down the road with the meal-bag over my shoulder.

When I entered the carriage, a leisurely gait was kept for half a mile, lest, by undue haste, we might attract attention. We then struck a piece of woods, where we changed the gait considerably, making the dirt rattle about the dasher of the old vehicle.

We drove down the road to my farm, and without attracting attention went by the house and into the barn. My brother was there when we entered, and while I went with him to decide about the setting of a flight of stairs which he was building, Howard took the bag from the buggy and hid it in the hayloft. He then unharnessed the mare, and in just one hour after leaving Concord, she was rolling in the dirt in a vacant lot in the rear of the barn. This was just what we wanted her to do, for she very soon removed all traces of her twelve-mile drive.

I then took a bushel basket and went up to the hay loft, where Howard had hidden the bank's property in the hay. Placing the bag in the basket, I carried it carelessly under my arm into the house and up to my chamber. I then undressed and jumped into bed, and sent Howard for my sister, to whom I stated I was sick and needed a doctor. The nearest physician was at Natick village, two and a half miles away. No sooner had she left the yard, than I jumped out of bed, dressed, and locked the door. Then the bag was emptied on the bed and the work of sorting began.

We divided equally. Howard made his part into small packages, which he placed about his body. I concealed my share under the haymow in the barn, and then became an invalid again.

Two days afterward, I buried the property at the base of an old hemlock tree in plain sight of the farmhouse. After covering the spot over with dirt and rubbish, I went back to bed.

Leaving the Concord Bank
carrying the bag of swag ($310,000)

L. W. Moore at the time
of the Concord robbery.

Henry Hauck,
alias Harry Howard

214

In the meantime, the town of Concord had become an excited place. When the cashier returned from dinner he found the street door unlocked, and of course was unable to open the vault door because he had no key to throw back the bolt. He did not know whether the bank had been robbed or not, but looked for the worst and at once telegraphed President George Heywood, in Albany, who had a duplicate set of keys. Not until his arrival did the bank people know that the burglar-box had been cleaned out as neatly as though a feather duster had been in operation.

* * * * *

More about Langdon Moore

by Alton Hall Blackington

IT WAS NOT UNDERSTOOD UNTIL THE NEXT DAY, however, that the little man standing in front of the Concord National Bank with a feed bag over his shoulder had just committed the greatest bank robbery of all time. There he was, waiting to be picked up in a farm surrey by his partner, with no less than $310,000 in currency, notes and bonds. The two drove away behind a walking horse along the Maynard Road to Natick.

It is unlikely, even if Concord residents had taken notice of the pair (one woman did), that any of them would have recognized the men as the hardened criminals they were. But the police, detectives, and underworld knew them well; the one with the beard, who had carried the feed bag, was Langdon W. Moore, alias Charles A. Adams, alias Stephen Sherman; the other, Henry Hauck, alias Harry Howard, just out of Sing Sing.

At Natick, where Moore had been passing as a gentleman farmer, the two divided the loot in equal shares. Moore hid his in the ground under a hemlock tree. Hauck concealed his in a money belt around his body and took off for New York City.

This dirty deed will never be long forgotten. Nor will Langdon W. Moore, its author—the only bank robber in this country whose memory is perpetuated every year at the time of the full moon in July. Each year, also at this time, someone will endeavor to solve a mystery which is indeed a part of this celebration.

Born at East Washington, New Hampshire, at 10 A.M. on May 7, 1830, Moore was raised in Newburyport, Massachusetts, and on a farm in Lisbon, New Hampshire. At 11 o'clock on the Fourth of July, 1853, he walked into a gambling den called The Chestnut Cottage on Portland Street in Boston. It was his first experience at "shaking pops," and he was there to "beat the game." But the game beat him and, by his own confession, all he won was an addiction to gambling, a vice he was unable to overcome.

This addiction led him to New York where, as Charles A. Adams, in a high hat and velvet-collared coat, he set up an amazing chain of gambling houses, counterfeiting presses, and organizations of phony bond and bill salesmen of which even the underworld of today would be proud. To fill the ever-growing sales of this organization, Moore couldn't run his printing presses fast enough. He had to supplement these with actual bank robberies—such as the one at Concord. This required what were, to Moore, "disillusioning" payoffs to police, detectives, and judges.

Not really a vicious man, Moore had certain traits not usually found in a criminal of his standing. It must be noted that during his career of crime, Moore would never peddle any

More about Langdon Moore

bonds or bills taken by his accomplices with guns or force. Nor would he have any truck with men who found the bottle good company. One example of this was seen at Francestown, New Hampshire, a short time before the Concord episode. There, Moore and two contemporaries from New York had "piped" the local bank and were readied for the "haul." It turned out, however, that Moore discovered his partners in premature celebration—doused in alcohol. Whereupon, Moore hired Hauck (who later helped him at Concord) to come to Francestown on the night of the robbery, there to pose as watchman of the bank, and Moore's two partners

A page from a rare copy of Moore's autobiography.

Suffolk County Jail, Feb. 21, 1880.
1. Giving my pedigree.
2. Locked in.
3. Leaving for a sixteen years' sojourn at Concord.

were frightened away.

Eventually, double-crossed himself, Moore landed in the Rockland (Maine) State Prison. Still later, at age 57, on March 30, 1880, he was sentenced to 16 years in a Massachusetts prison. "As three score and ten is the average span of life," remarked Judge Bacon as he read the sentence to the prisoner, "I guess that will finish your criminal career."

It did, and with some six years off for good behavior, September 8, 1890 (the date of his release) found Langdon W. Moore reformed and ready to devote the rest of his years to the suppression of crime—and to the support of honesty in public official life.

Dates are important here—especially as these parallel the dates in the life of Denman Thompson, author of the now-famed "The Old Homestead"—a play which has been seen by 30,000,000 Americans. Denman Thompson was born on October 15, 1833 (three years after Moore), in Girard, Pennsylvania, of New England parents. When he was 14, his family moved back (1847) to the old homestead in Swanzey, New Hampshire. In 1850 he turned to the theater as a profession. His first appearance on the stage was in "Lady Macbeth" at the (Old) Howard Athenaeum in Boston. In 1852 he had a speaking part in "The French Spy." Thus, Thompson and Moore, who at that time was running a grocery store in Scollay Square, were making their way together in this year of 1852 within a block or two of each other in Boston and may have begun a friendship, the mystery of which now is buried with them.

In 1875 (while Moore was in Rockland Prison), Thompson conceived the idea of a play about a New Hampshire farm boy turned bank robber. By April, 1886 (when Moore was rotting away in the Charlestown, Massachusetts, jail), this idea came to its first public performance under the title of "The Old Homestead" at the Boston Theater. It is conceivable, yet unproved, that Thompson called on his old friend in the Charlestown jail—perhaps for his character "Reuben Whitcomb" in the play. Conceivable or not, many followers today of "The Old Homestead" believe this to be true.

After Moore's release from prison in 1890, he not only wrote for and gave interviews to the *Boston Herald* about his personal life of crime but also exposed the officials whom he had in one way or another bribed. In 1892, Moore published a 659-page book, *Langdon W. Moore, His Own Story of His Eventful Life.* Thus both the book and the play—each of which was purportedly an object lesson in "crime does not pay"—by the year 1896 were going strong.

Was it this coincidence then which explains why in 1896 Langdon W. Moore came to live with Denman Thompson in the latter's home in Swanzey? Or does it still seem odd that Thompson, a simple, retired author, should have invited into his own home this ex-criminal? There was one real fuss between the two while they lived together (1896-1900). Thompson became so angered about the Moore autobiography that he bought the printing plates and had them shipped to Swanzey to be destroyed. No more copies were ever printed. Today the

book is a collector's item. Was there something in it Thompson did not like? Was there a personal reference to him which the modern reader is unable to translate?

In any event, after this quarrel, Thompson built for Moore a cottage of his own on the shores of Swanzey Lake. There Moore lived until his death from cancer on June 28, 1910.

Not far away, Denman Thompson is buried, his end coming within a year (April 14, 1911) of his departed friend's. Thompson had no children. His nieces, after his death, apparently remained friendly, too, with the memory of Moore. The latter's portrait hangs in a West Swanzey home today.

The two men can be said to live on together. Every year, around the time of the July full moon, Thompson's perennial play, "The Old Homestead," is reenacted in the Potash Bowl in Swanzey. Thousands thrill to the charm of the play—and the supposed prototype of Langdon W. Moore: one "Reuben Whitcomb"—the greatest bank robber New England has ever known—big as life in his perennial role.   END

Denman Thompson's "Old Homestead" in West Swanzey, New Hampshire.

8.
HORRIBLE HOMICIDES

The Story of Bloody Half-Acre

by Jim Barrows and Oscar Nelder

The first and last lynching in Maine—memories of those dreadful days back in April of 1873 still linger in the North Country . . .

THEY TOOK CULLEN FROM THE STORE, TIED HIM to the pung, and started off for Presque Isle, hauling his 220 pounds across the still-frozen surface of the snow. It took a half dozen men to control him as he cried, twisted, dragged his big feet—the ones that got him into all the trouble to begin with.

Hard to tell what was going through his mind when the mob intercepted the horse-drawn conveyance. After all, Cullen wasn't the brightest man alive, but he was one of the strongest in Aroostook County, Maine, where strong men came a dime a dozen.

The mob—maybe 75 or 100 men, enough to fill the Main Street at Ball's Mill in Mapleton Plantation—was hooded. Not one face showed, except for the few men deputized as members of the posse.

It took some doing. They had to haul Cullen up the steep hill. There was a big enough tree there, and they threw the freshly-soaped rope around a good stout limb 20 feet off the ground and hauled Cullen up.

By the neck.

Cullen was later buried alongside the Mapleton Road in a bog, where airmen from the Snark missile base at Presque Isle now practice small arms firing. A phrenologist got his skull —he said it was Cullen's, anyway—and used it for years to demonstrate his science.

* * * * *

That was the only time the easygoing farmers and woodsmen in Northern Maine ever took the law into their own hands. It was back in April of 1873 when they took Cullen from the constable and his posse and lynched him.

Winter held on late in the central part of the county, and in the Spring of 1873 the folks who worked in Ball's Mill were still snowshoeing into Presque Isle after the first of May. Big Jim Cullen had lived in Ball's Mill for two years. The other residents of that pioneering community cared not a hoot for him or his type. Tales of his brute strength had been making the rounds in town since his arrival from

Rogue's Roost, a group of shacks on the American side of the international border below Mars Hill.

Cullen was a big man, six-three. They claimed he'd once toted a 40-foot timber that five men couldn't budge. Ugly-tempered, his red beard and over-sized feet were his trademark. He lived with a Mrs. John Twist. The son of their illicit union was aptly nicknamed "Dummy" by the townspeople.

On the morning of April 28, 1873, David Dudley slogged through the knee-deep snow to his store in Ball's Mill. There were huge footprints outside the front window. A heavy shutter was torn off its hinges, a window smashed. Dudley ran inside to take stock. It took only a short while. Missing was a pair of boots. A big pair.

Deputy Sheriff Granville A. Hayden was summoned from his store in Presque Isle. He arrived in Ball's Mill on horseback shortly before noon and inspected the big prints, rapidly disappearing in the warming sunlight, outside the window. Their size left little doubt as to the thief's identity. A warrant was issued and given to Hayden for Cullen's arrest. Hotel owner M. L. Stewart, joining the swelling crowd outside, was heard to observe that the crackerbox jail at Houlton, the county seat, hadn't held Cullen on at least two previous occasions. The intimation was a slap at the locked room with the boarded-up window that served as Presque Isle's drying-out tank for soggy woodsmen with pockets emptied at whatever saloon they might find.

Hayden wiped at the frost on his beard, snuffed, spat.

"Tracks lead off toward Swanback's," he mused. It would be a hard, five-hour push through the woods to Swanback's shingle mill in Chapman Plantation, and he'd be lucky to make it by dark. Snow was still pretty deep in the woods. If Cullen were holed up at the mill, Hayden figured, a tired deputy sheriff would need some help. He wasn't a big man. Then,

221

too, if Cullen had gone from there, word could be sent back while he continued on Cullen's trail.

"Anyone want to come along?" Hayden asked, scanning the faces of the crowd. They murmured, began to slip away at the fringes of the gathering. Few of the taciturn Maine farmers or woodsmen liked the idea of meeting Cullen in the dark forest with less than a dozen men at their sides.

The sheriff, exasperated at their timidity, picked the two nearest him—William T. Hubbard, a Castle Hill man, and Minot C. Bird. The sunlight, silhouetting Bird's face, showed the fuzz on his cheeks. They made no protest. Prodded by Hayden's reassurances, and afraid of appearing cowardly to their neighbors, the two set out with Hayden, snowshoeing for Swanback's mill. Once in the privacy of the forest, following the wide swath left by the trudging Cullen, Hayden made his decision.

"Got it figured," he told his reluctant deputies. "All we can do is to keep Cullen moving, and away from here. We don't want any more of his troublemaking, and that's the only way I can see to do it."

They reached Swanback's mill, seven miles from Ball's Mill and three from any other camp, late in the afternoon. Darkness was beginning to ring the horizon in the east.

Cullen and Swanback greeted them at the doorway to the small cedar-logged cabin.

"All kinds of company today," the shingle mill operator commented. "Jim just got here after lunch. C'mon in and sup with us."

"Where you headed, Cullen?" asked the sheriff. Bird and Hubbard stood close at his back.

"Well, now, Mister Hayden, I kinda got into a little trouble back a ways . . . you know . . . and I figured it'd be best if I went in to Daniel's Mill to work for a while."

Hayden and his diminutive posse said no more about the matter until after supper, according to testimony at the coroner's inquest four days later. Then, as Swanback stoked the fireplace at one end of the cabin, Hayden motioned Cullen outside.

"Look, Cullen," the sheriff said, "it's too dark for us to go back to Ball's Mill right now. I have a warrant here for your stealing the boots." Cullen started to speak, but was shushed by Hayden with a wave of the hand. "We talked it over back there, and there's no sense in taking you to Houlton. It's such a little thing—even if it is stealing—and we figured if you'd keep right on going across the line and never show your face around here again, we'd all be better off—and you, too. I shan't tie you up; there's no sense to it. And I won't say anything about this matter to Swanback, if it'll make you any happier. Come morning, though, you'd better light out. You come back, we'll slap the warrant on you."

Hayden returned to the camp's warmth. Cullen stayed outside brooding for some time. He reentered as the others were settling in their beds, Hubbard and Hayden between the door and the fire, Bird and Swanback on the makeshift bunk at the other end of the cabin. Swanback's dog curled on a mat at his master's feet.

Cullen's bed was near the bunk, but he sat quietly staring into the flames in the fireplace long after the others had fallen asleep. His thoughts slipped back to his birthplace in Florenceville, New Brunswick, just a little ways over the line; to his mistress, Mrs. Twist, and her two children by her first marriage; to their own "Dummy," or whatever Cullen knew him as. If he went back to New Brunswick, he wouldn't be there more'n a day or so before the Mounties came after him. They never left a fellow alone—not Cullen's kind of fellow, anyway, in his simple mind. If he went away, that was the end of the family life. Oh, she wasn't much on looks, but she could set a good table. If he stayed on, it might mean another trip to Houlton, unless . . .

The night passed slowly for Cullen. Finally, along toward morning, he glanced at the sleeping forms of the four men. Hubbard lay on his back, snoring softly. The deputy slept fretfully on his stomach. Bird and Swanback, farthest from the fire, were huddled together for warmth. Cullen stood up quietly, pulled on the stolen boots. He kicked at the half-burned wood in the fireplace. The sparks swirled; the logs settled. No one stirred.

Lifting a double-bitted axe from its pegs on the wall, Cullen lumbered softly across the corner of the room, silhouetted against the fresh flames.

Standing between Hayden and Hubbard, he paused, raised the axe and swung with all his brute strength, splitting Hubbard's head from crown to base. The axe imbedded itself with a thud in the dirt floor.

Hayden stirred and began to sit up as Cullen pulled the weapon free and swung on him. Hayden fell back, dead, the side of his head torn away.

Swanback said he heard a noise "between the whack of an axe and the stir of a puddin'." He and Bird sat up as Cullen turned from the two corpses and advanced toward them.

Swanback lunged for the door. Cullen swung the axe at his head, missed. The door took the full force of the blow. Made of dry cedar, it shattered and fell from its leather hinges, tangling Cullen's big feet in the debris. Swanback disappeared into the darkness. Bird cowered on the bunk, unable to move or cry out. He stared at the two dead lawmen. Cullen stood over him, breathing heavily, the bloodied axe in his two big hands.

Bird's stomach knotted as he tried to shrink through the mattress of pine boughs. The wall stopped his backward movement. Too frightened to speak, he raised his hands in supplication to Cullen.

The axe dropped ever so slowly to the floor. Cullen jerked the frail youth up by his shirt front, holding him off the floor. Bird's eyes were wide with terror. Cullen threw him back onto the bunk. It collapsed. Bird lay amid its rubble, still unable to speak or scramble for the doorway.

Cullen's ankle began to hurt him. Must've got it tangled with the damn door. Swanback's lit out, he thought, probl'y for help. Never catch him.

"Go get Swanback," he ordered. "Bring in some wood from outside. We'll burn the place down. Then I'll let you both go if you never tell no one what just happened here."

Bird only half believed the words, but he rushed outside anyway, returning shortly with Swanback. The two began lugging wood feverishly, piling it next to the fire, around and atop the two bodies as Cullen directed. Swanback had escaped, but without his boots; the prospect of freezing his bare feet in a hike to Ball's Mill and Bird's message from the murderer, in his state of shock, were sufficient convincers.

Cullen doused the corner with kerosene from a jug, motioned Bird and Swanback outside, and threw a faggot from the fire onto the pyre.

He stumbled outside, favoring his twisted, aching ankle. The threesome watched the flames as they began to lick through the cedar logs. The roof collapsed five minutes later. Cullen chuckled, then turned, ready to finish off the two remaining witnesses. Swanback and Bird had hesitated only a moment before they struck off for safety. Their five-minute head start and Cullen's wrenched ankle gave them their needed margin of safety.

Back in Mapleton Plantation, Mary Judkins pulled the covers up around her head. It was no use. The pounding wouldn't stop. She sat up in bed, staring out her window into the darkness. It was nearly two o'clock. She heard her father's slow steps on the stairs, his muttered exasperation, the bolt on the door slide back.

Andrew Judkins surmised there was trouble, even before he opened the door. After all, nobody's up at two o'clock in the morning unless something's wrong. Bird and Swanback stood in the doorway, gasping for breath. They had no snowshoes. They were in their stocking feet, hatless. Their hair was standing "straight up," Judkins said afterward.

"They'd been running just as fast as they could for three miles," he said, "and were just about beat out. If there hadn't been that heavy crust on the snow, their feet would've been cut to pieces." The pair gasped out their gruesome tale between gulps of air and coffee, warmed from the night before on the back of the stove. Cullen, they feared, was only a short distance behind them, and intent on killing them before they could tell of his misdeeds.

Judkins finished hearing their story, ran next door and roused the Eben Garlands. Mary went from house to house in her nightgown awakening the other neighbors, who quickly began to ssemble at Judkins' farm home.

Judkin's small home filled with neighbors. A watch was set up; a runner sent to Presque Isle to take word to the marshal at Houlton. The farmers surrounded the house in the darkness. Cullen stumbled out of the woods shortly afterward, saw the bobbling lanterns, and guessed correctly that Bird and Swanback had reached safety. In the darkness he headed for his home near Haystack Mountain.

After sunrise, Judkins gathered a few men from among the farmers, and, leaving a score of men at his farmhouse to protect the two survivors of the slayings, set off for Swanback's clearing.

Only a pile of charred wood remained. Prodding through it with sticks, they uncovered the remains of the two men and Hayden's keys. The group then returned to Judkins' home with what remained of the sheriff and Hubbard in a shoebox, "all of which would not weigh ten pounds."

Mrs. Twist heard the angry crowd as it marched up the hill toward her house. Cullen swung open the trap door to the cellar, and, descending, cowered in its darkest corner. His mate shoved the kitchen table over the trap.

Colomore L. (Lew) Griffin shouted the mob to silence, and, from a healthy distance, hailed the house. Mrs. Twist's face appeared at a window.

"We want Cullen," Griffin shouted.

"I haven't seen him for two days," she cried. "Why? What do you want him for? He hasn't done anything. He's not here, anyway. I don't know when he'll be home."

"He killed Gran Hayden and Bill Hubbard last night. He took an axe to 'em at Swanback's camp and set fire to the place. We know he's in there. His tracks lead right here. Send him out."

"I tell you, he's not in this house," she protested, crying. Griffin advanced to the door.

"Come out and surrender, Cullen," he roared. "We know you're in there. If you don't come out, we'll put a torch to the place." There was no answer. "If you try to run for it," another in the crowd yelled, "we'll gun you down." Nearly a dozen rifles and shotguns graced the mob. Cullen peered out through a crack in the outside cellar door.

"I ain't goin' to give up," he shouted defiantly. "I won't, and anyone comes after me'll get the same as the other two at the cabin."

A few men in the crowd suggested that they go in after the murderer, but they were quickly shouted down. A lighted torch was produced. One member of the crowd advanced on the house.

"Here's the torch, Cullen," he shouted. "Better come out, or up goes the house and everyone in it." There was a shriek from Mrs. Twist.

"Don't let 'em, Jim," she screamed, crying, and it was enough. The cellar doors opened slowly, and Cullen, blinking in the sunlight, walked out toward the crowd.

Constable B. J. Hughes took charge of the prisoner. He called on Lieutenant James H. Phair, later postmaster at Presque Isle, and Dr. Fred G. Parker to help him. Cullen, trussed tightly, was taken to Dudley's store, more than 50 angry men trailing around and behind him.

"Cullen discussed the brutal affair readily and without emotion," according to the account of the incident in the Presque Isle *Sunrise*, the local weekly paper. "He said he was convinced that the people would not let him live, and that he was willing to tell the truth. He explained that he had no particular reason for committing the murders, except that, he thought, if he could get hold of the papers which were in the possession of Deputy Sheriff Hayden, he could not be held, and so he determined to kill both men."

Word of the slayings had already spread through the county. Another mob was formed at Houlton, some 42 miles distant, and headed on horseback for Presque Isle.

Cullen was seated in the store on a salt box, his arms pinioned behind him. These bonds were in turn tied with stout ropes to two upright timbers supporting the roof. All day, scores of the curious came to view the hulking redhead who had killed the popular deputy and his assistant. As the sun took a reddish, bloody tinge in the west, a horseman rode up to the store, a shoebox in his hands. He dismounted and whispered a few words to several of the bystanders, pointing at the box.

Striding into the store, he stopped in front of the trussed murderer, opening the box. "That's all that's left of 'em," he gritted between clenched teeth.

"They look well," Cullen said stupidly, then nodded, stonefaced. His face blanched as he drew a breath of the pungent contents of the box, sickish-sweet smelling, and he screamed, "I'm sorry I didn't kill the others, too."

Then, according to the *Sunrise* account, Cullen "treated the ashes and bones of his victims to an indignity so rude and coarse that we cannot repeat it here." That settled things, if they hadn't been already settled.

A strapping farm lad sidled up to a corner of the store, selected a neat length of rope and a bar of soap. With great deliberation, he seated himself cross-legged on the floor in front of Cullen and began soaping it.

Cullen whistled softly to himself as he watched the boy work.

"As the hours wore on," the *Sunrise* observed, "it became quite evident that public sentiment demanded summary vengeance and proposed to secure it without waiting for any process of law."

Mysterious strangers moved around Presque Isle from house to house, the paper observed, not explaining how, in a county with only a few thousand inhabitants there could be many strangers.

And, the account notes slyly, "just what was said perhaps will never be repeated. A man would come to the door, whisper to the householder, and then say out loud, 'Will you be there?'" The person so addressed would usually nod assent.

"All this resulted in a company of one hundred or two hundred people who that evening proceeded out on the road toward Ball's Mill."

Constable Hughes, meanwhile, had formed a guard of a half dozen men, including Dr. Parker and Lieutenant Phair. They strapped Cullen to a wood sled—a pung—and the horse-drawn affair set out with an ever-growing crowd of curious toward Presque Isle and its tiny inadequate jail.

They had gone less than a mile when they were halted by a crowd of hooded men. "There may have been fifty with their features concealed," witnesses estimated later. "Without much argument they put a rope around Cullen's neck, dragged him out of the conveyance along the ground one hundred feet or so, then four or five rods into the woods, and hanged him to a maple tree." The well-soaped rope did its work well.

The entire mob was dispersed in half an hour. They left Cullen hanging there. The view is still beautiful from that spot—at least, they say it's the same spot—but the tree where Cullen was hanged has long since been cut up into small pieces that were sold as souvenirs.

The *Sunrise* editor published an extra the next morning, "deploring the event, and stating that the lynching was done by a party of roughs from neighboring towns, and that some of the citizens of Presque Isle were concerned in the matter."

"The editor called upon the United States marshal to come and investigate the facts," the account reads, "and punish the perpetrators of the base deed, which he said had brought a lasting disgrace upon the town and the county."

"I met him (the marshal) on the street about four o'clock in the morning," the editor wrote, "and he was in a perfect rage and even prohibited me from sending anything about the matter to outside papers that would in the least indicate that Presque Isle people had anything to do with the matter.

"My despatches had already gone, a horseman taking them . . . to Houlton, where they were telegraphed to the paper I represented. As soon as the extra was on the street, the editor was informed that he must suppress the edition, and not allow any matter to appear in his regular edition.

"When he objected, he was told that if he did not comply, not only his office, but even his house would be destroyed by the enraged people, who would not for a moment let such as expression of disapproval be published to the outside world. After such vigorous arguments, the editor concluded that discretion was the better part of valor, and complied with the request."

But the discreet publisher apparently had allowed several copies of his extra to be sold: copies are still bound in the files in the city's library.

A coroner's inquest returned a verdict that Cullen came to his death "by some party or parties to the jurors unknown."

That was Maine's first and last lynching. The participants are all dead now, but some of their sons and many of their grandchildren still recall versions of the incident.

The scene of the murders is marked on most detailed maps of the area still, as "Swanback's Clearing." It's known as the "Bloody Half-Acre," though—and a queer, spooky place to be in the uneasy night.   END

by Lowell Ames Norris

The preacher, the choir girl, and the debutante—

A Tragic Triangle

HIGH ON A BLEAK HILL IN HYANNIS, DOWN ON Cape Cod, where the wintry winds sweep the broad expanses of the Atlantic Ocean, sleeps Avis Linnell—the attractive choir girl who was once belle of this then little village and daughter of a prosperous Hyannisport contractor.

In this lonely grave lies buried a plain gold ring—a wedding ring that once glowed white in the moonlight of love-filled summer nights—the symbol of all that might have been, but never was.

More than a quarter century later, the body of another woman, once a Boston debutante and heiress to millions, lay in New York City awaiting burial, her frail form wasted by the illness which caused her death.

These two women had never met. Yet their lives were intertwined by the overpowering influence of a man, the third member of this tragic triangle—the Reverend Clarence V. T. Richeson, scion of an influential Virginia family.

But on a summer's night in June, 1909, death must have seemed far away to Avis Linnell. She was slim and attractive, although quiet and reserved at only sixteen. Her interest that night lay in the wedding of her sister Vida to William J. MacLean of Brockton. That was—at first. Later, all her interest became focused upon the young student minister who officiated at the service, Clarence V. T. Richeson of the Hyannis Baptist Church. Interest and friendship between the two young people progressed to such a degree that, by December 17, 1908—Avis' seventeenth birthday—the Reverend Mr. Richeson gave her a plain gold band ring. This ring was later to cause much talk, some even going so far as to hint that a secret marriage had been consummated. This despite the fact that friends of Avis were beginning to make plans for a rainbow wedding.

Richeson first came to Boston in 1906, where he enrolled at the Theological Seminary in Newton. Here, Moses G. Edmands, one of the trustees and a member of an old Boston family, became interested in this spirited young Southerner. He did all he could to further Richeson's career and entertained him quite frequently, with the assistance of his daughter Violet, a current debutante.

Two years later, still in the seminary, Richeson, while serving a church in South Yarmouth, was called to the pulpit of the Hyannis church where Avis was a choir girl and where, a few months later, he was to officiate at the MacLean wedding. Back in those days when romance had not yet been dubbed old-fashioned, the whole town was watching this love story unfold between the attractive girl and the handsome man of God. To Avis he was "the Prince in White" and her "All in All."

After graduating from the theological school in June, 1908, Richeson preached some sermons of an inflammatory nature, and town sentiment began to turn against him. Disregarding friendly warnings to change his ways, he continued to preach sensationalism from the pulpit; in the spring of 1910 he was forced to resign. This produced conflicting emotions among the townsfolk. Many were glad to see the Southern Firebrand leave town. Those who regretted his action were mostly women, including, of course, Avis Linnell.

Later that spring, a call came to Richeson from the Immanuel Baptist Church at Cambridge, Massachusetts, and in June he took up his duties in this fashionable house of God across the Charles River from Boston.

During the summer, he returned to Hyannisport to see Avis, who quickly became her former happy self. During one of their favorite walks

Avis Linnell—the choir girl. *Courtesy Curtis B. Norris.*

among the dunes, he suggested that she come up to Boston that fall and attend the New England Conservatory of Music.

"You can never tell when that sort of training will be valuable," he said, "and we can be near each other again." And the minister hinted that this was not all the future held. True enough!

Avis again began to plan on an October wedding although the man may have said nothing to encourage her in her dreams. But she was very young and very much in love.

There was no wedding that year. Avis left her home and enrolled as a music student at the Conservatory, getting a room at the Boston Young Women's Christian Association on Warrenton Street. Whenever the opportunity offered, Richeson saw Avis, although he grew more and more busy as time went on.

In March of the next year, the townsfolk at Hyannis were surprised to read in the Barnstable *Patriot* the announcement of the engagement of Reverend Clarence Richeson to Miss Violet Edmands of Brookline. Simultaneously, Mrs. Linnell received a letter from Avis stating that her engagement to Mr. Richeson had been terminated at the minister's request.

Yet, during the summer that followed, Richeson spent much time in the company of Avis after convincing her father and mother that the announced engagement was all "newspaper nonsense." Folks thought a reconciliation had been reached when the minister returned to Cambridge and Avis went back to the Conservatory and her room at the Y.W.C.A.

So started the eventful fall of 1911. Richeson was more than busy and Avis was still hoping.

Above: Violet Edmands—the debutante. (From a 1911 issue of the *Boston Post.*)

Right: Reverend Clarence V. T. Richeson— the preacher. *Courtesy Curtis B. Norris.*

It was after supper on Saturday evening, October 14, 1911. Avis had come in from an afternoon spent with her "boy friend" and joined a group who were sitting around the table in the social room. They were discussing a concert they were planning to attend later that evening. Avis remained silent although she had helped arrange the party. Finally, after a long period of silence, she announced she was going to her room.

"What!" exclaimed Inez Hascomb. "Not going? But you helped plan the party."

"I know I did," Avis admitted. "Nevertheless, I'm going upstairs, take a bath, and go to bed." Disregarding protests from the chattering group, she pushed back her chair, made her way slowly up the stairs, and disappeared.

A girl whose head was buried in an evening tabloid looked up as Avis vanished above stairs. "No wonder the girl doesn't want to face us," she cried excitedly. "Get a load of this!"

She pointed to an article replete with pictures. "That boy friend must have told Avis to skidoo. He's going to marry a society bud from Chestnut Hill."

The girls clustered around the flaming headlines. There it was in black and white. The Reverend Mr. Richeson was going to be married on October 31—only 17 days away—to the heiress daughter of a well-known Brookline family.

While they were talking, a shrill scream came from above. A girl in negligee leaned over the stairs. "Come quick," she said. "Something has happened to Avis."

While they stood in shocked surprise, Juliet C. Patterson, the Y. W. Superintendent, elbowed her way through the sobered group and disappeared up the stairs. Seated inside her room was the limp body of Avis Linnell—her clothes piled neatly on a nearby chair and her feet immersed in a tub of hot water. She lay apparently in a coma. A woman doctor was hastily summoned. She gave one hurried look at the purpling lips and the darkening fingers. Quickly she felt for a pulse. "This girl is dead," she stated, "apparently from some powerful drug, evidently self-administered." Then she added, "You'd better notify the Medical Examiner at once." There was a shocked, bewildered silence as the door closed behind the doctor.

"Suicide!" somebody whispered. "She killed herself! That isn't like Avis."

"Why doesn't somebody do something?" another broke in. "Where's her family? Somebody ought to know."

"Her family are somewhere upstate," Inez told them. "But that boy friend of hers ought to know where to reach them."

Minutes later, she had the "boy friend" on the wire. The news was clearly a shock to Richeson. Inez heard his quick, in-drawn breath. There were a few seconds of silence. "Poor child," he sympathized. "She was a member of my Hyannisport congregation. I baptized her into the faith. And I knew her folks quite well." He suggested that they get in touch with the girl's sister, Mrs. William J. MacLean of Brockton. He paused. "But I fail to see why I am drawn into this matter," he added coldly.

Inez was so incensed she could hardly speak. Then words fairly tumbled from her mouth. "Because you're the only friend the girl thought she had close at hand," she replied. "Besides you had lunch with her just a few hours ago!"

This the minister denied. He seemed about to hang up, then hesitated. "By the way," he asked casually, "did she say anything before she died? Leave any message?"

The indignant Miss Hascomb slammed down her receiver.

Meanwhile, in the glare of powerful lights in the morgue of the Boston City Hospital, Medical Examiner Timothy J. Leary went forward with a most careful examination of the body of Avis Linnell.

Hours later—in the early morning hours—lights still burned in Police Headquarters, then in Pemberton Square, as the usual routine investigation of the case proceeded under the direction of Deputy Superintendent William B. Watts. The report of the Medical Examiner lay upon his desk as he talked with William J. MacLean, brother-in-law of the dead girl, who had come to take charge of the body.

"Do you know any reason why your sister-in-law should want to commit suicide?" the Deputy Superintendent asked.

"I feel positive she didn't commit suicide," MacLean replied. "She was not the kind of person who would do such a thing."

"Do you know of any men with whom she might have become too friendly?" Watts continued.

"What do you mean?" the brother-in-law exclaimed.

Watts reached over and picked up the report. "According to the Medical Examiner," he said, "she was about to become a mother."

MacLean recoiled as though from a bodily blow. Then he recovered. "All the more reason not to kill herself," he replied. "No matter what she had to fear, she would be more afraid of death. I tell you she was murdered." He brought his clenched fist down hard upon the desk.

"You feel sure of this?"

"I am positive," returned MacLean.

"Then wait until I call in the Medical Examiner," Watts said. "He feels somewhat the same as you." He spoke into the telephone. "We have got to be certain of our facts before we make any announcements." A few moments later, Leary appeared. "What makes you think, Leary, that the girl was not a suicide?" he asked.

"For various reasons," the Medical Examiner answered, swiftly marshalling his facts. "First because of the type of poison used. It is one of the most violent known and kills almost instantly. Therefore, she must have taken it a few seconds before death. Secondly, because she had not prepared for death. The bed covers were carefully turned back and there was an opened book on the pillow. She had laid out fresh undergarments for the next day. And when they found her, she was in a bathrobe and nightgown instead of being fully dressed."

Watts did not fully agree. "Couldn't that have been planned?" he countered. "Couldn't she have made a sudden decision even after making those preparations?"

"Not when she was lying with her feet in hot water," the doctor emphasized.

"Somebody tricked her," MacLean broke in hotly. "She took that poison believing it was something else."

Watts turned to Leary. "Let me put it my way," he said. "I do not consider it safe for you to overlook that angle."

The Deputy Superintendent assured him that he would not. Then he asked MacLean to stand by ready to tell him the name of every person that his sister-in-law knew.

"And the charge?" questioned the brother-in-law.

"Murder," said Deputy Superintendent Watts.

* * * * *

When the sensational charge of murder was made public by the Deputy Superintendent and Medical Examiner Leary, all New England was shocked.

At Police Headquarters, Watts was painstakingly considering all points which had been brought out in the investigation so far and was restudying all evidence in the light of murder. Newspapers were called upon to assist in learning all recent purchases of the poison that had caused the girl's death. A reward of $1000 was offered by the *Boston American* to anyone who would come forward with information which would lead to the arrest of the murderer—if murder it was.

Former acquaintances of Avis Linnell were checked, and, presently, Watts learned of the girl's love affair with the Reverend Mr. Richeson. However, nothing of advantage to the police could be made of the information he had uncovered. Nor could Watts see any evidence which would lead him to conclude that the minister was in any way mixed up with the case.

The announcement of his engagement to Violet Edmands had been made earlier in the spring. Merely their marriage plans had been announced on the night of Miss Linnell's death. During the summer, after the minister's betrothal had become known, he and Avis Linnell had been seen together on several occasions in Hyannisport.

As a matter of routine, Watts had checked all drugstores in the vicinity of the Boston Y.W.C.A. and had discovered no records of sales of any poisons that could be fitted into the case. Now, because of knowledge of the love affair between the minister and the dead girl, he visited all drugstores situated along the street car route by which Richeson traveled from Cambridge to Chestnut Hill.

He returned to headquarters discouraged and grasping for even the slightest clue. He had worked day and night on the case and had uncovered nothing of any consequence. As he sank in his desk chair exhausted, the telephone bell rang at his elbow. His hand fumbled as he took off the receiver and said hello into the mouthpiece.

"I want to see you," a man's incisive voice said briskly. "I think I know something about the poison in the Avis Linnell case."

Minutes later, the Deputy Superintendent was closeted with a stylishly dressed man in his late thirties with well-groomed mustache. "My name is William Hahn," he began, "and I run a drugstore in Newton Center. (Newton Center is a part of Newton which lies a few miles west of Boston.) Four days before this Linnell murder, a young man whom I have known for quite some time walked into my store and said he wanted some poison which would kill a dog.

"I asked him why he didn't try chloroform, and he replied he didn't like the smell of it and besides he wanted something that would work more quickly. Finally, I suggested this other poison and told him it would do the work. However, I warned him that he would have to be very careful in handling it for it was very dangerous. He nodded and stood by while I weighed it out, telling me to be sure to give him enough to do the work.

"I told him there was enough there to kill two or three dogs. He laughed and told me to throw in three or four more hunks as the dog was going to have pups and he wanted to be sure it did the job."

"Is that all that was said?" asked the Deputy Superintendent.

"No, we talked of other things, and he started to leave. When he got to the door, he turned back. 'This request may sound queer to you,' he said, 'but can you keep a secret? I haven't bought this stuff from you and I don't know you.'"

"And what did you say?"

"Nothing. In fact, I didn't think anything about it," Hahn went on, "until I saw that piece in the paper asking for information on sales of this poison. I got in touch with my lawyer, and he advised me to see you."

"He advised you well," agreed the police officer. "You say you know this man?"

The Immanuel Baptist Church in Cambridge, Massachusetts, where Richeson was pastor of a fashionable congregation. *Courtesy Curtis B. Norris.*

"I've known him ever since he was a student here in Newton," was the reply. "He's a preacher—the Reverend Clarence Richeson of Cambridge."

* * * * *

Watts lost no time in going to the minister's boarding house in Cambridge. But he was not there. Nor did anyone in the family know where he had gone.

"Did he own a dog?" Watts inquired.

"No," reported a member of the family with which he lived.

"Is there a female dog on the premises?"

"No."

Returning to Boston's Police Headquarters and prepared to go to any length to ensure Richeson's capture, Watts discovered the man had not fled town. He had merely sought seclusion at the Edmands' home. Efforts to gain entrance to this Chestnut Hill mansion were ignored. Nor was there any answer to the telephone.

By midnight Watts had assembled a police task force. In it were officers from Boston, led by Chief Inspector Dugan, representatives from the office of District Attorney Joseph C. Pelletier, as well as police and detectives from the Brookline police. Hurrying to the Edmands' estate, they threw a cordon around the house and grounds. Just beyond the police lines, reporters and cameramen waited impatiently in taxicabs.

Deputy Superintendent Watts and Chief

231

Inspector Dugan mounted the front piazza and rang the front door bell. There was no answer from within, and the bellpull came free. It had been cut. The hours dragged by, the silence broken every now and then by the explosion of flashlight powder. The house remained dark. But the police pickets still maintained their vigilance.

At daybreak, Watts and Dugan again hammered on the front door, as the Deputy Superintendent was positive that the minister was within. This time the door opened a few inches. The face of Moses Edmands appeared. "What's the meaning of all this racket?" he began.

"We're police officers," Watts explained. "We want the Reverend Mr. Richeson."

Edmands hesitated, then asked the officers inside. While they waited in the hall, he telephoned his lawyer. Finally, he led them down a long hall and halted beside a closed door. "He's in there," he said.

Watts knocked sharply on the panel.

"What do you want?" a weak voice cried.

Watts pushed the door open and the two officials went in. Before them on a disorderly bed—unshaven and on the verge of collapse—was Clarence Richeson. He readily admitted his identity, and Watts informed him he was under arrest for the murder of Avis Linnell. It was evident Richeson was under awful strain. He staggered from the bed and slowly dressed himself. Watts brought him a glass of milk. He sipped it slowly. Slowly he put the glass down.

"May I say good-bye to my fiancée?" he asked. "She's lying ill in another room."

Watts gave him permission. Richeson stumbled down the hall to the room of the girl he had expected to marry. At the sound of his voice, she sprang from bed and threw her arms around his body, all the while crying bitterly.

"Oh, they can't take you away from me," she sobbed. "They mustn't. I can't let them!"

"It's all right," the minister reassured her. "I tell you there's nothing to worry about. Everything will be all right." He reached up and gently removed the girl's arms from about his neck. Then he turned to the officers. "I'm ready, gentlemen," he said.

* * * * *

From behind prison walls, Richeson continued to proclaim his innocence and thousands

Medical examiner T. J. Leary had reason to believe Avis did not kill herself. *Courtesy Lowell Ames Norris.*

of persons, including members of his Cambridge church, believed him guiltless, as did a certain very few of his former congregation in Hyannis. Despite Richeson's denials, investigation disclosed he had lunched with Avis Linnell on the day of her death at a sea grill on Dartmouth Street near Huntington Avenue in Boston, not far from the Y. W. Later he took her for a long walk in the Fens. Inspection of the minister's room disclosed, among other things, dozens of locks of feminine hair which devoted admirers had sent him.

In order to prevent the accused from claiming that the girl had taken her own life, the body of the former choir girl was quietly exhumed and brought to Boston for reexamination. Also her clothing was searched to make certain that neither a farewell note nor the poison container had been buried through accident with the girl. On her finger, investigators found the same gold band which the minister had given her during their early acquaintance. It was reburied with her.

Delving deep into Richeson's past, Watts learned that many women had figured in his early life, including a young woman in the far west who lent him money and still considered herself engaged to him. Investigators also learned he had been expelled from one college for cribbing. He had been a bread salesman, a street car conductor, and a labor agitator. He

232

Deputy Superintendent William B. Watts of Boston, who was in charge of the case. *Courtesy Lowell Ames Norris.*

had been forced to resign from several pulpits because of alleged unsavory episodes with women.

When the grand jury met on October 26, more incriminating evidence was revealed. He had been engaged to Avis Linnell, and he had given her a diamond ring which he later took back under pretense of having it cleaned. He had been responsible for her going to Boston after all preparations for a wedding had been completed. It was also established to the complete satisfaction of all that he had the sort of poison which was the direct cause of the girl's death. But the defense stood firm with over a million dollars in their coffers. They said they would explain everything in their own good time. The trial was set for January 15, 1912. Charles Richeson, a brother, came to Boston, prepared to assist in any way.

In November, members of the Immanuel Baptist Church reluctantly removed the name of Richeson from their church boards. A goodly majority still believed him innocent, as did a great many others who felt a terrible mistake was being made. A few days later, Richeson was found in his cell lying in a pool of blood. He had unsuccessfully tried to mutilate himself, following the example set by St. Origen.

When this became known, the world recoiled with horror. Close upon this came a 200-word confession:

Deeply penitent for my sin and earnestly desiring, as far as in my power lies to make atonement, I hereby confess that I am guilty of the offense of which I stand indicted.

I am moved to this course by no inducement of self-benefit or leniency. Heinous as is my crime, God has not wholly abandoned me, and my conscience and manhood, however depraved and blighted, will not admit of my still wronging by a public trial her whose pure young life I have destroyed.

Under the lashings of remorse I have suffered and am suffering the torture of the damned. In this I find a measure of comfort.

In my mental anguish I recognize that there is still, by mercy of the Master, some remnant of the Divine Spark of goodness still lingering with me. I could wish to live only because within some prison's wall I might, in some small measure, redeem my sinful past, help some despairing soul, and at last, find favor with my God.

Sincerely yours
Clarence V. T. Richeson

Outside State's Prison in Charlestown on May 20, 1912, a few minutes past midnight, crowds waited for the electrocution of the minister; inside the stone walls in Murderer's Row, within sight of the little green door, men's voices were raised singing "Safe in the Arms of Jesus." The deep bass notes of Richeson were heard above the rest.

While the throngs outside waited, Richeson walked with steady tread to the death chair. He calmly reaffirmed his Christian faith as guards adjusted the leather straps that held the lethal head electrode in place. "I am ready to die," said Richeson, and Warden Benjamin J. Bridges raised his gold-headed cane as a signal to the executioner.

But the final curtain on this dramatic love-crime saga did not ring down until 27 years after Richeson went to his death. Violet Edmands came into the news again. She had disappeared from sight in 1912, and Boston knew her no more. She was reported in Japan, where she spent years in social service work, and finally in New York City, where she devoted herself to unselfish and untiring philanthropies. In 1939 her frail body could stand no more. Friends say she died of a broken heart at the age of 54. May she, too, rest in peace.   END

Murder Most Fowl

**Investigators were convinced that
somehow the motive was revenge . . .**

by Frederick John

ON THE MORNING OF APRIL 9, 1926, GEORGE Washington was found sprawled on the floor of the bird house at Franklin Park Zoo in Boston, Massachusetts. The coroner ruled that George had been strangled.

This must be considered a remarkable accomplishment since George was an ostrich: the murderer would have had to cover a lot of territory in order to throttle the long-necked bird properly.

There was a bloodstained handkerchief on the ground next to the deceased, and an old overcoat had been tossed into a corner. The only witnesses were a lot of peacocks, parrots and other noisy birds.

"Motive!" declared Boston Police Captain Bradley C. Mason, who was in charge of the

(Editor's Note: *Certain names have been changed to protect the innocent.*)

investigation. "We've got to come up with a motive for this crime. Once we discover the motive, we'll find our murderer."

At the outset, investigators were convinced the motive was revenge. In order to get into the bird house, they theorized, the murderer would have had to scale a ten-foot-high rear fence. Next, it would have been necessary to sneak across a large yard and force open the door of the cage where the unsuspecting 250-pound ostrich was sleeping, then tiptoe up behind the innocent bird, perform the dastardly deed, and escape before the guards at the park discovered the murder. Obviously, reasoned veteran investigators, the man who had throttled George had been motivated by a bizarre desire to revenge himself on the ostrich for some twisted reason.

The first break in the case came a few hours

The bird house at Franklin Park Zoo, where George Washington slept.

after the murder was discovered. "Why don't you drop over to South Boston and question Francis X. McMurphy?" said a voice on the phone.

"What for?" Sergeant Charles B. Ryan, who answered the call to police headquarters, wanted to know.

"'Cause Francis X. McMurphy gave his wife a big ostrich plume for her hat. Last night he didn't have a penny to his name. That ostrich feather he bought his Agnes for her birthday must have cost all of a dollar."

In a matter of minutes, a police wagon was in front of the McMurphy home on J Street, and Francis X. was hauled away for questioning.

"Where did you get that feather, McMurphy?" the police inquired.

"I bought it this morning down at Ray-mond's," insisted Francis X. "I got a bill of sale back home to prove it."

"Don't try to bluff us, McMurphy," snarled the police. "We know you didn't have any money last night. You couldn't have bought that plume."

"I borrowed the money from a friend. It's my Agnes' birthday. I wanted her to have a nice gift."

"Confess!" insisted the police. "You murdered George Washington last night to get that plume! Confess, and clear your conscience!"

McMurphy refused, and a short time later authorities released him from custody. He did have a bill of sale, and a friend came forward to verify that he had loaned McMurphy some money. In addition, it was determined as nearly as possible that the ostrich still had all its feathers.

The case broke that evening. An officer, who had been home sleeping during the day after working all night, reported to his superior that he had questioned a man during the wee small hours near Franklin Park. The patrolman said he had stopped the man because his clothes were torn, and there was blood on his face. Before allowing the suspect to continue on his way, the officer had written down his name and address in his police book.

"I did it!" cried the suspect, who shall be hereafter referred to as Mr. Nemo, when he was confronted by authorities. "I didn't mean to do it, but I did it."

It turned out that Mr. Nemo had been drinking a cheap brand of prohibition brew the night before with a few of the boys.

"I didn't want to upset the little woman by disturbing her sleep when I got home," said Mr. Nemo, "so I decided to sneak in the back way. Right off the bat, I should have known I was at the wrong place. That fence I climbed seemed a lot higher than the one we have at home. After that, I had trouble getting my key in the lock. I finally had to force the door open. And once I got inside, right away something attacked me and started hitting me on the head. All I did was grab hold of the thing and hold on for my life. That's all I did, so help me. It was self-defense."

Mr. Nemo was arraigned in Dorchester District Court the following morning, charged with drunkenness.

"So help me, Your Honor," pleaded the defendant, "my friend liquor and I have parted company."

The judge knew a repentant sinner when he saw one. He fined Mr. Nemo a mere $15, ordered investigators to return the overcoat he had left behind at the zoo, and ruled that the case was closed.

Not so! Ostrich lovers across the nation protested the decision. They claimed Mr. Nemo should have been shipped to State Prison for his crime. And they sent nasty letters to many Bay State political leaders.

Malcolm E. Nichols, who was Mayor of Boston at the time, called a press conference.

"I have," he declared, "investigated this matter fully, and I am satisfied that justice has been served. The real culprits in this case are those people who sold the poor man that illegal alcohol. We have laws against such things, and I intend to see that they are strictly enforced."

Massachusetts Governor Alvan Fuller also disclosed to the press that he had "looked into that episode at the zoo."

"I love birds as much as any man," he declared. "But you can't expect a man to rot in jail simply because he defended himself against one."

Several poems were written about the episode. The most famous is a long narrative poem written by an anonymous author. In part, it reads:

Then I leaped across the darkness,
Just a bruised and battered wreck,
And I grabbed a hold of something
That felt like a fellow's neck.

But I felt no Adam's apple,
And the neck was long and thin.
But what troubled me the most was
That I couldn't find no chin.

In addition to the poems, both humorous and serious, countless protest meetings were held across the nation by animal lovers. Hundreds of letters to the editors poured in. Everybody had something to say about the Ostrich Murder Case.

At the time, there was a great deal of doubt that Mr. Nemo could have whipped George Washington in a fair fight. Daniel Harkins, Franklin Park curator, had informed the press that the odds were 25 to 1 against a human emerging victorious in a fight with an ostrich.

A South African expert on ostriches wrote the Boston *Herald*: "To an unprotected man, an infuriated ostrich is as dangerous as a lion."

A Boston *Transcript* reader demanded to know, "how much does this man who overpowered the 250-pound ostrich weigh?"

Mr. Nemo, it was revealed, weighed 120 pounds soaking wet and was therefore a most unlikely person to whip an ostrich twice his weight in hand-to-hand combat.

As a result, to this day there are those who remain convinced that the real murderer got away. END

George Washington (250 pounds) was more than twice the weight of his confessed slayer (120 pounds).

The "death ship" *Herbert Fuller* put into Halifax Harbor flying the black flag of mutiny and towing a black-draped jolly boat loaded with corpses. (From a faded old newspaper photo.)

Death aboard the *Herbert Fuller*

by John U. Ayotte

Wholesale homicide aboard an ill-starred barkentine.

THE *Herbert Fuller* WAS A BARKENTINE—THAT is, her foremast was square-rigged, and her main and mizzen masts rigged fore-and-aft, as the masts of a schooner are rigged. She was launched from a Down East shipyard in 1890 and wound up 27 years later, the target of a German U-boat, at the bottom of the Mediterranean. But long before she ran afoul of the Kaiser's underwater navy, the vessel from Harrington, Maine, had figured in a more tragic and mystifying adventure—an affair still the object of conjecture and surmise. Into this adventure, which began in mid-Atlantic on July 14, 1896, the ill-starred ship was sailing in the first dark hours of the new day.

Five of the 12 persons on board were quartered in the after-house: the captain and his wife, the two mates, and the lone passenger, a Harvard student, Lester Hawthorne Monks. Ellery Sedgwick, a family friend, in his reminiscences *The Happy Profession*, records that at 19 the young man from Brookline had become so talented a drinker that his health was affected. His doctors, his college dean, and his family all agreed that the best possible solution was a long voyage on a ship where boon companions and liquor would be in short supply. The *Herbert Fuller*, about to sail from Boston to Rosario, Argentina, seemed to meet these requirements, and Lester Monks—whose life was to be a compound of the thunder and the sunshine—unwittingly embarked upon a perilous undertaking.

On the evening of July 13, the fifth day out, with a smooth sea and a fresh breeze on the starboard quarter, the *Herbert Fuller* was moving at a speed of seven or eight knots. After watching the sunset from the main deck, piled high with the overflow of the lumber cargo, Monks went below at eight o'clock. The large main cabin was in the middle of the after-house, with doors opening into the chart room and the three staterooms of Mrs. Nash and the mates Bram and Blomberg. Next to the Captain's wife—her husband's companion on all voyages—was the passenger's cabin. Access was from the chart room where 42-year-old Charles I. Nash, the ship's master and part owner, habitually slept.

As Lester Monks turned in for the night, he may have been thinking of the strangers who had suddenly become his shipmates. Captain and Mrs. Nash understandably had tried to make him feel at home, and seemed to enjoy his talk of books and college, and of topical news items, one of which was the current Cuban rebellion against Spain. The mates were less responsive. The first officer, Thomas Mead Chambers Bram, was in his early 30s, a swarthy, mustached, and enigmatic native of the West Indian island of St. Kitts. When Monks first visited the barkentine at Mystic Wharf, Bram had given him unexpected and mysterious advice not to sail on the *Herbert Fuller*. Between Bram and the second mate, the big Russian Finn August W. Blomberg, strong mutual dislike had already flared out in several exchanges of hot words. By contrast, the young mulatto steward, Jonathan Spencer, also a West Indian, seemed popular with everyone. The six sailors bunked in the forecastle were probably still unknown by name to the passenger. Three were Swedes: Folke Wassen, Oscar Anderson, and Charley Brown, whose real and somewhat formidable name was Justus Leopold Westerberg. France, Holland, and Germany were represented by Francis Loheac, Henrik Perdock, and Henry J. Slice, now a naturalized United States citizen. These were obscure men, but their names would soon be widely known, and spelled and misspelled in scores of newspapers.

239

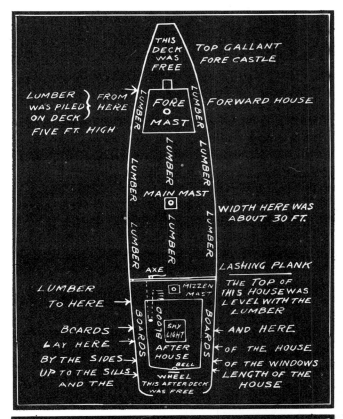

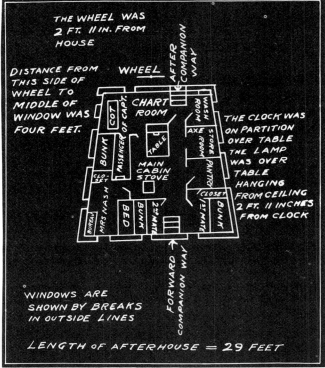

Top: Deck plan of the *Herbert Fuller.*
Above: Interior of the afterhouse.

Because his cabin door rattled with the roll of the ship, Monks set the lock and shoved a sea chest against the bottom of the door. Under his pillow at night he kept a revolver, a parting gift from his uncle, Dr. George Monks, who had warned Lester that the crew of a lumber schooner was not like that of a yacht, and that a pistol might come in handy before the long voyage was over. The revolver, however, was not loaded, and the cartridges were stowed in a drawer under the bunk.

While Monks lay in his bunk, a brief rain squall brought Captain Nash on deck for a few words with the second mate, who had the starboard watch. At midnight, Bram and the port watch relieved Blomberg and his men. Henry Slice relinquished the wheel to Charley Brown who, after a two-hour trick, would in turn be replaced by Loheac. Meanwhile, under cover of the nightly routine, a murderer had finished a probably long-thought-out plan, and was about to strike.

As he testified later, Monks was awakened shortly before two o'clock by a woman's scream. While pondering its significance, he heard another disturbing sound, a "gurgling noise," from the direction of the chart room. After listening intently and with increasing alarm, he loaded his revolver and donned a dressing gown and slippers. Shoving back the chest, he unlocked the door, and stepped cautiously outside. In the dim light from a flickering oil lamp in the main cabin, he saw Captain Nash lying on the chart room floor beside his overturned cot. The gurgling noise came from his throat, his body was bloodstained, and he made no response when the passenger called urgently:

"Captain Nash! Captain Nash! CAPTAIN NASH!"

Unable to arouse the ship's master, Monks went to summon Mrs. Nash, but his knocks were unanswered, and a hasty glance through her cabin's open door disclosed a heap of blood-splashed bed clothes. Monks now had his fill of the after-house. Avoiding the stairs leading aft to the wheel deck, he started up the forward companionway. As he ascended, he saw the first officer approaching in the half darkness of the main deck, and called out "Mr. Bram!" but at sight of Monks and his pistol, the mate snatched up a plank and threw it. The missile fell short, and Monks hastily shouted an explanation for his sudden appearance, revolver in hand.

"Come below," he cried, "the Captain has been murdered! Come below, for God's sake!"

"No! No!" Bram protested, in what appeared to be shocked disbelief, but he acceded to the passenger's insistent request. Below, the mate went to his room for a revolver, Monks to his cabin for more clothing. Captain Nash still gasped feebly, but Bram did not go near him. For his part, Monks was only too glad to leave the terror-ridden atmosphere of the cabins and to hurry back with the first officer to the open space of the deck. To a suggestion that they look for the second mate, Bram replied:

"There is a mutiny. Blomberg is forward with the crew."

The two men sat down on the lumber-topped deck; one covered the forecastle with his revolver, the other the wheel deck and the after-house. The barkentine was still making about eight knots, and Monks could easily imagine that mingled with the noise of wind, ship, and water were other sounds in the semi-darkness of the stealthy approach of the mutineers. Presently the mate became hysterical. Grasping Monks' knees, he begged to be saved from the vengeance of the crew. He whimpered that when his watch had come on at midnight, the second mate had given him drugged whisky. With mention of this, Bram became violently ill; after a few minutes the nausea passed, and the first officer seemed to regain his self-control.

Partly in talk, but mostly in silence, the pair kept vigil until dawn. When Loheac became visible at the wheel, they walked aft and questioned him; he professed to know nothing of the tragic happenings below. Bram and Monks then went forward and told the momentarily skeptical steward of the Captain's murder. When convinced they were not joking, Spencer announced he would go down and see for himself. Bram proffered his revolver; and pointing it over the side for a trial shot, the steward pressed the trigger. At the ensuing report, the mate jumped. Later, the other cartridges in the cylinder were found loaded, but the bases were marked from some previous attempt at firing.

The steward returned from his reconnaissance of the after-house visibly shaken. Not only had he found Captain Nash dead, but Blomberg also, dead in his bunk and not, as Bram had reported, in the forecastle plotting with the crew. Both men had been hacked and slashed with a cutting weapon.

As the trio stood amidships, Bram suddenly pointed to an area of the deck and exclaimed that he saw an axe. Spencer and Monks could not identify the object until they had walked much closer; it was a short-handled axe from the main cabin storeroom, now bloodstained and half hidden under a plank. As Bram picked up the weapon, Spencer said:

"That's the axe that done it."

Bram repeated the words several times and then asked:

"Shall I throw it overboard?"

Still unsure about the mutiny, Monks assented.

"Yes," he said, "for fear the crew may use it against us."

Before the steward could interfere, Bram hurled the axe into the sea.

"You shouldn't have done that," Spencer remonstrated, "the axe was important evidence."

In a confidential tone, the mate answered:

"Then we don't find no axe."

"Do you take me for a fool," Spencer snapped back, "don't you know a man (Loheac) has seen you with the axe?"

At the steward's suggestion, the crew was assembled. As the men came out of the forecastle, there was no sign of a mutinous attitude and this, coupled with Bram's earlier lie about Blomberg's whereabouts, and the incident of the axe, deepened the first uneasy suspicions which Monks and Spencer had begun to entertain against the first mate.

After news of the murders had been broken to the crew, all except the helmsman entered the after-house. Now a third body was found, the badly gashed corpse of Mrs. Nash in her cabin bed. Back on deck, the men held a council. Monks opened a box of cigars, while Bram tried to conciliate everyone. He gave no orders, but instead offered suggestions. One was quite startling.

"Now," he said casually, "we will take those bodies out and throw them overboard, and wash up the blood in the cabin."

Henry Slice was the first to object. The bodies, he said, should be sewed up in canvas and placed in the jolly boat for preservation, and the after-house left untouched for police examination when the ship reached port. Slice's recommendation was strongly seconded, and Bram accepted it. When the three encased bodies were laid in the boat, Monks read the applicable burial service from the Book of Common Prayer. Several days later, the jolly boat was lowered, and thereafter towed behind the ship.

At Bram's request, Lester Monks prepared an account of the tragedy, including a highly implausible explanation of how it had occurred. Blomberg, wrote Monks, had attacked Mrs. Nash, whereupon her husband had assailed the mate with the storeroom axe. In the struggle, Mrs. Nash was killed and both men mortally wounded, but Blomberg for some strange reason had carried the weapon on deck before going below again to die. Not only the murderer, but everyone else, knew this theory to be absurd, but in the prevailing climate of suspicion and fear, it was in the interest of all to affect to believe the "official" version and to sign their names to it.

Bram's suggestion that a course be set for Cayenne, 1500 miles away, was overruled, and a decision made to sail for Halifax. On July 15, suspicion fell on Charley Brown, and he was put in irons. Four days afterward, when the Swedish sailor made a serious countercharge against Bram, Spencer and Monks covered the mate with a revolver and placed him in confinement. A pilot boat was sighted two days later off Halifax, and the nightmare week came to an end.

* * * * *

From Nova Scotia, the *Herbert Fuller* personnel were transferred to Boston, where, after an extensive investigation, Thomas Bram was indicted by a Grand Jury and came up for trial, December 14, 1896, before the Circuit Court of the United States on a charge of murder. Presiding were Circuit Judge Colt and District Judge Webb. The United States' District Attorney, Sherman Hoar, and his assistants, John H. Casey and Frederick P. Cabot, represented the government; James E. Cotter and Asa P. French appeared for the defense.

The prosecution's case was based on circumstantial evidence and on the direct evidence of Charley Brown, who testified that shortly before two o'clock on the morning of July 14, from his post at the wheel, he had seen Bram through the rear window of the after-house, holding a weapon by the handle and striking a man lying on the chart room floor. Other telling points were made against the mate in the testimony of Monks, Spencer, and members of the crew. Bram was shown to have done nothing to help the dying captain, as he lay gasping on the chart room floor, to determine the fate of Mrs. Nash, or to start an immediate search for the murderer. Instead, the first mate had told Monks a patent falsehood, which placed the already dead Blomberg alive in the forecastle, engaged with the crew in a mutiny. Bram had thrown the bloodstained axe overboard, and had proposed disposing of the murder victims in a similar way, while at the same time destroying all evidence of the slaying in the cabins. There was also evidence that the first mate had exhibited animosity toward both Nash and Blomberg, had spoken with gross disrespect of Mrs. Nash, and had used language which indicated a plan in mind to seize the ship.

Many believed at the time of his trial, and have believed since, that Bram expected to take over the *Herbert Fuller* easily, once the Nashes, Blomberg and Monks were dead, and intended to sell the barkentine to the Cuban insurgents, or to some other not too inquisitive buyers. It has been thought also that Bram, like Lady Macbeth, had fortified himself with liquor before entering the rooms of his prey, and that his plan failed because of Monk's locked door, the passenger's later arrival armed on deck, and the gradual evaporation of the murderer's alcohol-inspired courage.

The defense introduced evidence that in Holland Charley Brown had once been "out of his head" for 14 days, a time when he had shown delusions of persecution by firing a revolver bullet through a window at an imaginary

enemy. Exploiting this incident, Bram's counsel tried to convince the jury that the Swedish seaman was a homicidal maniac, and thus the only person on the barkentine who could have committed the three "senseless" murders.

Testifying in his own behalf, Bram proved a cool, polite and painstaking witness, unperturbed under searching cross-examination, but he offered little in rebuttal of the evidence brought against him.

After 26 hours' deliberation, the jury returned a verdict of "Guilty." Execution of the mandatory death sentence was stayed by an appeal and, because of certain inadmissible testimony by a Halifax detective, the United States Supreme Court ordered a new trial. This took place in Boston from March 16 to April 20, 1898. Boyd B. Jones and John H. Casey acted for the government; defense counsel was unchanged. Again the verdict was "Guilty," but the law now empowered the jury to fix the punishment at either death or life imprisonment, and the latter penalty was imposed.

After 15 years in prison, Bram was paroled in 1913 by President Wilson and in 1919 granted a full pardon, apparently because the Chief Executive harbored doubts of the mate's guilt. These may have been planted, or at least nurtured, by the popular novelist and mystery writer, Mary Roberts Rinehart, who had recently published *The After House*, a fictional work based on the *Herbert Fuller* homicides, with the setting transferred to a yacht, where the first mate was an innocent suspect in the murder of the captain, a passenger and a lady's maid, and the real killer a maniacal helmsman, "Charley Jones." Years later in an autobiographical volume, Mrs. Rinehart stated flatly that Bram was not the barkentine murderer and gave credit to her novel for the reopening of his case.

The decision of the President is a puzzling one. No new evidence had come to light since 1898, yet he chose to repudiate the verdicts of two juries, both of which had seen and heard the nine survivors on the witness stand, and could assess the credibility of their testimony at first hand. Probably his act is an example of a phenomenon often present in murder cases. A murderer whose identity is still shrouded in mystery is a sinister and terrifying figure, whom the general public is most anxious to see hunted down. Once captured, however, and brought to trial, the killer usually loses his ghoulish aura and becomes a mere human being, seemingly quite out of character as a bloodthirsty assassin. Then with many individuals there is a tendency to disregard the actual evidence against the defendant, and to cast about for some other person who more nearly fits their image of what a murderer should be. The Borden case is a striking example of this type of thinking, and it may be there were those who just could not believe that Cain was the type to have murdered his brother Abel.

The massacre on the *Herbert Fuller* was certain to impress some men and women as the deed of a human fiend, who could not have had any rational motive for the triple slaughter. Thomas Bram, convicted of the crime, was almost certainly a sane man; therefore they felt it necessary to find someone else for the role of pirate-assassin. Discarding the mate left only two other possibilities: the passenger and the Swedish-born helmsman.

Lester Monks was soon eliminated save by a few diehards. His sanity was not in question, he had no possible motive, and moreover was exonerated by Charley Brown, who pointed the finger of accusation, not at the young man from Brookline, but at the ship's first officer.

Because of one authenticated episode of mental disturbance, Charley Brown was vulnerable. By a slight feat of anyone's imagination, he could be pictured as a persecution-haunted madman, who dealt out death blindly and remorselessly. It is doubtful, if Woodrow Wilson, Mrs. Rinehart, and others who may have embraced this theory, ever really explored two conditions vital to such a deduction: the physical difficulties in the way of the "maniacal helmsman," and the inexplicable actions of Bram after the first murder was reported to him.

Before Charley Brown could begin his round of murders, he would have had to lash the wheel. Descending the aft companionway, he then must find the axe and, moving from room to room, methodically hack three persons to death. As attested by a trail of blood spots, the slayer left the cabin area by the forward companionway, laying his weapon first on the after-house roof, before moving it again to a plank on the main deck. After doing all this, without attracting the attention of Mate Bram on watch, Brown must return to the wheel and remove the lashing ropes. The time consumed would have been at least eight minutes (probably more), yet the best expert opinion, based on tests with the *Herbert Fuller*, held that if the wheel had been lashed for more than two minutes, the barkentine would have come up into the wind with sails flapping, forcibly alerting Bram and the seaman forward

If we do concede that Charley Brown could somehow have committed the murders undetected by the personnel on watch, we still must account for the conduct of the first mate after Monks rushed up the companionway to give the alarm. From that time on, the list of Bram's strange acts and omissions is long: the callous ignoring of the fatally wounded Captain Nash; the failure to check at once the cabins of Mrs. Nash and Blomberg; the hasty retreat from the after-house; the lie to Monks about the mutiny; the throwing overboard of the axe; the attempt to bury the dead at sea and to destroy the evidence of how they had died; and finally the effort to bring the barkentine into a port far distant from the United States. Everything Bram did, or failed to do, helped cover the tracks of the assassin, and as the mate had no conceivable reason to protect either Charley Brown or Lester Monks, the conclusion is inescapable that the murderer he shielded must have been himself.

A minor mystery is posed by the "nicked" cartridges in Bram's revolver, markings probably caused by a worn firing pin or defective ammunition. It may be that Bram intended to kill his last victim by shooting, afterwards claiming that he had surprised the murderer at work and had fired in self-defense. The first mate may have stood over the sleeping Blomberg, repeatedly drawing the pistol trigger, only to hear each time a harmless click as the hammer fell. Forgetting that one round (the cartridge later fired by Spencer) was untouched, Bram would then have turned again to a surer weapon, the bloodstained, short-handled axe.

After his release from prison, Bram tried several business ventures, and eventually became captain and owner of the schooner *Alvena*. But although he cruised the sea lanes until well into his 70s, it is doubtful if any other survivor of the fatal 1896 voyage ever expressed the slightest wish to sail again in the company of his old shipmate, Thomas Mead Chambers Bram.   END

Exonerated by Somnambulism

Rufus Choate hit upon a line of defense that would make American legal history . . .

by W. A. Swanberg

IN 1845, THE WEALTHY TIRRELL FAMILY OF Weymouth, Massachusetts, was holding frequent grave conferences with one question on the agenda: What to do about Albert?

Tall, 25-year-old Albert Tirrell seemed determined to dive head-first into ruin and drag the proud family name with him. The possessor of a pretty wife, Prudence, and two small children, he had made a commendable start only to fall into horrendous error. When his father died in 1843, he was left a large inheritance and the nominal control of the Tirrell shoe factory, the biggest in Weymouth. Such a young man could scarcely be given full authority over an enterprise employing scores of men and machines, but he labored diligently and was showing considerable promise late in 1844 when he made that regrettable business trip to New Bedford. It was in New Bedford, then a rip-snorting whaling port, that he met a brunette young lady named Maria Bickford whose aims in life were as dubious as her appearance was alluring.

That was when the Tirrell troubles began. Albert promptly dropped the shoe business, forsook his family, and concentrated his time on Maria Bickford. Maria, described in an old account as "a beautiful and designing wench who played the concertina with skill," fell in wholeheartedly with this arrangement, charmed not only by Albert but by the largesse he tossed her way. The next thing the Tirrells knew, he had installed her in a Boston apartment and seldom put in an appearance except to draw money.

Time and again, Nathaniel Bayley, Albert's 32-year-old brother-in-law, sat down with him to deliver a stern lecture on the duties of a husband and a business man. Albert would raise his hand and vow, "So help me, I will put that woman out of my life." Yet he seemed mesmerized by Maria, and although they often quarreled violently he always returned to her. His forlorn wife was in tears. The Tirrell inheritance was dwindling at a merry clip, for Maria had expensive tastes in jewelry and clothing. Gossip was rife both in Boston and nearby Weymouth. In September, 1845, Albert and Maria were ejected from the staid Hanover House in Boston after an uninhibited party climaxed by a fight. That was the last straw. To teach him a lesson, the family had Albert arrested and charged with adultery.

No sooner had they done this than they realized what a disgrace it would be to have one of their clan besmirched with a criminal record. They now begged the court for leniency. On October 21, Albert was freed after paying a bond and agreeing to keep the peace for six months—above all, to shun Maria.

He kept his word for less than 24 hours. Maria had meanwhile taken lodging in a house on Cedar Lane in Beacon Hill. Sure enough, Albert, hopelessly bewitched, showed up there on October 22. He was with Maria so much during the next five days and home so little that the Tirrell family must have wondered what, if anything, would bring the black sheep back to the fold.

At about four on the morning of October 27, smoke issued from the house on Cedar Lane and someone raised the alarm. Firemen, coming on the run, discovered a smouldering mattress in the upstairs landing. Another mattress was

245

blazing in Maria Bickford's room. More important, Maria herself lay on the floor in her chemise, dead, her throat cut deeply. A bloody razor lay some eight feet away. Matches had been stuffed into the mattresses, making it clear that someone had murdered Maria and tried to burn the house to destroy the evidence.

Next to arrive were the police, who learned that Albert Tirrell had been with Maria that night and, in fact, had left without taking his fancy figured vest.

Meanwhile a disheveled Albert was racing across nearby Bowdoin Square and pounding at the door of Timothy Fullam, who kept a livery stable. Fullam knew him, having previously furnished him with rigs at odd hours. He got up and harnessed a horse while Albert muttered vaguely, "Someone tried to murder me—I'm in a scrape." He seemed in a stupor, speaking in a disconnected way, but Fullam was not surprised for he had seen the young aristocrat in his cups on other occasions.

They drove to Weymouth where Albert had a quick conference with Nathaniel Bayley. The brother-in-law, well aware that he had violated his probation, advised him to keep out of sight. It was not until later that the police came looking for Albert and the shocked Bayley found that he was wanted not for a petty misstep but for murder. Bayley told the officers he had no idea of Albert's whereabouts. After they left, he sought out the scapegrace, accused him of the crime, gave him some money, and told him to clear out of the country.

According to Bayley's later story, Albert seemed "strangely confused" and denied any knowledge of the murder. Nevertheless, he apparently agreed that his position would be embarrassing if he stayed. He took the money, went to Boston, shipped as a seaman aboard the freighter *Sultana*, and vanished for four months. Not until February, when the *Sultana* docked in New York, was he arrested and brought back for trial.

It was the sensation of the decade. The whole Boston area was agog when County Attorney Samuel Parker opened the trial on March 24, 1846, with the demand that Albert Tirrell be hanged for murder. There was evidence aplenty that he had been with Maria on the fatal night

and that they had often quarreled violently. There was proof that he had fled to the livery stable after the crime and been driven home. Nor did his flight to sea seem the act of a man with unsullied conscience. All in all, seasoned observers said that Prosecutor Parker's job was easier than rolling off a log, since nothing could save Albert from the gallows.

By this time one might think the long-suffering Tirrells would have decided that hanging was, all things considered, the most certain and permanent method of keeping Albert out of trouble. On the contrary. No Tirrell had ever been hanged, and they did not propose to start now if they could help it. They retained Rufus Choate to avert such a family disgrace.

Choate, who had recently completed Daniel Webster's unexpired term in the United States Senate, was one of the most eloquent pleaders of the day, a man whose services came high. Some observers sniffed that the Tirrells were carrying their snootiness pretty far when they insisted on paying a fat fee for an attorney who could no more save the defendant's neck than the courthouse chimney sweep.

But Choate, a resourceful fellow, had made a close study of the evidence. He had been struck by the statements of both Timothy Fullam and Nathaniel Bayley that Albert seemed in a stupor after the crime, as if he did not know where he was. After talks with the family, he hit on a line of defense that would make American legal history. When he rose in the courtroom, he staggered Prosecutor Parker, the judge and the jury by what he said.

"If Albert Tirrell murdered Maria Bickford," he told them, "he was not responsible for what he did because he was asleep at the time and unaware of what he was doing."

As people stared at him pop-eyed, he proceeded to paint Albert as the champion sleepwalker of the whole New England area. From earliest childhood, Choate said, the boy had been even more active while asleep than when awake. When he was three, his parents had found him missing from his crib. They were horrified to discover that he had climbed out on the roof of an adjacent porch and was toddling along the edge of it, sound asleep, only a step from disaster. His father rescued him and

Rufus Choate, advocate extraordinary.

put him back to bed. The lad remembered nothing of it in the morning. On another occasion he had paid a night visit to the kitchen, taken a quart jar of maple syrup and distributed its contents over the parlor rug so thoroughly that the rug had to be discarded.

His nocturnal athletics were so alarming that for his own safety his parents had been forced to bar his windows and lock his door after putting him to bed. However, as he grew older he complained about this restraint, so that the practice of locking his door was discontinued for a time. One night when he was 16, he had left the house clad only in his nightshirt and his father's best beaver hat, harnessed the horse and driven to his uncle's home a mile distant. The uncle, aroused by the arrival of the horse, was amazed to find Albert unhitching the beast at the stable. He was clearly asleep, performing this operation in a daze, heedless of the early-winter chill. When the uncle shook him, he awoke with a start, unaware of how he had got there.

Young Prudence Tirrell related that Albert, a lover of whist, had once left his bed in the small hours. When she became aware of his absence, she found him in the library, playing whist with mechanical motions in his sleep although he had no companions. Again, she had awakened to find him pressing his fingers around her neck, apparently bent on strangling her. Her sharp cry brought him to his senses, whereupon he apologized profusely.

A seaman from the *Sultana* testified that Albert had slept alone on deck by choice, saying he was a restless sleeper and did not wish to disturb the others. Early one freezing morning the second mate had seen him climbing at a perilous height on ice-covered rigging. Everyone was in a sweat until he got down safely, when it was seen that he was in a daze. The mate seized him by the arm. Albert started, stared around in surpise and said, "Mate, where have I been?"

"That was precisely my client's condition on the morning of October 27 when he reached the livery stable," Choate said. "He was just awakening from somnambulistic sleep. He did not know where he had been or what he had been doing."

Drs. Walter Channing and Samuel Woodard gave expert testimony for the defense about the remarkable things sleepwalkers could do. "In this somnambulistic state," said Dr. Woodward, "a person can dress himself, set a house on fire or commit a homicide. The somnambulist, however, is not insane. He is dreaming asleep, while the insane person is dreaming awake."

During the beginning of all this talk about sleepwalking, Prosecutor Parker had assumed the expression of a man enjoying a hilarious joke. As it progressed, however, his amusement gave way to indignation. When his turn came, he allowed that he had never heard such nonsense in all his life. Albert's condition of semi-stupor after the crime, he declared, was due simply and solely to an excess of rum, a beverage of which he was known to be inordinately fond. If the jury found him anything but guilty, Parker hinted, they must indeed be sleepwalking.

But Attorney Choate had cast his spell. As the jurors retired to deliberate, according to one waggish reporter, "many of them appeared to be in a somnambulistic state." They returned two hours later and pronounced Albert Tirrell not guilty. A free man, Albert walked happily out with his family.

Very probably he pinched himself to make sure he was awake. END

Memories of Jolly Jane

Autopsies of the exhumed bodies showed that all four members of the Davis family had died of morphine and atropine poisoning . . .

**by Elmer W. Landers
(as told to Margaret H. Koehler)**

I NEVER MET JANE TOPPAN. YET, IN MANY WAYS, she has been one of the most memorable women in my life.

I was twelve when my family moved into the old Jachin House in Cataumet, Massachusetts. For years it had been a rambling summer hotel, a big old wooden frame building with wide porches where guests from the city could sit rocking on summer evenings, enjoying the cool breezes that swept in from nearby Buzzards Bay.

For a number of years prior to the time when we moved in, the Jachin House had been owned by Alden Davis, the leading citizen in Cataumet at the close of the last century. Mr. Davis

was the town's postmaster, station agent, ran the General Store across Depot Square, and also was an accomplished marble worker. He owned a good bit of real estate locally too, including a large summer cottage not far from the hotel. This he had rented for several seasons to Nurse Toppan of Cambridge.

In a period of two months—July and August, 1901—the entire Davis family died: Mr. Davis, his wife, and their two daughters.

You might say that I grew up with the story of Jane Toppan. Captain Irving Gibbs—husband of one of the women she murdered—was a frequent visitor to the Jachin House when we

248

Nurse Jane Toppan, who started life as Honora Kelly. *Courtesy Elmer W. Landers.*

lived there, and I well remember the tales he told. A tall, bearded man, he looked exactly as most people think a New England sea captain should look. For a few years after the murder, he left Cataumet with his two young sons. Then, after marrying a cousin of the Davis family, he moved back to the very cottage in which Jane Toppan had lived.

I can remember him saying that often Jane had offered him a drink of some sort, saying that "it would be good for him." He always refused these drinks, even though in those days he certainly had not been suspicious of Jane. Like everyone else in Cataumet, he had thought

highly of her. For Jane *was* popular with the townspeople, and there are still those living around Cataumet who remember members of their families saying what a fine and likeable person "Jolly Jane" was.

Jane used to rent the Davis cottage for the sum of $250—a princely sum in those days. She always brought a lot of things with her, and usually a lot of people as well. She used to say that the reason she rented a cottage on the Cape was so that city friends of hers would have a chance to enjoy the delightful weather and beaches.

Sometimes neighbors would leave their children with Jane while they were away. People in the village spoke of seeing her—usually wearing a white dress and a striped sailor cap —leading a group of children down to the beach at Scotch House Cove, or maybe below the bluffs on Squiteague Bay. They would be carrying baskets of food, off for a glorious day with "Jolly Jane."

No one ever knew just where Jane accumulated the money to make these summers on the Cape financially possible. But one day while she was occupying the cottage, a neighbor, Mrs. Hill, noticed smoke coming from the chimney and at the same time saw Jane running across the law, carrying with her a capacious handbag.

"Where's the fire?" Mrs. Hill called as Jane came into the kitchen.

"There's no fire," Jane insisted. "I just left the house." Despite this assertion, she seemed agitated, Mrs. Hill thought, and she dropped the handbag that she was carrying. The clasp came undone, and bills—which had been folded individually, as tightly and small as possible— scattered out across the floor. "That bag was really stuffed full of money," Mrs. Hill said afterwards.

Many years later I owned the Davis cottage myself—in fact my own children grew up there. In one part of the kitchen the paint kept chipping off, exposing black charred wood beneath, which certainly seemed to negate Jane's statement that there had been no fire. I remember, too, that when I was living in the old hotel there was charred black wood in a back room. It was later shown that Jane had been responsible for a number of fires in houses where she nursed.

Jane started life as Honora Kelly, the daughter of a Boston tailor. Her mother died when she was small, and she and her sisters were placed in charge of a grandmother, who was finally forced to put them in a Boston orphanage. It was here that Jane was "discovered" by Mr. and Mrs. Abner Toppan of Lowell, Massachusetts. They adopted Jane, and the plump, pleasant little girl was almost a model daughter as she grew up. She was popular, a good student in school, active in the affairs of the local First Congregational Church, and her

friends later remembered that, wherever she was, Jolly Jane was always the life of the party.

In due course, Jane had a romance with a young man who gave her a golden ring with a bird embossed upon it. He then went off to Holyoke to get a better job so that they could get married. But, once there, he fell in love with his landlady's daughter and married her.

Jane was despondent. Friends remembered that, years later, if anyone showed her a picture of a bird she would scream, "Take it away!"

After this unhappy romance, Jane's whole character altered, at least temporarily. She fell to brooding, and she seldom left the house. Then, quite suddenly, she had a change of heart. She entered nurses training at Cambridge Hospital where she quickly became a favorite of the staff. She was cheerful, capable, diligent. However, before finishing her course she transferred to Massachusetts General Hospital. Here, she won an excellent reputation for her nursing ability. Leaving the hospital and entering private practice, she was highly recommended by the best doctors in Boston—and for miles around, for that matter. It was not until some years later that it was discovered she had left Massachusetts General without completing her course and, therefore, was not legally qualified to be a nurse. But this was not until after those dark days of 1901 in Cataumet.

It was on July 3, 1901 that the strange, tragic, fatal events began to unfurl.

Mrs. Alden Davis had decided to go to Boston. She wished, first, to see her daughter, Genevieve Gordon, who had come on from Chicago to spend a few days with her in-laws. She also wanted to see Jane Toppan, to collect some money from the previous year still owed Mr. Davis for rental of the cottage, and to ask her if she would like to rent it again.

So, Mrs. Davis took the Boston train on a particularly hot morning. That entire summer of 1901 was in fact unseasonably warm. For this reason, when Mrs. Davis—hurrying to catch the train—became dizzy on reaching the station, everyone considered it just a little "spell" due to the unusual weather. Some suggested that she would be wiser to go home and make

Above: Jachin House in Cataumet, Massachusetts, the rambling summer hotel owned by the Davis family.

Below: Not far from the hotel was the Davises' large summer cottage which Nurse Toppan rented for several seasons for herself and her friends. *Photos courtesy Elmer W. Landers*

Right: Mary Davis Gibbs, for whose murder Jolly Jane was finally brought to account. *Courtesy Elmer W. Landers.*

Below: The Cataumet depot where Mrs. Alden Davis boarded the train for her last trip. *Courtesy Elmer W. Landers.*

the trip another day. Meantime, the conductor held the train for her, and after a few minutes she insisted she was all right and got aboard.

She still did not feel well when she got to Boston and so decided to first go to Miss Toppan's home in Cambridge. And it was from there, that evening, that Miss Toppan called the Davis home in Cataumet to tell old Mr. Davis that his wife had arrived in a dazed and numbed condition, and was quite ill. Mrs. Davis had had diabetes for years; the nurse attributed her illness to the disease, and promised to watch over her and make her as comfortable as possible. She also agreed to call Mrs. Gordon, and to tell her of her mother's indisposition.

That same afternoon Genevieve Gordon came to the Cambridge house, where she found her mother in a darkened room, weak and gasping for breath. The next morning, Mrs. Davis died. Grief-stricken, Genevieve pleaded with Nurse Toppan to go back to Cataumet with her, accompanying her mother's body. Jane agreed.

There was sorrow in Cataumet, but no great sense of shock. Mrs. Davis, the townspeople said, really hadn't been well for quite awhile.

The funeral took place on a sizzling July day. Afterwards, back at the Jachin House, Genevieve Gordon looked pale and worn and complained that she had begun to feel ill.

Jane Toppan had already announced that she must return to Cambridge on the next train, telling the family that she had "nursing engagements" to attend to. Now, in the face of Genevieve's illness, Mr. Davis begged her to stay on, and once again she agreed to comply.

Genevieve lingered through much of that hot July, sometimes she seemed to have taken a turn for the better, sometimes she obviously was worse. On July 31 she died—31 years old.

Alden Davis was then 75. In the space of a month, he had lost his wife and his daughter. When he too became ill, no one in town was the least surprised. "The cross of grief he's been bearing, it's no wonder," people said.

Now it was Mary Davis Gibbs, who lived nearby with her husband and two young sons, who asked Jane to stay on and care for her father. Mary's husband, Captain Irving Gibbs, was at sea. But her father-in-law, Captain Paul Gibbs, was at home in nearby Pocasset; she left her boys in his care and went to the Jachin House to be with her father.

On the morning of August 5, Captain Paul drove over to Cataumet with his two daughters hoping to give Mary whatever consolation he could. When they reached the Davis house, it took only a single glance at Nurse Toppan for Captain Paul to know that something was dreadfully wrong.

"There's been more trouble, more terrible trouble," she said mournfully. "During the night, Mr. Davis died. When he failed to come down for breakfast this morning, I went up and found him. The doctor has just left. He tells me it was a cerebral hemorrhage."

Another funeral over, Captain Gibbs tried to persuade his daughter-in-law to go back with him to Pocasset, with her two boys, until her husband got back from the sea.

"I'd like to," she admitted, "but there is just too much to do to settle things here. Nurse Jane has agreed to stay on a little while longer, and Cousin Beulah (Jacobs) is coming down from Cambridge to be with me."

Satisfied that with Beulah Jacobs and Miss Toppan on hand his daughter-in-law was being well looked after, Captain Paul Gibbs went back to Pocasset. Then, toward mid-August, he received an urgent message to return to Cataumet. Arriving at the Davis house, he went directly upstairs to a darkened room where Mary lay unconscious, gasping for breath. Alarmed, he told his daughters, who had again accompanied him, to fetch Dr. Leonard Latter, the family's physician in Falmouth.

Going to Mary's bedside, he spoke to her, but there was no response. The captain later said that he suddenly sensed another presence in the room.

"I turned," he related, "and Nurse Toppan was standing in the doorway. She went to Mary's side, and, with a hypodermic needle, swiftly gave her an injection. Then she said to me, 'The Doctor has ordered Mrs. Gibbs to be kept absolutely quiet. I must ask you to leave immediately.'

"I was only interested in my daughter-in-law's best interest," the Captain said later, "and I had no reason not to believe Miss Toppan.

After all we, just as had the whole Davis family, trusted her implicitly. So I left."

The next word Captain Paul Gibbs had of his daughter-in-law was the news of her death. He promptly sent a message to his son, Captain Irving Gibbs, who was reached aboard his ship at Norfolk, Virginia.

The more Captain Paul thought of his daughter-in-law's death, the stranger it seemed to him. Troubled, he went to Dr. Latter.

"Somehow," he said, "I feel that there's something wrong. I feel that there's something wicked about Jane Toppan. I should never have left the house that afternoon when she told me to go."

The doctor agreed that the case, in his experience, had been unusual. "But not without precedent," he added. "Although Mary's case has puzzled me, I have not a shred of evidence against Nurse Toppan."

"Nor have I," replied the Captain. "But the last day I was at the house—when Mary seemed unconscious—watching Nurse Toppan give her that injection gave me the shivers, I'm frank to say."

Injection? He had given no orders for an injection of any type, Dr. Latter replied.

This put an entirely new light on the subject. A neighbor and good friend of the Gibbs family was then on vacation in the area—Major General Leonard Wood, a native of Pocasset who was the Governor General of the Philippines. General Wood was a doctor; his brother Edward was a Professor of Pathology at Harvard University. Both agreed that, while the deaths of the two elder Davises might well have been due to natural causes, there surely was suspicion attached to those of both Mary and her sister Genevieve.

Rufus Wade, a state detective, was called into the case, with the thought of seeking out any possible motives that would lend logic to the growing suspicions about Jane Toppan.

At a drug store in Falmouth they found a clerk who remembered that Miss Jane Toppan had bought morphine there—with a doctor's prescription, of course. At Waters' Drug Store

The Davis family monument in Cataumet. It was here that the bodies of the poison victims were buried, exhumed, and later reburied. *Photo by Charles R. Koehler.*

in Wareham she had also bought morphine, and later returned to ask for a fresh supply, stating that because of the hot weather the original medication had "melted together." The druggist obligingly had yielded to her wishes.

The prescriptions—many attributed to Dr. Latter—were forgeries.

This was sufficient evidence to permit the police to proceed further. On a chill autumn night, lanterns flickered through the old graveyard across the County Road from the Methodist Church as a party of men started toward the large monument topped by a Grecian urn that marks the final resting place of the Davises.

For a time, only shovels chopping at the hard, cold ground broke the stillness. State Police Officer Simeon Lettney had also been assigned to the case, and he and the two Gibbses, father and son, stood in silence—with the Rev. James Docking of the Methodist Church standing by both to keep away intruders and to make certain that this ghastly act was, nonetheless, conducted with "fitting decorum"— as the earth yielded up the bodies of the four members of the Davis family.

The coffins were carried to the old barn on Major Allen Swift's property, adjoining the burying ground. There Professor Wood, Professor Whitney, also of Harvard, Dr. Faunce and Dr. Harris performed autopsies, removing the vital organs. These were taken to Boston, analyzed, and the report came back. All four members of the Davis family had died of morphine and atropine poisoning.

An order was issued for Jane Toppan's arrest, and Detective Lettney set out to find her. Her trail led first to Lowell, where she had stayed for a time with Mr. O. M. Brigham, widower of her dead foster sister. Another foster sister, Mrs. Edna Banister, was at the Brigham home at the time, en route to the Buffalo Exposition. Jane looked her over carefully, told her that she really wasn't looking too well and suggested that she take some medicine which would fix her up.

Mrs. Banister wasn't interested, but Jane had a way of insisting in such matters. She gave Mrs. Banister the tonic—and not very long afterwards there was a funeral in Lowell.

Now George Nichols, a long-standing friend, asked Jane if she would come up to Nashua, New Hampshire, and look after his sister, who had been ailing. It was at the Nichols home in Nashua that Detective Lettney found Jane. Later, she confessed that had he not arrived when he did, she might very well have poisoned both George and his sister that very evening. At the time she protested her innocence and willingly returned to Barnstable, insisting that she couldn't even "kill a chicken."

On December 6, 1901, Jane Toppan appeared in the great old gray stone courthouse in Barnstable, where the Grand Jury indicted her for the murders of Alden Davis, Genevieve Gordon, and Mary Davis Gibbs. An indictment was never issued against her in the case of Mrs. Alden Davis, but under the circumstances it hardly was necessary.

Jane was confined until June in the Barnstable County Jail. Almost daily, Dr. Henry Stedman, a leading alienist of the day, visited Jane in her cell. As the weeks wore on, he talked to her of many things. Finally, it seemed to him that she was becoming both increasingly confiding and increasingly tense. He sensed that there was something she wanted to tell him.

He began to talk to her of murder, and finally he posed the question. "Did you kill them, Jane?"

"Yes," she whispered. "I killed them all. They were sick and I eased their suffering. I had to do it. It relieved something in me. No one will ever know—I don't know myself—when I will have another impulse to kill. The Davises were not the first."

And indeed they hadn't been. When, finally, the story had all emerged and facts were checked, it was proved that Jane Toppan had killed at least 31 persons, starting with the murder of her step-parents, the Toppans.

"Thirty-one is all I can remember," Jane said. "My memory is not so good."

Actually, she was tried in only one case—the murder of Mary Davis Gibbs. A jury was impaneled on June 23, 1902. The case was heard, and deliberation was brief. Jane Toppan was found "not guilty by reason of insanity" and she was committed to "the Taunton Insane Hospital" for life.

As fate decreed it, that proved to be a period of some 36 years.

In Cataumet, the members of the Gibbs family who lived on tried to forget her. Captain Irving Gibbs married Beulah Jacobs—then widowed—in 1909, and they came back to live in the Davis cottage which Jane Toppan had rented in earlier summers. Captain Gibbs was willing enough to talk about Jane and the murders, but this was not the case where Mary Gibbs' two sons were concerned. They would never mention the murders, nor would they discuss the nurse.

As for Jane, when she died at Taunton in 1938 there was no one to mourn. The Boston papers ran stories about the fact that the body was unclaimed in the Taunton morgue, and that unless someone came forward with funds for a funeral she would be buried in potters' field. No one came forward.   END

The Scandal of Jaffrey

by Sumner Kean

Dr. William Kendrick Dean. Photo taken about 1908.

Who murdered Dr. Dean? German spies or somebody everyone knew? Hysteria and suspicion split the town wide open . . .

IN FEBRUARY, 1919, SELF-STYLED PSYCHOLOGIST, European-born William De Kerloff, stood on the platform of the East Jaffrey, New Hampshire, town hall. With a straight face and apparent sincerity, he told of photographing blood spots, which, upon magnification, revealed the murderers of William Kendrick Dean.

His talk followed an address by the then county solicitor, Roy M. Pickard of Keene. In his sane dissertation, the tall prosecutor attempted to explain to the overflow gathering the difference between evidence worth consideration by a grand jury and the imagination-embellished rumors which were then, and to some extent have been ever since, pervading the town. Mr. Pickard answered questions dispassionately, despite their antagonistic tenor. Only when the questioners became so aggressive that it seemed the solicitor himself were the guilty party did the presiding officer call a halt.

Neither talk aided in the solution of the case which had torn the town asunder, nor did the voluntary offers of clairvoyants contribute anything. So sharp was the line of demarcation which separated adherents of one theory from another that households were riven, religion was pitted against religion, and even politics was unwittingly drawn into the furious controversy. Members resigned from lodges, and a tiny country club died aborning. Staunch defenders of one or another unpopular theory either left town or were forced out of business.

Chief among the theories advanced to explain this extraordinary case—one of New Hampshire's few unsolved mysteries—were:

That Jaffrey was the center of a German spy ring which used Mount Monadnock's commanding height as a beacon point to flash signals to the Kaiser's submarines lurking off Boston harbor.

That the banker, Charles L. Rich, was involved because he suffered a black eye and bruised cheek the night Dean was killed.

That Dean's aging wife, his first cousin, Mary, killed him because of jealousy.

Attorney Pickard said that Federal agents, despite lengthy shadowings and interrogations, were unable to pin the crime on anyone with avowed German sympathies. He further contended that the lights seen to flash from Monadnock's 3186-foot summit were not signals connected with a spy system; that Mr. Rich's explanation of his injury—that he had been kicked by his fractious mare—was plausible and not open to doubt; and that Mrs. Dean was so physically infirm that she could not have committed the crime.

The afternoon of August 13, 1918, Mrs. Horace Morison of Boston and Peterborough, a summer resident, called on Dr. Dean with two other women to solicit contributions for a benefit sale. At that time, Dean and Mrs. Morison conversed in private about the lights on the mountain. She told him she planned a trip to Boston the next day, and he asked her to stop at the office of the Secret Service there and ask that they send their best man up to see him as he had important information to impart. He could not go himself, he explained, because he could not leave his ailing wife for such a long period. Although pressed by Mrs. Morison, he refused to divulge the information. He contended that its possession might jeopardize her. She complied with his request the next day, only to read later in a Boston paper of his murder.

That evening, a Tuesday, when the East Jaffrey stores were open until nine o'clock, Dean drove to town for supplies. There was conflicting evidence about the exact time of his arrival and departure. He did some shopping at Goodnow's store and at Duncan's drug store, chatted with a few acquaintances. He drove home in his rubber-tired buggy, the jog of his sluggish horse getting him there about 10:30 P.M.

City born and bred, Dean had never attuned himself to country habits. He liked to stay up all night, then sleep during the day. His farm animals were trained to accommodate such habits. He milked his Jersey cow at noon and again at midnight. When he arrived home that evening, he drank some milk and ate some currant buns he had bought in town. Then he smoked a hand-rolled cigarette, changed into an old coat, caught up a lantern and milk pail. Then, telling his wife he would be back about midnight, he left for the barn about 500 feet away.

Investigators, reconstructing the crime, believe he was attacked 15 minutes later. A blow on the head rendered him unconscious and fractured his skull. A light horse blanket was wound around his head. He was garrotted with a hitching rope. He was tied at ankles, knees and wrists, and a grain sack containing a 27-pound rock was pulled over his head and shoulders. This was fastened to the belt loops of his pants. He was then tossed into a well about 12 feet deep. The heavy stone kept his body submerged in the six feet of water in the well.

William Kendrick Dean, son of missionary parents, was as a boy a familiar figure in the royal household of Siam (Thailand). He attended Columbia University Medical School for two years. Prior to these medical studies he had graduated from the University of Rochester. Although he never obtained a medical degree or license, throughout his life he used the unearned title of "Doctor." From the age of fifteen, he made his home with a wealthy physician, his uncle. He fell in love with the latter's daughter. Cutting short his medical career, he married her in 1878. They made their home in Boston. Here he was employed by a publishing firm but soon after, because of his health, left for the country. They finally settled in East Jaffrey in 1889, on a hillside farm on the old Jaffrey-Peterborough road near where he was to meet his death.

He built a pretentious hilltop home. There they lived for many years, quietly but comfortably, on the income from his wife's inherited money. Dean was well read, had a large library, and was a brilliant conversationalist. This, coupled with the fact that his wife was an accomplished pianist, made their home a center for the intellectuals, particularly summer residents. A register kept by Mrs. Dean showed 600 signatures in a single summer. No one, however, stayed the night and only rarely did anyone stay for meals.

Dean was a small man, five feet six and 135 pounds. Physical development was a fetish with him. He exercised with heavy dumbbells and went in for other strenuous exercise. His dress was considered flashy for the time and place. When he drove to town that evening before he was murdered, he wore knee-length khaki pants (forerunner of Bermuda shorts), white shirt, high starched collar, bright pink tie and a dark coat. He appeared much younger than his 63 years. His wife was three years his elder. However, her infirmities made her seem more aged than her actual years.

Some say that Dean was a "ladies' man;" others disagree. Regardless, there was never any indication that he was anything but faithful to his ill and fast-aging wife. He cared for her, did the housework and, during the last years of her life, prepared all the meals with little or no outside help. His name for her was Polly. She called him Billy and, perhaps because of his diminutive stature, "my baby."

On the night he was killed, she readied some hot soup against his return from the barn at midnight. When he did not return at the usual time, she waited, huddled in her chair, afraid to brave the dark and search for him. Poor, feeble Mrs. Dean, it must have been a night of anguish for her; her darkened mind was unable to cope with the real and fancied horrors of night.

When daylight came, she searched for him. The only clue was an extinguished lantern on the stable floor, its reservoir still half full of oil. Piteously she called again and again for her Billy. There was no response. Then she called neighbors. They, the selectmen, and the police chief, Perley Enos, eventually found her husband's body in the well. Mr. Pickard and Dr. Densmore, the county medical referee, were called.

Mrs. Mary Dean in 1880.

258

Dean's trussed body was hauled from the well. Even to untrained investigators it was patently a case of murder. Ignorance on the part of those present destroyed some valuable clues: a bloody imprint on the barn door handle and a bloody footprint. There were no trained state police detectives who could be consulted. The only undestroyed clue was a hand weeder, a three-pronged claw with a one-foot handle, found tucked into a nearby stone wall. This appeared to be the weapon used to fell the small gentleman farmer. No autopsy was conducted until several months later. At that time the body was exhumed. Examination disclosed that the victim had a paper-thin skull. The blow had fractured it, but apparently failed to kill him.

In the absence of modern police methods, the case immediately degenerated into a bizarre "whodunit" with suspicion, not concrete evidence, the principal factor.

First, because Mrs. Dean had told somebody, before the body was found, that "Billy is dead in the deep water," she was a suspect. Many, including the then State Attorney General, the late Judge Oscar Young, held to that belief. As a result, she was not informed that her husband had been murdered or his body found until weeks later.

Next in the line of suspects was the Deans' close friend, Mr. Rich, cashier of the local bank, judge of the municipal court, a former state senator and a man of spotless reputation. Suspicion's horrible pointed finger was directed at him for the sole reason that he had suffered an injury to his face similar to that suffered by Dean when he was felled with the weeder.

But far beyond these two, in ever-widening circles, suspicion was directed at German agents.

Prescott Duncan, Jaffrey businessman, was then a student at Cushing Academy. Home on vacation, he was on the scene when Dean's trussed body was pulled from the well. He phoned in the story to *The Boston American*. The slaying had all the elements of mystery so dear to sensational Hearst journalism. The managing editor assigned a top feature writer, Bert Ford, to the case. Ford, recently returned war correspondent with a book to his credit, *The Fighting Yankees Overseas*, a combat history of the 26th Division, knew his business. Daily for a month he dug up details. He interviewed witnesses and eventually broadcast his theory that Dean was a victim of German spies —a hero killed in combat back of the lines.

The entire Monadnock region was pictured as the operating area for a ring of spies. Its proximity to Fort Devens and the fact that the mountain's bald top is one of the first high

The Dean barn in East Jaffrey, N.H.

points of land visible to incoming mariners were cited to bolster this belief. There were reports of night-riders, in cars and on horseback, and it was not long before Jaffrey residents were looking for spies beneath their beds and casting a suspicious eye at anyone of German origin or sympathies. Actually it was merely localization of national war hysteria—hysteria which reached its apogee when the name of the comic strip, "The Katzenjammer Kids," was whitewashed into "The Captain and the Kids."

State and county authorities did their best. They hired Pinkerton detectives. The Secret Service sent agents to run down spy rumors. In addition, relatives of the Dean family hired De Kerloff, the psychologist-detective. They all worked hard, perhaps none of them harder than De Kerloff, searching, shadowing, interrogating. If the latter had stuck to sleuthing, Jaffrey might have had faith in him, but the detection

Diagram of the Dean farm and surroundings.

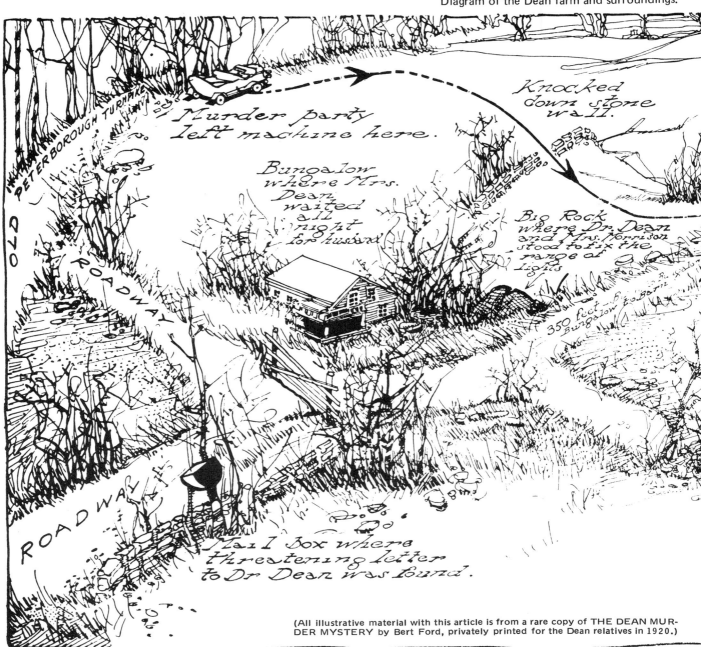

(All illustrative material with this article is from a rare copy of THE DEAN MURDER MYSTERY by Bert Ford, privately printed for the Dean relatives in 1920.)

of a murderer through photographs of blood spots was too much to swallow. Another thing which made many gag was a bit of charlatanism. When Dean's body was exhumed for autopsy seven months after his death, De Kerloff made a drawing of the peculiar three-pronged wound on his skull. Then, at a public meeting he slapped the paper over the wound on Judge Rich's face in an effort to show resemblance. De Kerloff eventually sued the town for $4000

Pack Monadnock Mt.

...n where Dean murdered

200 feet

Body carried from barn and thrown into cistern.

The Dean home.

for his expenses and services. It is little wonder he failed to collect from either town or court.

There was a popular radio serial going at the time—"The Green Hornet." A gray Marmon automobile frequently seen on back roads was promptly dubbed the Gray Hornet. Then, a Hooded Terror which gazed in windows or peered in factory skylights at night-shift workers was reported to be at large.

All added to the general terror which gripped the town.

Hysteria died down a bit when the Marmon's owner convinced Federal investigators that his actions were not against the best interest of the nation, and faded away when the Hooded Terror turned out to be nothing more than a disgruntled policeman who, because the town had refused to pay him, had adopted this disguise to strike back at a community which did not appreciate his services.

At the demands of prominent citizens, a grand jury was impanelled to hear all the evidence. It heard everybody but indicted no one.

Today, decades after the crime, authorities still mark it "unsolved." Certain conservative elder residents, however, hold to what they call a "hoss sense" solution:

There existed in the town and its environs a group of young toughs below draft age. They and their girl friends were in the habit of cavorting in empty houses. The Deans, because of financial reverses, had rented their big house and moved to an old cottage about 300 yards away. The big house tenant, because of suspected German sympathies, had but lately, at Dean's insistence, moved to a nearby farm. A circuitous road passed near the big house. This showed tire marks the day after the murder. It is believed that two or more persons, one perhaps a woman, were in the big house when they saw the light of Dean's lantern. The theory is that they investigated, were recognized by Dean, then struck him down with the weeder, the first weapon that came to hand. Panicking when he dropped with the blow, they tied him up, weighted the bundle so it would stay down, and dumped him in the handiest spot—the well.

Prosaic solution perhaps, but again perhaps the only one which will ever come out of this explosive World War I mystery.   END

9.
NATURE'S HEAVY HAND

"Heavy Squall and That's Not All"
The December Tempest of 1839
Becket's Runaway Reservoir
HURRICANE! September 21, 1938

"Heavy Squall and That's

A malignant funnel of swirling wind came to where its kind had never been seen—

On South Street, Shrewsbury, reconstruction begins of the wreckage caused
by the tornado in minutes. It took months. *Courtesy* Worcester Telegram.

JUNE OF '53, AND SUMMER WAS ON ITS WAY IN New England as usual—winter cool growing warm to the first late May/June heat; occasional showers, with a few nights of lightning to brighten the hushed, late spring/early summer nights.

In Worcester, Massachusetts, the weather was seasonal—pleasant at the end of a wet spring. Occasional thunder showers cleansed the air, and the night breeze caressed young leaves into living vibrancy. Tired of winter, residents had begun to appear on their front porches, relaxing out-of-doors after the day's work.

A year like most, 1953, and early June was college commencement time in Worcester, a college town. The daily newspaper solemnly described a commencement speaker exhorting

the graduating class of Holy Cross College to "walk in truth" that "they might be an honor to their teachers."

That was Sunday, June 7. In Arcadia, Nebraska, a tornado killed ten people as they sat down to family reunion dinner in the farmhouse that was their ancestral home. It, too, was destroyed by the storm. The story was a small item in the news across the nation.

But that, of course, was Nebraska, not New England, where residents of the six states congratulated themselves over toast and morning coffee for living in a sensible climate, where things like that didn't happen.

Didn't happen, that is, until Tuesday, June 9, when at 5:08 P.M. the world came to an abrupt end for many Worcester area residents. Many others lost, if not their lives, their life savings, homes, shops or livelihoods.

The tornado hit.

---

*Weather forecast for the first part of June 1953 in *The Old Farmer's Almanac*.

264

Not All"*

by Tom Koch

Massachusetts—Petersham, Quabbin Reservoir, Worcester, and Shrewsbury . . .

Top: Battered automobiles, twisted metal and shattered glass mark the passage of the monster. *Courtesy the Norton Company. Above:* All that was left of a home—a bent fan and rubble. *Courtesy* Worcester Telegram.

Born in the Midwest of unsettled air, raised above the earth by storms and wind, it attacked Nebraska in adolescence. Unsated and furious, it left the earth and, growing greater still, moved east, touching Flint, Michigan, before disappearing into the upper reaches of the atmosphere until it was ready to come down again.

Large, too large for the earth, and with more power than any creation or dream of man, the unthinking, malignant funnel of swirling wind came to where its kind had never been seen: first Petersham, Massachusetts, then Quabbin Reservoir in central Massachusetts, where it excavated a crater 100 feet in diameter as, full-grown and unreasoning, it moved southward towards Worcester.

The great, black, swirling, horrible funnel, like a nightmare ice-cream cone, attacked Holden, a town next to Worcester, bulldozing a path of total destruction through what had been quiet streets of homes. From Holden, now at the height of its fury, it went on to northern Worcester to demolish a machine shop before sweeping east to the Worcester Poor Farm. The tornado crushed Assumption College and decimated three churches, then moved into Shrewsbury and eastward.

Finally, all fury spent, it left the earth and died.

* * * * *

That Tuesday evening, James P. Abdella and Melvin G. Johnson, construction workers, were driving home from work to Shrewsbury. "All of a sudden," as Abdella tells it, "I saw a chimney flop over."

A roof next sailed over his truck, and he saw row after row of Maple Street homes topple like card houses upset by the kick of a naughty child. "That's when my stomach came into my mouth," he said.

A few minutes before, workers from local factories had begun to go home. The 9:00-5:00 shift at the Norton Company was punching time clocks on the rim of the machine shop. J. Roy Erikson of the purchasing department had left work a few minutes early.

"It was hailing and a few minutes to five, so I decided to go home," he said. "Traffic was backed up on Brook Street, below the plant, the sky was dark, and I thought—maybe it's another hurricane like 1938—more probably just another summer thunderstorm. I was going to get out of my car and walk up the road to see what the tie-up was, but decided not to."

A good thing he didn't. Glass from a broken greenhouse was whipping through the air. He still thought it was "just a bad storm because who the hell ever heard of a tornado around here."

Turning around, he looked for another route home. Nearing his house later, he found branches down and some homes collapsed, but his was intact. His wife told him she thought that an unscheduled freight train had passed on the tracks near their house and maybe there had been an accident.

"It sounded like a train's roar," she said, "and there were all these cars with their lights on, beeping horns, so I thought there had been an accident."

There were no trains passing his house at 5:08 P.M. that day. The roar she had heard was the tornado sweeping through.

Erikson's brother Harold was putting his car in the garage near Roy's home when the tornado struck, dropping the roof on him. He was pinned inside until neighbors freed him and took him to a hospital.

When Roy heard the news, he and his older brother Andrew, an ex-navy medical corpsman, began to tour the city's hospitals, looking for Harold.

"There was no time to fill out admittance forms," Roy recalled. "Bodies were just put wherever there was room, and doctors looked after them when they had a chance." At City Hospital, the third or fourth one they had visited, Andrew stopped looking in order to lend a hand preparing blood for the injured; Roy continued the search. Around midnight, the two brothers got together again, having

looked through all the hospital wards. An undertaker they met suggested they look in the morgue.

"It wasn't like a morgue on TV. It was just an area, the only open one around, with bodies laid out wherever there was room, like a field station after a rout," Erikson said. And Harold was there. Harold Erikson, deceased—one of more than 90 dead that day in June.

Others were luckier. When the storm struck, Hilding H. Anderson's family was in the den of their Holden house. Hilding, a Norton employee, was working late when the storm struck. It was an hour before he knew that anything unusual had happened. The building he worked in was on the side of the plant opposite the decimated machine shop. It was hours more before he knew that his home had been destroyed.

Preceding the tornado had been a milder storm of rain, hail and wind. As it grew worse, Mrs. Anderson contemplated going to the cellar for refuge, but her teenage daughter said, "Naw, Mom, it's just a storm." When the tornado hit the home, it tore the chimney cap from its foundation, dropping it through the roof, a half foot from Mrs. Anderson's head.

The house was a total ruin, yet his parents' home only three-quarters of a mile away was not damaged. "It was no worse than a windstorm there," Anderson said.

Anderson's seven-year-old son was playing with a friend at a house nearby when the storm dropped on residential Holden. The boys, alone in the house, were scared by the darkening sky and overturned a sofa to crouch under it. The tornado shattered windows and hurtled glass through the room, cutting the sofa but not the boys.

"I'll never understand how they knew to do that," Anderson said. "It saved their lives."

In the Anderson's garage was a power lawn mower and a 12-cubic-foot refrigerator. The lawn mower never moved, but the refrigerator was picked up by the storm and never seen again.

Although his house was totally destroyed, its cupola, hand carved by Anderson's father, was found intact the next day lying in the woods, 100 yards away. A canceled check from Anderson's records, stored in the house's attic, was later found 65 miles away in Southwick. It came to rest, ironically, on the lawn of a bank president, who returned it to him via a Worcester acquaintance. He kept it as a souvenir.

Not only roofs but people were carried away by the storm. One mother and child were reportedly carried yards through the air to a safe landing, only to have the baby snatched from its mother and hurtled another 100 yards to its death.

As it bounced through Worcester County, the tornado of '53 did over $70 million damage, injured at least 800 people, killed nearly 100, and did it all in about ten minutes.

The night of the storm, there was widespread pillage. The National Guard was called out to control looting and assist the injured. "I can't believe, I never could, the looting that went on after the storm, but I know if I could have laid my hands on a gun, I would have shot the guys who looted my house," Anderson says.

In the weeks that followed, as the hospitals emptied, reconstruction began. It took Erikson a week to decide to rebuild because "at first, all we wanted to do was move. It was as if we would never feel safe there again." Some did move, but most, like the Eriksons, rebuilt because "where can you go and be safe, at least safer than we were? Nowhere. It was a freak of nature, and there was no place we could think of that was safer than Holden; so we rebuilt, as did most of our neighbors."

Federal and state aid poured in, private companies like Norton donated transportation, building materials, technical assistance and financial aid to the stricken. Spokesmen for the company say it gave over a million dollars in disaster relief in the weeks immediately after the tornado struck.

Two days after the storm, Worcester police stamped out what they described as an illegal lottery to benefit tornado victims. On the 11th of June, members of the Worcester police vice squad seized 125 books of lottery tickets that were being sold at five cents a ticket. The drawing was for a $50 bond; the seller was to receive, all told, a profit of $625 dollars. Things were nearly normal!

A tornado is one of nature's most powerful and climatologically unique contributions to the misery of man. Most storms, from rainy downpours to devastating hurricanes, are broad-based furies which sweep across the land in a moderately predictable fashion. A tornado is different. It is not earthborn but a creature of the atmosphere—a funnel of swirling wind bouncing across the country, touching down only at certain points. Its fury is contained in a narrow band of power less than a mile across, and it is difficult to plot, difficult to predict, and difficult to prepare for. The revolving mass of air and vapor, preceded by winds of 40 to 50 miles an hour, is a vacuum. The destruction comes not so much from the fury of the wind as from the power of this vacuum.

When a tornado hits a building, the pressure in the storm center is lower than in the building and, in an attempt to equalize inside and outside air pressure, buildings collapse "like a house of cards." The closest analogy is when a paper bag filled with air is clapped between two hands: it explodes, not just because you are strong but because the compression creates a higher air pressure inside the bag, which must escape. The "pop" when the bag bursts is the air pressures equalizing. It is the same with a tornado. The pressure inside a house, office or shop is higher than in the storm outside. In attempting to equalize the air pressure, the atmosphere forces the building out. On June 9, 1953, within a half hour Worcester barometers fell an unprecedented one-half inch in about 30 minutes.

Soon after this storm, meteorologists instituted a "tornado watch" to give area residents time to prepare in case another blow appeared. The chances, however, are very slim. Weather bureaus with new, sophisticated systems are prepared for such storms and can give people warning. Despite these early warning systems and 20 years of time, some Worcester area residents still wonder whenever a storm approaches, and wait in fear when a thunderstorm brings night hours early and wind whips the trees. Survivors of the '53 storm, like Mrs. Anderson and the Eriksons, head for their cellars and wait out the storm.

There are some things which, never experienced, can never be understood and, once known, can never be forgotten. Among these are love and close brushes with death—and tornadoes seen from the inside.   END by Lawrence A. Averill

The December Tempest of 1839

The appalling scene in Gloucester harbor furnished the setting for Longfellow's "Wreck of the Hesperus" on the "reef of Norman's Woe."

CAPE ANN THRUSTS ITS HEAD DEFIANTLY INTO the Atlantic, like a sullen wolf, its snout worn down by the rasping gales of centuries. Fierce storms flay the coast when "nor'easters" roar in off the ocean, or when the wind blows on shore from the southeast. Uncowed by the uplifted arm and clenched fist of Cape Cod that guards the Bay on the south, raging storms plunge fiercely into the upper Bay and bite at Gloucester. On the way in, they snap viciously at Nahant and Marblehead, and at Annisquam, Plum Island, and Ipswich on the way up the coast.

Descendants of the old Gloucester fishermen will tell you still about what was the most disastrous gale ever to strike Gloucester. It was bitter winter weather that 15th day of December, 1839, when cyclonic winds and stinging snow blasted the New England coast. The appalling scene in Gloucester harbor furnished the setting for Longfellow's "Wreck of the Hesperus" on the "reef of Norman's Woe," which the poet wrote shortly after the storm.

All day and all night on that dreadful Sunday, and throughout Monday, the tempest smote the plunging vessels and the splintering docks. Anticipating trouble, 50 to 60 ships out of Portland had put into Gloucester harbor to ride out the tempest, joining possibly a dozen others already sheltered there. When the sickly morning light of Monday broke over the scene, no more than *six* vessels still rode at anchor, all of them denuded of masts and spars.

Roaring in from the northeast, the furious gale tossed huge schooners about like toothpicks. By Monday morning the shore was strewn with wrecks, scattered cargoes, mangled and frozen corpses. All day the murky low ceiling echoed and re-echoed with the deafening boom of the breakers, the crash of falling masts, and the almost human shrieks and moans of

vessel fragments in constant collision. Intermittently above the tumult could be heard the piteous cries of perishing sailors pleading for help across mountainous waves through which no help could come. Some of the vessels broke open and sank at their moorings; more of them were dashed to pieces on the ledges; still more were blasted by the gale down the coast and out to sea where they were lost forever.

Among the schooners that plunged to the bottom were: two from Wiscasset, the *Favorite* and the *Sally*; the *Neutrality* of Portland; the *Milo* and the *Sally & Mary* of Bristol; the *Mary Frances* of Belfast; the *Brilliant* of Mt. Desert. Twenty-six schooners were dismasted, either by the rending gale or the desperately swung axes of crewmen struggling to parry some of the storm's sledgehammer blows at the groaning hulls. The schooner *Antioch* of Ellsworth—her masts having been axed down—continued for some time to tug at her anchors until one of the chains ruptured. The crew succeeded in getting off only minutes before the second one parted. The rearing ship then pirouetted dizzily out to sea, to be broken to pieces on Cohasset Rocks. A similar fate overtook the *Mary Frances* of Belfast, whose anchor lines snapped almost as soon as her crew was removed.

A 90-foot section of the stone breakwater at Sandy Bay was torn away, and the stone fillers weighing seven and eight tons were wrenched aside. Two vessels were flung onto a ledge nearby and went to pieces. All hands were lost. The *Brilliant*, a large schooner deep laden with stone from Mt. Desert, swung adrift for some time, only to be inexorably driven inshore. The sea was running over her so high that the crewmen were forced up into the rigging where their position was extremely precarious. The towering breakers shortly swept her broadside into

Gloucester Harbor during the storm.

Wreck of the Pocahontas.

the ledges, and she began to break up rapidly. Through the howling storm and blinding sleet, the helpless onlookers from the bank could make out men clinging to the starboard fore rigging. Their doom came swiftly. A mountainous wave snapped off both masts offshore, with the men sepulchred beneath them. One only survived. Others were found later under the shattered masts.

Crewmen on another wildly careening vessel succeeded in getting a line to shore, having first made themselves fast to it. Although frantically willing hands and knotted muscles of those on land exerted superhuman effort to draw them to safety, the line fouled in the whirling debris and the rescuing battle came to naught. The men perished, although one end of the line to which they were lashed was in the hands of half-crazed men straining to save them.

There were other heart-rending frustrations as rescuers sought to pit their puny strength against the slashing elements, failing more often than succeeding in their struggles. Half-frozen wretches, stiffening with the icy cold, were plummeted hither and yon in the death clutches of the breakers and the winds. In awful scenes, impotent crewmen were heaved on mountainous waves almost to shore, only to be sucked back into the abysses. Fragments of vessels to which men had lashed themselves collided in the cavernous troughs, broke up, and wrenched men free only to be hurled downward into watery graves before the startled eyes of observers shivering on the shore. Some of the victims were suffocated in the whirlpools and spewed out lifeless upon the beach. Others were caught in the yawning crevices of ledges and reefs, from which their battered and frozen bodies were extricated next day when the tide was out.

We have no very reliable records of the number of victims of the holocaust around the port of Gloucester. Only 12 bodies were found. Most were swept to sea. Even before the gale had died down, a public meeting of citizens was called and a purse of $500 was immediately raised for aid of the shipwrecked men.

The great hurricane of the 15th and 16th of December in that tragedy-packed year of 1839 continued to be a most devilishly persistent visitation, refusing to die until it had wrought further evil. For more than a week it raved and snarled along the coast of New England. On the 23rd of the month, the brig *Pocahontas*, from Cádiz bound for Newburyport, went ashore stern first in the most exposed and dangerous spot of Plum Island. All 13 on board perished. The funeral of her captain and seven of his crew whose bodies were recovered was attended by a throng of people estimated at the time to be 2500. An American ensign was thrown over each coffin. Notwithstanding that it was one of the roughest and coldest days of the winter, several hundred persons followed the bodies to the cemetery. All the bells tolled in Newburyport, and every flag was half-masted.

On the 27th, an ENE storm of great fury raged through the entire night along the already battered New England coast. There was great destruction in Boston. Wharves were inundated. Dykes were demolished. All the low land between Front and Washington Streets was flooded. Eleven vessels were severely damaged or completely destroyed.

The paralyzing tempest continued intermittently into early January. Altogether, 192 vessels were lost in six weeks' time. About 340 persons lost their lives in the rampaging floods. The disaster was unparalleled in the previous history of the New England coast.   END

A great roar boomed out, and what seemed like a
cloud of black smoke appeared at the head of the valley—
a dark, foam-bordered mass 40 to 50 feet high . . .

Becket's Runaway Reservoir

by Holcomb B. Noble

CLINT BALLOU PEELED OFF HIS WET CLOTHES AND
fell exhausted into bed. But he didn't plan to
sleep long. It had poured sheets of rain all day.
It had rained steadily all fall, and now there was
a grave danger that the reservoir dam high above
town would collapse. He knew there would be
little chance for sleeping until the threat had
passed—if it passed.

* * * * *

In November, 1927, rains bore down on the
mountain towns of Vermont and the Massachusetts Berkshires as they rarely had before or
have since. Every stream and brook was full;
rivers began overflowing their banks. Residents
of some valley towns had been able to move out
if the flooding became bad, wait for the sun to
reappear, the water to recede, and the chance
to move back to wet but substantially undamaged homes. Ballou and other residents of Becket in the Berkshires knew they would have no
such privilege. If there was going to be a flood,
there would be no moving out and moving
back. In their case, there would be nothing to
move back to.

They had a beautiful town in a valley among
three wooded hills that rose at some points almost straight up from the beds of three mountain streams. Even in normal times one of the
streams swirled and foamed down some 250
feet of moss-grown ravine. It joined another
that flowed cleanly, harmlessly, quietly along a
main street shaded with maples, and the three
streams came together in the center of town.
There were summer homes scattered around the
hills and five lakes, but most of the residents
lived in the valley. Up near the end of one of

the gorges, winding into the hills, lay the highest body of water in the state, the Wheeler
Reservoir, held back by an earthen dam. Normally, the reservoir fed the stream on the main
street as it flowed gently down over a series of
waterfalls and under a series of bridges. But if
the dam burst, it would unleash from its height
of 1,800 feet a body of water that would crush
everything in its path—in this case, the main
part of a town of 700 people.

On November 3 it really began to rain as
though someone, somewhere, had decided to
turn all New England into one huge swamp.

About four o'clock in the afternoon, Clint
Ballou and two employees of one of his basket
shops drove up in the pelting rain to check the
reservoir. They went out onto the 30-foot-high,
200-foot-long stone wall that held the earth and
stone dam in place. Everything looked all right.
There, stretched out behind them, was a 50-acre
body of water, not peaceful in the rain and
wind, but harnessed and harmless. Despite the
rainfall only a little water was going over the
spillway. The dam showed no signs of weakening, but just to be safe they opened the main
sluice gate at the base of the dam to a two-thirds
head. Then back to town and a fresh change to
clothes.

At about ten o'clock the downpour ceased—
"the rain factory stopped for lack of raw material," as one of the townspeople put it—and
by 11:30 P.M. the stream had begun to sub-
side. Ballou and his brother Will went back up
to the dam and found the reservoir had risen
four inches since late afternoon and the spillway was now taking in a river. But the rain had

The runaway reservoir turned the little valley village of Becket into a wide, deep gully of boulders, stumps and debris.   Few houses were spared.

let up. That was the important thing, and because of it, they thought the worst was over. They opened the gate a full head, returned to their homes, and by 1:30 A.M. Clint Ballou was finally getting sleep that had been so long in coming.

At 3:30 he jumped out of bed, called his grain store man, Fred Crochiere, and they started for the reservoir again. The water had gone down two inches. The night was still in the darkness —beautiful after the rain. The water was peaceful, like a sleeping lion, and the air was light again as they walked along the top of the dam.

Then they saw what they had come up there so many times not to see—what generations before them had feared as well. There along the top of the dam, like a long, lethal dagger, was a crevice about two feet wide and nearly 12 feet long, the first indication that something was wrong underneath. At that moment the dam was probably honeycombed and, if it let go, the men would be hurled into the pit below.

Ballou and Crochiere hurried down to the gatehouse to see whether the water was discharging through the gate and cylinder all right. Ballou peered through the gatehouse flood

with his flashlight and heard something crack, like timber snapping.

"For God's sake," Crochiere said, "let's get out of here! I don't like those sounds!"

A second crack warned them that it was time to move. No sooner had they got out of the gatehouse when part of the wall burst and smashed the little building like an eggshell— the two men less than 30 feet away. They broke into a run, perhaps never faster, reached the first house directly in line with the dam and banged on the doors and windows.

"If the dead sleep like that," Ballou thought, "Gabriel himself would have some trouble waking 'em up." He thought the water would be upon them at any moment. Finally, the man of the house came downstairs and let them in. Ballou and Crochiere blurted out what was happening and told him and his family to hurry to high ground. Ballou rushed for the telephone.

Mac McCormick, who operated the town switchboard from a room in his house in the valley, answered on the first ring. He was not sleeping much that night either.

"Mac, this is Clint. Something terrible has happened here at the dam. The water is coming

Forty-eight buildings, eleven bridges and two miles of railroad were destroyed.

down on us just as sure as there is a God in heaven. Call my wife first, my brother second, then everybody on the low ground. Do you get it?"

Mac said he did. He called the Ballous and roused his own wife and two daughters and sent them up to Middlefield Hill. Then, although his house was bound to be in line with the onrushing water, he sat back down at his switchboard. One by one, the bells began to ring on every circuit in the village.

Meanwhile, Ballou and Crochiere raced their Paige touring car around the eight narrow curves and over the narrow bridges on the road down to town, blasting their horn and shouting the warning to everybody. "If I live to be a thousand years old, I shall see the lights flashing in the houses and see the people leaving their homes as we came down the street," Ballou said. Most of the people did leave their houses. But some did not.

Frank Prentice couldn't believe there was so much danger. Although he thought he probably ought to get out of his house, near the main railroad lines that winds through the Berk-

shires from Boston to the west, he was in no great rush. A 90-year-old man and his wife, whose house was right on the bank of the swollen, angry stream, respected the danger all right but insisted that, if anything was going to happen, they would prefer that it happen with them together in their own house. A housekeeper, Mrs. Justine Carroll, had been caught in a flood once before in another town and thought she would be safer inside than out. Repeated attempts to persuade them to leave were to no avail.

Others rushed to the hills. Generally, they were able to take nothing with them except the clothes they were wearing. Some brought personal papers or a trinket or two. One man brought his neckties and a bag with one onion in it. It was still dark and they could not see what was happening below. Esther McCormick, from a friend's back yard, could not pick out her own house from among the others in the darkness. She could not see that her father still had not left the telephone switchboard or that Ballou was still below trying to get everyone to safety. Finally, Ballou joined his wife on higher ground, but McCormick would not leave.

They all waited. And waited.

"Now and again I would see a lantern bobbing rapidly along the main street . . . an automobile would speed by, carrying others seeking refuge in the hills," McCormick said. "An hour passed and nearly two. The suspense was terrible."

Perhaps the alarm had been false. Perhaps the dam was going to hold after all. Only one chunk of it had collapsed; perhaps the rest of it would stand. Perhaps the town was safe. Gradually people began to go back to their homes. Ballou, with five others, headed back up to the mountain reservoir for another inspection.

They got to within about a quarter of a mile of the dam when they saw in a sickening instant that the alarm had indeed been true. The dam had fallen, and the water was coming straight for them. Some of the men jumped from the car and dashed up the bank, and others urged that they all do the same. But there was a wide place in the road with a good place to turn around, and Ballou decided to try it. He thought he could beat the flood if he did not stall the engine in turning around. Then with the big wave in sight and water already up to the running board, he wheeled the car around and raced for town. Down the mile and a half of narrow winding road he sped, blowing the horn all the way—Paul Revere in a touring car, sounding the warning, with the water rushing down the valley behind him.

The Rev. Charles Ramsay and his family, who had gotten cold waiting on a hilltop after the first alarm and returned home thinking the danger over, had just started eating a breakfast of oatmeal and coffee when they heard Ballou's horn. They hurried up the hill behind their house, turned and saw the water. For them and for most of the townspeople of Becket, there came—at just about dawn—the worst sound they would ever hear, the worst sight they would ever see.

A great roar boomed out and what seemed like a cloud of black smoke appeared at the head of the valley and approached in a dark mass some 40-50 feet high, bordered with seething white foam. It pushed through the first bridge and crushed the house from where Ballou had telephoned. It rolled across the gorge and began tearing out the road behind him, then collapsed a two-story sawmill, shooting lumber and logs into the air.

As the water poured down toward the village, it sliced the front porch cleanly off the Ramsay house but left the rest of the house intact. Next came the big brick silk mill. The giant wave splashed into the mill pond in front and stormed inside, knocking out bricks and pushing out walls and caving in the roof as though the mill were a child's castle crumbling with the brush of a hand. Then another bridge. Then the Lyman house. Then Will Ballou's house. Here and there a great root or chunk of rock or concrete would stick out for an instant only to be sucked under again. With irresistible force, the water smashed building after building.

Clint Ballou and his men had beaten the flood to the center of town by several minutes and taken to high ground. McCormick, however, was still at his post at the telephone switchboard, still trying desperately to get word to everyone, still apparently in the path of destruction himself.

Before he fled, Bob Burnham, whose house was not far from the reservoir, telephoned McCormick to tell him the dam had broken. The water was coming down on the town for sure. The operator decided he would not leave his switchboard. He told himself he was not afraid. The water was not going to hit his house anyway, he said; it would bank off before it got there and head for the opposite side of the valley. He began checking the circuits again and found most everyone had gotten the warning of Ballou's auto horn and hurried to the hills. Now he was nearly alone. But there was still Mrs. Carroll, who had already refused all urging to leave, and there were still others to call.

Suddenly he heard a mighty roar. He looked up the street; the water had just come in sight. It was attacking the silk mill, knocking bricks in all directions. There was an explosion, black smoke, and then nothing but the steady roar and crash of water. Somehow, he thought, it didn't seem to be coming very fast. But before he knew it, water had torn away the front half of the house next door. His switchboard went dead and water swirled in around his knees. McCormick threw his headphone aside and raced for the back porch, but the water outside was already some 15-20 feet high. He was trapped.

Frank Prentice was still in his house, a few doors down, when the torrent picked it up and began bobbing it about like a toy boat. The water forced him to the second floor. From a bedroom window he just managed to grab the branch of a tree that had held fast and pull himself to safety. Seconds later the house broke into pieces when it crashed into the railroad bridge at the lower end of town.

Other buildings, homes, barns, stores, followed the same pattern. They were picked up whole or in sections by the powerful, demented force and floated almost lightly and gently away—to be suddenly broken apart against the railroad bridge or Middlefield Hill as the water veered to the right and headed down toward the Connecticut Valley.

Mrs. Carroll's house floated airily away, then rolled on its side, and finally broke into shreds and washed away. She was never seen again.

Ballou and his family stood on a hill between the Baptist and Congregational churches. They saw the water hit the little dam above his grist mill. Like a volcano, it shot logs, rocks, trees and timbers, bricks, silk, machinery, furniture, sacks of grain into the air. Ballou stood in a trance, watching helplessly as the work of a lifetime was washed away before his eyes. The basket shop collapsed. Then his house rose off its foundation, and he watched as it floated away and smashed against the twisted iron remains of the bridge.

"My God, our property!" he murmured.

In what was once the center of town, a tall tree withstood the force of the thousands of pounds of water hurtling against it, and, because it did, the old couple who insisted on staying together in their own home were saved. So much debris began piling up against the tree that it split the wave in two, one half going one side of their house and the hotel and the other half around the other. Against all reasonable odds, neither building was damaged, and the old man and his wife were not harmed.

McCormick was still on the porch of his house when the crest of the high wave approached. Seconds before it reached him, the current twisted, and the bulk of it missed his house entirely—just as he had predicted—though without fully believing himself. Houses on both sides of him were washed away but his was spared. He left the porch and went back inside. Although the telephone switchboard and most of the first floor were covered with water and mud, he tried by force of habit to make a connection. Most of the lines in town were down and the entire exchange was out of order.

In about 10 minutes the water began to recede. He waded out into the main street, the first to survey the awesome damage.

Heartsick, others began slowly coming back to see the village that was no longer there. Many wept. Many had lost all they possessed. Although some had lost nothing personally, the loss of the community they had known was almost too much to bear. Most just stared and said little.

What was once their town was now a wide, deep gully of boulders, tree stumps, debris, and aimless, eddying, flowing water. A solitary hen walked up and down looking as though she had been through a clothes wringer. A dog roamed around and around the spot where his master's house once stood. People wandered aimlessly, too—wondering what they were going to do, what was going to happen to them now.

The town was a ruin. Forty-eight buildings were gone, eleven bridges, two miles of railroad.

Except for Mrs. Carroll, the people of the town were all right. The raging flood had passed, and they were safe. No one else had been hurt. The alertness and brave actions of Ballou, McCormick and others had saved scores of lives.

A woman employee of one of Ballou's two basket shops, the one which was damaged but not destroyed, came to him the morning after the flood as he stood amid the rubble. She was in tears and asked:

"Mr. Ballou, what are we going to do?"

"What are we going to do?" he replied. "I'll tell you what we're going to do. We're going to open that basket shop Monday morning and go to work."

END

Hurricane!
September 21, 1938

Photo by Stephen N. Lemanis

1

In Springfield, Massachusetts

**At the Eastern States Exposition, the stock was turned
loose when the hurricane hit; horses, cows, bulls,
steers, pigs, geese, chickens, rabbits—a veritable
Noah's Ark of animals—were all running wild . . .**

by Isobel F. Hoffman

I WAS IN SPRINGFIELD, MASSACHUSETTS, FOR THE week of the Eastern States Exposition in September, 1938, where I had gone to show my three-gaited saddle mare, "Jasmine," in the horse show held in the Coliseum. I was staying at the house of friends across the street from the Fair Grounds and was anticipating an enjoyable time, unaware of the coming disaster.

There had been some wind and rain, with hurricane warnings which no one at first seemed to take seriously. But on the morning of September 21, 1938, the wind now blew a gale (estimated at 186 miles an hour at the height of the storm), and the rain came down in torrents.

By early afternoon all Exposition activities had been cancelled, and the spectators were leaving to seek shelter. The grandstand collapsed, injuring many persons and killing one. Trees and poles were being blown down, telephone wires and power cables hopelessly broken and tangled. Men were hard at work sandbagging the bank of the river on the east border of the Fair Grounds—the water was rising rapidly.

Apparently, the horses were safe in the stable at that time. One of the grooms in charge of some hackney ponies belonging to a woman in California said to me, "Why don't you go on home? We will be sleeping here in the tack room and if anything happens in the night, and we have to get out, we will take your mare along with our ponies."

I left, and as I neared my friends' house, the chimney was blown off, the bricks and debris narrowly escaped hitting me. This was the beginning of my horrifying experience. In the house, the family was very much frightened and excited. Up in my room the large panes of glass in the window seemed to be bending in and out, and the sound of the wind and rain was

deadly. The National Guard had been called out and from a loudspeaker in a car was ordering everyone to evacuate—the Connecticut River was flooding.

I was dreadfully frightened. My first thought was for the mare, so, not having time to dress, I ran across the street in my nightgown and robe, to see if she had been taken out. By chance, my groom, George, who was rooming about half a mile away, arrived at the gate at the same time. "You can't go in there," yelled a guard. "You could get trapped." But I had a valuable mare that had been shown in Madison Square and Boston Gardens, winning many ribbons, and I wanted to make sure that she had been taken out. We went in, regardless, and found she was still there, standing frightened and alone—the place deserted. We didn't stop for the tack or anything, but George grabbed a lead rope, and we worked as fast as we could. Getting her out was something to remember—or forget. We were drenched from the rain and groping around in the dark, trying to keep clear of the wires which were down.

At the gate the guard yelled, "Get over the

The Midway area of the Eastern States Exposition grounds in Springfield, Massachusetts, September 22, 1938.

bridge quick and head for Agawam Race Track before the bridge gets covered!"

Over the bridge we ran into big trouble. The stock had been turned loose and were running wild—horses, cows, bulls, steer, pigs, dogs, geese, chickens, rabbits, all kinds like Noah's Ark—but they weren't going two by two. Panic reigned. Weird cries and noises were heard from the animals; some were being trampled to death. It was a scene of dire confusion—the rain, wind, muddy and slippery ground, downed wires, darkness, women and children leaving their homes in their nightclothes pathetically carrying their pets to safety, and a Brahma steer goring a large Percheron horse in its side, sending it down a bank—all in all an utterly harrowing experience.

We could hear some of the frightened animals running towards us. A man shouted, "Get up against a tree or lie down." There was a car parked a short distance from the side of the road. My groom said, "Get in that." I opened the door to jump in and sat right on top of some woman. She said nothing—anything went.

Then we continued on the long, eventful walk to Agawam, where we had been told we might find shelter, only to find on our arrival that the stables had been blown down. Some of the animals had been tied to stakes driven into the ground. George held the mare on the lead rope all night. Some of the fellows there built a big fire, and we all hung around that trying to dry out and get warm. An elderly man spoke to me and said, "I was on the *Titanic* when it sunk and sat on an ice floe for a long time before I was rescued. What a terrible experience that was, but take it from me, this is worse by a long shot!"

After some difficulty, we obtained a horse van and finally got Jasmine home to Southport, Connecticut, after running into many hindrances and detours. Trees and wires were down, and roads were mostly underwater. We arrived safely, only to find that the home stables were flooded. Our other horses had been taken out and moved up the street to the Hunt Club, and we took the mare there. Jasmine developed a strep throat as a result of her dreadful night, but recovered and went on to win many more ribbons. ∎

Photo by Stephen N. Lemanis.

Author Isobel Hoffman and her show mare, Jasmine.

277

2 On Nomansland Island

Great seas were coming in twenty feet high; you couldn't see the breakwater nor the tops of the spiles in the basin . . .

by Cameron E. Wood

MY WIFE HAD LEFT NOMANSLAND ISLAND ON September 12 for her fall vacation and to get our winter's supply of groceries, etc. So I was all alone on the island on September 21, 1938.

In order that you may understand what happened, I will explain where I kept our two boats. At a short distance from our house is a stone breakwater which used to form a little sheltered anchorage. Unfortunately, this has silted in with sand and beach stones, so that now no boat can lie there. The only boats I can keep are a 16-foot dory and a 10-foot skiff. These I have to haul out on the beach. In order to do this alone, I have placed two masts in the ground which are about 25 feet high; one is set 50 feet above normal high-water mark and one at low-water mark. They are about 100 feet apart. At the top of these masts is fastened a heavy wire cable. From the top of each mast is a guy wire, or backstay. The one on the inshore mast is anchored about 50 feet inshore, the other one to the breakwater; all the wire cables are drawn tight by means of turnbuckles. On the top of the cable are two trolleys to which are fastened two four-ply tackle blocks, with which I can hoist my boats and run them for launching or for hauling up.

On Wednesday morning, September 21, I heard over the radio that a gale was coming up the coast. I went down and pulled my boats way up to the inshore mast and tied them. At about 4 P.M. I saw that the water was up to my boats, so I put on my rubber boots and went down again. I waded out and hoisted the skiff a little higher on the cable. I thought the water would not come any higher, as it had never been even this high before.

After I had hoisted the skiff, a large sea came and filled it. I climbed in, bailed it out and hoisted it higher. Then I saw that the water was rising very fast and had become so deep that I could not touch the bottom. The seas were running so swift that I didn't dare try to wade ashore for fear I would be swept off my feet by the undertow. I thought the water would soon start to go down and then I could go ashore without danger, so I stayed in the skiff. But the sea got higher and higher, and I had to hoist the skiff and myself as high as I could, about 20 feet from the ground.

In the meantime, the wind had increased to a hurricane and was blowing (they later said over the radio) 100 miles an hour. The skiff was swaying on the cable at a frightful rate. Great seas were coming in 20 feet high; you could not see the breakwater or the tops of the spiles in the basin. The water would strike the mast and fly into the air and drench me to the skin with each sea. After every three or four seas, I would bail out the skiff, as I was afraid it would get so heavy that it would break the ropes and drop me into the water. It was an awful sight to see those great seas come rushing in under the skiff—some were so high they broke over the stern (the bow was toward the beach).

Water began to eddy and swirl between and under the buildings on the shore, and they started to go to pieces like packs of cards, whirling by me and out to sea. The strength of those waves was terrible to watch, especially from where I was. I thought, "What chance will I have if I get tossed into those seas?"

I was not frightened, but I did think that I would never get ashore alive. One does a lot of thinking when he feels his time is most up. I thought, "Well, we all have to go sometime and I have always said that I wanted to die with my boots on"—and I surely had them on—they were full to the top with salt water.

I did feel sad for my dear, faithful wife. I thought of how bad she would feel when she came back and could find no trace of me. Indeed, nobody would ever know what became of me. After all the buildings along the shore were gone, I looked out at our house, which was about 200 yards away, and could see the big white waves go by the house. Then I thought, "Our cozy little home that my wife has always taken so much pride in will go next, with all of our belongings."

But by some miracle it did not go. I had been in the boat for over two hours, holding on for my life and bailing water. Now it was commencing to get dark. The waves were not coming quite so high, and when they ran back I could see the ground about half way from the shore. I was beginning to feel weak and starting to tremble. I realized I could not hold on in that awful wind much longer, and I knew nobody could help me as I was alone on the island. I thought, if I could climb to the top of the mast, maybe I could slide down the backstay, which ran about halfway to the bank. Then, when the sea ran down, maybe I could make the shore before the next wave could catch me and pull me back. So I got out of the boat and tried to climb, but I was too weak and could not hold on and fell into the water. I tried to grasp the mast, but the first big sea caught me and snatched me away as if I were a straw and rolled me underwater. I thought, "Well, I guess this is the end."

The next I knew I felt the ground with my knees and hands. I grabbed my hands into the ground and grass roots and held on until the sea ran back. I was too far gone to get on my feet so I started to crawl on my hands and knees for the shore. That was the only time I was scared and the first time I had spoken through it all. I could hear myself saying (and I remember how strange my voice sounded), "Oh! If I can only make it before the next sea catches me and pulls me back." I got as far as a large stone and got a firm grip on that, as I knew the next sea must be close behind. When that one ran back, I crawled over the bank and sank face down in the grass, gasping for breath.

The first thing I did when I realized that I was safe was to thank God that I made it. I do not know how long I lay on the ground, as I was nearly gone and could hardly breathe. I was full of salt water and so weak that I could not stand, so I started to crawl to the house, which was about 100 yards away.

I finally got there; then I had a hard job to get my rubber boots and clothes off. When I did get into bed, sand and all, and pulled all the blankets over me, how I did wish my dear wife was there to help and comfort me, but I had to fight it out alone. I was trembling so badly that I shook the whole bed. The trembling went on for hours. I suppose it was from shock, as I did not feel cold. I knew there was a bottle of whiskey in the closet and that a little would do me good. But when I was a young man I made a vow to myself that I would never drink a glass of intoxicating liquor and I never have; I did not then, but I could not sleep all night. Strangely enough, I was more frightened after I was safe in bed than when I was within reach of those great seas. I could see them come rushing towards me all night; then I would think of that crawl up the beach, so weak that I could hardly move, but kept going just by will power, expecting the next wave to catch me and pull me back. It was like a nightmare.

The next morning I was so sore and lame, all over, that I could hardly get out of bed and do my chores, cook breakfast, etc. The cows and hens did not get fed or milked the night before so I had an extra lot of milking and carrying to the house. Thursday, the 22nd, I slept nearly all day and all night. Friday morning I felt pretty good, but lame. I walked part way around the island to see what the storm had done. My dory was gone, all the year's wood was stored in one of the buildings that was washed away, with many other things. The whole shoreline was changed. Some places the cliffs were washed away 25 feet inland, where they were 30 feet high.

Saturday morning, September 24, a Coast Guard cutter came at about 10 A.M. They sent a boat ashore, and were very kind to me. While they were there a plane came and dropped a letter, newspapers and food. My wife was aboard the plane, but I did not know it then.

On Thursday, September 29, my wife came home on the *Emily H.* of Newport, Rhode Island. So everything is all O.K. again, and God is in His Heaven. ∎

3

Conimicut, Rhode Island

The hurricane was piling and pushing the whole Atlantic before it into the wedge-shaped bay—TIDAL WAVE!

by James H. Readio, Jr.

FIRES ARE BURNING OVER ON CONIMICUT POINT, sending heavy billowing clouds of smoke toward Providence. Planes drone overhead, passing and repassing along the shore line; presumably, they are looking for submerged bodies in the shallow water. Yesterday, we heard dull reverberations, as though the National Guardsmen were dynamiting the wreckage in their search for more bodies. Presumably, they are now burning up the debris to check the spread of typhoid.

I say presumably for, although we live on the waterfront, just south of the point which juts out about a mile into Narragansett Bay from the west shore, we cannot pass through the cordon of military police who turn back all morbid sightseers and hold in check marauding bands of looters.

Just one week ago, this shore was covered with scores of beautiful houses, the homes of people who lived and worked and played. Today, not one house stands; scarcely a stick of timber remains. Dozens of bodies have been removed; more are being found daily. We look across the point to the eastern shore of the bay, then up toward Providence, an unobstructed view; the water—calm, benign, serene; the land —a picture of stark desolation.

For we have lived through a hurricane and a tidal wave; we have saved our home and our lives; we have survived a searing catastrophe that will go down in history as the worst disaster than ever occurred on the North Atlantic seaboard.

* * * * *

Our home, an old two-story, wood-frame building, is on fairly high ground about 300 feet back from the high-water mark. A sloping lawn runs down to where the Lodge stood on the edge of the beach—a heavily timbered, single-room building, originally designed for the storage of boats during the winter, with a massive, hewn-stone fireplace. Here was an accumulation of years of collecting—Indian relics, whaling harpoons, muskets, dueling pistols, sextants and compasses, antique furniture, and a miscellaneous assortment of collectors' "junk" which lent atmosphere for the numerous parties, stag and otherwise, that were held the year round not only by the grownups, but by the children as well.

As I write, I try in vain to recall the weather on Wednesday morning, September 21. I do know that at noon the skies were ominous. The atmosphere was humid, sultry and oppressive; the wind had begun to blow quite violently. Business conditions were such that I required only the flimsiest of excuses to close up the office and head for home. Accordingly, at 2:30 I left to pick up the children at school, as I knew they were not prepared to walk home in the wind and rain which had begun to fall fitfully.

Harry, the youngest and only boy, had been detained for discipline by his teacher. She said he had run out of line at recess; his version of it was that he had merely walked fast. While the punitive period was being absorbed, I remained outside in the car. The wind had risen to gale velocity. The car rocked and swayed. I watched a group of boys playfully learning backwards into the wind. A sudden blow would overbalance them and throw them forward to the ground, a quick letup would send them tumbling backward with shrieks of laughter.

Then Marjorie was picked up in the nearby junior high, and lastly, Elizabeth, who was teaching her first year at still another school. Della was attending art school in the city and would be home later on the bus, with her grandmother. By this time it was 3:30, and the wind was blowing as hard as I ever remembered having seen it; still there was no foreboding of the full extent of the violence that was to come. Driving slowly homeward to avoid the fallen trees, poles and wires, we stopped to pick up a few broken pieces of rotted branches to burn in the Lodge fireplace in the evening. Mother was acting as hostess to the Rhode Island Wheaton College Club. The husbands were coming along to share the broiled steaks, and I had forgotten to get any wood to make a nice bed of live coals over which to broil the said steaks.

I had no sooner placed the last piece of wood in the car than it really began to rain—large drops at first, then solid sheets of water that hit the hard road like a waterfall, bounded back into the air and obscured all vision! The car windows were closed tightly. The heat and humidity were oppressive. Occasionally, the rain would let up for a few seconds, the vision would clear, and we would crawl slowly and cautiously homeward. Just in the nick of time, we saw a sagging telephone or lighting cable stretched across the road. A machine careened crazily past us on the left; he hadn't seen it. We jammed on the brakes and held our breaths. Miraculously, the wind shipped the cable overhead, and the car passed through unharmed. Another gust, and the pole supporting it snapped off and fell away from the road, carry-

ing the cable with it and clearing a path for us.

Before entering the driveway to the garage, we decided to drive to the foot of the dead-end street and look out over the bay at the storm. Mountainous surf was rolling in, and we could scarcely see 100 feet offshore. A group of boys were laboriously trying to fasten their boats to the dock, or to beach them safely beyond the high-tide mark. The tide was rapidly rising. This was no place for us! Turning around to regain our driveway, we saw that our willow tree, a beautiful towering specimen three or four feet through at the trunk, had blown over across the road and blocked our return. In the howling of the storm, we hadn't even heard it crash to the ground 50 feet behind. We fought our way to the fence that separates our lawn from the street, pulled down a section of it, then drove through the opening and across the lawn to the garage.

Once inside the house, we breathed a sigh of relief. Wet clothes were changed and preparations were under way for the club meeting at the Lodge. Away from the howling wind and the driving rain, we could breathe easier; the storm would pass, and we could begin to clear away the old fallen willow and repair the fence in the morning.

Crash! The kitchen window blew in, carrying the wooden fastening splines with it and letting in a torrent of water that flooded the floor. Crash again, as some object, hurtling through the air, broke the pane in another window and filled the room with flying fragments of splintered glass.

We rushed to the front of the house. The piazza awnings were torn to shreds. Another crash, and the piazza roof ripped apart and began blowing away in sections.

Instantly, all was confusion. The two younger children were whimpering, visibly frightened —this was certainly a storm that we could remember in the years to come. The phone rang, and we heard Mother agree that maybe it would be better to postpone the club meeting until the next night.

There seemed to be comfort in physical contact. Hand in hand, Mother, the three children, Auntie and I crowded up the stairs to look out from the bedroom window on the waterfront.

By now I had lost all track of time, but it was probably about 4:30. The water was higher up on the beach than I had ever seen it before. All of a sudden it occurred to me that the tide had been high at 6:00 the previous night; it would be high an hour later tonight at 7:00! Over two hours more of rising water, with a hurricane piling and pushing the whole Atlantic before it into the wedge-shaped bay. Still, of course, it couldn't hurt *us*. It never had, and even the historic September gale of 1815 couldn't have reached our house. An overawing sense of futility and helplessness came over us. We stood away from the windows to avoid being hit if they should blow in, and through the wiped openings on the steamed panes we watched the water rush up.

The Lodge was surrounded by water. The rear door facing the house was open. (I remember wishing that I had closed it that morning—the water might get in and wet the floor and the rugs.) The stone chimney toppled over, the building swung around and faced down the bay, paused for a moment, then raced across the beach and disappeared in the seething cauldron. In the length of time it has taken to write these few words, the water had engulfed the Lodge, carried it off, and completely submerged the tall spruces that were still standing beside the foundation.

I groaned and covered my head with my hands. A light, firm touch on my elbow, and I turned to see Elizabeth, white-faced but smiling. "Never mind, Daddy. I'll save up my teaching pay, and we'll rebuild it." A kiss on my cheek, a reassuring pat on the back, and she was off to mop up the water coming in around the window casing.

Shades of the good monk Mendel! What forebears had passed down such dominant strength and courage to my daughter and had skipped me by in so doing? I glanced at her mother and knew the answer. Calm, poised,

soft-spoken, she was cuddling the two younger children, trying to calm their fears, assuring them that the danger was all over, and that of course Daddy would find the Lodge, and of course if he couldn't, he would rebuild a better and a bigger one.

Still the water kept coming, tremendous rollers broke over our lawn. A shriek of terror from one of the children as our neighbor's home, a large, yellow, two-story cottage appeared through the blinding haze, sailed majestically over our lawn, heaved convulsively, broke up into walls, floors and roof, and passed out of sight.

Shrieking wind! Driving rain! Roaring water! House after house floating off, three in sight at one time, racing to destruction! A sudden tremor shook the house. Some heavy object had crashed against a corner of the foundation, the floor of the room where we were standing trembled, the walls swayed. The room had been built out over part of the piazza—over the corner that had been hit.

Little Harry clutched my hand and pulled me into the den.

"Sit down, Daddy."

I sat beside him on the couch and put my arm around his trembling, pathetic little figure.

"Pray, Daddy."

I looked into his pleading, tear-stained face and was momentarily stumped. My annual Easter service stood me in stead.

"Dear God," I faltered.

"Dear God," he repeated tremulously.

"Hear our prayer. Guide us safely through this storm, protect our home, save the lives of our neighbors who are less fortunate than we, grant us all strength and courage in this hour."

It was the best I could do. Phrase by phrase, in a sobbing voice, he repeated the words after me, and with the final "Amen," jumped to his feet, threw back his shoulders and pulled me up beside him.

"We'll be all right now, Daddy," he said in

House after house floating off, three in

a firm, brave voice. And somehow I, too, caught his spirit and believed with him.

I glanced out of the den window in the rear of the house—we were entirely surrounded. I heard and felt the surf breaking against the front door. Marjorie ran down the stairs and called up that water was pouring over the sill and into the living room. Now was the time to leave if we were ever going to. Hastily gathering up a few prized possessions, we left. A soggy, wet football and a bedraggled dolly were numbered among them. Auntie, bless her soul, carefully locked the rear and side doors from the inside, carried the keys in her hand, went out through the front door, leaving it unlocked, and immediately lost the keys.

We locked arms, with the children in the center, plunged through the surf in the back yard and waded to higher land and safety with our neighbors.

I left the family and plowed back to the house, then crawled along the south side and around to the front. Looking toward the bay, I saw a solid wall of water in all directions, several houses still floating by, boats, furniture, mattresses, debris of all kinds everywhere.

Fifty feet from where I stood, in the lee of the house, I noticed a floating object rising and falling in the surf. In the weird, yellow light of dusk, it glared startlingly white in the water. I watched it for a few moments, fascinated, trying hard to orient it and to assure myself that it couldn't be what it must be. A wave caught it and turned it over. An arm was flung out, and the head rolled from side to side. No doubt about it now.

A neighbor appeared from nowhere. I cupped my hands and shouted into his ear. He couldn't hear, so I pointed. We dashed out and, grasping a flimsy garment that was torn almost to shreds, pulled it to shore. Together we half dragged and half carried the limp, yielding form to a knoll beyond reach of the water. The flesh was so soft, the skin so white, the woman so young.

We covered it with an old, water-soaked blanket, then piled heavy planks on it to keep the blanket from blowing off. Nothing else could be done. Faint and nauseated, I bent over with my hands pressed to my stomach. It was all over in a moment.

I must have been in a daze for some time, for suddenly I realized that the wind had lessened, the rain had practically ceased, and the water was receding as rapidly as it had come up. The storm had passed! Our house was badly damaged, but it was still intact on its foundation! We were safe!

Grim-faced men came from out of the dusk. Flashlights and lanterns flickered. Were we safe? Did I know whether this, that and the other family got out in time from their homes? Had I heard from the K. family? Two children had been taken from their floating roof, three more were missing. It was rumored that some boys had taken them off in a skiff. The mother was last seen by the two children as she lost her hold and was washed into the water. She was still missing. I led them around to the knoll and pulled back the blanket from the still form. A flashlight cast a momentary light on the features, not a word was said—the search was over.

It was now about 7:30. The wind had died down, the water was still rushing out, the rain had stopped. Two hours later I gathered the family together and, sloshing through the muck and debris, we entered our home. Someone brought us word from the city that Della and her grandmother were safe; they had had harrowing experiences, both had narrowly escaped drowning, but they and we were safe. What else mattered? Candles were sought out and lighted.

Overhead the stars were shining brightly.

* * * * *

Weary and haggard we greeted the cold, gray dawn! So I might write if this were a novel. Actually we slept soundly (perhaps the psychologist can explain why), more so than usual, and

ght at one time, racing to destruction!

Once thickly settled Conimicut Point, Rhode Island, was swept almost clean of even the wreckage of its homes by the force of the tidal wave in the Hurricane. *Courtesy the* Providence Journal-Bulletin.

awoke late, to find the room flooded with brilliant sunshine, the air balmy and mild. It was Mark Twain who said, "If you don't like New England weather, wait a moment!"

Looking out over the landscape we saw that most of the familiar landmarks were gone or were so altered as to be hardly recognizable. Not a shore house in sight, wreckage of all kinds strewn everywhere; enough lumber in the yard to rebuild three Lodges. Deposited in the middle of our front lawn was a bathtub, a washing machine, several sinks, toilets, metal beds, dishes, radios, and a miscellaneous assortment of household equipment, all practically whole and intact. In the center of the debris, still standing upright, grimly guarding it all, was a brick chimney.

A gaunt young man prowling around through the wreckage approached and inquired about the body we had found the night before. His mother and brother were missing, and he had been up all night searching for them. Their bodies were discovered the next day.

This was one week ago. Today, while looking under some heavy planks that had been sheared and twisted from the oyster dock a mile south of us, I noticed a round, silvery object. It was the crystal glass ball from our gazing globe in the garden—absolutely intact and unscathed.

We understand from the news bulletins that we get over the radio in the car (we have no gas, water or electricity) that 241 bodies have been recovered, hundreds still are missing; 2500 homes are absolutely destroyed, 6000 homes are badly damaged. And this along the shores of Little Rhody, the smallest state in the Union. What must it be along the rest of the North Atlantic coast!

The state meteorologist tells us that the wind reached an official velocity of 96 miles an hour in Providence, 120 miles an hour on the coast. We who were on the coast, and live, commend him for his conservatism.

It is impossible to get carpenters and masons —they are all in the city trying to repair the damage to the utilities and business properties. Nevertheless, we're going to repair and rebuild just as soon as we can, for this is New England and we are New Englanders.   END

INDEX

287